James E. Matthew

A handbook of musical history and bibliography from St. Gregory to the present time

James E. Matthew

A handbook of musical history and bibliography from St. Gregory to the present time

ISBN/EAN: 9783337717155

Printed in Europe, USA, Canada, Australia, Japan

Cover: Foto ©ninafisch / pixelio.de

More available books at **www.hansebooks.com**

A HANDBOOK
OF
MUSICAL HISTORY
AND
BIBLIOGRAPHY

FROM ST. GREGORY TO THE PRESENT TIME

BY

JAMES E. MATTHEW

Author of "The Literature of Music," etc.

WITH

ONE HUNDRED AND TWENTY-EIGHT ILLUSTRATIONS, REPRI-
SENTING REPRODUCTIONS OF OLD INSTRUMENTS, FAC-
SIMILES FROM RARE MUSICAL WORKS, AND
PORTRAITS OF MUSICAL COMPOSERS

LONDON
H. GREVEL & CO.
33, KING STREET, COVENT GARDEN, W.C.
1898

Printed by Hazell, Watson, & Viney, Ld., London and Aylesbury.

PREFACE.

SINCE the issue of my "Manual of Musical History" in 1892, death has been very active in the ranks of musical composers, and the world is the poorer by the loss of Brahms, Gounod, Rubinstein, and Ambroise Thomas—to mention a few of the most eminent only.

As the work is now out of print I have availed myself of the opportunity to subject it to further revision, and to bring it down to the present date; it has also been thought well to add to its utility by including some notice of the labours of the more prominent contemporary musicians.

J. E. M.

January 1898.

CONTENTS.

	PAGE

CHAPTER I.
EARLY HISTORY OF MUSIC .   1

CHAPTER II.
THE HISTORY OF MUSICAL INSTRUMENTS . . . 20

CHAPTER III.
THE MUSICAL INFLUENCE OF THE NETHERLANDS . . 56

CHAPTER IV.
MUSIC IN ITALY AND GERMANY 67

CHAPTER V.
EARLY HISTORY OF MUSIC IN ENGLAND . . 79

CHAPTER VI.
THE ORIGIN OF THE OPERA AND ORATORIO . . . 92

CHAPTER VII.
THE RISE OF THE OPERA IN FRANCE . . . 111

CHAPTER VIII.
MUSIC IN GERMANY 137

CONTENTS.

CHAPTER IX.
MUSIC IN ENGLAND AT THE TIME OF THE RESTORATION . 179

CHAPTER X.
THE RISE OF OPERA AND ORATORIO IN ENGLAND . 202

CHAPTER XI.
FURTHER HISTORY OF MUSIC IN ENGLAND . 229

CHAPTER XII.
MUSIC IN FRANCE DURING THE EIGHTEENTH CENTURY . 241

CHAPTER XIII.
MUSIC IN VIENNA . 269

CHAPTER XIV.
THE MODERN ITALIAN OPERA 303

CHAPTER XV.
FURTHER HISTORY OF MUSIC IN GERMANY AND IN NORTHERN EUROPE . . 328

CHAPTER XVI.
MUSIC IN FRANCE AND ENGLAND DURING THE PRESENT CENTURY . . . 405

ILLUSTRATIONS.

FIG.		PAGE
1.	Facsimile of a portion of the *Antiphonarium* of St. Gregory belonging to the Monastery of St. Gaul (A.D. 790) . . .	5
2.	Nomenclature of the Neums, given in the Breviarium de Musica, a MS. of the eleventh century (from Gerbert)	7
3.	Commencement of the " Prose," or Hymn for the Festival of the Holy Cross (MS. twelfth century)	8
4.	Notation on four lines (from a Lombardic gradual of the fourteenth century)	10
5.	Diaphony in fifths, for four voices (from the *Enchiridion Musicæ* of Hucbald, ninth century)	13
6.	Diaphony, passing from the unison to the fifth and back to the unison (from a MS. of Francon from the Ambrosian Library, Milan ; eleventh century)	14
7. 8. 9.	Crowned minstrels playing on various instruments (from a MS. in the National Library, Paris)	15
10.	The air *L'Homme Armé* (thirteenth century) in modern notation .	17
11.	Song of the Foolish Virgins (from the liturgical drama of *The Wise and Foolish Virgins*). Notation in neums (from a MS. of the eleventh century in the National Library, Paris) . .	18
12.	Egyptian sistrum	21
13.	Oriental Nacaire	23
14.	Musician playing the tambourine and pipe (from the House of the Musicians at Rheims)	24
15.	Triangle of the ninth century (from a MS.)	25
16.	Hand-bell, ninth century (from a MS. at Boulogne) . .	25
17.	Bell of St. Cecilia at Cologne, made of rivetted plates . .	26
18.	Bell in the tower of the cathedral at Siena, twelfth century . .	26
19.	Carillon played with a hammer (from a MS. of the ninth century at St. Blaise, in the Black Forest)	27
20.	Syrinx (MS. in the Library at Angers) . . .	28
21.	Double flute.	28
22.	Musicians playing the flute and other instruments (from Jost Amman, sixteenth century)	29

ILLUSTRATIONS.

FIG.		PAGE
23.	Chorus (from a MS. of the ninth century at St. Blaise)	30
24.	Cornemuse, or bag-pipe (from the House of the Musicians at Rheims)	31
25.	Primitive organ (sculpture in the Museum at Arles)	32
26.	Sculpture on an obelisk erected by Theodosius at Constantinople in the fourth century, representing organs in which the pressure of air is produced by the weight of the blowers	33
27.	Organ with bellows worked by levers (from a MS. of the twelfth century in the library of Trinity College, Cambridge)	34
28.	Organ (from a MS. Psalter of the fourteenth century, National Library, Paris)	35
29. 30.	Small organs, called "Portative," "Positive," or "Regal"	36
31.	Oliphant (fourteenth century)	36
32.	Shepherds' trumpets (eighth century, from a MS. in the British Museum)	37
33.	Bent trumpet (eleventh century, Cottonian MS. British Museum)	38
34.	Trumpet with support (eleventh century, Cottonian MS. British Museum)	38
35.	Military trumpet (from Jost Amman, sixteenth century)	39
36.	Ancient lyre (from a MS. at Angers)	40
37.	Lyre used in the north (ninth century)	40
38.	Psalterium (ninth century, from a MS. in the National Library, Paris)	41
39.	Round psalterium (twelfth century)	42
40.	Psalterium (ninth century, MS. Boulogne)	42
41.	Cithara (from Gerbert)	42
42.	Nablum (ninth century, from MS. at Angers)	43
43.	Triangular Saxon harp (ninth century, from the Bible of Charles the Bald)	43
44.	Harp (tenth century, Saxon Psalter, British Museum)	43
45.	Harp (tenth century, University Library, Cambridge)	43
46.	Harp (twelfth century, MS. National Library, Paris)	44
47.	Harp of O'Brien, King of Ireland (tenth century, in the Dublin Museum)	44
48.	Players on the harp (twelfth century, from a Bible, National Library, Paris)	45
49.	Harpist (fifteenth century, from an enamel found near Soissons)	45
50.	Minstrel's harp (fifteenth century)	46
51.	Harp with pedals, made by Vaderman in 1780 for Queen Marie Antoinette (now in the South Kensington Museum)	46
52.	Dulcimer (fourteenth century, MS. National Library, Paris)	47
53.	Clavichord (beginning of the sixteenth century, from Martin Agricola)	48
54.	Lute (thirteenth century)	48
55.	Crwth of the ninth century	49

ILLUSTRATIONS. xi

FIG.		PAGE
56.	King David playing the rotta (from a window of the thirteenth century in the cathedral of Troyes).	49
57.	Concert (portions of a bas-relief of the capital of a column at the	50
58.	Church of St. George, Boscherville)	51
59.	Organistrum (ninth century, from Gerbert)	52
60.	Devil playing the viol (thirteenth century, Amiens Cathedral)	53
61.	Minstrel playing the viol (fifteenth century, Book of Hours, of King René, MS. Library of the Arsenal, Paris)	53
62.	Viol-player (thirteenth century enamel found at Soissons)	53
63.	Angel playing the viol (Amiens Cathedral)	53
64.	Rebec (sixteenth century)	54
65.	Monochord (fifteenth century, from a MS. Froissart, National Library, Paris)	54
66.	Viol-players (after Jost Amman, sixteenth century)	58
67.	Orlando di Lassus	64
68.	Hans Leo Hassler	71
69.	Ludwig Senfl	74
70.	Michael Prætorius	76
71.	Title-page of the volume of plates of the *Syntagma* of Michael Prætorius (1620). [Reduced size.].	77
72.	Arcangelo Corelli .	105
73.	Girolamo Frescobaldi (1587-1654).	108
74.	The *Ballet Comique de la Royne*, performed before Henri III. and the court (facsimile of the frontispiece of that work, 1582)	113
75.	Tritons playing on instruments of music (from the *Ballet Comique de la Royne*, 1582)	115
76.	Jean Baptiste Lully (after the portrait by Mignard, engraved by Roullet, seventeenth century).	123
77.	Title of the opera *Alceste ; ou, Le Triomphe d'Alcide*, by Lully, with a view of the Tuileries (after the drawing by Chauveau, 1674).	125
78.	Title of *Atys*, tragedy set to music by Lully, published by Christ. Ballard in 1676 (drawn by Chauveau and engraved by Lalouette)	127
79.	Title of the opera, *Armide*, by Lully (engraved by J. Dolivar, after a drawing by Berain), published by Christ. Ballard, 1686	129
80.	*Les Noces de Thétis et de Pélée* (scene from the opera of Colasse, with a view of the Pont Neuf, designed and engraved by Sebastien Leclerc, 1689)	131
81.	A player on the musette (engraved by Leblond, after C. David, seventeenth century)	133
82.	Adam Gumpelzhaimer .	139
83.	Johann Sebastian Bach.	141
84.	Louis Marchand .	143
85.	Johann Joachim Quantz	145
86.	Carl Philip Emanuel Bach	149

ILLUSTRATIONS.

FIG.		PAGE
87.	John Peter Sweelinck.	151
88.	Heinrich Schütz.	153
89.	Title-page of Keiser's *Hannibal*.	155
90.	Johann Adolph Hasse	165
91.	Carl Heinrich Graun.	167
92.	Johann Adam Hiller.	169
93.	Dr. John Blow (from the frontispiece of his *Amphion Anglicus*, drawn and-engraved by R. White, 1700)	185
94.	Henry Purcell (from the engraving by Zobel after Klosterman's portrait in the possession of the Royal Society of Musicians).	189
95.	George Frederick Handel.	207
96.	Dr. Arne, from a sketch by Bartolozzi.	231
97.	Rameau (from the portrait of Restout, engraved by Benoist)	247
98.	Gluck (after Auguste de St. Aubin, 1781).	257
99.	Grétry at his pianoforte (after the picture by Isabey)	263
100.	Franz Josef Haydn	271
101.	Wolfgang Amadeus Mozart.	275
102.	Ludwig van Beethoven	285
103.	Franz Schubert.	297
104.	Cherubini.	306
105.	Rossini	310
106.	Verdi.	317
107.	Pietro Mascagni.	322
108.	Leoncavallo	324
109.	Carl Maria von Weber	331
110.	Lachner	340
111.	Spohr	342
112.	Felix Mendelssohn Bartholdy	347
113.	Robert Schumann	359
114.	Franz Liszt	374
115.	Richard Wagner.	378
116.	Johannes Brahms	389
117.	Robert Franz	391
118.	A. Dvořák.	393
119.	Engelbert Humperdinck	397
120.	Anton Rubinstein	399
121.	P. Tschaikowsky	401
122.	D. F. E. Auber.	410
123.	Giacomo Meyerbeer	414
124.	Hector Berlioz.	419
125.	Ambroise Thomas	422
126.	Charles Gounod.	424
127.	C. Saint-Saëns.	428
128.	Jules Massenet.	430

THE HISTORY OF MUSIC.

CHAPTER I.

EARLY HISTORY OF MUSIC.

Music among the Romans—Effects of Christianity on Music—St. Ambrose—St. Gregory—Introduction of " Neums "—*Antiphonarium* of St. Gregory and its History—Improvements in Notation—Guido d'Arezzo—Boethius—Infancy of Harmony—The Troubadours and Minstrels—Minnesingers and Meistersingers—" Confrérie de St. Julien " in Paris—Adam de la Halle—*Robin et Marion*—Liturgical Plays.

HOWEVER widely the appreciation of art may have been diffused among the inhabitants of ancient Rome, it is certain that the Romans themselves showed but little originality in its practice. For their sculpture, which was probably the manifestation of art in the greatest favour, they were almost entirely dependent on Greeks, who were attracted to Rome in large numbers by the liberal patronage which they received. In music they relied equally on foreign talent, its professors being also almost invariably drawn from the shores of Greece. All the treatises on music which have come down to us from ancient time are written in the Greek language. No original work on the subject in Latin is known earlier in date than the treatise of Boethius.

A new direction was given to the practice of music by the spread of the Christian religion. The persecution which they suffered in their own land drove many of the early Jewish converts into Rome, where they performed their religious rites in secrecy. It is reasonable to suppose that they brought with them many regretful memories of the sacred melodies of their beloved land. But music was in those days an unwritten language, which had a natural tendency to become deteriorated, especially as the ranks of the early Christians were soon recruited by converts from among the people whose hospitality they had sought, who added the melodies of their pagan hymns to the common stock. The practice of music was carried on with difficulty, for, owing to a constant succession of persecutions, their meetings for public worship were held by stealth—most frequently in the secrecy of the catacombs.

It is no wonder, then, that the ancient melodies, thus handed down by tradition alone, should become corrupted. Under Constantine a happier time was in store for the Christians, and they were enabled to celebrate their worship in public. It soon became evident that great variety of practice existed in the performance of the vocal portions of the services. St. Ambrose, who had become Bishop of Milan, was about the year 384 engaged in building his cathedral there. He determined that the music performed within its walls should be the purest obtainable. As a first step he collected all the melodies at that time in use, and then proceeded to lay down fixed rules for the future guidance of his choristers.

He allowed the four following tonalities only, in which all the melodies receiving his sanction were written. We have attached to them the equivalent terms according to the Greek nomenclature, and have marked the position of the semitone with a circumflex.

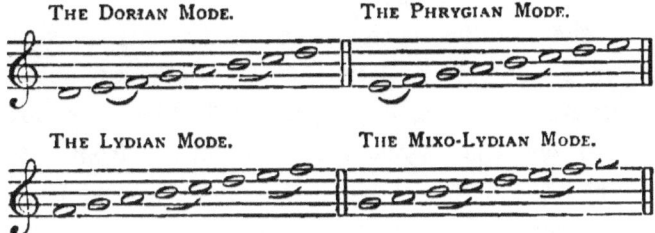

It is said that Pope Damasus was the first to introduce, at Rome in the year 371, the practice of chanting the Psalms, which up to that time had been recited in a loud voice by the congregation; and no doubt the introduction of music in public worship spread rapidly. Gregory of Tours records that the baptism of Clovis in the church of Rheims was accompanied by beautiful music, which impressed the royal catechumen so deeply that when he signed a treaty of peace with Theodoric, King of the Ostrogoths, he made a condition that the prince should send him from Italy a party of singers and a skilful performer on the cithara.

Two centuries after the time of Ambrose, St. Gregory the Great, who was elected pope in 590, supplemented the work of his predecessor by making a further collection of the melodies in Church use. He increased the number of modes to eight, but in addition to this he drew up an *Antiphonarium*, consisting of hymns, with suitable melodies, adapted to all the principal seasons of the Church's year. These have ever since remained in use in the Roman Catholic Church, and are now familiar to all under the name of "Gregorian," which they owe to their collector, although the proper name for them is Plain-Chant or Plain-Song.

For the notation of his melodies Gregory is said to have made use of the letters of the Latin alphabet, the capitals A, B, C, D, E, F, G standing for the seven lowest notes of his scale, while the small letters, from a to g, continued the octave above. The enthusiasm of Gregory for the worthy performance of the musical services of the Church does not admit of question. He established in Rome schools for the education of choristers, and insisted on a knowledge of music among the bishops, refusing to ordain to that dignity a priest who was wanting in a sufficient knowledge of plain-song.

For Gregory also has been claimed — on doubtful grounds—the system of musical notation which came into general use soon after his time,—that of "neums," a word supposed to be derived from the Greek word πνεῦμα, breath. As an example, we refer to the facsimile of part of the so-called *Antiphonarium* of St. Gregory (fig. 1), supposed to be the oldest musical manuscript in existence, the historical value of which cannot be exaggerated. It has been for many centuries the property of the monastery of St. Gall, in Switzerland. Towards the end of the eighth century, Charlemagne was desirous of introducing uniformity of practice in ritual throughout the whole of his vast empire. With

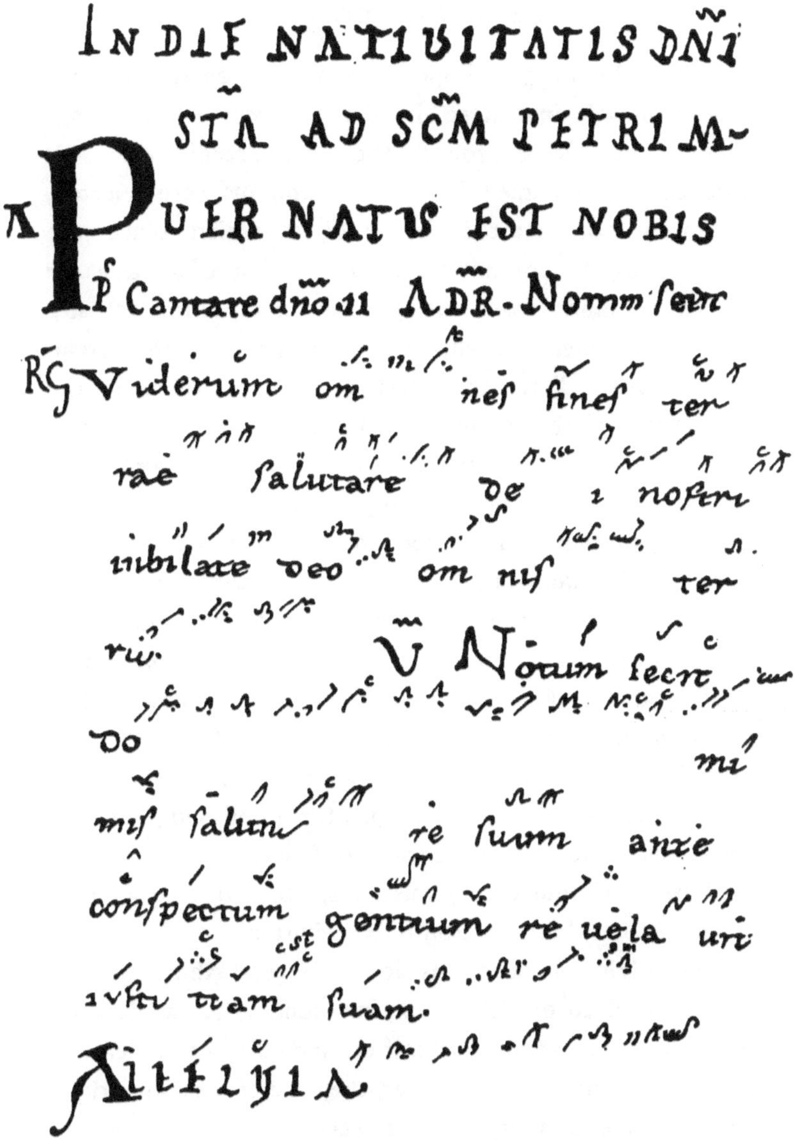

IN DIE NATIUITATIS DNI
STA AD SCM PETRI M-
PUER NATUS EST NOBIS
P Cantare dño. II ADR. Nomm secr
RG Viderunt om   nes fines ter
rae salutare   De   i nostri
iubilate Deo   om nis   ter
ru.   U Notum fecit
Do
                                        mi
mis salutu   re suum ante
conspectum gentium re uela uit
iusti tiam suam.
Alleluia

Fig. 1.—Facsimile of a portion of the *Antiphonarium* of St. Gregory belonging to the Monastery of St. Gall (A.D. 790).

that view he begged Pope Adrian I. to send him two choristers well instructed in the practice of plain-song. To so laudable a request the Pope readily acceded. Two choristers named Peter and Romanus were selected, and they both started for Metz, at which place the reform was to commence, each in charge of a copy accurately made from the precious manuscript actually drawn up under the supervision of Gregory the Great. On the road, Peter fell ill, and was glad to claim the hospitality of the monks of St. Gall. By the express command of Charlemagne, he was received as a permanent resident in the monastery,—possibly with a view of making another centre for the diffusion of the true principles of plain-song; and thus the *Antiphonarium* has become the most cherished possession of the monastery. By a fortunate accident, Père Lambillotte, one of a small body of men who have been instrumental of late years in restoring the ancient practice of the Roman Church, was enabled to make a facsimile of it in the year 1848, which was subsequently published; and in 1885 the actual manuscript itself was shown in the exhibition of musical manuscripts, etc., which was held in the Albert Hall at South Kensington.

The origin of neums is lost. Several theories have been started to explain them, but none quite satisfactory. According to some authorities, including the learned historian of music, Kiesewetter, they are of Roman origin, having some analogy with a species of shorthand invented by Tiro, the freedman and secretary of Cicero. Fétis claimed for them an Oriental origin, while Coussemaker thought they were simply the acute, grave, and circumflex accents. The question will probably never be settled. Their interpretation into modern notation presents equal difficulty, especially as the practice of writing them varied considerably. It may be taken for granted that no absolute pitch was intended. The rising and falling of the voice were indicated by the distance at which the neums were placed above the words, although

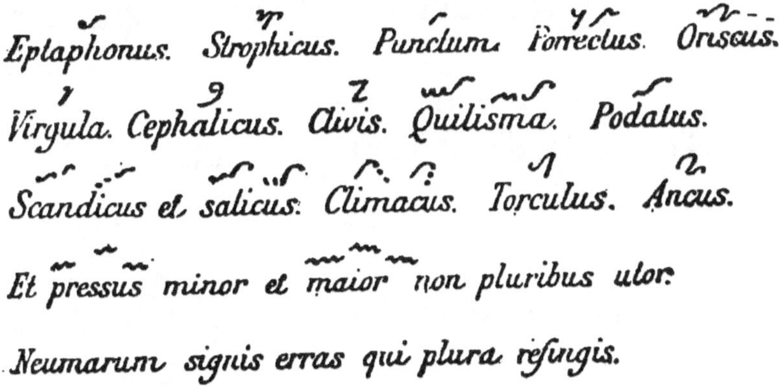

Eptaphonus. Strophicus. Punctum. Porrectus. Oriscus.

Virgula. Cephalicus. Clivis. Quilisma. Podatus.

Scandicus et salicus. Climacus. Torculus. Ancus.

Et pressus minor et maior non pluribus utor.

Neumarum signis erras qui plura refingis.

Fig. 2.—Nomenclature of the Neums, given in the Breviarium de Musica, a MS. of the eleventh century (from Gerbert).

the interval could not be clearly defined by this method. It must be borne in mind, however, that the melodies were familiar to the singers, so that but little assistance was required for that purpose. When the signs became a little more definite in shape, they probably represented certain well-known and frequently recurring sequences of notes so constantly met with in plain-song. Of these Gerbert gives a "memoria technica" from an eleventh-century manuscript, in which the names of the figures are arranged in hexameter verses, with the signs representing them (fig. 2). The use of neums was not confined to ecclesiastical music alone, and many manuscripts exist in which they are added to secular poems.

In confirmation of the opinion that neums were of

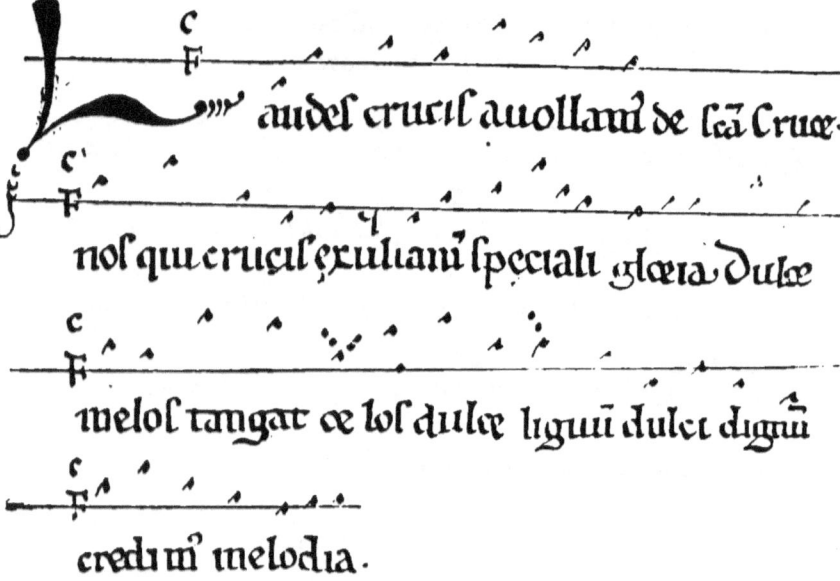

Fig. 3.—Commencement of the "Prose," or Hymn for the Festival of the Holy Cross (MS. twelfth century).

assistance to those only who already were familiar with the melodies they were designed to represent, the contemporary testimony of St. Isidore, Bishop of Seville, a friend of Gregory, may be brought forward. He says expressly: "Unless sounds are retained in the memory they perish, for they cannot be written down." A very simple invention paved the way to a reversal of this opinion. It occurred to some scribe, whose name has, unfortunately, not come down to us,— for without doubt he deserves to be remembered with gratitude,—to draw with his bodkin a line across the parchment above the words to which the music was to be given. At the beginning of this line was written the letter F, signifying that all the neums placed upon the line represented the note of that name (fig. 3). At once we have a definite pitch to start from, and the germ of the musical staff, which soon suggested itself.

The first step was the addition of another line above the F, representing the note C; and it became the practice to use a red line for the F, while the upper line was drawn in yellow or green ink. It was a natural advance to draw a line, either with a bodkin or in black ink, between the coloured lines, and another line below the red soon followed. The four-line stave was now complete (fig. 4), and embraced a sufficient portion of the scale for most purposes of plain-song; but, if necessary, another line was added either above or below the four-line staff, as convenience dictated. The introduction of the single line appears to have been made at the end of the tenth century, although it was some time before its use became general. On the introduction of the complete staff, neums were gradually abandoned in favour of notes bearing more resemblance to those with which we are now familiar.

The invention of the use of coloured lines has been attributed to Guido d'Arezzo (*circa* 990-1070), apparently without foundation, and it is only fair to say that he does

10 THE HISTORY OF MUSIC.

not claim it. M. Fétis remarks that "Guido's fame has rested far more on what has been attributed to him than on what he really did." There can be no doubt that he was a very successful teacher of youth, in which capacity he invented the method of reading music now known as "*Solfeggio.*" He observed that the melody sung to the hymn to St. John the Baptist—

Fig. 4.—Notation on four lines (from a Lombardic gradual of the fourteenth century).

Ut queant laxis
*R*esonare fibris
*Mi*ra gestorum
*Fa*muli tuorum,
*Sol*ve polluti
*La*bii reatum,
    Sancte Johannes—

rose a degree of the scale with the commencement of

each line. It occurred to him to use these syllables—Ut, Re, Mi, Fa, Sol, La—to designate those notes of the scale, and he taught his pupils to sing these intervals by carrying back their thoughts to a melody so familiar to them all, instead of referring to the interval on an instrument.

The important part which music filled in the service of religion made some acquaintance with it a necessary part of the education of every ecclesiastic. The mild wisdom of the writings of Boethius, which caused him to be looked on as a Christian, led to their extraordinary popularity. Among them was unfortunately a treatise on music, and this was selected as the text-book. It has been abundantly proved that he entirely misunderstood the subject which he attempted to explain; and the blind confidence which for so long a time was placed in his knowledge proved a great hindrance to the true study of the science. But in truth it was a subject on which the divorce between theory and practice was almost complete. The priest and the chorister were content to acquire sufficient knowledge to go through their duties with credit, while the student indulged in the useless inquiries then so popular.

We are fortunately not called on here to decide whether the ancient Greeks and Romans were acquainted with harmony, a question which has been discussed with great warmth by many learned musicians; there can be no doubt, however, that rude attempts at harmony were made at a very early period of the Middle Ages. It must be admitted that they were of such a nature that the preformance of them in the present day would strike the musician with horror; but it is equally certain that at the time in which they were in use they were received with enthusiasm. A monk who wrote soon after the time of Charlemagne mentions that the Roman singers taught the French singers the art of "organising,"—the term by which the earliest attempts at harmony were described. On this statement Coussemaker makes the very sound reflection that if the monk was mistaken in the fact which he reports, it proves at least that the practice existed at the time when he wrote, which was in the early part of the ninth century.

The first attempt to describe the principles of harmony as then understood is given by the monk Hucbald, who lived at the end of the ninth and the beginning of the tenth centuries, in his treatise entitled *Musica Enchiriadis*. In the earliest specimens the melody was accompanied by notes of equal length, preserving the same interval throughout the whole of the composition. The intervals allowed were the octave, the fifth, and the fourth, which were admissible when the work was in two parts only, but these parts might be doubled in the octave above when a larger number of parts were employed. This style of writing was called diaphony or organum. The meaning of the former term offers no difficulty; Hucbald explains it to be so called "because it consists, not of a melody produced by a single voice, but of a harmonious composition of sounds of a different nature heard at the same time." But the term "*organum*" is not so easy of explanation. The word had been in use before the time of Hucbald, who makes no attempt to unravel the difficulty. The first to do so was the monk John Cotton, who fancied that it was so called from the resemblance it had to the sounds of the organ. We will now give from Hucbald a specimen of this method of harmonising (fig. 5), and this was considered by the critics of the time to be a "*suavem concentum*"!

Soon after the adoption of "organum," "discant" was

Fig. 5.—Diaphony in fifths, for four voices (from the *Enchiridion Musicæ* of Hucbald, ninth century).

introduced, which made its way almost simultaneously. It was originally in two parts only, the principal melody called the "tenor," while the accompanying part was called the "discant"; but at a later time other parts were added. The main difference between diaphony or organum and discant consists in the fact that while in the former the accompanying parts were note against note, in the latter these parts might consist of notes of different value from those of the "tenor" which they accompanied. In its earliest days the discant was often improvised by the singer, for whose guidance certain rules were current; but it is difficult to suppose that the practice was possible except with the smallest number of singers. This was called in France "chant sur le livre," and in Italy "contrapunto a mente." It is not surprising that the practice led to abuses; a desire for display would naturally lead the singer into a style of singing quite foreign to the spirit of plainsong; and thus we find that several of the popes attempted to suppress it.

Fig. 6.—Diaphony, passing from the unison to the fifth and back to the unison (from a MS. of Francon from the Ambrosian Library, Milan; eleventh century).

From such humble beginnings the modern science of harmony was developed.

Secular music was kept alive by the troubadours, who were both poets and musicians. Their art is supposed to have had its origin in the East, and to have passed into Provence from the neighbouring country of Spain. The troubadours were the aristocrats of the world of art, many of the body being of noble and even royal origin, among whom may be numbered Thibaut, King of Navarre, the Châtelain de Coucy, the Count of Anjou, the Count of Soissons, and the Duke of Brabant. But a more humble birth, if accompanied by commanding ability, was no obstacle to admission to the honoured ranks, and among such we find Adam de la Halle, Blondeau de Nesle, the devoted friend of Richard Cœur de Lion, Richard de Fournival, and others. Their rules compelled them to choose some lady whose charms formed the prevailing subject of their songs, and their efforts sufficed to enliven the tedium of the courts to which they generally attached themselves.

Fig. 7. Fig. 8. Fig. 9.

Crowned minstrels playing on various instruments (from a MS. in the National Library, Paris).

Unlike the troubadours, the jongleurs and minstrels wandered about from place to place, certain of being well received in the houses of the rich, where their lays ensured them a welcome; they were always well lodged and fed, and dismissed with an ample reward. This roving life was far from exercising a beneficial effect on them, and they were too apt to deserve the character of being rogues and drunkards.

In Germany the troubadours and minstrels existed under the names of minnesingers and meistersingers.

The minnesingers were selected from the members of the noble classes, while the meistersingers, who took their rise early in the fourteenth century, when the minnesingers were abandoning their functions, answered to the professional musicians or minstrels. Election into the body was a proceeding of great solemnity. The candidate performed before four judges, who were hidden from sight by a silken curtain. One of these had to watch carefully for any grammatical error; the others paid attention to the rhyme and metre, and the melody of the postulant. If the judges agreed in thinking him worthy, he was admitted with all due ceremony, being decorated with a silver chain and badge, on which was represented David playing the harp. To be a meistersinger was not incompatible with a much more prosaic calling; Hans Sachs, of Nuremburg, one of the most celebrated, was, it will be remembered, a shoemaker.

Among the troubadours whose names we have mentioned was Adam de la Halle, who was born early in the thirteenth century. Thanks to the researches of M. Coussemaker, the most learned authority on the music of this period, we possess a very large collection of his works, which comprise numerous songs, rondeaux, motets (a word which had not at that time acquired the meaning of a *sacred* composition); in all of these both words and music were of his composition; but what is still more interesting, we find a regular drama set to music, entitled *Li Gieus de Robin et de Marion*, which one is almost justified in calling an opera. The story is one of the simplest. Marion is betrothed to the shepherd Robin, when a knight appears on the scene who tries to steal away her affections: however, she proves faithful, and everything ends happily. In the course of this piece Adam de la Halle introduces the famous air *L'Homme Armé* (fig. 10), which was so often in after-times used as a subject for musical treatment. Tradition has it that this was the air which the Crusaders sang on their entry into Jerusalem.

Allied to this little musical play are the liturgical

Fig. 10.—The air *L'Homme Armé* (thirteenth century) in modern notation.

dramas of the Middle Ages, which were performed in churches as a means of instructing the people in the main facts of the Christian religion. Several of these have also been published by the indefatigable M. Coussemaker, and among them we find such subjects as the Resurrection, the Adoration of the Magi, the Massacre of the Innocents, the Holy Women at the Sepulchre, and other subjects of a like nature. The characters were personated by the priests and choir of the church; they were performed at the appropriate seasons of the

Church's year, and no feeling of irreverence had any place whatever in thus representing the principal facts of religious belief. It is interesting to notice that the melodies in *Robin and Marion* are decidedly light in character compared with the music of these dramas, which are of the nature of plain-song. M. Coussemaker prints twenty-two of these compositions, ranging from

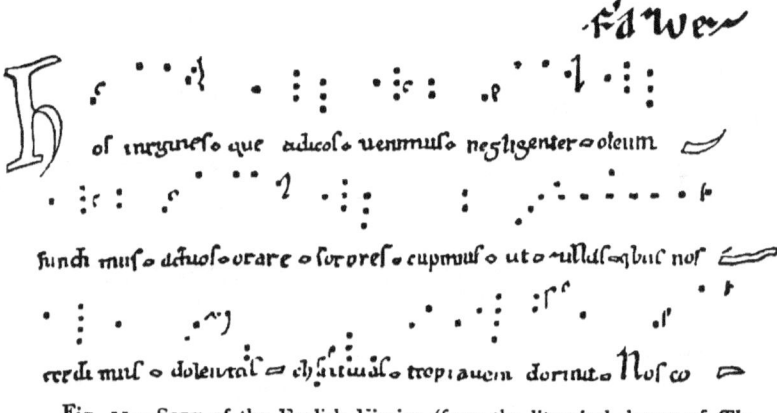

Fig. 11.—Song of the Foolish Virgins (from the liturgical drama of *The Wise and Foolish Virgins*). Notation in neums (from a MS. of the eleventh century in the National Library, Paris).

the eleventh to the fourteenth centuries. The earliest of these is the Parable of the Wise and the Foolish Virgins; the music to this is inserted in neums. We are enabled to give a facsimile of a portion of this interesting work (fig. 11).

The knowledge and cultivation of music spread rapidly over Europe, but it was in the Low Countries that the greatest advance was made, as will be seen in our third chapter.

BIBLIOGRAPHY.

Kiesewetter, R. G. Geschichte der europäisch-abendländischen oder unsrer heutigen Musik. Darstellung ihres Ursprunges, ihres Wachsthumes und ihrer staenweisen Entwickelung; von dem ersten Jahrhundert des Christenthums bis auf unsre Zeit. Leipzig, 1834. 4to. (The above was translated into English by Robert Müller, London, 1848. 8vo.)

Ambros, W. A. Geschichte der Musik. Leipzig, 1862-78. 4 vols., 8vo.

David, Ernest and Lussy, Mathis. Histoire de la Notation musicale depuis son origine. Paris 1882. 4to.

Coussemaker, E. de. Histoire de l'Harmonie au Moyen Age. Paris, 1852. 4to.

Lambillotte, L. Antiphonaire de Saint Gregoire. Paris, 1851. Bruxelles, 1867. 4to.

Paléographie Musicale, par les Bénédictins de Solesmes. Solesmes, 1889, etc. 4to. (The work is still in progress.)

Chappel, W. The History of Music. London, 1874. 8vo (1 vol. only published).

Coussemaker, E. de. Mémoire sur Hucbald. Paris, 1841. 4to.

Hueffer, Francis. The Troubadours. London, 1878. 8vo.

Vidal, Antoine. La Chapelle St. Julien-des-Ménestriers et les Ménestrels à Paris. Paris, 1878. 4to.

Coussemaker, E. de. Œuvres complètes du Trouvère Adam de la Halle. Paris, 1872. 4to.

Drames Liturgiques du Moyen-Age. Paris, 1861. 4to.

CHAPTER II.

THE HISTORY OF MUSICAL INSTRUMENTS.

Difficulties of the Subject—Instruments of Greece and Rome—Classification of Instruments—Instruments of Percussion : Drums, Cymbals, Bells, Carillons, Change-ringing—Wind Instruments : Syrinx, Flute, Chorus, Bagpipes, The Organ, Trumpet, Shophar, Oliphant, Sackbut, Hautboy, Bassoon—Stringed Instruments : Lyre, Psalterium, Cithara, Nablum, Harp, Dulcimer, Clavichord, Virginal—Spinet, Harpsichord, Pianoforte, Lute, Theorbo, Guitar;—Bowed Instruments : The Crwth, Rotta, Hurdy-gurdy, Organistrum, Viol, Violin, Monochord.

THE investigation into the nature and construction of the musical instruments of early times is surrounded with many difficulties. The earliest are known to us only by the representations which have been preserved on sculptured monuments, with such scanty descriptions as contemporary writers have given. Nor can these representations always be accepted in perfect faith. Even in our own day many of the attempts at the representation by otherwise skilled artists of instruments perfectly well known to musicians frequently result in abject failure. In such trivial details it is thought perfectly allowable to draw on the imagination. There is no reason to suppose that any greater conscientiousness actuated the artist of a former age, and it is therefore unsafe to rely too implicitly on representations of this character for such details, for instance, as the number of strings with which a particular instrument was furnished. In addition to these difficulties, the nomenclature is much involved, the same instrument receiving during the course of years a succession of different names, while, on the other hand, the same name, from a fancied but false analogy, has, in many cases, done duty for an instrument of an entirely different nature. Many attempts have been made by men of learning to investigate the nature of the instruments of Biblical and classical times,—it must be added, with a very inadequate result. A similar attempt, embracing instruments of a more modern day, was made by Father Bonanni, an industrious writer, in his *Gabinetto Armonico* (Rome, 1722), but with no greater success. He had no special knowledge of the subject; his aim was to produce a book of handsome plates of instruments, into the design of many of which an exuberant fancy entered, for it is certain that nothing of the sort ever existed. No scientific investigation was made till the question was taken up in our own day by the late Mr. C. Engel, whose excellent catalogue of the musical instruments at the South Kensington Museum contains nearly all the solid facts on the subject which are available.

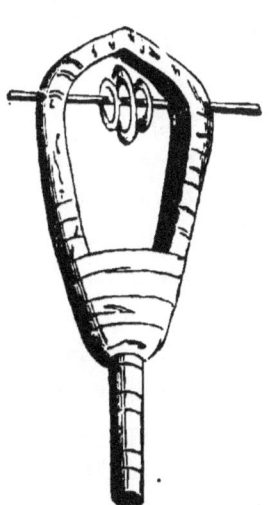

Fig. 12.—Egyptian sistrum

The favourite instruments of Greece and Rome belonged

mostly to the families of the lyre and the flute, but the latter nation seems to have adopted many of the instruments in use among the peoples which they conquered; thus drums and trumpets are supposed to have been borrowed from the warlike nations of the North, while the sistrum (fig. 12), a frame of bronze, through holes in the side of which metal rods were loosely inserted, producing a jingling noise when shaken, was introduced from Egypt with the worship of Isis. The Romans seem also to have possessed the hydraulic organ, which is represented on a coin of the time of Nero, now in the British Museum. The organ is mentioned by St. Jerome in a letter in which he speaks of the different kinds of musical instruments of his day (A.D. 331–420). His account of it is a very good example of the difficulties which have to be contended with in trying to understand these ancient descriptions. He says it was composed of fifteen brazen tubes, and two reservoirs of air of elephant skin, and of twelve forge bellows to imitate the sound of thunder. He goes on to describe, under the generic name of *tuba*, several sorts of trumpets: that which gathered together the people, that which directed the marching of troops, that which proclaimed a victory, that which sounded the charge against the enemy, that which announced the closing of the city gates, etc. He further mentions the cithara of the Hebrews, an instrument triangular in shape, with twenty-four strings; the sambuca, a wind instrument of wooden tubes sliding one in the other, something like the modern trombone; the psalterium, a small harp of ten strings; and the tympanum, which resembled the tambourine.

THE HISTORY OF MUSICAL INSTRUMENTS.

The obvious division of musical instruments is into three classes—instruments of percussion, wind instruments, and stringed instruments. Indeed, a modern writer on the subject, Mr. J. F. Rowbotham, maintains that in uncivilised nations musical instruments have always been invented in the successive order of "the drum, the pipe, and the lyre"; and he supports his theory with much learning and research.

INSTRUMENTS OF PERCUSSION.

There can be no doubt that some form of the drum is known to almost every nation, however low in the scale of civilisation. It is so familar that description is needless. At a very early date the kettledrum was in use in France, as it is referred to by Joinville under the title of "Nacaire" (fig. 13), and was an Oriental importation. The modern tambourine, so associated with Spanish life, under different names was popular in most countries. A curious sculpture is to be seen on the House of the Musicians at Rheims (fig. 14), in which a musician is represented as playing on a pipe, while he strikes the tambourine, which is fastened to his elbow, with his head. The tabour was long popular in England, associated with the pipe, both instruments being played by the same person. It was a small hand drum, and has its counterpart down to the present time in Provence, under the name of tambourin, where, in conjunction with the flageolet, it serves for village dances.

Fig. 13.—Oriental Nacaire.

It should be mentioned that most of the instruments of the drum order give no definite musical pitch. Their use is simply to accentuate the rhythm. This, however, is not the case with the modern orchestral kettledrums, which are susceptible of tuning by tightening or relaxing the heads. These instruments are generally used in pairs.

We have already mentioned the Egyptian sistrum. Allied to it are cymbals, also of Oriental origin, and even now those in general use are nearly all made in Constantinople. The crotala were small cymbals used in dancing, much in the same way as castagnettes are employed in Spain. The triangle is also of great antiquity (fig. 15).

Fig. 14.—Musician playing the tambourine and pipe (from the House of the Musicians at Rheims).

The use of the bell was soon appropriated to the purposes of religion, for calling together the congregation. At first it was no larger than a hand-bell (fig. 16), which was rung in front of the church door, or from a raised platform; but with increased skill the size was developed, and the bells were hung in the towers and campaniles—the word signifies bell-towers—and required mechanical assistance to ring them. In early times these large bells were made of

THE HISTORY OF MUSICAL INSTRUMENTS. 25

hammered plates of metal, riveted together, as in the large bell of St. Cecilia at Cologne, represented in fig. 17. But the practice of casting them soon became general. One of the most ancient now existing is that of the cathedral at Siena (fig. 18), which bears the date 1159. It is barrel-shaped, and gives a very acute sound. The variety of pitch in different bells soon suggested the chime or carillon, which first consisted of a series of bells struck

 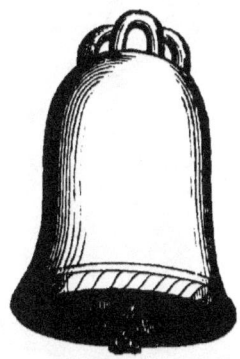

Fig. 15.—Triangle of the ninth century (from a MS.).　　Fig. 16.—Hand-bell, ninth century (from a MS. at Boulogne).

by the performer with a small hammer (fig. 19). But with the increase in the size and number of the bells it became necessary to replace the hammer of the performer by mechanism. Carillons were a source of great delight to the inhabitants of the Low Countries, where they are still to be heard in their greatest perfection. They are generally set in motion by a system of pins on a barrel, so disposed as to produce the melody, as in the familiar musical box; but they can also be played upon by trained performers, some of whom have been musicians of eminence, as, for instance, Matthias van den Gheyn, of

Louvain, who was an excellent composer and a fine organist.

The Russian bells are among the largest in the world. The great bell at Moscow is a familiar example; but this has never been rung, as it was cracked, immediately after it was cast, by an unfortunate influx of water before the bell was cold. The habit in Russia appears to be to ring all the

Fig. 17.—Bell of St. Cecilia at Cologne, made of riveted plates.

Fig. 18.—Bell in the tower of the cathedral at Siena, twelfth century.

bells at once, the din from which is terrific. The practice of what is called change-ringing, by which is meant a continual variation of the order in which the bells are sounded, according to certain rules laid down, is peculiar to England.

WIND INSTRUMENTS.

The reed gave to our progenitors a musical instrument almost ready to their hands. It was a natural step to the combination of reeds of different lengths into the syrinx or Pan's pipes (fig. 20), now only associated in our minds with the ancient and popular drama of *Punch and Judy*. The tibia or flute was originally made out of

Fig. 19.—Carillon played with a hammer (from a MS. of the ninth century at St. Blaise, in the Black Forest).

a shin bone of an animal, and its shape was retained when it came to be constructed of other materials. It was blown at the end, and was frequently used double, either with a common mouth-piece (fig. 21) or separately; and in Greece or Rome it was usual to employ a *capistrum* or bandage round the cheeks, which embraced the mouth.

The flutes were of different lengths, to produce a more extended range of sounds. The horizontal flute, blown through a hole in the side, was in use in early times (fig. 22), but was for a long time abandoned. The modern flute was in its earliest days known as the "German" flute, to distinguish it from the flute à-bec, which was

Fig. 20.—Syrinx (MS. in the Library at Angers).

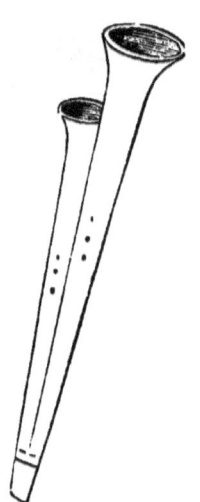

Fig. 21.—Double flute.

blown into by means of a mouthpiece containing some modification of the reed, having greater resemblance to the flageolet.

The "chorus" (fig. 23) was an instrument of one or two speaking tubes attached to a bladder, or sometimes the skin of an animal, as a pig, into which a mouthpiece was inserted to blow it by. To show the confusion in which the subject of these ancient instruments is involved, the name of chorus was also applied to a stringed instrument. That which we have been describing evidently paved the way to the *cornemuse*, or bagpipe (fig. 24), a contrivance to which some have refused the name of a musical instrument, while, on the other hand, it is held in exaggerated

Fig. 22.—Musicians playing the flute and other instruments (from Jost Amman, sixteenth century).

reverence in the northern parts of these realms. The bagpipes consist of a wind-bag, which is usually supplied from the mouth of the player; a reservoir to contain the wind, a certain number of the tubes forming the drones, which are not under the control of the player; and the chaunter, a pierced tube on which the melody is performed.

It is an instrument of great antiquity, and is found, even in our own day, over a wide extent of the globe. It exists in Italy in the rude "*zampogna*" of the Calabrian peasant, the bag formed of the skin of a pig; and in Scotland in the finished instrument of torture of Her Majesty's pipers.

Sometimes the wind was supplied to the wind-bag by

Fig. 23.—Chorus (from a MS. of the ninth century at St. Blaise).

means of a pair of bellows, worked by the pressure of the elbow. This is the case with the Irish and also with the Lowland Scotch bagpipe. Under the name of "musette" a similar instrument, of smaller dimensions, became very fashionable in France during the reign of Louis XIV. It was constructed in very ornamental fashion, and was a favourite instrument in the hands of ladies.

It is evident that the bagpipes contain all the elements

of the organ. A sculpture now in the museum at Arles (fig. 25) shows that in its most primitive form the organ was actually blown by the breath of two attendants, who of course had to blow alternately to keep up the pressure of wind. The difficulty of doing this successfully seems to have suggested the hydraulic organ. Of that instrument there is an elaborate description in Vitruvius, which has greatly exercised the ingenuity of those interested in the question. There can be no doubt, however, that it was "hydraulic" only so far that the weight of a column of water was used to produce the necessary pressure of wind. The pneumatic organ soon came into use, for on an obelisk erected by Theodosius, who died in 393, is a representation of an organ (fig. 26), in which the pressure of air is produced by a couple of attendants who are standing on the upper board of the bellows. There were probably two pairs, side by side, or the pressure could not have been uniform. Here we have the method which has been retained in Germany even to the present day.

Fig. 24.—Cornemuse, or bagpipe (from the House of the Musicians at Rheims).

The suitability of the organ for use in religious service appears to have soon suggested itself. It is stated to have been common in the churches of Spain as early as A.D. 450. In France its introduction was later. In 757 the Byzantine emperor Constantine Copronymus sent one for a present to Pépin, and seventy years later Haroun Alraschid made a similar gift to Charlemagne.

Fig. 25.—Primitive organ (sculpture in the Museum at Arles).

In the next century organs had become common. The earliest representation of an organ in which the bellows are worked by means of levers is given in a MS. Psalter of Edwin, in the library of Trinity College, Cambridge (fig. 27). It is played upon by two performers, both of whom appear to be chiding the unfortunate blowers,

THE HISTORY OF MUSICAL INSTRUMENTS. 33

a custom which even now has not gone out of use. That two performers were required for so small an instrument may be accounted for by the fact that keys had not come into use. Each particular pipe was allowed to speak by the withdrawal of a broad piece of wood which slid under the foot of the pipe. In 951 an organ of considerable dimensions was erected in Winchester Cathedral, which was described with great enthusiasm in a poem by a monk named Wolstan, although it must be admitted that the description is by no means easy of comprehension. When first introduced the keys were vastly broader than we are accustomed to in the present day, for they required to be struck by the whole fist, and thus performers on this instrument came to be called organ-beaters.

Fig. 26.—Sculpture on an obelisk erected by Theodosius at Constantinople in the fourth century, representing organs in which the pressure of air is produced by the weight of the blowers.

While the dimensions of organs continued to increase, those of small size still remained in use, under the names of Portative, Positive, or Regal (figs. 29, 30), in the accompaniment of the plain-song, and also for domestic enjoyment. The addition of pedals, which have so largely added to the resources of the organ, is attributed to Bernhard, a German living in Venice about the year 1470. With the invention of the swell, a box containing the pipes which opened with Venetian or sliding shutters, thus allowing of a crescendo,

Fig. 27.—Organ with bellows worked by levers (from a MS. of the twelfth century in the library of Trinity College, Cambridge).

the organ may be considered complete. This improvement was first applied to an organ by Jordan in the Church of St. Magnus, by London Bridge. It is almost confined to England, as the use of it on the Continent has been very rarely adopted.

The instruments of the trumpet order were numerous. The earliest were made from the horns of animals, and this type is preserved in the Jewish "*shophar*," made of ram's horn, which is still used in the synagogues at the Festival of the New Year. Another was the "oliphant" (fig. 31), so called because it was constructed from the tusk of an elephant, and was used in the Middle Ages as a hunting-horn, and also for announcing the arrival of distinguished guests. Many of these still remain, and are frequently so exquisitely carved that they are

Fig. 28.—Organ (from a MS. Psalter of the fourteenth century, National Library, Paris).

admirable works of art. In mountainous districts enormous trumpets were used as a means of communication between the shepherds on neighbouring hills (fig. 32). These were generally constructed of wood, bound together by metal bands or thongs of hide. In this form they are familiar to Swiss travellers at every spot where there exists an echo.

But it was for military purposes that the trumpet was chiefly brought into requisition. The use of metal soon

Figs. 29 and 30.—Small organs, called "Portative," "Positive," or "Regal."

became almost universal in its construction. In the earliest times it was made perfectly straight, or only slightly curved; and when the length was excessive, some sort of prop or support became necessary (figs.

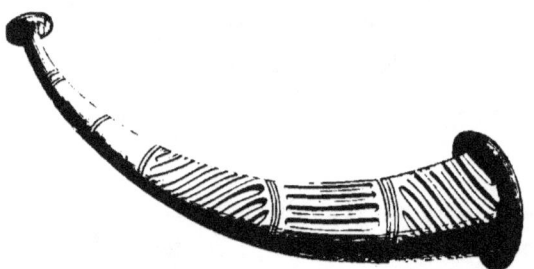

Fig. 31.—Oliphant (fourteenth century).

33, 34). It was soon found, however, that the tube could be doubled on itself with no harm to the quality of tone, but with the advantage of much greater convenience of handling (fig. 35). With the addition of the slide, by which the pitch of the instrument could be varied, the trumpet became available as an orchestral instrument, and as such was a great favourite of Handel, who has written *obbligato* parts for it to several of his songs. The sackbut was also made of metal, furnished with a sliding

Fig. 32.—Shepherds' trumpets (eighth century, from a MS. in the British Museum).

piece, and was the equivalent of the modern trombone, forming the bass to the trumpet.

The "shawm" (*i.e.* "chalumeau"), which was a reed instrument, developed into the modern hautboy, to which the bassoon serves as a bass. These were the only reed instruments in general use in the orchestra till the adoption of the clarionet in the latter part of the last century. The "recorder," which is often mentioned in seventeenth-century works, was also a reed instrument, but on the side, near the mouthpiece, there was a hole covered with a piece of bladder, which modified the quality of sound.

STRINGED INSTRUMENTS.

The fabled invention of the lyre does not concern us here, but the instrument remained in use for a long period,

Fig. 33.—Bent trumpet (eleventh century, Cottonian MS. British Museum).

Fig. 34.—Trumpet with support (eleventh century, Cottonian MS. British Museum).

and continued to be represented in the illuminations of manuscripts (figs. 36, 37). The psalterium, which succeeded it, differed in name rather than character, being simply a frame on which the strings were stretched (figs.

38, 39). The resonant chamber indeed was smaller, or even absent, so that the tone must have been less powerful. The only advantage would seem to have been the increased number of the strings. The frame assumed several different shapes. In fig. 40, for example, the upper part

Fig. 35.—Military trumpet (from Jost Amman, sixteenth century).

of it was prolonged to enable it to rest against the shoulder. Differing only in having the strings arranged diagonally is the instrument figured by the Abbot Gerbert (fig. 41) from a manuscript in the library of his monastery at St. Blasius in the Black Forest, under the title of "cithara." The "nablum" has a semicircular frame (fig. 42), and it will be noticed in this that the resonant chamber became larger. The strings of these instruments were plucked with the finger, but in many cases with a plectrum, in the way the zither is played in the present day.

Some form of the harp was almost universal (figs. 44-51), and its shape was the natural result of the different lengths of string required to produce the musical scale. In its earliest construction it was simply a wooden framework for carrying the strings, but the want of a "sound-board" to reinforce the tone was soon felt. This was supplied by making the portion of the frame nearest the body of the performer to consist of a hollow box. That this plan soon suggested itself is proved by the "Harp of O'Brien" (fig. 47) in the museum of the Royal Irish Academy, Dublin, for which the date of the tenth century is claimed. The Welsh "triple" harp, on the merits of which the inhabitants of the

Fig. 36.—Ancient lyre (from a MS. at Angers).

Fig. 37.—Lyre used in the north (ninth century).

Principality are eloquent, is so named from the fact that the strings are arranged in three parallel rows. The outer rows on each side are tuned in unison, and thus by

Fig. 38.—Psalterium (ninth century, from a MS. in the National Library, Paris).

plucking the string on each side successively it is possible with great skill to produce almost the effect of a sustained note. The inner row contains the chromatic intervals. In this position they must be very difficult of access.

The harp is an instrument around which numerous

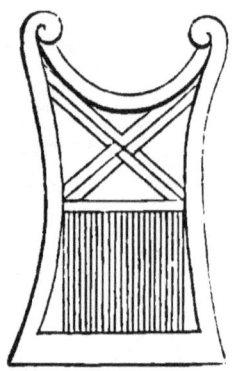

Fig. 39.—Round psalterium (twelfth century).

Fig. 40.—Psalterium (ninth century, MS. Boulogne).

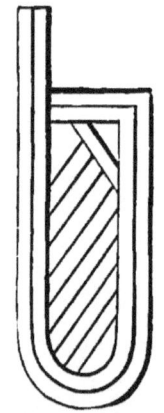

Fig. 41.—Cithara (from Gerbert).

poetical associations have gathered, from the days when David played before Saul, and Alfred entered the Danish camp; but its resources were very restricted until the invention of the "pedal" harp in the year 1720, by a Bavarian named Hochbrucher. By means of a pedal working a little plate armed with projecting pins, it was in the power of the performer to raise the pitch of each string a semitone (fig. 51). The mechanism passed up the front pillar, and each note was affected in all its octaves. Up to this time the only way of altering the pitch of the string was by pressing it with the finger. This mechanism was subsequently much improved by Erard.

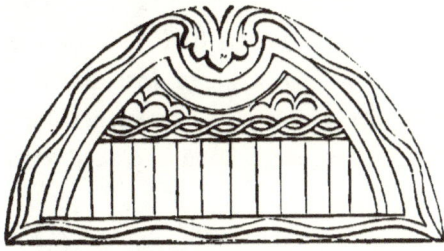

Fig. 42.—Nablum (ninth century, from MS. at Angers).

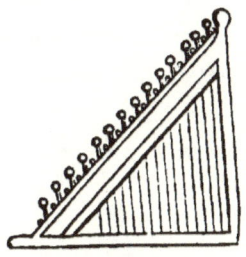

Fig. 43.—Triangular Saxon harp (ninth century, from the Bible of Charles the Bald).

A favourite instrument was the dulcimer (fig. 52), which

Fig. 44.—Harp (tenth century, Saxon Psalter, British Museum).

Fig. 45.—Harp (tenth century, University Library, Cambridge).

even now may occasionally be met with. It consisted of a flat box, acting as a resonating chamber over which the strings of wire were stretched. They were struck by little hammers. This instrument was also known as the psaltery.

An attempt was made as early as the first half of the sixteenth century, to apply keys to stringed instruments; in the first attempt, under the name of "clavicytherium," the strings were of gut, but these were soon replaced with

Fig. 46.—Harp (twelfth century, MS. National Library, Paris).

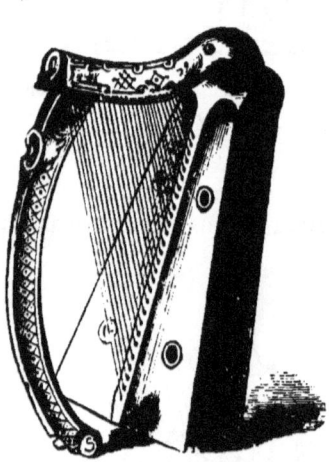

Fig. 47.—Harp of O'Brien, King of Ireland (tenth century, in the Dublin Museum).

wire, and the instrument was then called the clavichord (fig. 53). The use of these instruments was mainly confined to Germany. The peculiarity of them was that one string only served for each tone and the semitone above, the vibrating length of each string being shortened by the action of the same key which set it in vibration. This latter was produced by the impact of a metal "jack," which was raised by the key. In the "virginal" or

THE HISTORY OF MUSICAL INSTRUMENTS. 45

"spinet" the string was set in vibration by the plucking of a slip of quill or leather on the "jack." It is supposed by some that the name of virginal was given it in honour of Queen Elizabeth, with whom it was a favourite. This

Fig. 48.—Players on the harp (twelfth century, from a Bible, National Library, Paris).

Fig. 49.—Harpist (fifteenth century, from an enamel found near Soissons).

in its turn was superseded by the harpsichord, a much larger instrument, resembling in shape our modern grand pianofortes. The action was still that of the "jack" and quill, but more than one wire was used to each note, sometimes even as many as four; and there were elaborate contrivances to enable a part of these only to be set in vibration, so as to produce variety of power. Kirkman, whose house has just ceased to exist, and Tschudi, the founder of the well-known firm of Broadwood, were both eminent makers of harpsichords. The dulcimer no doubt suggested the application of hammers instead of quills. This invention has been claimed

Fig. 50.—Minstrel's harp (fifteenth century).

Fig. 51.—Harp with pedals, made by Vaderman in 1780 for Queen Marie Antoinette (now in the South Kensington Museum).

for both Germany, France, and Italy, but there can be little doubt that the latter country was a few years the earliest, in the person of Bartolomeo Cristofali. The new "pianoforte" was destined in a very short time to drive the harpsichord quite out of the field.

THE HISTORY OF MUSICAL INSTRUMENTS. 47

Among the most popular instruments during a long period commencing with the sixteenth century, although of much earlier origin, was the lute (fig. 54), and that throughout the greater part of Europe. The strings were

Fig. 52.—Dulcimer (fourteenth century, MS. National Library, Paris).

arranged in pairs tuned in unison, with a single string called the *chanterelle*, on which the melody was performed. The neck had frets at the required distances for producing the semitones. These frets were generally made of catgut, tightly fastened round the neck. Lutes were made of various sizes, and in the seventeenth century such instruments, of very large dimensions, with extra strings at the side of the finger-board, became very popular, under the names of theorbo, archlute, and chittarrone. The use

Fig. 53.—Clavichord (beginning of the sixteenth century, from Martin Agricola).

of the guitar, which requires no description, was more popular in Spain, but it also had its period of fashion both in France and England.

It will be noticed that all the stringed instruments of which we have spoken as yet were incapable of sustaining the sound. This was rendered possible by the use of the bow, which came into use in very early times. In Europe the most ancient was the Welsh crwth (fig. 55), pronounced "crowd," although some such instrument was no doubt known even earlier in the east. On the Continent a similar instrument was known under the name of *"rotta"* (fig 56), which

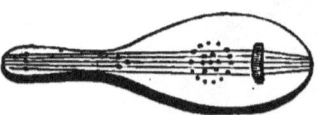

Fig. 54.—Lute (thirteenth century).

has been by some supposed to be an attempt to represent the same word. The term has been productive of

Fig. 55.—Crwth of the ninth century.

Fig. 56.—King David playing the rotta (from a window of the thirteenth century in the cathedral of Troyes).

some confusion, on account of its similarity with "*rota*," *a wheel*, by which was understood the hurdy-gurdy, an instrument of great antiquity. It may be found repre-

50 THE HISTORY OF MUSIC.

Fig. 57.

THE HISTORY OF MUSICAL INSTRUMENTS. 51

Fig. 58.

Figs. 57 and 58.—Concert (portions of a bas-relief of the capital of a column at the Church of St. George, Boscherville).

sented on a bas-relief from the Church of St. George's, Boscherville (figs. 57 and 58), in Normandy, dating from the eleventh century, and still earlier in a manuscript of the ninth century, described by Gerbert, under the title of "*organistrum*" (fig. 59). It will be seen from the figure that instead of frets the string was stopped by turning the handles at the side of the neck, which brought the projecting "feather" on the axis sufficiently above the level of the neck to effect that purpose. It appears that two performers were necessary. The size of the instrument was soon reduced so as to adapt it to the powers of a single performer, and at a later period it became very fashionable in France, under the name of the "*vielle*," and in the eighteenth century shared with the musette the attention of the ladies.

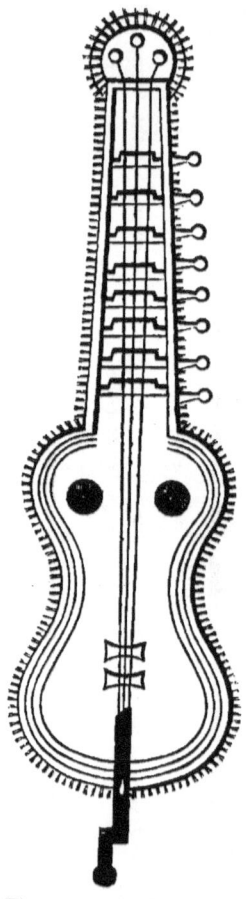

Fig. 59.—Organistrum (ninth century, from Gerbert).

For many years the viol (figs. 60–63) under various shapes, put in vibration with the bow, remained in vogue. The position of the tones and semitones was fixed by frets attached to the finger-board. For completeness it became necessary to have a "chest of viols," which contained two treble viols, a tenor and a bass-viol. The

Fig. 60.—Devil playing the viol (thirteenth century, Amiens Cathedral).

Fig. 61.—Minstrel playing the viol (fifteenth century, Book of Hours, of King René, MS. Library of the Arsenal, Paris).

Fig. 62.—Viol-player (thirteenth century enamel found at Soissons).

Fig. 63.—Angel playing the viol (Amiens Cathedral).

latter was also known as the Viola da Gamba, as it was held between the knees.

But the violin and its family were soon to oust the viol. Its invention is claimed for Gaspar Duiffoprugcar, of Bologna. It is probable that, although living in Bologna, he was in reality a Tyrolese, and his real name Tieffenbrücker. It was certain, however, that at almost the same

Fig. 64.—Rebec (sixteenth century).   Fig. 65.—Monochord (fifteenth century, from a MS. Froissart National Library, Paris).

time in the second half of the sixteenth century, both Gaspar di Salo in Brescia and Andreas Amati in Cremona began to make violins, agreeing in all important particulars with those now in use. From that time the town of Cremona acquired a reputation for these instruments which is universal. Several members of the Amati family sustained its reputation, and they were succeeded by Antonius Straduarius and Joseph Guarnerius, who carried their skill to a pitch of excellence which more modern times have not succeeded in equalling.

The monochord was more used for purposes of scientific investigation into the division of the scale than as a musical instrument, but an old manuscript of Froissart's *Chronicles* serves to show that it was occasionally brought into requisition (fig. 66). Allied to this was the "trumpet-marine," the favourite instrument of M. Jourdain in the *Bourgeois Gentilhomme* of Molière, which, in spite of its name, was a stringed instrument.

BIBLIOGRAPHY.

Coussemaker, E. de. Essai sur les Instruments de Musique au Moyen age. Paris. S.A. 4to.

Engel, Carl. A descriptive Catalogue of the Musical Instruments in the South Kensington Museum. Preceded by an Essay on the History of Musical Instruments. (2nd Edition.) London, 1874. 8vo.

South Kensington Museum Art Handbook. No. 5. Musical Instruments. London. S.A. 8vo.

Hopkins, E. J. The Organ. . . . Preceded by an entirely New History of the Organ by E. F. Rimbault, LL.D. (2nd Edition.) London, 1870. 8vo.

Rimbault, E. F. The Pianoforte, its Origin, Progress and Construction, with some Account of Instruments of the same Class which preceded it; viz., the Clavichord, the Virginal, the Spinet, the Harpsichord, etc. London, 1860. 4to.

Hipkins, A. J. A description and History of the Pianoforte and of the older Keyboard stringed instruments. London, 1876. 8vo.

Rühlmann, Julius. Die Geschichte der Bogen-Instrumente. Brunswick, 1882. 1 vol. 8vo, with 1 vol. oblong, Plates.

CHAPTER III.

THE MUSICAL INFLUENCE OF THE NETHERLANDS.

Dufay—Binchois—John of Dunstable—Hobrecht—Okeghem or Okenheim—Tinctoris—Obligations to Glareanus for our knowledge of these Early Musicians—Josquin de Prés—Willaert—The Invention of the Madrigal—Early Music Printers—Orlando di Lassus.

AS we have seen in Chapter I., the plain-song of the Church had now assumed a definite form, which the improvements in musical notation placed beyond the reach of those corruptions inseparable from oral tradition, while in secular music the same improvements had also been adopted, as shown by examples that have come down to us.

The progress of music was destined to receive a great impetus from the genius of a school of composers which arose in Flanders. The influence of this school in a short time made itself paramount over the whole of Europe, both by the originality of the works which it produced and by the personal influence of its members, whose assistance was in request at all the centres of musical life. Its founders were Guillaume Dufay (1350–1432), Egidius Binchois (1400–1465), and John of Dunstable, the latter of whom was of English birth. Their reputation is based on the testimony of contemporaries rather than on any specimens of their powers which have been handed down to us, although Dufay became attached as tenor singer to the Pontifical Chapel in Rome in the year 1380, retaining this position until his death, and while thus employed he wrote several masses, which are still preserved in its archives.

In the second half of the fifteenth century three other distinguished musicians came to the front: Hobrecht, Okeghem or Okenheim, and Tinctoris. Hobrecht was master of the music at the cathedral of Utrecht, and it is interesting to note that in that capacity he had as pupil the eminent Erasmus, who sang there as a choirboy about the year 1471. For our acquaintance with the works of Hobrecht and several other of the distinguished musicians of those early times we are indebted to a distinguished philosopher and mathematician named Glareanus, from the fact that he was a native of the canton of Glarus. He enjoyed the intimacy of Erasmus, and among the many fields of learning which he cultivated, took great delight in music, on which subject he wrote two works, in addition to editing Boethius, whose treatise on music was then looked on as containing the highest knowledge on the subject. The most important of the works of Glareanus on the subject of music was called *Dodecachordon*. The theory which it was designed to support does not concern us here; its interest for our present purpose lies in the fact that a large number of specimens of the compositions of contemporary and earlier musicians, which it would be exceedingly difficult to find elsewhere, are preserved in this work, as well as many interesting particulars of their composers. The book, which is an excellent example of typography and music printing, was published at Basle in 1547. Speaking of Hobrecht, he tells us that he was a man who composed with remarkable facility, one night sufficing for the composition of a mass, which was the admiration of musicians. In 1492 he was elected musical director of the cathedral

Fig. 66.—Viol-players (after Jost Amman, sixteenth century).

at Antwerp, from a number of competitors who, during a whole year, took charge of the services in turn; and this appointment he held till his death, about the year 1507. He exercised important influence on the development of music, and was looked on as a great authority, receiving visits from all the principal musicians of his time. A collection of five of his masses, as well as many of his motets, were published during his lifetime by Petrucci.

It is supposed that Okenheim, who was born about 1430, began his career as a choir-boy in Antwerp Cathedral, and there are strong grounds for believing that he continued his studies, after the breaking of his voice, under Binchois. It is certain, however, that in 1461 he was chaplain to Charles VII. of France, and afterwards to his successors Louis XI. and Charles VIII.; he subsequently became treasurer of St. Martin at Tours without resigning his other appointment. The testimony of contemporary writers unites in showing the respect in which he was held, and his death formed the subject of a poem, *La Déploration de Crétin sur le Trépas de feu Okeghem,*— which has been reprinted in Paris within the last few years by M. Thoinan, -as well as of dirges to his memory by more than one of his pupils. Glareanus claims for him the invention of the form of musical composition called "canon." Many of his works remain in manuscript, and of those which were published the original editions are of the greatest rarity. As a teacher, Okenheim's reputation was equally great, many of the leading musicians at the end of the fifteenth and beginning of the sixteenth centuries having been his pupils; among these the most famous was Josquin de Prés, of whom we shall have to speak presently.

Tinctoris is better known as a theorist than as a composer. He was born at Nivelles, seemingly about 1434 or 1435, and at an early age went to Italy, where he became *maître de chapelle* to Ferdinand, King of Naples, by whom he was held in great estimation. He there founded a school of music. To Tinctoris belongs the merit of writing the first dictionary of music, under the title of *Terminorum Musicæ Definitorium*, a book of the very greatest rarity, being the first work printed on the subject of music. It is distinguished by great clearness of statement, and has been reprinted several times during the present century.

But a still greater light appeared in the person of Josquin de Prés (1450?-1521), a man who having been taught all that could be taught by his master Okenheim, possessed in addition that true genius which enabled him to use his vast learning as a means to an end—the production of works of true beauty. Till that time no one had appealed so directly to the heart. Early in life he was master of the music at the cathedral of Cambrai, but he was soon called to become one of the singers in the Pontifical Chapel at Rome, under Pope Sixtus IV. At the death of the latter he entered the service of Ercole d'Este, Duke of Ferrara, and subsequently that of Lorenzo de Medici, of Louis XII. of France, and of the Emperor Maximilian I. Josquin appears to have been a man of much address, as the following anecdotes will show. Louis XII. wished him to write a piece of music for several voices, in which he could himself take part. The King was an indifferent musician, with a weak voice, and sang much out of tune. The composer wrote a part which he called *vox regis*, consisting of the repetition of a single note throughout—an example which many years later was followed by Mendelssohn in his *Son and Stranger*. At another time the King promised him some preferment, but delayed to perform his promise, on which the composer wrote and executed a motet to the words *Memor est verbi tui.* The hint was not taken, whereupon he tried the effect of a second motet, *Portio mea non est in terra viventium.* At last he received the long-wished-for benefice, and expressed his gratitude in a third motet, *Bonitatem fecisti cum servo tuo, Domine.* A number of his masses were printed by Petrucci and others, as well as a large collection of motets and other sacred music, in addition to many chansons, etc.

We have spoken only of the leaders of the Flemish school, but it was very numerous, and comprised many men whose works were only inferior to those of the great masters whose scholars they were. Among these we must name Pierre de la Rue, Brumel, Jannequin, Mouton, Arcadelt, Verdelot, Gombert, Clemens non Papa, Goudimel (who settled in Rome and founded a school, but was subsequently killed in Lyons during the massacre of St. Bartholomew), Philippe de Monte, Waelrent, and Claude le Jeune.

Another distinguished Fleming, Adrian Willaert, founded a school in Venice, from which issued, among others, Constanzo Porta, Cypriano di Rore, and the great theorist Zarlino.

We have seen how widely extended was the influence of the Flemish school. One of its greatest achievements is the invention of the madrigal—a form of composition which at once met with the greatest favour both in the Netherlands and in Italy. Circumstances greatly favoured this result. The art of printing music with movable type had just been invented by Ottaviano dei Petrucci, of Fossombrone, in the duchy of Urbino, about the year 1503, who set up a press in Venice. Others quickly followed. Gardano, Vincenti, and Scotto in Venice, Phalèse in Antwerp, as well as others, printed edition after edition of sets of madrigals, for which the demand seems to have been inexhaustible. Everything published in Italy was at once reprinted at Antwerp, frequently at Nuremburg also, and *vice versâ*. They were invariably printed in separate parts for convenience of performance,—a score was unknown. It naturally follows that complete sets of parts of early madrigals are among the rarities of musical literature, for singers were doubtless no more careful in those days of the music they took home to practise than they are at present. This remarkable multiplication of copies proves that the knowledge of music and the power of singing must have been very widespread.

We have still to speak of one more of the glories of the Flemish school—with whom it seems to have died out—Roland de Lattre, better known as Orlando di Lasso or di Lassus, for he adopted both forms of his name. He was born at Mons, most probably in the year 1520, according to some authorities in 1530. At an early age he became a choir-boy at the Church of St. Nicolas, and so beautiful was his voice that three separate attempts were made to kidnap him. On the first two occasions his parents were fortunate enough to recover their child, but on the third they allowed him to remain with Ferdinand Gonzaga, Viceroy of Sicily, who was at that time in command of an army of the Emperor Charles V. at St. Dizier. By him the young Orlando was taken to Milan, and subsequently to Sicily. He appears to have remained three years at Naples with the Marquis of Terza, and then to have gone to Rome, where for six months he was the guest of the Archbishop of Florence, until he received the appointment of director of the choir at St. John Lateran, a post which at that time was always entrusted to a musician of eminence. After two years he returned to his native land, and entering the service of Julius Cæsar Bracanio, visited in his train the court of our Henry VIII., by whom he was well received. He had decided on settling in this country, when he was called to Antwerp to assume the post of director of the music. There he made himself so much esteemed that he proposed to make that city his permanent abode. But his reputation had become so great that Duke Albert V. of Bavaria, a true lover of music, made him the most flattering offers, with the result that in 1557 he removed to Munich, which from that time became his home.

The intercourse between the Duke and the musician was of the most intimate nature, and did honour to them both. The Duke took a deep and personal interest in all the works of the musician; the latter was a man of charming and courtly manners, whose knowledge was not confined to the art which he practised. He married a young maid-of-honour attached to the court, and was subsequently ennobled by the Emperor Maximilian II. He died in

Fig. 67.—Orlando di Lassus.

MUSICAL INFLUENCE OF THE NETHERLANDS.

Munich in 1594, having passed his life in the most congenial surroundings which could fall to the lot of a musician.

The number of works which he left behind him was enormous, in all departments of musical composition. They comprise 51 masses, 180 magnificats, 780 motets, and many other works of sacred music, while among the secular are contained 233 madrigals and 371 chansons, altogether 1,572 sacred and 765 secular works. A magnificent collection of his works is still to be seen in the Royal Library at Munich, superbly written on vellum, with illuminations, and in the richest binding. These volumes alone are a splendid testimony to the consideration in which he was held. Many of his works are included in the *Patrocinium Musices*, printed by Adam Berg in Munich, a sumptuous work, of which seven volumes only were issued, of the largest folio, and printed in notes which could be read by a whole choir. After the death of Orlando di Lassus, his sons Ferdinand and Rudolph brought out a complete collection of his motets in separate parts, in six volumes, under the title of *Magnum Opus Musicum*. It is most clearly printed, and if the bars were inserted, could be read from by any choir in the present day. An admirable edition of the works of the great musician is now in course of publication by Messrs. Breitkopf and Härtel.

With Orlando di Lassus ceases the predominance of musical activity in the Netherlands. As we have seen, its influence had extended over the whole of the continent of Europe. From this time Italy became for a while the chosen home of music.

BIBLIOGRAPHY.

Kiesewetter, R. G., and Fétis, F. J. Verhandelingen over de vraag: Welke verdiensten hebben zich de Nederlanders vooral in de 14ᵉ. 15ᵉ. en 16ᵉ. eeuw in het vak der toonkunst verworven. Amsterdam, 1829. 4to. (Kiesewetter's essay is in German, that of Fétis in French.)

Schmid, Anton. Ottaviano dei Petrucci da Fossombrone der erste Erfinder des Musik notendruckes. Wien, 1845, 8vo.

Dehn, S. W. Biographische Notiz über Roland de Lattre. (This contains an admirable catalogue of the works of Lassus. Dehn is said to have scored the *whole* of the *Magnum Opus Musicum*.)

Ambros, A. W. Geschichte der Musik, *vide* p. 19.

CHAPTER IV.

MUSIC IN ITALY AND GERMANY.

The Papal Chapel—Palestrina and his Reforms—His Successors—The Music for Holy Week in the Sistine Chapel—Music in Venice—Writers on the Theory of Music—Early German Composers—Isaak and Senfl—The Influence of the Reformation on Music—German Writers on Musical Instruments and Theory.

IT will scarcely appear surprising that Rome, the centre of all that was most magnificent in the pomp of religious ceremonial, should attract within its walls the most eminent artists of the day, and we have seen how many of the Flemish musicians were drawn to it; indeed, the majority of the Papal Chapel were of that nation. Under the influence of Josquin de Prés, and still more of Orlando di Lassus, the school of the Low Countries had in a great measure broken away from the mere exhibition of technical contrivance—although that was not wanting—in favour of greater beauty of expression. The practice, however, was still maintained of employing secular melodies as the subjects of religious compositions; for instance, every writer of the day felt it due to his reputation to write a mass on the air *L'Homme Armé*; and many of the subjects in vogue were even more mundane in their associations.

In addition to this practice, which to the musicians

of those days suggested no lack of reverence, corruptions had also crept into the authorised text of the mass, the singers even venturing at times to sing the very words of the secular melodies on which the masses were written; in fact, great laxity had become common, and had been the occasion of grave scandal.

The Council of Trent was now (1564) sitting, and this abuse was one of the subjects which it was called on to consider. It is needless to say that it was condemned absolutely, a proposition being very seriously entertained to forbid any other music than the plain-song. Pope Pius IV., however, decided on referring the whole question to a commission of eight cardinals, with the saintly Carlo Borromeo at its head. The commission appears to have taken great pains to act rightly, and sought the advice of many of the papal singers. Cardinal Borromeo was personally strongly opposed to the proposition of confining ecclesiastical music to the ancient plain-song, and persuaded his fellow-members to suspend their judgment, having in the meantime requested Palestrina, who had already attained some eminence, to compose a mass which should reconcile the claims of religion and of art.

The composer was not content with writing a single mass; he submitted three, which were sung in succession by the papal singers before the commission. It was at once seen that the great composer had solved the problem. Both the first and the second mass were heard with delight, but the third with absolute enthusiasm. Nothing so solemn had been heard up to that time. This was the famous *Missa Papæ Marcelli*, so named in memory of Pope Marcellus, who filled the office for a few days only. It remains a model of all that religious music should be—the highest type of unaccompanied vocal music, and at the same time most devotional and expressive. It was at once sung before the Pope in the Sistine Chapel, when it impressed all hearers with its beauty.

Giovanni Pierluigi da Palestrina was so named from the place of his birth, the date of which was 1524. At an early age he went to Rome, singing in the choir of Santa Maria Maggiore. He became a pupil of Claude Goudimel, and, after holding different offices, was in 1555 appointed by Julius III. a singer in the Sistine Chapel. Shortly afterwards Paul IV., who had succeeded to the papacy, deprived him of his office on the ground that he was not in orders, and that he was also married. In the same year, however, he was made director of the music of St. John Lateran, and in 1561 at Santa Maria Maggiore. As a result of the success of his *Missa Papæ Marcelli*, the office of composer to the Sistine Chapel was created for him. He was a man of great saintliness of character, living in the greatest intimacy with St. Philip Neri, in whose arms he expired in the year 1594. His works, which are very numerous, including no less than ninety-three masses, are masterpieces of the art of writing for unaccompanied voice; they are full of learned contrivance, but the learning is kept in the background by the devotional feeling which is their prominent characteristic; no vocal music is capable of giving greater delight to the true musician; no music is more admirably suited to the requirements of religious worship. Such fitness had never been attained before his time, and the term "alla Palestrina" has ever since been applied to the highest development of sacred music. Many of his compositions are still unpublished, but this reproach is being removed by Messrs. Breitkopf and Härtel, of Leipzig, who are bringing out a complete and critical edition of his works, now approaching completion.

It will be supposed that the traditions of such a master would be perpetuated. Among those who followed in his footsteps were Giovanni Maria and Bernardino Nanini, Felice and Francesco Anerio, Giovanni Animuccia, Luca Marenzio, and Gregorio Allegri. The Papal Chapel had always numbered among its members several Spanish musicians. Among the most eminent of these were Christoforo Morales—a motet by whom, *Lamentabatur Jacob*, is a masterpiece of expressive music—Bartolomeo Escobedo, Francesco Guerrero, and, perhaps greatest of all, Loreto Vittoria.

The choir of the Sistine Chapel carried the practice of unaccompanied vocal music to the highest pitch of excellence, and was the admiration of all musicians. The performance of the music during Holy Week was especially admirable. This was the composition of Palestrina, Allegri, and Bai. The *Miserere* of Allegri was so jealously guarded that no member of the choir was allowed to take one of the parts out of the chapel, under pain of excommunication. Our own Dr. Burney, however, succeeded in obtaining a copy, which he published in 1771, and it will be remembered how the youthful Mozart, when only fourteen years of age, wrote it down from memory after hearing it once, taking his manuscript in his hat for correction on a second occasion. When it is remembered

Fig. 68.—Hans Leo Hassler.

that the composition is written for two choruses of four and five parts, and that the two choruses finally unite, the wonderful nature of the feat becomes the more remarkable.

We have already mentioned that a school of music was

founded at Venice under the auspices of the Flemish musician Adrian Willaert. It produced many good musicians, among whom were Cipriano di Rore, who, in spite of his name, was of Flemish origin; Giovanni della Croce, renowned for his madrigals; Andrea Gabrieli, and his nephew Giovanni Gabrieli. Its influence made itself felt in its turn in Germany. Hans Leo Hassler (fig. 68), was among the earliest musicians of Nuremberg, having learned his art in Venice at the feet of the elder Gabrieli. Among other musicians of Northern Italy, we must name Orazio Vecchi and Giangiacomo Gastoldi, who both pursued their art in Milan, and Costanzo Porta, another pupil of Willaert, who was successively director of the music at Padua, Ravenna and Loretto.

In addition to the numerous composers of whom we have spoken, there was no lack of writers on the theory of music. Among the earliest of these was Franchinus Gaforius, who published his first work in the year 1480; and it is a proof of the interest taken in the subject, so soon after the invention of printing, that several editions of his treatises were called for. We must also mention Peter Aron, and somewhat later Zarlino, who was director of the music of St. Mark's at Venice. It was the fashion of those early days to bring out handbooks to the seven liberal arts, of which, of course, music formed one; these were generally dry treatises epitomised from Boethius, and as a knowledge of plain-song was part of the education of every priest, it naturally follows that the works on this subject were almost countless.

In Germany, among the earliest musicians of eminence

we find Heinrich Isaak. The place and time of his birth are doubtful, but he was a contemporary—some say a pupil—of Josquin de Prés. He became director of the choir of St. Giovanni in Florence, from which place he was called back to Germany by Maximilian I. Many of his works remain in manuscript, but some were published, and several handed down to us in the works of Glareanus and other writers. His pupil Ludwig Senfl (fig. 69), of Swiss birth, wrote masses, as well as many motets, and among his miscellaneous writings set to music some of the odes of Horace. The names of Jakob Händl and Gregoir Aichinger must also be recorded.

About this time the Reformation took place. It is well known that Luther was a profound lover of music, several well-known chorales being attributed to him. There can be no doubt that one of the effects of the Reformation was to alter the direction of musical activity. The laity were encouraged to join in the musical portions of the service. It is obvious that works of any elaboration were unsuited for such a purpose, and to this feeling must be attributed the multiplication of chorales, many of which form the cherished inheritance of the Protestant portions of the German nation, to whom they are universally familiar. Among the best known of these, and one identified with the great Reformer's career, is *Ein' feste Burg ist unser Gott*, and this is additionally familiar from its introduction by Meyerbeer in his *Huguenots*, by Mendelssohn in the *Reformation Symphony*, and by Wagner in his *Kaiser March*. *Nun danket alle Gott* is another, which in Germany occupies much the same position that the Old Hundredth Psalm

Fig. 69.—Ludwig Senfl.

does with Englishmen. The beauty and appropriateness of the German chorale are incontestable, but there can be little doubt that its exclusive use has tended to cramp the development of religious music in that country.

Germany produced a large number of didactic and theoretical works, among the earliest and most curious of which is the *Flores Musicæ*, by Hugo von Reutlingen, printed by Pryss at Strasburg in 1488, although probably written more than a century earlier. As its title indicates, it is in Latin, and while printed as prose, in reality consists of hexameter verses, with a running commentary by a later hand. Among our greatest obligations to the Germans is the information they have given us on the form and construction of the musical instruments of that time. The *Musica Getutscht* of Sebastian Virdung (Basle, 1511) gives descriptions, with figures, of most of these. It is a work of very great rarity, five copies only being known, three of which are in public libraries abroad, the others both in this country in private hands. Fortunately an excellent facsimile has been published. It is written in the German language, but in 1536 Ottomar Luscinius (*i.e.*, Nachtigall) brought out a similar book in Latin, illustrated with the identical blocks used for Virdung's work, of which it was in great part a translation. Lastly, we must mention another and a later work, also of the greatest rarity, the *Syntagma Musicum* of Michael Prætorius (fig. 70) (Wittemburg and Wolfenbüttel, 1615-1620), designed by the author to be a complete encyclopædia of the art and practice of music, which also contains descriptions and woodcuts of the instruments then in use (fig. 71). Of these plates an excellent facsimile has been issued, but the letterpress has not been reprinted. As the date of the work is nearly a century after that of Virdung, its historical value is important.

Fig. 70.—Michael Prætorius.

We have already spoken of the debt we owe to Glareanus for preserving to us in his great work *Dodecachordon* many compositions by distinguished musicians of an earlier date which would have been otherwise lost. For the same reason must be mentioned Sebaldus

Fig. 71.—Title-page of the volume of plates of the *Syntagma* of Michael Prætorius (1620). [Reduced size.]

Heyden's *Ars Canendi* (Nuremberg, 1537). The number of books on the science of music published in Germany during this period is very large, and the Germans soon became, as they have since remained, the most prolific writers on the art.

BIBLIOGRAPHY.

Adami, Andrea. Osservazioni per ben regolare il coro dei cantori della cappella pontificia. Roma, 1711. 4to. (Contains memoirs and portraits of seven of the more eminent members of the Papal Chapel.)

Baini, Giuseppe. Memorie storico-critiche della vita e della opere di Giovanni Pierluigi da Palestrina. Roma, 1828. 2 vols., 4to.

Caffi, Francesco. Storia della musica sacra nella già capella ducale di San Marco in Venezia dal 1318 al 1797. Venezia, 1854, 1855. 2 vols., 8vo.

Koch, E. E. Geschichte der Kirchenlieds und Kirchengesangs der christlichen, insbesondere der deutschen evangelischen Kirche. (2nd ed.), Stuttgart, 1852-3. 4 vols., 8vo.

Winterfeld, C. von. Der evangelische Kirchengesang und sein Verhältniss zur Kunst des Tonsatzes. Leipzig, 1843, 5, 7. 3 vols., 4to.

CHAPTER V.

EARLY HISTORY OF MUSIC IN ENGLAND.

Sumer is icumen in—Fairfax, Sheppard, Mulliner, Taverner, Merbecke, Tallis, Redford, Edwards, Tye and Byrd—Patent for Music-printing granted to Tallis and Byrd—Farrant—The Madrigalian Era—N. Yonge's *Musica Transalpina*—Watson's *Italian Madrigals Englished*—Morley, Bateson, Ward, and O. Gibbons—*Triumphs of Oriana*—Widespread Knowledge of Music—Morley's *Introduction*—*Parthenia*—Dr. John Bull—Foundation of Gresham College—Ravenscroft—Hilton—Barnard's Cathedral Music—Metrical Version of the Psalms.

IF, in consequence of its geographical position, England was in a great measure cut off from the musical influences which were at work in the Continent of Europe, there is one fact to which it may point with pride—the possession of the earliest secular composition in parts existing in any country. This is the famous *rota*, or *round*, *Sumer is icumen in*, contained in one of the Harleian manuscripts at the British Museum. An excellent facsimile forms the frontispiece of Mr. W. Chappell's *Popular Music of the Olden Time*, and another is to be found in Sir George Grove's *Dictionary of Music* (vol. iii.). We do not therefore reproduce it here. In the judgment of those best qualified to form an opinion, the manuscript belongs to the first half of the thirteenth century. This was the opinion of the late Sir F. Madden among others, and lest it should be supposed that national feeling may have influenced this decision, it may be well to mention that M. Coussemaker concurred in it. The composition is a canon for four voices, with two others forming the *pes*, or burden. The style of the composition, both in melody and harmony, is far in advance of anything known at that time, which was a hundred and fifty years before the rise of the Flemish school.

With so long a step in advance, it is humiliating to be unable to continue the record, and we are forced to suppose that much music was lost at the suppression of the monasteries in the time of Henry VIII. We have already spoken of John of Dunstable. Of musicians before the Reformation very little beyond the names has come down to us. Robert Fairfax, Doctor of Music (and England is the only country in which degrees in music have been conferred), was organist, or perhaps precentor, of St. Albans in the reign of Henry VII. About the same time flourished John Sheppard, organist of Magdalen College, Oxford, who received his education from Thomas Mulliner, master of the boys of St. Paul's, London. Taverner was organist of Boston, and subsequently of Cardinal College (now Christchurch), Oxford. Having joined the Reformed religion, his life was in some peril, but fortunately his skill in music helped to secure his acquittal.

We now come to one whose name is more widely known in our own time—John Merbecke, to whom was entrusted the duty of arranging the musical portions of the first reformed Prayer Book of Edward VI., which was published in 1550, under the title of *The Booke of Common Praier Noted*. This was an adaptation of the plain-song to the new form of liturgy. The author was a man of some learning in other departments of knowledge, having compiled a concordance to the Bible. He was a very staunch adherent to the new doctrines, and nearly fell a martyr to his opinions, having been condemned to death with two of his friends, who were actually executed, his own life being saved by Bishop Gardiner's intervention. The choral portions of the services of the Reformed Church were also set to music by the celebrated Tallis. He made use of the resources of harmony, and his noble setting has held its place to the present day wherever the choral service of the English Church is performed.

John Redford succeeded Mulliner as master of the boys at St. Paul's Cathedral; he wrote many services and anthems, one of which, *Rejoice in the Lord*, is still in use. Richard Edwards, also a writer of much Church music, is better known to us as the composer of the beautiful madrigal, *In going to my naked bed*. Some of the works of Dr. Tye also are still performed. He formed the idea of making a rhymed translation of the Acts of Apostles and of setting it to music, but does not seem to have advanced beyond the fourteenth chapter.

Tallis was one of the most learned composers in an age of learning. In proof of this we may point to his canon in forty parts, which is still extant. One of his familiar works is the well-known tune to Bishop Ken's evening hymn, which contains a canon between the treble and tenor parts. William Byrd is known to most by his canon *Non nobis Domine*, so often sung as a grace. It has remained a matter of discussion whether Byrd conformed to the Protestant religion or continued in the Romish faith; but it is certain that he composed several masses. One of these, for five voices, forms the earliest publication of the Musical Antiquarian Society. With Tallis, who was his master, he published a set of *Cantiones Sacræ*, and other sets by himself alone, under similar titles. Of his English works we have *Psalms, Sonets, and Songs of Sadnes and Pietie, Songs of Sundrie Natures, some of gravitie and others of myrth*, and *Psalms, Songs, and Sonnets, some solemne, others joyful, framed to the Life of the Words*. To Tallis and Byrd, and to the survivor of them, was granted by Queen Elizabeth the exclusive right of printing music and of ruling music paper. Tallis died in 1585, and the patent devolved wholly on Byrd, who is believed to have gained largely by it.

We must not pass by Richard Farrant, gentleman of the Chapel Royal, without mention. The beautiful subject of his still favourite anthem, *Lord, for Thy tender mercies' sake*, is alone sufficient to preserve his name from oblivion, although by some it has been attributed to Hilton.

We have now come to the golden age of music in England, a time when its composers will bear comparison with any contemporary writers on the Continent. This period has been happily called the Madrigalian Era, and is covered by a space of exactly fifty years from the year 1588, which is the date of the first collection of madrigals published in this country. The title is worth transcribing:—

"*Musica Transalpina:* Madrigales translated of foure, five, and sixe parts, chosen out of divers excellent Authors, with the first and second part of *La Verginella*, made by Maister Byrd, upon two stanz's of Ariosto, and brought to speak English with the rest. Published by N. Yonge, in favour of such as take pleasure in musick of voices. Imprinted at London by Thomas East the assigné of William Byrd. 1588."

It will thus be seen that this first collection was almost exclusively, as its title infers, a collection of the work of foreign musicians; in fact, it contains, among others, four by Palestrina, four by F. di Monte, ten by Luca Marenzio, two by Orlando di Lassus, and fourteen by Ferrabosco. In his quaint preface Yonge says:—

"Since I first began to keepe house in this citie, it hath been no small comfort unto mee that a great number of gentlemen and merchants of good accompt (as well of this realme as of forraine nations) have taken in good part such entertainments of pleasure, as my poore abilitie was able to affoord them, both by the exercise of musicke daily used in my house, and by furnishing them with bookes of that kinde yearly sent me out of Italy and other places, which beeing for the most part Italian songs, are for sweetness of aire verie well liked of all, but most in account with them that understand that language. . . . And albeit there be some English songs lately set forth by a great master of musicke which for skill and sweetness may content the most curious; yet because they are not many in number, men delighted with varietie have wished more of the same sort."

To the praiseworthy desire so quaintly expressed we are indebted for this collection, which Yonge followed up with a second in the year 1579. From the wording of the preface it was generally supposed that Yonge was a merchant in London; from Mr. W. Barclay Squire's researches there seems little reason now, however, to doubt that he was really one of the vicars choral of St. Paul's.

Another collection of foreign madrigals was published in 1590 by Thomas Watson: *The first set of Italian. Madrigalls Englished, not to the sense of the originall Dittie, but after the affection of the Noate.* Whether this introduction of foreign madrigals directed the efforts of our own musicians into that channel we are unable to say, but certain it is that from that time set after set by native musicians followed each other in quick succession. The principal composers were Morley, with a set for four voices and another for five, besides ballets and canzonets, or *Little Short Aers*; Weelkes, five or six sets of madrigals and one of *Ayeres, or Phantastike Spirits*; Wilbye, two sets, comprising the well-known *Flora gave me Fairest Flowers*, and *Sweet Honey-sucking Bees*; Bateson, also two sets; Ward and Orlando Gibbons each wrote a set. They were among the later representatives of the school. Gibbon's *Silver Swan* is a little masterpiece of dramatic expression. We have selected only the most prominent writers for mention, but together they produced a large body of works, mostly of the greatest interest and merit.

There is one set which we have not mentioned that, called the *Triumphs of Oriana,* a collection of twenty-five madrigals, two of which were by Ellis Gibbons, brother of Orlando Gibbons ; but with this exception, each was by a different composer, and each ended with the same burden in praise of Oriana, under which title is meant Queen Elizabeth, who has been accused of having encouraged the delicate flattery. Certainly it is flattery of which any monarch might be proud. The work was collected by Morley.

The publication of so much vocal part music supposes a very wide knowledge of music, and this, we find, was the case. Every gentleman was expected to be able to take his part. For instance, in Morley's *Plaine and Easie Introduction to Practicall Musicke* (1597), Philomathes, the disciple, gives the following reason for seeking instruction : " Supper being ended, and musicke-bookes, according to the custome, being brought to the table, the mistresse of the house presented mee with a part, earnestly requesting me to sing. But when, after manie excuses, I protested unfainedly that I could not, eurie one began to wonder. Yea, some whispered to others, demanding how I was brought vp. So that, vpon shame of mine ignorance, I go nowe to seeke out mine olde friende master Gnorimus, to make my selfe his scholler." To this his friend Polymathes replies, " I am glad you are at length come to bee of that minde, though I wished it sooner. Therefore goe, and I praie God send you such good successe as you would wish to your selfe."

It is much to be regretted that a very small portion only

of all these riches is available for performance, or even for study. We have already spoken of the rarity of original copies of music of this character, which was invariably published in parts, and in consequence is seldom found complete. Some attempt was made about the year 1840 to remove this reproach by the foundation of the Musical Antiquarian Society, which during several years republished, with some luxury, many of these masterpieces, in score. After a time, as too frequently is the case with such undertakings, the work got into arrears, and the subscribers fell away, and thus the Society came to an end when its work was but just beginning. Fortunately, thanks to the enterprise of a musical amateur, Mr. G. E. P. Arkwright, a new series of old English composers is in course of publication, and already comprises the madrigals of Kirbye, songs of sundry natures by Byrd, madrigals by Alfonso Ferrabosco from the *Musica Transalpina*, ballets and madrigals by Weelkes, and a Mass by Dr. Christopher Tye. The enterprise deserves the support of all who are interested in these five specimens of our national music.

Many of these madrigals are described as "apt for viols," and no doubt formed the principal resource of the instrumental performers of those days, although Orlando Gibbons wrote a set of *Fantasies in three parts*, and a few by other composers exist. Of some of the foreign madrigals, parts are found without the words, expressly arranged for instrumental performance. The year 1611 saw the publication of *Parthenia the Maydenhead of the first Musicke that was ever printed for the Virginals, by the famous masters William Byrd, Dr. John Bull, and Orlando*

Gibbons, Gentlemen of his Majesties most Illustrious Chapell. It is said to be the earliest work printed from copper plates, and is engraved on a double stave of six lines in each. The music consists of *preludiums, pavanas,* and *galiardos,* and its difficulty speaks well for the executive power of those days. Dr. John Bull, whom we have just mentioned, was a very skilful performer on the organ, and a musician of great attainments, much in favour with Queen Elizabeth. His health having given way, he travelled in France and Germany, being everywhere received with the respect due to his abilities. James I. having appointing him his organist, he returned to England, but starting again on his travels, became the organist of Antwerp Cathedral. He must have been a man of a restless disposition, for he died at Lübeck in 1628; some, however, say in Hamburg. To him is attributed, we fear on somewhat slender grounds, the composition of our national anthem, *God save the King.*

By the munificence of a citizen of London, Sir Thomas Gresham, provision was made for the foundation of a college to afford instruction in the principal branches of knowledge, among which music had a place. The bequest was not to take effect until the death of his widow, who survived him for some years, so that it was not until 1597 that the scheme could be matured. On the express recommendation of Queen Elizabeth, Bull was appointed the first professor. Precise injunctions were drawn up as to the course to be adopted by the holder of the office. "The solemn music lecture is to be read in manner following; that is to say, the theoretic part for one half-hour or thereabouts, and the practical part, by help of voices or instruments, for the hour." All the other lectures were to be read both in Latin and English ; but, in deference to Bull's small acquaintance with Latin, this requirement was waived in the case of the music professor, and this arrangement has continued to the present day. Bull's inaugural lecture is extant; but when his health gave way, Thomas Byrd, a son of William Byrd, seems to have undertaken his duties. It is disgraceful to have to state that the intentions of the founder, at least with regard to the music lectures, were absolutely neglected. The subsequent professors were completely ignorant of the art they undertook to illustrate, and it was not until the present century that a better state of things was inaugurated by the appointment of R. J. S. Stevens, a musician of adequate attainments. In 1609 was published by Thomas Ravenscroft, under the title *Pammelia*, the first collection of catches, rounds, and canons printed in this country. This was followed in the same year by *Deuteromelia*, which contains the favourite Nursery catch *Three Blinde Mice*, and it is worthy of note that it is written in the minor, not in the major, as it is now almost invariably sung. Hilton's *Catch that Catch Can*, first printed in 1652, was another favourite collection, which was frequently reprinted.

The first attempt to form a collection of cathedral music was made by the Rev. John Barnard, one of the minor canons of St. Paul's in the year 1641. It comprises both services and anthems by most of the eminent Church musicians who had written before that time. No complete copy of this valuable work is known. It should consist of ten vocal parts. Of these Hereford Cathedral possessed eight, of which several were imperfect; in 1862 the Sacred Harmonic Society, at that time in the height of its prosperity, became the fortunate possessor of eight parts; and, strange to say, these two libraries each had the parts wanting to complete the other set. Soon afterwards one of the missing parts was purchased for Hereford, and at a later period the Sacred Harmonic Society also acquired one of the parts which it lacked, so that the two libraries each possessed nine parts out of ten. Lichfield has seven of the parts. There is strong ground for supposing that an organ part must also have existed, but this has never been seen. That an edition of an important work should disappear so completely is very remarkable, and it is generally thought that the bulk of the copies must have been destroyed during the political troubles which resulted in the Commonwealth. The very valuable library of the Sacred Harmonic Society, which contains an almost complete collection of the English madrigals, such as it would be hopeless to try to get together now, has passed into the possession of the Royal College of Music. It is not a little remarkable that, in addition to the printed volumes of Barnard's *Church Musick*, it contains seven volumes of manuscript collections made by him for this work.

As a natural result of the Reformed religion, the people asserted their right to take part in the common praise of the Church, and this impulse found its embodiment in metrical psalmody. The version that received official sanction was that by Thomas Sternhold, John Hopkins, "and others." It was a sorry production. The whole sublimity of the original was lost in a flood of maundering verbiage. In one or two instances the versifiers stumbled on a rendering which showed some rugged dignity, as, for instance, in the hundredth Psalm, which still is in use, but such examples are apparently due to a fortunate chance. The first complete edition was dated 1562, and this contained the melodies of the tunes, which were mostly derived from German sources. Several editions were subsequently published in vocal parts, one by Est in 1594. The tunes in this were harmonised by John Douland, Farmer, Allison, Farnaby, and others, the melody being assigned to the tenor voice. But perhaps the best-known is that published by Ravenscroft in 1621, in which a melody is assigned to each psalm. Some were German tunes which by this time had become naturalised, others were by Ravenscroft himself, while among other composers the name of John Milton, the father of our great poet, appears.

The Psalms were again paraphrased by George Sandys, and set to music by Henry Lawes, but this version, which had far greater literary merit, was never adopted for public use in churches. The "old" version of Sternhold and Hopkins maintained its position for many long years, till it was supplanted by the equally prosaic productions of Brady and Tate; in some country places that change had not taken place even in living memory. Both are in these days deservedly shelved.

We have now brought down the history of English

music to the time of the civil war, which, we need scarcely add, put a complete stop to the cultivation of music in this country. To the ears of the Puritan, music was anathema, and its professors were compelled to seek for some other livelihood.

BIBLIOGRAPHY.

Barrett, W. A. English Church Composers. London, 1882. 8vo.
Rimbault, E. F. Bibliotheca Madrigaliana. London, 1847. 8vo.
Ward, John, LL.D. Lives of the Professors of Gresham College. London, 1740. Folio.

CHAPTER VI.

THE ORIGIN OF THE OPERA AND ORATORIO.

Influence of the Renaissance—Study of Greek Music—Vincenzo Galilei—Giulio Caccini and Jacopo Peri—Rinuccini's *Euridice* set to Music by both these Composers—Monteverde—His Instrumentation—The Opera in Venice—Origin of the Oratorio – Carissimi—Alessandro Scarlatti—Durante—Pergolesi—Jomelli—Lotti—Marcello—His Psalms—*Il Teatro alla moda* — Porpora — Corelli and his School — Tartini — Frescobaldi — Domenico Scarlatti.

OF all the movements which have affected the intellectual and artistic development of the civilised world, there has been none so great in its results as that consequent on the discovery of the remains of classical literature and classical art, which is called the Renaissance. Of that movement Florence was the centre.

One of the natural results of this great impulse was a tendency to attach an excessive admiration to everything which descended from classic times. The literary men of the time could appreciate the beauty of the ancient Greek and Roman works which were gradually opened to them. The artists could judge how far the sculptures which were continually being brought to light excelled the works of themselves and their fellows. Finding the ancient nations so greatly in advance both in literature and the plastic arts, it was naturally supposed that ancient music stood at a height of similar pre-eminence; and this notion was fostered by the accounts which the ancients themselves gave of the effects produced by their own music.

It is not surprising therefore that the thoughts of those interested in music should at that time be directed towards the study of the art as practised in ancient Greece. The subject was one of great difficulty and complication, and the materials then available were insufficient for a solution of the problem. But such considerations generally act as a stimulus to investigation; of all musical questions none has perhaps engaged more attention, while none has produced less satisfactory results, many points, even in our own day, being still in dispute.

Among those engaged in the investigation of this question was a small body of friends who were in the habit of meeting in constant intercourse at the palace of Giovanni Bardi in Florence. In addition to the host, these consisted of Vincenzo Galilei (the father of the still more celebrated astronomer), a man of great ability and learning, who was a good practical musician, and the author, among other works, of a dialogue comparing ancient and modern music. In this work, which was dedicated to Bardi, he proved to his own entire satisfaction the complete superiority of ancient over modern music. Three short fragments of Grecian music only were known to Galilei; in fact, these, with another of doubtful authenticity, are all that have been discovered till a few years back. In the year 1581, when this work was published, Orlando di Lassus and Palestrina were at the height of their celebrity. The *Missa Papæ Marcelli* had been produced for sixteen years, and yet a man could persuade himself that these scraps of ancient melody proved that modern music was in comparison worthless! The other members of the society were Pietro Strozzi and Giacomo Corsi, Florentine noblemen; Rinuccini, a poet; Giulio Caccini, Emilio del Cavaliere, and Jacopo Peri, musicians. All these were burning with the desire to restore the ancient Greek tragedy, with its musically accompanied declamation. The first attempt was a drama by Jacopo Peri, *Dafne*, which was privately performed in 1597. Galilei wrote a cantata on the story of Count Ugolino to exemplify the principles he had enforced, while three dramas were brought out by Emilio del Cavaliere.

None of these works have come down to us. But about the year 1600, or somewhat earlier, the poet of the coterie wrote a libretto on the subject of Euridice; both Peri and Caccini at once set it to music, and the setting by Peri was chosen to be performed in honour of the marriage of Henri IV. of France with Maria de' Medici. The work of Caccini appears never to have been performed, but both were published in 1600 at Florence. Both are of the utmost rarity. A second edition of Peri's work was brought out in Venice eight years later, and both operas have been reprinted in cheap form by Guidi, of Florence, within the last few years.

This *Euridice* of Peri was the first opera ever represented. It cannot fail to appear remarkable that an attempt to turn back the current of musical thought into ancient channels should have developed during the course of years into the modern Italian opera, but the chain of connection is continuous. In the preface to his *Euridice* Peri has preserved the names of his singers and instrumentalists, and he has also told us what instruments composed the band. This consisted of a clavecin, a *chitarrone*, a large lira or viol, and a great lute. With the views which the composer was endeavouring to enforce, it will readily be supposed that the work is mainly in recitative; but another composer shortly appeared who materially developed the operatic style. This was Monteverde, a musician of the Venetian school, and director of the music at St. Mark's. In such estimation was he held that on his election to this post the salary was at once raised from two to three hundred ducats, and subsequently to four hundred, in addition to which he received from time to time several valuable marks of favour. No public occasion, either in Venice or in other towns of Northern Italy, was complete without a work from his pen. Thus he composed for the Duke of Parma four interludes on the subject of Diana and Endymion, a requiem for the funeral of Cosmo de' Medici, Duke of Tuscany, and other works. He also composed a large number of madrigals. But it is as a writer of opera that we speak of him here. In 1607 he composed his opera *Ariana* for the court of Mantua, which was a great advance on other works of that kind. "Widely superior," says Fétis, "to Peri, to Caccini, and even to Emilio Cavaliere as regards invention of melody, he gave us in that work passages the pathetic expression of which would even in our own day excite the interest of artists. . . . In his *Orfeo* he discovered new forms of recitative, invented the scenic duo, and without any previous example to serve as a model contrived varieties of instrumentation with an effect as new as it was piquant." He seems in some measure to have anticipated the *leit-motiv* of Wagner, in so far that particular instruments were assigned to the accompaniment of the different characters. Thus two harpsichords played the symphonies and accompaniments of the prologue, which was sung by a personification of Music; two lyres or great viols of thirteen strings accompanied Orpheus; two treble viols gave the interludes of the recitative sung by Euridice; a large double harp accompanied the chorus of nymphs; Hope was announced by two "French" violins and a harpsichord; Charon's song was accompanied by two guitars, the chorus of spirits by two organs, Proserpine by three bass viols, Pluto by four trombones, Apollo by a "regal," or small organ, and the final chorus of shepherds by a flageolet, two cornets (which were reed instruments resembling a coarse-toned hautboy), a clarion, and three muted trumpets. The aim would seem to have been variety of tone, as the instruments were not used together. The effect on the musical world of that day was marvellous, so much so that shortly afterwards we find instruments other than the organ introduced into churches, resulting in gradual but complete alteration in the character of ecclesiastical

THE ORIGIN OF THE OPERA AND ORATORIO.

music. Monteverde was, in fact, essentially an inventor. Among other things due to him is the *tremolo*, a form of accompaniment which his successors have not failed to make use of. But he was still more noticeable for his innovations in harmony, which caused much controversy in his day, one of the foremost of his opponents being Artusi, in a book called *L'Artusi ovvero delle imperfezzioni della moderna musica* (Bologna, 1600). So radical were the changes which he effected that he may be considered as the father of modern music. Space forbids us to give a complete list of his operas, one of which only, *Orfeo*, has been printed.

In 1637, six years before the death of Monteverde, to whom the opera is so largely indebted, the first theatre for the public performance of opera, which till then had been performed only in the palaces of princes, was built at Venice by Benedetto Ferrari and Francesco Manelli, the former a poet, the latter a musician. It was called the Teatro di San Cassiano. It was opened with a joint work of the proprietors, who had taken Monteverde as model. The veteran composer was at once attracted by the sweets of popular approbation, and several of his works were performed at other theatres in Venice. In 1643 he died.

From the year 1637, the date of the building of the Teatro di San Cassiano, there is published a detailed list by Antonio Groppo of all the *drammi in musica* brought out in Venice, which shows how this form of composition at once gained a footing. Two other theatres were soon afterwards opened, with a succession of operas by Francesco Cavalli, Ferrari (who was a poet as well as a musician), Francesco Paolo Sacrati, Cesti, and others too numerous to enumerate here. Opera-houses were opened in most of the larger Italian cities: the fashion spread to Germany, and soon extended to France also.

We must now turn our attention to the infancy of a form of composition with very different aims from those of the opera.

We have already had occasion to speak of the liturgical dramas of the early days of music. Of these the oratorio may in some sort be considered the descendant, although its later development was due to a desire to make use of the attractions of music as a means of bringing the people to a discharge of their religious duties. In the year 1564 St. Philip Neri united his disciples at Rome in the religious order called the *Oratorians*, for the reason that they stood outside their church exhorting the passers-by to come in to *pray*. In furtherance of this object, and especially with the view of gaining the attendance of youth, St. Philip introduced music of an attractive character, which he employed Amimuccia, a native of Florence, to compose. He produced motets, psalms, and other works, both in Italian and Latin, under the general title of *Laudi Spirituali*, the first book of which was published in 1563. These were sung at the conclusion of the regular services.

The range of subject of these compositions was gradually widened, but the first work on a scale at all corresponding to that which we now call an oratorio was *La Rappresentazione di Anima e di Corpo*, by Emilio del Cavaliere, and it was performed in the Church of Santa Maria della Vallicella in Rome in the year 1600. The recitatives were composed by his friend Jacopo Peri. It will be seen therefore that both opera and oratorio owe their origin to the same composers, and agree in the date of their first production. From the place of their first performance this species of composition acquired its name of oratorio. It appears that Cavaliere's oratorio was performed on a stage erected in the church, with action and scenery.

But it is to Carissimi that the development of the oratorio is chiefly indebted. He was born near to Rome about the year 1604. It is not known to whom he owed his musical training. He appears never to have written for the stage, and but little of his service music is extant; he devoted himself almost exclusively to the production of sacred cantatas and oratorios. In his hands recitative acquired a power of expressiveness which till then it had not known, and which indeed has seldom been surpassed. A few only of his works have been published, but four of his oratorios—*Jephtha, The Judgment of Solomon, Jonah,* and *Belshazzar*—have been issued in a volume edited by Dr. Chrysander, the well-known critic and Handel scholar. The traditions of this fine composer were continued at Naples by Alessandro Scarlatti, who is by some thought to have been a pupil of Carissimi. He was a composer of great originality and learning, excelling both in oratorio and in opera.

To him we are indebted for the invention of *accompanied* recitative, that is, recitative not simply supported by the harpsichord and bass, or, as in later days, by the principal violoncello and contrabasso (a practice, however, which has almost died out), but accompanied with the orchestra, the phrases of the recitative being connected by suitable interludes. Of this form of recitative, *Comfort ye* in the *Messiah* is a familiar instance. He also was the first to make a return to the principal subject of an air after the second part, a practice which soon became universal in the music of that period. His fecundity was extraordinary and inexhaustible. He became director of the Conservatoire of St. Onofrio at Naples, and there trained many pupils (amongst others Durante and Hasse) who formed the glory of the Neapolitan school.

Durante devoted himself exclusively to religious music, and excelled more in the treatment and development of his subjects than in the invention of them, but all the vocal parts have such "singing" qualities that they have served as models for vocal writing. Leonardo Leo, who was also one of the ornaments of the Neapolitan school, wrote both for the church and for the theatre. He had at his command great majesty of style, and at the same time knew how to touch the heart.

The name of Pergolesi, so called from his birthplace, is perhaps better known at the present day. He also was Neapolitan by education. The sweetness and charm of his melody have preserved the popularity of several of his works, among others his *Stabat Mater* for two female voices. He died of consumption at the early age of twenty-six, but not before he had written enough both for the stage and for the church to show how great was the loss to music. His operetta *La Serva Padrona* may almost be said to keep the stage. The extraordinary excitement caused by its production in Paris will be described later. The mention of Jomelli, who was equally celebrated as a writer both of sacred and of operatic music, will conclude this notice of the Neapolitan school.

We must now return to Venice. Lotti was one of that chain of distinguished men who devoted their services to the Cathedral of St. Mark. He served the successive offices of second and first organist and of director of the music, and in these capacities he composed much sacred music, written in a clear, simple, and expressive style. His operas, which were humorous, are somewhat wanting in dramatic power. He composed much vocal music for the chamber, among which is the madrigal *In una siepe ombrosa*, to which we shall have to refer when we come to speak of Bononcini. Lotti's song *Pur dicesti* is well known even in the present day. His pupil Galuppi, although wanting in science, hit the taste of the Venetian public in his light and sprightly operas. He also became musical director at St. Mark's. On the invitation of the Empress Catherine II. of Russia, he was induced to visit St. Petersburg, but he found the orchestra wretched, and was soon glad to return to his native city, which he continued to delight with his works, preserving to an advanced age the gaiety of his disposition.

We have still to speak of one other distinguished Venetian musician : Benedetto Marcello. He was born in the year 1686, of a noble family, and received, under his father's supervision, the most solid and brilliant education it was possible to obtain. Among other accomplishments, he was taught the art of music, learning first the violin. The mechanical difficulties of this instrument he had not the perseverance to overcome, and he shortly abandoned it in favour of singing and composition, but even the serious study of the latter was somewhat irksome to him. His musical tastes soon began to absorb all his energies, and his father, who wished him to devote his time to the study of law, sent him into the country, to be out of the the reach of all musical influences. The passion was too deep-seated to be subdued. His father had to yield, and dying soon afterwards, his son returned to Venice.

There he pursued his calling of advocate, receiving several public appointments, leading the life of a brilliant man of the world, and availing himself to the full of all those pleasures which the light and easy society of the theatre offered. Such was Marcello, when a remarkable circumstance entirely changed the direction of his thoughts. He was attending at the Church of the SS. Apostoli, when a stone which covered a grave gave way beneath him, and he fell to the bottom of the tomb. He was uninjured ; but he looked on the circumstance as a providential warning, and from that time changed his habits of life, broke away from his old associates, and almost renounced his taste for music.

The work by which Marcello is best known is his setting of Giustiniani's paraphrase of the first fifty Psalms. Of these the first twenty-five were published at Venice in 1724, under the title of *Estro Poetico Armonico, Parafrasi sopra i primi venticinque salmi*, the following twenty-five being brought out in 1726 and 1727. They are written for one, two, three, or four voices, with figured bass for the organ, sometimes with *obbligato* string parts. The variety which they show testifies to the great powers of their composer; in fact, they are a mine of beauty which in the present day has been lost sight of. Several editions were brought out in Venice, and an excellent one, with English words, in London by John Garth, organist of Durham, at the suggestion and probably with the assistance of Avison, organist of Newcastle-on-Tyne, whose name has been brought into notice by Mr. Browning in his *Parleyings with Certain People*. Avison was an enthusiast for the works of Marcello, having written an *Essay on Musical Expression*, the main purpose of which was to exalt Marcello at the expense of Handel.

But Marcello has other claims to attention. In addition to his musical works, he was the author of a brilliant little satire, *Il teatro alla modo*, the first edition of which was published in 1727,—possibly earlier. It professes to give instructions in their duties to all the persons engaged in a theatre, much in the style of Swift's *Directions to Servants*, the publication of which (1745) it preceded by several years. For example, it is by no means necessary that the virtuoso should be able to read or write, or that he should pronounce his vowels well, or that he should understand the meaning of the words, but very desirable that he should jumble up sense, letters, and syllables, in order to show his taste in shakes, etc. He must always take care to say that he is not in voice, that he has a toothache, or a headache, or a stomach-ache, and that the music is not written for his voice. The prima donna will make a point of absenting herself from most of the rehearsals, sending her mother instead to make her excuses, etc., etc., and in this style through all the persons employed about a theatre.

A word of mention also must be given to Porpora, a composer of many operas, but still better known as the most eminent master of singing who ever existed. Among others, he trained the great singers Farinelli and Caffiarelli.

A few remarks on the progress of instrumental music in Italy will close this chapter. The skill of the Italian instrument-makers had definitely settled the forms of the instruments of the violin family, when a musician appeared qualified to turn them to the best account in the person of Arcangelo Corelli (fig. 72), who was born in 1653. He was a pupil of Bassani, but his great powers were the fruits of genius, and there can be no doubt that he was the greatest performer of the time in which he lived. Nothing could exceed the amiability and modesty of his character. He found a protector in Cardinal Ottoboni, in whose palace he passed the greater part of his life, leaving it only to make a journey to Naples, which did not conduce to his happiness. In fact, he was of so retiring a nature that he does not appear to have done himself justice before strangers, nor in unusual surroundings. Of him is told the characteristic anecdote that, playing on one occasion to a large company, he found they were all talking, on which he

THE ORIGIN OF THE OPERA AND ORATORIO. 105

put away his violin, fearing, as he said, to interrupt conversation. His works are well known (or, at least, *used* to be) to all violinists. They consist of four sets of sonatas for two violins, violoncello and figured bass for the

Fig. 72—Arcangelo Corelli.

harpsichord, which formed a model for much similar music by his successors, a set of sonatas for violin and bass, which even now are a capital study for the violinist, and a set of concertos for two violins and violoncello, with two *ripieni* violins, viola and bass. Of these, No. 8, written for the night of the Nativity, is especially charming. A school of violin players was the product of his teaching. Among these were Veracini, Alberti, Albinoni, Geminiani, who passed the greater part of his life in England, Locatelli, and Vivaldi. The latter modified the concerto. In his hands it became more similar to that which we now understand by a concerto: a principal and leading part for the first violin, the other instruments forming an accompaniment.

Giuseppe Tartini was one of those whose genius irresistibly surmounted the obstacles of their education. His father intended him for a monk, but this being distastful to him, he was sent to Padua to study law. His quickness rendered this study so easy to him that he found ample time to devote to the art of fencing, into which he threw himself with great enthusiasm. Having secretly married a young lady at Padua who was related to the Bishop, he was compelled to fly, and sought an asylum in a monastery at Assisi. Here he devoted himself with equal ardour to the study of the violin. At the end of two years the anger of the Bishop was appeased, and he was enabled to return to Padua and to his wife, who had been left there without any knowledge of the place of his refuge. Shortly after this, being with his wife in Venice, he chanced to hear Veracini. His remarkable playing convinced him that he had still much to learn, and he retired once more for a lengthened period to Ancona, devoting himself, with that singleness of purpose which seemed part of his nature, to further studies, the management of the bow receiving great attention. He came forth from his retirement a violinist of the first rank, for whom difficulties as understood at that time did not exist. He composed much for his instrument, and his works show how greatly he had advanced on the mechanical skill of Corelli. One sonata of his may still be heard in our own day, that known as *Il trillo del diavolo*, which derives its name from the circumstance that the devil appeared to him in a dream and performed a piece of music of a difficulty which to Tartini appeared impossible. He was fortunately at once able to write it down and preserve it for posterity. Tartini was also much occupied with the scientific aspect of music. Although previously observed by the German theorist Sorge, he was the independent discoverer of the "*third sound*"—*i.e.*, the resultant tone produced when harmonic intervals are sustained with some force, in perfect tune, on the violin or other instrument. For example, the interval of a fifth produces the octave below the lowest primary tone—the major third a note two octaves below. This phenomenon has received the name of "Tartini's tones." Tartini trained many excellent pupils, the most famous among whom was Nardini.

The organ seems in Italy never to have obtained that prominence which was accorded it in Germany. Its use was restricted mainly to the accompaniment of the services. Even at the present day St. Peter's at Rome possesses no instrument at all worthy of the church, those in use being wheeled about from place to place as convenience dictates. Among the few organists who have attained to eminence as such must be named the two Gabrielis, uncle and nephew, both organists of St. Mark's at Venice (Andrea 1510-1586; Giovanni 1557-1613). To the latter is attributed the first

108   THE HISTORY OF MUSIC.

use of the term "sonata." A man of greater eminence was Girolamo Frescobaldi (fig. 73) (1587-1654), who was not

Fig. 73.—Girolamo Frescobaldi (1587-1654).

only a great performer, but an eminent composer for his instrument. The principal part of his life was passed in

Rome as organist of St. Peter's, and so great was his celebrity that it is related that thirty thousand persons assembled on the occasion of his first performance there. He published much for his instrument, and it may be interesting to add that, as originally printed, the part for the right hand is engraved on a stave of six lines, while that for the left has eight lines. It would be difficult to find anyone at the present day ready to undertake to play from the original copies.

Domenico Scarlatti (1683-1757), son of Alessandro Scarlatti, of whom we have already spoken, was also celebrated as an organist, adding another to the eminent men who filled that post at St. Peter's at Rome. He was somewhat fond of wandering, and filled this office for a short time only. But he was still more eminent as a performer and composer for the harpsichord; in fact, he was the most eminent player of those days. His works for that instrument are distinguished by much grace and variety; they are also exceedingly difficult, and would tax the skill of many a pianist of the present day. He made much use of the practice of crossing the hands, which he was able to do even in rapid passages with great skill and neatness. It was observed, however, that in his later works this practice was much less frequently indulged in, the explanation being that the composer had become so immoderately fat that this method of execution had become quite impossible to him.

BIBLIOGRAPHY.

Edwards, W. Sutherland. History of the Opera. London, 1862. 2 vols., 8vo.

Fétis, F. J. Résumé Philosophique de l'Histoire de la Musique. Prefixed to the first edition of his Biographie Universelle des Musiciens. Bruxelles, 1833. 8 vols., 8vo.

Hogarth, George. Memoirs of the Opera in Italy, France, Germany, and England. London, 1851. 2 vols., 8vo.

Tartini, G. Trattato di Musica secondo la vera Scienza dell' Armonia. Padua, 1754. 4to.

Stillingfleet, B. Principles and Power of Harmony. London. 1771. 4to. An abridged translation of Tartini's Trattato.

CHAPTER VII.

THE RISE OF THE OPERA IN FRANCE.

Chapel Music of the Kings of France—Clément Marot's Psalms—*Ballet Comique de la Royne*—Claude Lejeune—E. de Caurroy—Italian Singers brought into France by Mazarin—Skill of Louis XIV. in Music—Introduction of French Opera by Perrin and Cambert—Jean Baptiste Lully—His Career and Influence—Colasse—Desmarest—Campra—Destouches—Cultivation of Instrumental Music—Descartes—Père Mersenne.

MANY of the early kings of France showed an interest in music, and maintained a body of musicians attached to their chapel for the dignified performance of the rites of religion. The names of some of these are recorded, but the first of any eminence was Jehan Okenheim, who entered the service of Charles VII. as chaplain or director of the choir, another testimony to the acknowledged pre-eminence of the Flemish school. We have already spoken of the relations between Louis XII. and the director of his music, Josquin des Prés; under him the King's chapel was considered to be the best in Europe. Francis I. and Henri II. aspired to be considered composers, and Charles IX. had an even greater passion for the art. "At mass," says Brantôme, "King Charles would often rise and, in imitation of the late King Henri, his father, go to the lectern and sing, and he sang the tenor and the upper part very well, and he was very fond of his singers, and especially of Etienne Leroy, who had a very beautiful voice."

In those parts of France where Protestantism was in the ascendant, metrical psalmody was introduced. The first fifty Psalms were translated into French verse by Clément Marot, and the work was completed by Theodore Beza. The translation was carried out at the express desire of Calvin, and popular melodies were adapted to the words by Guillaume Franc, but without harmony. Calvin's views on the subject of sacred music are well expressed in his letter "to all Christians and lovers of the word of God" prefixed to Marot's translation. "Among the various things which are suitable for man's recreation and pleasure music is the first, or one of the foremost, and leads us to the belief that it is a gift of God set apart for this purpose. . . . It is always necessary to be careful that the song be not light nor flighty, but that it have weight and majesty, as says St. Augustine, and therefore that there be a great distinction between the music designed to delight men at table and in their houses and the Psalms which are sung in church in the presence of God and His angels."

In spite of the political and religious struggles which were agitating France during the latter part of the sixteenth century, the amusements of the court were carried on with great gaiety. Among the most popular of these, were ballets, a form of diversion introduced from Italy in which the highest personages themselves took part. Among the most famous of these was the representation

Fig. 74.—The *Ballet Comique de la Royne*, performed before Henri III. and the court (facsimile of the frontispiece of that work, 1582).

known as the *Ballet Comique de la Royne*, on the subject of Circe, which was performed on the occasion of the marriage of the Duc de Joyeuse with Marguerite de Vaudémont de Lorraine, sister of the queen of Henri III. of France. The words and music, illustrated with engravings of the different characters and decorations, were published by Adrian le Roy in the year 1582, and we are thus able to judge of the magnificence and disregard of expense with which the work was mounted. The general design of the work was due to Baltasar de Beaujoyeulx, an Italian musician who had been induced to come to France by the Maréchal de Brissac, where he became director of the music to Catherine de' Medici, but the music in it was actually composed by two French musicians, Beaulieu and Maistre Salmon. The performance took place at the Château de Moustier, and it lasted from ten o'clock at night until four o'clock the next morning, the Queen and her sister both taking part in it. In this work occurs the melody so popular a few years back under the title of the gavotte of Louis XIII. We give a general view of the appearance of the hall (fig. 74), and also of a group of Tritons performing on various musical instruments, both extracted from the original work, which is now of great rarity (fig. 75).

The fashion having been thus set by the court, ballets at once became the favourite amusement of the upper classes; and it is worthy of note that much of the pleasure consisted in taking part in the actual performances, which was thought by no means inconsistent with the dignity of the highest in the land, for even Henry IV., Louis XIII., and Louis XIV. loved to appear

THE RISE OF THE OPERA IN FRANCE. 115

in them. Nor was the practice confined to France alone. It was in consequence of his reflections on

Fig. 75.—Tritons playing on instruments of music (from the *Ballet Comique de la Royne*, 1582).

Henrietta Maria, who had engaged in similar entertainments at Somerset House, that Prynne drew on himself the cruel sentence of the Star Chamber for his *Histrio-Mastix*. It must be borne in mind that these ballets consisted not simply of dancing, but that they also comprised much vocal as well as instrumental music. While mythology furnished the subjects for a large number of them, the choice was by no means restricted, and we find such titles as *Les Grimaceurs, Les Barbiers, Les Coqs, Don Quichotte, La Délivrance de Renaud*, the latter arranged from Ariosto, in which Louis XIII. represented the demon of fire. This was a work on a large scale, and had received the care of three several composers: Mauduit, who conducted a concealed chorus of sixty-four singers, accompanied by twenty-eight viols and fourteen lutes; Guesdron, who was in charge of ninety-two voices and forty-five instruments; these two composers had written the vocal music, while the dance music was the work of Belleville, who directed that department.

Claude or Claudin Lejeune was in the service both of Henri III. and Henry IV. as composer of the chamber, and at the same time Eustache de Caurroy was director of the chapel. To him is assigned the composition of the popular air *Vive Henri IV.*, and also of *Charmante Gabrielle*.

Public performances of music, in distinction to those given at the houses of the rich for the entertainment of their friends, were as yet unknown. The first company of Italian singers which was heard in France was induced to visit that country by Cardinal Mazarin during the regency of Anne of Austria, whose tastes his own interests prompted him to study. The Italians gave their first performance on December 14th, 1645, in the Salle du Petit-Bourbon, with the piece *La finta Pazza*, which was partly spoken and partly sung; but one of the great attractions was the mechanical effects, which had been arranged by Torelli, an Italian architect, with special gifts in that direction, who formed one of the company. A singer, Margarita Bertolazzi, won golden opinions, but the entertainment does not seem to have commended itself to French tastes. Of this there are interesting evidences in the *Mémoires* of Madame de Motteville, quoted by M. Chouquet. She says, "Those who are judges think very highly of the Italians. For my part, I find the length of the performance takes largely away from the pleasure, and that verses repeated in a simple manner represent conversation more naturally and touch the heart more deeply than the singing pleases the ears." Later on, however, she tells us : "On Shrove Tuesday" (1646) "the Queen had a performance of one of her musical comedies in the small hall of the Palais-Royal. We were only twenty or thirty persons in the place, and we thought we should die of cold and *ennui*." It is possible therefore that discomfort may have warped the lady's critical judgment.

The sums squandered by Mazarin on these amusements were enormous. The Italian company was again brought over during the years 1647 and 1648, and during February of the former year they produced the tragi-comedy of *Orfeo*, in mounting which it is said Mazarin expended the sum of 500,000 livres. The composer of this work is not known ; it has been suggested that it may have been the work of Monteverde, but the contemporary descriptions do not seem to agree with the existing score.

Although, in spite of the advantages resulting from such powerful support, the Italian company appears to have aroused no enthusiasm, there can be no doubt that their example was the means of turning the thoughts of French musicians into a similar channel. With a view of utilizing the expensive stage machinery which was constructed for *Orfeo*, Corneille was employed to write a comedy for music; he chose the subject of Andromeda, to which the music was composed by D'Assoucy, but no part of it is now to be found. The Italians continued their visits until the troubles consequent on the " Fronde " interrupted them for a time.

There can be no doubt that the true creation of opera in France was due to the fortunate combination of the powers of poet and composer in the persons of Perrin and Cambert. The former, always known as the Abbé Perrin, in obedience to a literary affectation of the day, although he held no Church preferment, filled the post of introducer of ambassadors to the Duke of Orleans, but after the death of the Duke and of Mazarin, who extended his protection to him, he appears to have become little better than a literary hack. At the least he deserves the credit of perceiving that the heroic verses of the fashionable poets of the day lent themselves with difficulty to musical treatment. On a hint from Mazarin, he wrote *La Pastorale*. Cambert was at that time master of the music to Anne of Austria, having been a pupil of Chambonnières, one of the most famous harpsichord-players of that time. From the position he held there can be no doubt that he was a capable musician. To him therefore Perrin applied to write the music for his new drama. The result justified the choice. The piece, *La Pastorale, première comédie française en musique*, as it was entitled, was performed at Issy, in the house of M. de la Haye. It received no advantages of scenic splendour, but the success was nevertheless prodigious. So great was it that Louis XIV. commanded a performance at Vincennes. The authors followed up their triumph by another work, *Ariane ; ou, Le Mariage de Bacchus*, which was in rehearsal at Issy when the death of Mazarin unfortunately put a stop to the performance.

The favourable reception which these works had received in the circle of the court led Perrin to entertain the idea that the public would be disposed to support him in similar performances. A considerable sum of money would be necessary to carry on so ambitious an enterprise, and Perrin was at all times impecunious, but he succeeded in finding a financier, Champeron, who was disposed to advance the necessary funds. After much scheming he at last, in 1669, obtained the required patent granting him the privilege of establishing throughout the whole kingdom "academies of opera or musical representations" in the French language. One thing alone was wanting—a suitable locality in which to give the performances. After long search a tennis-court was found, known as the "Jeu de Paume de la Bouteille," in the Rue Mazarin, and in this it was decided to begin the enterprise, but of course many alterations were necessary to fit it for its new purpose. With Perrin, Cambert, and Champeron had become associated the Marquis de Sourdéac, a man who had developed a peculiar talent for stage mechanism, to whom therefore this department was assigned. At last all was ready. On March 19th, 1671, the new theatre was opened with the joint work of Perrin and Cambert, as poet and composer, the opera *Pomona*; and this was the first occasion on which the public were admitted by payment to such a performance. The poem does not seem to have pleased, and indeed it must be admitted that Perrin was a very poor poet, but the public were delighted with the music of Cambert, as well as with the splendour of the spectacle which the ingenuity of Sourdéac had arranged. The spectators were in rapture; the house was full to overflowing night after night, although the prices of admission were very high, a pit ticket costing as much as ten livres, a sum equal to about thirty francs of the present day. The piece ran for eight consecutive months, during which the partners made a net profit of 120,000 livres. So great was the struggle for places that the police had to be called in to maintain order. Unfortunately no complete copy exists of this work, which is really a landmark in the history of dramatic music in France; an engraved copy of a portion of the score is in the National Library in Paris, but this contains forty pages only, comprising the first act and a fragment of the second. The manuscript copy at the Conservatoire stops at the same place, as does also that in the library of the Opéra. One is forced to believe that the engraving of the work was never completed, and indeed

THE RISE OF THE OPERA IN FRANCE. 121

circumstances soon arose which may have led to this result.

In spite—or perhaps in consequence—of the financial success of the undertaking, it was not long before differences took place between the partners in it. Perrin, always needy, had before the opening of the theatre borrowed money from time to time of the Marquis de Sourdéac. He was probably lavish as well as thriftless, and, in spite of the large amount of his share in the profits, was unable or unwilling to repay these advances, with the result that he was refused admission to the theatre which owed its existence to him. Law proceedings naturally followed. Sourdéac was already provided with another poet, named Gabriel Gilbert, and to him was entrusted the preparation of a pastoral poem in five acts, called *Les Peines et les Plaisirs d'Amour*, the music for which Cambert set to work at once to compose. It was produced in November 1671. Of this work also a few fragments only have been preserved, but there can be no reason to doubt that its popularity bade fair to rival that of its predecessor.

While these attempts at the foundation of a lyric drama were going on, another musician was pushing his way to the front, whose abilities and good fortune were to throw those of Cambert into the shade. This was Jean Baptiste Lully (fig. 76). He was by birth an Italian, having been brought from Florence by the Chevalier de Guise, who was pleased with the spirit and vivacity of the boy, then twelve or thirteen years of age. The Chevalier had promised Mademoiselle de Montpensier to give her a little Italian boy, and, in accordance with this promise, the young

Lulli—or Lully as the name was always spelled in France—was handed over to this lady, who had no better employment for him than to make him a scullion. But genius will always assert itself. A visitor having by chance heard him playing on the violin, urged his mistress to provide him with proper instruction, and he proved so apt a pupil that in a short time he was admitted among the number of the Princess's musicians. Gratitude was not a prominent feature of his character, and having been guilty of setting to music a copy of scurrilous verses against his mistress, he was turned away in well-merited disgrace.

But his talents both as a performer and as a composer had already gained him some reputation, and secured his ready admission into the band of Louis XIV. He had the honour of playing some of his own compositions to the King, who was so pleased with them that he appointed him inspector of his violins, and soon afterwards created for him a new band, with the name of the " Petits Violons du Roi." Under Lully's guidance these became the best in France, for in that time there did not exist a single musician able to play his part if he had not previously learned it by heart!

Attached to the court, he assisted in the composition of the ballets in which the King took part, and subsequently wrote entire works of this nature. He was an excellent mimic, and frequently performed in these ballets, and having become intimate with Molière, he wrote the incidental music to several of his comedies, among them *L'Amour Medécin*, *M. de Porceaugnac*, and *Le Bourgeois Gentilhomme*, in all of which he appeared on the stage

THE RISE OF THE OPERA IN FRANCE. 123

with great success. The King was greatly amused with

Fig. 76.—Jean Baptiste Sully (after the portrait by Mignard, engraved by Roullet, seventeenth century).

his buffooneries, and from that time overwhelmed him with favours, and would listen to no other music than his.

In this enviable position Lully found himself at the precise moment when the strife between Perrin and his associates broke out. No scruples of conscience ever stood in the way of the realisation of any project on which he had set his mind. He at once formed the resolution to oust Cambert and his friends, and to get the management of the opera into his own hands. The privilege had been granted to Perrin, who had sufficient reasons for entertaining no lively feelings of friendship towards his late partners. There seems little doubt that Perrin was induced to cede this privilege, which was for twelve years, to Lully for a sum of money, of which he had always need. The influence of Lully with the King had become so great that he had little trouble in obtaining a new privilege, securing to himself the exclusive right to carry on such an enterprise. The patent was not registered without some litigation, but eventually Lully, backed by the King's favour, triumphed. The person most injured was the composer Cambert, who found his occupation gone; he ultimately came to this country, and entered the service of Charles II., as we have stated elsewhere.

Duly provided with his privilege, Lully began his search for a home worthy of the Académie Royale de Musique. He found at last another tennis-court in the Rue Vaugirard, near the garden of the Luxembourg, which, with the assistance of an Italian architect named Vigarani, he transformed into a theatre. He got together some of the scattered members of Perrin's troupe, and the new house was opened in May 1672, with the *Fêtes de l'Amour et de Bacchus*, a pasticcio made in haste from the fragments of the incidental music written to Molière's comedies.

Fig. 77.—Title of the opera *Alceste; ou, Le Triomphe d'Alcide*, by Lully, with a view of the Tuileries (after the drawing by Chauveau, 1674).

From that time his fortune was made. He allied himself with the poet Quinault, whose reputation is mainly due to the celebrity he acquired as librettist to Lully. The first opera specially written for the new theatre was *Cadmus*, which at once placed him in the foremost rank as a dramatic composer. Others followed in rapid succession, to the number of nineteen; all were received with the greatest favour, and were published in a style of considerable magnificence, as the specimens of the titles which we give (figs. 77-79) will show. His works prove the possession of great dramatic power, and he was in addition an excellent director of a theatre, training singers, band, and chorus to perform their parts in a manner which had not been known before in France.

The king would listen to no other music, and loaded the composer with favours, even going to the length of making him one of his secretaries, to the disgust of the other members of the body. With his great genius, he was sordid and avaricious, grovelling to the great, overbearing to those under his command. He married a daughter of a musician named Lambert, who brought him some fortune and every disposition to second him in his desire to accumulate wealth.

He was a man of considerable wit. During an illness his confessor required him to burn the score of *Armide* which he was then writing. The Prince de Conti, visiting him the same day and hearing what had passed, exclaimed, " Surely, Lully, you cannot have burned so fine a work!" "All right!" replied Lully; "I knew what I was about. I had another copy in my drawer!" His death was caused by what may have seemed to be a trifling accident. In conducting a new work he hit his foot with his stick. He was in bad health, and an

Fig. 78.—Title of *Atys*, tragedy set to music by Lully, published by Christ. Ballard in 1676 (drawn by Chauveau and engraved by Lalouette).

abscess was the result, followed by graver symptoms. He was advised to have the toe, then the foot, and finally the leg, amputated, but he fell into the hands of a quack who undertook to cure him without resorting to such desperate remedies, and in a short time he died, in his fifty-fifth year, on March 22nd, 1687. His operas kept the stage for many years; the last performance of one of them, *Thésée*, took place in 1778, *i.e.*, one hundred and three years after its first production.

In addition to his operas, on which his fame mainly rests, he composed much Church music, including a large number of motets and other larger works. Although an instrumental performer himself, he seems to have paid but little attention to the scoring of his works. His practice was to write the vocal parts and the figured bass, handing the orchestration over to one of his pupils, Lalouette or Colasse.

The animosity which his overbearing behaviour had aroused showed itself in several works which were published after his death, and in none with more bitterness than in a curious little book with the title *Lettre de Clément Marot a Monsieur de * * * touchant ce qui est passé à l'arrivée de Jean Baptiste Lully aux Champs Elysées*. The author was Antoine Bauderon, Sieur de Sénéce, who had a grudge against Lully on account of the composer's rejection of a libretto which he had written. In it Cambert is made to appear covered with wounds and accusing Lully of having caused him to be assassinated in England. For this accusation there are no grounds whatever.

During the lifetime of Lully the composer's jealousy allowed no one else to occupy the stage; but he had no reason to fear any rivalry. For many years after his

Fig. 79.—Title of the opera *Armide*, by Lully (engraved by J. Dolivar, after a drawing by Berain), published by Christ. Ballard, 1686.

death each new work was but a feeble reflection of the style of the master. For some time his favourite pupil,

Colasse, who had scored most of his operas and had also acted as assistant conductor, was the composer most in request. His operas reached the number of ten, the only one which achieved any popularity being *Les Noces de Thétis et de Pélée* (fig. 80), for he was in truth completely wanting in genius, and it is said that the most successful portions of his works were, in fact, airs written by Lully, and cast aside as unsuitable, which his pupil had been careful to preserve. Late in life he abandoned music for the search after the philosopher's stone, and ultimately became imbecile. The two sons of Lully, Louis and Jean Louis de Lully, were also composers, and together wrote the opera *Zéphyre et Flore*. The younger died at the age of twenty-one; his career was therefore short, but his brother produced several operas alone or in conjunction with Colasse or Marais; but these young men possessed the name only, and not the genius, of their father.

Desmarets was among the most able of the immediate successors of Lully, several of his operas having been well received. The circumstances of his life were romantic. Having been "page of the music" to the King, he tried to obtain the appointment of one of the *maîtres de chapelle*, and was passed over on account of his youth alone, the King granting him a pension to compensate for the disappointment. In 1700, while on a visit to a friend at Senlis, he made the acquaintance of, and married secretly, the daughter of a high official, who set the law in motion, with the result that Desmarets was condemned to death. He was compelled to seek refuge in Spain, where he became chapel-master to Philippe V., and although Louis XIV. had been well disposed towards

Fig. 80.—*Les Noces de Thétis et de la Pélé* (scene from the opera of Colasse, with a view of the Pont Neuf, designed and engraved by Sebastien Leclerc, 1689).

him and admired his abilities, he refused to pardon him, and it was not until the Regency that he was allowed to return to France and his marriage was declared valid.

The only musician of the time who showed any disposition to break away from the stereotyped monotony of the ruling style was Campra, who, although not a genius, was a musician of great ability, and the composer of a score at least of operas which were very popular, as they were characterised by a greater vivacity and a more strongly marked rhythm than was then usual. Campra was educated as a Church musician, and it was while in office at Nôtre Dame in Paris that he produced his first two operas, which had in consequence to be brought out under the name of his brother, a musician in the band of the Académie de Musique. He was also favourably known as a writer of Church music, five books of motets of his composition being extant. We must also mention Destouches, who began life with a voyage to Spain in company with the Jesuit fathers, a body which he proposed to join. On his return, however, the profession of arms had greater attractions; this he abandoned for the pursuit of music. His opera *Issé* was performed in 1691, and it pleased by its natural melody. But his knowledge of music was so small that he was only able to compose his melodies, and was therefore obliged to call in assistance to score it. Sensible of his deficiencies, he went to Campra for instruction. Unfortunately an increase of knowledge seems to have destroyed his originality; and although several of his operas were played, he never renewed his first success.

It may be interesting to mention that nearly all the operas of this time were published in score, in which

THE RISE OF THE OPERA IN FRANCE. 133

the violin parts were invariably printed in what is called

Fig. 81.—A player on the musette (engraved by Leblond, after C. David, seventeenth century).

the French violin clef, with the G clef on the *first* line in place of the second line, in accordance with present practice. We may also note the fact that the contra-basso was first introduced into the French orchestra by Montéclair, in his opera *Les Festes de l'Eté*, in the year 1716.

Instrumental music appears to have received increased attention in private circles. The guitar became very popular, which may in part have been the result of the King's skill on it; but a more remarkable outbreak of fashion was the adoption of the musette, which was taken up by both sexes alike (fig. 81). An excellent and handsomely illustrated guide to this instrument was published at Lyons in 1672 by C. E. Borjon, an amateur, a learned advocate, who was the author of several works on jurisprudence.

During the reign of Louis XIII. the study of musical theory began to attract the attention of men of science. Descartes, at that time barely twenty-two years of age, published in 1618 his *Compendium Musicæ*, a work not altogether free from error, of which the author indeed seems to have been conscious, as he would not allow it to be reprinted during his lifetime, although it was more than once republished afterwards, having been translated into French by Père Poisson, and into English by Lord Brouncker, the first President of the Royal Society and an able mathematician, under the title of *Renatus Descartes' Excellent Compendium of Musick: with Necessary and Judicious Animadversions Thereupon. By a Person of Honour*. A few years after, Père Mersenne, who enjoyed the intimacy, although he shared but little of the philosophic spirit, of Descartes, began his investigations in the field of music. Among the earliest of his writings was his commentary on Genesis—a work which, although it extended to twelve hundred pages folio, only allowed space for the consideration of the first six chapters. The text, "His brother's name was Jubal; he was the father of all such as handle the harp and organ," was an opportunity which he could not resist. and he entered on a disquisition on music in general and on that of the Jews in particular which takes one hundred pages at least. But he had long meditated a large work which should embrace the whole field of musical knowledge. It was some time before he was able to put this idea into practice. Probably no publisher was willing to undertake so vast a speculation. The delay he filled up by the issue of certain trial portions, some in French, some in Latin. Among these is the curious and characteristic *Préludes de l'Harmonie Universelle*, in which he discusses not only the temperament most suitable for a musician, but also the horoscope necessary to produce the perfect artist. At last in 1636 his great work, *L'Harmonie Universelle*, which is in the French language, appeared—a vast folio of upwards of fifteen hundred pages, full of woodcuts, copperplate engravings, and musical examples. The cost of producing it must have been enormous, and the outlay can never have repaid the publisher, Cramoisy. The erudition it contains is immense, but the critical faculty of the author was defective. For the history of music the work is of great interest, as it contains many specimens of compositions which it would be difficult to find elsewhere, as well as particulars about their authors. It is to be presumed that the sale of the book was small, for it is one of great scarcity.

BIBLIOGRAPHY.

Castil-Blaze. Chapelle Musique des Rois de France. Paris, 1832. 18mo.
Castil-Blaze. De l'Opéra en France. 2nd Edition. Paris, 1826. 2 vols., 8vo.
Celler, Ludovic. Les Origines de l'Opéra et le Ballet de la Reine (1581). Paris, 1861. 12mo.
Chouquet, A. G. Histoire de la Musique Dramatique en France, depuis ses Origines jusqu'à nos Jours. Paris, 1873. 8vo.
Pougin, A. Les vrais Créateurs de l'Opéra Français, Perrin et Cambert. Paris, 1881. 12mo.
Thoinan, Er. (*Ernest Roquet*): Les Origines de la Chapelle Musique des Souverains de France. Paris, 1861. 12mo.

CHAPTER VIII.

MUSIC IN GERMANY.

The "Stadt-pfeiffer"—The Bach Family—J. S. Bach—His Sons and Pupils—Foundation of the Gewandhaus Concerts—The Opera in Germany—Reinhard Keiser—Early Career of Handel—Johann Mattheson—Hasse—Graun—Musical Journalism—Marpurg—Music in Vienna—J. J. Fux—Gluck—His Musical Reforms.

IN the first half of the seventeenth century Germany was suffering from the horrors of the Thirty Years' War. Such a period was most unfavourable for the fostering of one of the most peaceful of arts. A few eminent musicians had survived from happier times, among whom may be mentioned Adam Gumpelzhaimer (fig. 82), famous both as a theorist and as a writer of sacred music, and Michæl Prætorius (Schultz), whose *Syntagma* we have already spoken of at p. 75. But it was of necessity a time of but little musical activity, Froberger, Pachelbel, and Buxtehude being among the few writers of any celebrity. Such musical life as existed was preserved among the "Stadt-pfeiffer," or town musicians, a body of men who were not held in great estimation either for their musical powers or for their private worth. The town musicians were the privileged performers on all occasions of public and private rejoicing. They formed a close body, like the company of minstrels in France, to which admission was gained by a regular term of apprenticeship, and the privilege of belonging to the body had a natural tendency to be perpetuated in the same family. In the year 1653 a desire to protect their common interests impelled the town musicians of some of the larger places in Northern and Central Germany to unite in the formation of a scheme of united action, in furtherance of which a series of rules was drawn up and submitted to the Emperor Ferdinand III., whose approval it received.

These rules, which are too long to transcribe here, prove that in their ranks were some anxious to improve the status of a body of men at that time held in scant respect. Among the most respectable musicians of the society were several members of one family named Bach, all of whom followed the musical calling with enthusiasm. They traced their descent from a certain Veit (*i.e.* Vitus) Bach, a baker and miller of Wechmar, in Thuringia, who died in 1619. His chief delight was to play on his cithern while the corn was grinding, and so great was his love of music that he sent his son Hans to Gotha to be instructed by Caspar Bach, another member of the family, who was town piper. Hans combined the occupations of carpet-weaver and musician, and died of the plague in 1626, but not before he had brought up three sons, out of his large family, to the profession of music. From that time this course became traditional. The Bachs had large families, all of whom were devoted to music, and thus it came about that in the towns of Thuringia—Arnstadt, Erfurt, Gotha, and Eisenach—they seem to have monopolised the offices of organist and town musician.

The Bachs became a musical power, the name being

Fig. 82.—Adam Gumpelzhaimer (1560-   ).

considered as almost synonymous with "musician," and it is an interesting evidence of their family unity that they were all in the habit of meeting together once a year in Erfurt, Eisenach, or Arnstadt for social and musical intercourse, the meetings always opening in simple and pious fashion by the singing of a chorale.

In 1685 was born at Eisenach Johann Sebastian Bach (fig. 83), a great-grandson of Hans Bach, who was destined to raise the fame of the family to the highest pitch, and to become one of the greatest musicians of all time. As a child his father taught him the violin, but both his parents died before he had reached his tenth birthday. His elder brother, Johann Christoph, was organist of Ohrdruf, and he undertook the charge of the orphan boy, grounding him thoroughly in music, teaching him the clavichord (for he had himself been a pupil of Pachelbel), and sending him to the Lyceum, where he was instructed in Latin and Greek, acquiring a fair knowledge of the former language. This went on till he reached his fifteenth year. He had exhausted his brother's teaching, and with a school companion travelled to Luneburg, in which place they both joined the choir of the Church of St. Michael, where, in addition to musical instruction, his general education was not neglected. The organ was already his favourite instrument. In 1703 he left Luneburg to join the band of Prince Johann Ernst at Weimar, but in the same year was appointed organist at Arnstadt. The fame of Buxtehude, a Dane, who was organist at Lübeck, induced him to make use of his first month's holiday to visit him, walking the whole distance of fifty leagues. The musical attraction of Buxtehude's playing was so great that his one month's leave extended to three; on his return the authorities at

Arnstadt naturally demanded an explanation. In short, his position ceased to be comfortable ; and he was glad, on

Fig. 83.—Johann Sebastian Bach.

an early opportunity, to transfer his service to Mühlhausen, a position of greater importance. On the strength of this preferment, he married, and shortly after received the appointment of organist and court *musicus* at Weimar, a post which was very congenial to him, for both the Duke and his brother took much pleasure in music. He was called on to write a number of Church compositions, and acquired a great celebrity as an organist, and thus was frequently invited to different towns to give performances. On one occasion he visited Dresden, where at that time was living a harpsichord-player of great skill, a Frenchman named Marchand (fig. 84). The friends of the rival musicians arranged a trial of skill in the house of one of the ministers. At the appointed time Bach was ready. Marchand did not appear. After waiting some time a messenger was sent to his house; and it appeared that, dreading the result, he had left Dresden that morning.

For what reason is not ascertained, but in 1717 Bach left Weimar to enter the service of Leopold, Prince of Anhalt-Coethen, himself an enthusiastic musician. While here he lost his wife, but after a year and a half married again. His second wife, Anna Magdalen Wülken, who was court singer, was an excellent help to him. She was an admirable singer, and in addition wrote a fine hand, which enabled her to be of great use in copying his manuscripts.

But the circle of his influence at Coethen was a narrow one, and a vacancy occuring in the post of "Cantor" of the Thomas-schule at Leipzig by the death of Kuhnau, he offered himself, and was selected from several candidates, among whom was the celebrated Telemann. He was installed into his new office on the 31st May, 1723. It went somewhat against the grain with him to give up the title of "Capellmeister" for that of "Cantor," but the position offered a much wider field for his artistic

Fig. 84.—Louis Marchand.

activity. It did not prove altogether a bed of roses. The Thomas-schule was both a choir school and a grammar school, and his duty required him to teach Latin, although for this he was allowed to pay a deputy. He had to superintend the services at two principal churches, to each of which a choir of boys had to be sent, as well as to two subsidiary churches in the town. The school had been neglected, and was under the superintendence of the town council. There were thus all the elements of much heart-burning. In his own family Bach was a man of easy and amiable character, but in his public capacity he stood on his dignity. He seems to have been one of those men who rather enjoy an atmosphere of strife, and although he made one or two appeals to friends to obtain for him some more peaceful employment, he continued to fill this office to the day of his death. The salary was seven hundred thalers—say £105 per annum—with apartments and some few fees,—no very high pay for so great a genius. This was the time of his greatest activity. His fame continued to increase. He had always been fond of making journeys to the larger towns, both to hear and to be heard, but as age crept on these became less frequent. His son Emmanuel had become chamber musician and accompanist to Frederick the Great, who was an enthusiastic musician and a creditable performer on the flute; for this instrument Quantz (fig. 85), was his master; he was in the regular service of the King, and it was part of his duty to write a constant succession of new compositions for him, a lofty pile of which may still be seen reposing in a cabinet at Potsdam. Frederick was most anxious to make the acquaintance of the great master. At last he was persuaded to start for Potsdam, where he arrived on Sunday, May 7th, 1747. A concert took place every evening from seven to nine. The King was about to begin a solo on the flute, when the daily list of the strangers who had arrived was handed to him. He turned to the band with some excitement, and said, "Gentlemen, old Bach is come!" His flute was laid aside, and Bach was at once sent for, not being allowed

Fig. 85.—Johann Joachim Quantz.

time to change his dress. Much conversation then ensued, especially on the merits of Silbermann's pianofortes. The King had several, and Bach was carried from one to the other to test their merits and improvise on them. The next day Bach performed on the organ in the church, and in the evening he played a six-part fugue to the King's great satisfaction.

The closing years of his life were clouded by a gradually increasing blindness, which did not yield to the attentions of an oculist residing in Leipzig, who performed two operations without success. The medical treatment shook his constitution, and he died on July 28th, 1750, surrounded by his family and friends, at the age of seventy-five years.

Bach was a man of great industry, producing a constant succession of new works in all departments of musical composition. Of these his organ works will probably be considered his most enduring monument. His thoughts moved naturally in polyphonic forms of composition, and the strict rules of fugue seemed to him to be no trammel. As a performer on the organ he stood in the first rank. He was well acquainted with its mechanical details, and was frequently employed in trying new instruments, when his first act was to draw all the stops to see that the supply of wind was ample. As director of church choirs, he produced much music for religious worship, comprising among other works five complete sets of cantatas for every Sunday and holy day of the ecclesiastical year. In Germany it is a common practice to sing during Holy Week music appropriate to that sacred season, under the title of Passion music. It consists of solemn music illustrative of the Gospel narrative, interspersed with chorales, in which the congregation are expected to join. Of these Bach produced five, the one according to St. Matthew being that on the largest scale, and probably the best known. He also wrote a Christmas oratorio.

It may seem strange that a Protestant, and one whose abilities were devoted to the service of the Protestant Church, should have become the composer of masses. It would appear, however, that in Leipzig the form of worship had retained many Catholic practices, and even the occasional use of the Latin language. The B minor Mass was probably intended for Dresden—at least parts of it were certainly written with that destination—where the court was, and still continues to be, of the Roman Church. This is a work of great power and elaboration, on a scale hardly suited to the purposes of public worship, but it is well known in the present day by several careful performances of it which have been given by the Bach choir.

For the harpsichord he wrote much; in fact he may be said to have revolutionised the art of playing on that instrument. In those days the fourth finger was used but sparingly, the thumb not at all, being allowed to hang down in front of the keys in the way which one used to see affected by old-fashioned organists in our own time. Bach used the thumb equally with the other fingers. He wrote two sets of *suites*, one called the English *suites*, the other the French. The *suite* was a composition consisting of a succession of movements written in the rhythm of the dances of the period—the Allemande, Saraband, Gavotte, Minuet, Bourrée, Gigue, etc.—arranged in such order as to contrast in style. The *suite* was destined to develop into the sonata, of which we shall speak presently.

But the best known of his instrumental compositions is probably the *Wohltemperirte Clavier*, or *Well-tempered Harpsichord*. To explain this title, it is necessary to understand that in an instrument having fixed tones it is only possible for one key to be perfectly in tune. For convenience of performance the same note is made to do duty for C♯ and D♭, and so on throughout the scale; but this is not theoretically correct. In the days before Bach, the practice was to make the key of C in accurate tune, leaving the rest to their fate, and this fate was unbearable if the key involved several sharps or flats. This was still more the case where the sound was capable of being sustained, as in the organ, and it was therefore necessary to avoid remote keys altogether. A distribution of the error among all the notes of the octave is called the system of equal temperament. No one key is of course in *perfect* tune, but all diverge so little from accuracy that the difference is only perceptible to those of extreme nicety of ear. It is not claimed for Bach that he invented this system, but he was the first to bring it into practical use, tuning his harpsichords himself with great care. To enforce this system, he wrote the *Wohltemperirte Clavier*, or forty-eight preludes and fugues, in all the keys, major and minor. Many of these keys had *never* been used before, and the performance of them was only possible by means of his improved method of fingering.

He also wrote for stringed instruments; concertos for violins and other instruments; sonatas for harpsichord and violin, and also for violin alone. One is tempted to look on the latter as technical exercises; it is difficult to believe that the violin-player existed in those days who could execute them.

A few only of his works were published during his

Fig. 86.—Carl Philip Emanuel Bach.

lifetime; in fact, the expense was so great a bar to their publication, that he actually engraved with his own hand his *Art of Fugue*. It is in our time only that the greater part of his works have seen the light, or indeed that his powers have been fully appreciated. This reproach, however, may be withdrawn, as the Bach

Gesellschaft is bringing out a splendid and complete edition of his compositions, which is already well advanced.

His sons sustained the family reputation. They all received a careful and thorough musical training from their father. The eldest and most able of them, Wilhelm Friedemann, unfortunately was a man of an irritable and restless disposition, so that he led a wandering and purposeless life and did no justice to his great abilities. The next son, Carl Philip Emanuel (fig. 86), entered the service of Frederick the Great at Berlin as accompanist, subsequently removing to Hamburg. He adopted a much lighter and more graceful style of writing than his father, and there is no doubt that his works formed the model of the pianoforte compositions of Haydn and Mozart. To him may be attributed the settlement of the form of the sonata. He was an excellent performer on the harpsichord, and the author of an admirable treatise on the art, which undoubtedly paved the way for the modern school of pianoforte-playing. Friedemann and Emanuel were sons by the first wife, and to them were entrusted the manuscripts left by their father. Most of those which fell to the share of Friedemann were lost in his many wanderings; those in the possession of Emanuel were carefully preserved. The youngest son, Johann Christian, after visiting Italy and marrying a singer, settled in England, where he brought out many operas aud composed much instrumental music, dying here in respect, while a son of *his* fourth son died so recently as 1846, in his ninety-third year, in Berlin, where he filled the post of court musician. With him, at least as regards music, the annals of this remarkable family cease.

In addition to his sons, Bach trained many pupils,

Fig. 87.—John Peter Sweelinck.

among others J. F. Agricola; Altnikol, who married his daughter; J. C. Vogler, who was looked on as one of the best organists of his time; Ludwig Krebs, one of his favourite pupils; and Kirnberger, who became famous as a writer on the theory of music.

From very early days the organ had been much

studied in Germany. J. P. Sweelinck (fig. 87), a Dutchman, who after visiting Venice and sitting at the feet of Zarlino, became organist of the principal church in Amsterdam, may be looked on as the father of the great school of German organists which became so famous and received its highest development in the person of J. S. Bach. To that country we are indebted for most of its improvements, and especially for the addition of pedals, a resource opening a wide field to the powers of the composer, of which Bach and his followers availed themselves so ably.

Every town of importance possessed at least one fine instrument, which was in the hands of a competent performer. Many of the finest instruments were built in those days. Among builders the family of the Silbermanns was especially eminent, as they were also for their improvements in the harpsichord.

Telemann, who had competed with Bach for the appointment of Cantor of the Thomas-schule in Leipzig, formed a choral society in that place, of which he was conductor. But the first subscription concert in Leipzig took place in 1743, under the direction of Doles. The series was interrupted by the Seven Years' War, but they were subsequently resumed by J. A. Hiller, a musician of great attainments, who was the first to perform Handel's *Messiah* in Germany. In 1779 and 1780 the disused Cloth Hall (Gewandhaus) was turned into a concert-room; to this room the concerts were transferred in 1781. They have since been known as the Gewandhaus concerts, and for more than a century

Fig. 88.—Heinrich Schütz.

have maintained a character as the foremost, as they are now the most venerable, of all associations for the performance of classical music.

The Germans were by nature a grave and serious people, and thus the opera was for a long time an exotic among them. The eminent scholar Reuchlin arranged a comedy with music, under the title of *Scenica Progymnasmata*, for performance by the scholars of the Gymnasium in Heidelberg, so far back as the year 1497, which, from the number of editions it went through, may be supposed to have attained to considerable popularity : but the title of opera can scarcely be claimed for it. Certain Passion plays, with music, were also in vogue. The first real opera was composed by Heinrich Schütz or Saggittarius, more celebrated for his sacred music (fig. 88), to a translation of Rinuccini's *Dafne*, but this was for a court performance at a royal wedding, The first public performance was given at Hamburg by Johann Theile, on the story of Adam and Eve, and it was followed by other similar works, and thus Hamburg became the cradle of opera in Germany. A facile composer appeared in the person of Reinhard Keiser, whose first opera, *Basilius*, was hailed with enthusiasm by the inhabitants of that town. He followed up his success with commendable industry, opera after opera flowing from his pen for a space of forty years. During this time he brought out upwards of a hundred operas, a few only of which have been printed (fig. 89), some existing in manuscript, but all distinguished by an inexhaustible fund of bright and sparkling writing.

At this time appeared a composer who was destined

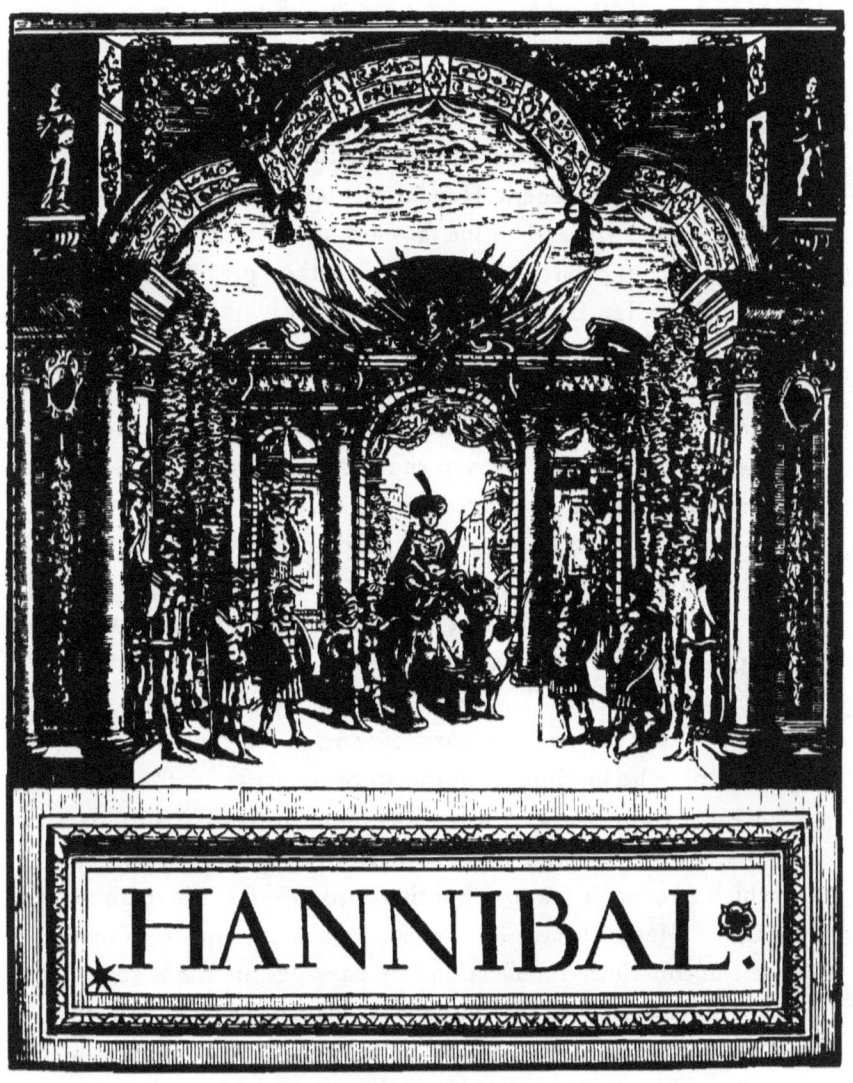

Fig. 89.—Title-page of Keiser's *Hannibal*.

to raise the opera to a pitch of excellence till that time undreamt of, but who was to be even more famous from the sublimity of his compositions in a still higher department of art. George Frederic Handel was borne at Halle in 1685 —the same year, and within a short distance of the place which saw the birth of Germany's other great musician, John Sebastian Bach. His father was originally a barber, but had developed, as was usual in those days, into a surgeon, who by a fortunate second marriage with the widow of another surgeon acquired a good practice and a position of esteem. His son showed a musical disposition; the father aimed to make him a lawyer. The boy was possessed of much firmness of purpose, and practised his music in secret, till at last a fortunate chance brought his powers under the notice of the Duke of Weissenfels, who impressed on his father that it was absolutely sinful to check such talent. The result was that on his return home he was put under the care of Zachau, organist of the Frauenkirche in Halle, a musician of no great depth, but a pleasing composer, and, what was more to the purpose, the possessor of a large and well-selected library of scores, which proved a happy hunting ground for his earnest pupil. Many of these he copied, and it is supposed that half-unconscious recollections of passages in these scores may account for the curious coincidences (to use no stronger word) which have undoubtedly been found in some of his later works. His industry was unbounded, for, in addition to his theoretical studies, he acquired great skill on the organ, as well as some command of the violin, and of the oboe, which remained a favourite instrument with him. After three years his master had to confess that he could teach him no more. He was then sent to Berlin, where he had the opportunity of increasing his experience by hearing works of the Italian school and by making the acquaintance of Ariosti and also of Buononcini, subsequently to be his most serious rival. The King was delighted with his precocious abilities, and proposed to send him to Italy, but to this his father would not listen, insisting on his return. His father survived this return but a few months. His mother, a woman of excellent sense, kept him to the regular studies of youth, while music was not neglected, and he acquired a reputation something more than local. He was at the age of seventeen appointed organist of the Schloss and Domkirche at Halle, where he had a fine organ at his command. This post he held while still studying at the university, and he also found time to form a choir of his old schoolfellows for the practice of sacred music, as well as to write several important compositions.

But the bent of his genius was essentially dramatic, and he was naturally drawn by the attractions of the Hamburg Opera. In the year 1703, therefore, he threw up his appointment at Halle, and started for Hamburg in pursuit of fortune, which came to him in the very modest guise of *ripieno* second violin in the orchestra of the opera. While there he made the acquaintance of Johann Mattheson, who was at that time singing as principal tenor at the opera. He was a man of great and varied accomplishments, as will be seen later, and to him we are indebted for many details of the great composer's life. Among others, we learn that the two friends went on a journey together to Lübeck, where Mattheson had been invited to become successor to the eminent Dieterich Buxtehude also. They tried together every organ in the place, and heard the veteran Buxtehude also. It appeared, however, that the acceptance of the post involved marrying the daughter of the retiring organist, a condition which neither was willing to adopt ; the appointment therefore went to a more compliant candidate.

One result of this friendship was to introduce Handel to society, and among other houses to that of Sir Cyril Wich, the English representative, to whose son he gave lessons on the harpsichord. Subsequently, however, Mattheson became tutor to the boy, supplanting Handel in his engagement as harpsichord-master.

While engaged in the orchestra, the fortunate absence of the harpsichord-player gave Handel the opportunity of distinguishing himself, and he also produced a Passion oratorio for performance in Holy Week. This, Mattheson, who was of a jealous disposition, criticised with some bitterness. Further differences arose. Mattheson had composed an opera called *Cleopatra*, which was produced in the ensuing winter season, the composer taking the principal tenor part, Antonius, while Handel was at the harpsichord. Antonius dying early in the action, Mattheson was not engaged on the stage, but insisted on taking Handel's place at the harpsichord. Handel refused to yield, and a quarrel ensued, ending in a box on the ear given by Mattheson. Such an insult in those days could of course only result in a duel, which was at once fought out before the opera-house, in the midst of a crowd of spectators. Fortunately Mattheson's sword broke against a button on Handel's coat, which terminated the encounter, or the world might have been all the poorer. By the intervention of friends, the combatants were reconciled, and became as good companions as ever, and we find Mattheson taking the principal tenor part in Handel's first opera, *Almira*, which was produced on January 8th, 1705.

It seems almost incredible, but opera in Germany retained so much of its Italian origin that it was performed in a mixture of the two languages. This was the case with *Almira*. As a question of art the custom was absurd, and it is difficult to see what practical advantage was gained by it. The reason was not ignorance of German on the part of the singers, for to several of them are allotted airs in both languages. The custom, however, was not confined to Germany, for it was introduced both into France and England.

The opera had considerable success, running for nineteen or twenty nights. The music has come down to us in an imperfect copy, which has been published in the German Handel Society's edition. In it is a saraband which was subsequently very popular when set to the words "Lascia ch' io pianga" in the later opera *Rinaldo*. Its success served to arouse the jealousy of Keiser, who shortly aftewards set the same libretto without the effect which the composer intended.

Handel's second opera, *Nero*, was produced the same year, but after three performances the theatre closed its doors, Keiser and his partner Drüsicke being compelled to fly from their creditors. Handel seems to have occupied himself for a time with teaching. He had been careful in his habits, and had saved a sufficient sum to enable him to visit Italy, where he arrived in the early part of 1707. It is supposed that his first resting-place was Florence, but at Easter he was undoubtedly in Rome, then and for long afterwards the goal of so many musicians at that season. His mind during this visit seems to have been receptive rather than productive, and after a few months he returned to Florence, where he brought out his first Italian opera, *Rodrigo*, in which he used up much of the material of his Hamburg operas, the overture, for instance, being in many parts the same as *Almira*. The Grand Duke of Tuscany, whose brother had made Handel's acquaintance in Hamburg and had been instrumental in inducing him to visit Italy, was so pleased with the work that he presented the author with a service of plate and a purse of a hundred sequins. The prima donna, Vittoria (probably Vittoria Tesi), a young lady of very impulsive disposition, fell madly in love with him. Whether the passion was returned is not certain, but in 1708, when Handel produced his *Agrippina* in Venice, she obtained consent to go there for the purpose of singing the principal part, and the work was received with great favour.

The spring of 1708 found him again in Rome, where he produced his first oratorio, the *Resurrezione*, for the Marchese Ruspoli, in whose house he lived. He also wrote *Il Trionfo del Tempo e del Disinganno*, a cantata which in after years served as the foundation of *The Triumph of Time and Truth*. It is à propos of the overture of this work that the well-known story of Corelli is told. His quiet style of playing did not suit the sprited passages of this overture. Handel made several attempts to instruct him in the way he wished them rendered. At last he lost his temper (which, in truth, seems not unfrequently to have happened), and snatching the violin from Corelli's hand, himself played the passages. Corelli's sweetness of disposition did not desert him. He replied, "Ma, caro Sassone, questa musica è nel stile Francese, di ch' io non intendo" ("But, dear Saxon, this music is in the French style, which I do not understand"). Eventually Handel modified it so as to be more in accordance with the Italian style.

While at Rome Cardinal Ottoboni arranged a trial of skill both on the organ and on the harpsichord between Handel and Domenico Scarlatti. On the latter instrument their merits were considered nearly equal, with a slight preference for Scarlatti; but on the organ there was no room for question. Scarlatti himself acknowledged the superiority of Handel, and said that before that time he was unacquainted with the capabilities of the instrument. Domenico Scarlatti took great delight in the society of Handel; and when people praised his great execution, he would cross himself and speak of Handel.

In July, 1708, he left Rome and visited Naples, where

he remained for more than a year, much courted by the best society. Here he wrote much, although no work of great importance ; and late in 1709 he prepared to leave those scenes through which he had made almost a triumphal progress. His route lay through Venice, and he there renewed his intimacy with the Abbate Steffani and Baron Kielmansegge, in whose company he started northward. As a good son, his first care was to visit his mother. He then proceeded to Hanover, where, through the kind offices of Steffani, he was appointed Capellmeister, with liberal arrangements as to leave of absence. His intention was to visit England, and he arrived in this country towards the close of the year 1710. It may be truly said that this formed the beginning of his real career. The history of the rest of his life will fittingly find a place in another chapter.

We have noticed the fact that Sebastian Bach and Handel were born at no great distance apart, and in the same year. It is not a little remarkable that these two great musicians never met. It was the wish of Bach's life to make the acquaintaince of his great rival. On two separate occasions he made the attempt. In 1719, hearing that Handel was staying with his mother in Halle, Bach started from Coethen, arriving in Halle only to find that Handel had started the day previous for London. On the second occasion, in 1719, Bach, being himself unwell, sent his son Friedemann from Leipzig to Halle with an invitation to Handel to visit him. On this occasion time did not allow him to accept his brother musician's invitation, and thus these two great men, so well qualified to understand each other, whose careers ran parallel for sixty-five years, never met.

Mattheson's last appearance on the stage was in Handel's *Nero*. We have seen that he had become tutor to the son of the English Ambassador; and, by his patron's influence, he was soon after appointed secretary of the Legation. He was a man of very great and varied abilities. When only nine years of age he was able to undertake the organ in several churches, and he soon acquired great proficiency in languages. He wrote several operas, and a great deal of music for the harpsichord, all of which is now forgotten except by antiquaries. It is as a writer on music that his fame is preserved, and he was without doubt the foremost critic of that time; in fact, it may almost be said that he was the inventor of musical criticism. His *Critica Musica*, the first attempt at a journal specially devoted to music, was commenced in 1722 and continued till 1725. Another work of the same character was started by him in 1728, under the title of *Der Musicalische Patriot*. The German writing of that day was distinguished by great pedantry; certainly Mattheson's was no exception, and in addition he was very bitter and overbearing in controversy, never entertaining any possibility of error on his own part. He was a most indefatigable writer, and a large number of his works are controversial, but he also wrote many of a didactic nature, one of the best known of which, *Der Vollkommene Kapellmeister*, for many years kept its place as a text-book.

Among the numerous ways in which his literary activity broke out, he conceived the fortunate notion of collecting the Lives of the most eminent German musicians of those days, as far as possible from information supplied by themselves, under the title of *Grundlage einer Ehrenpforte*, or *Foundations of a Triumphal Arch*. This book was published in 1740, and, with the *Lexicon* of Walther, published a few years previously (Leipzig, 1732), forms the main source of our knowledge of the earlier German musicians. It contains a Life of himself written with delightful self-satisfaction. Handel was, of course, invited with the rest to furnish particulars of his career for the work, but this, modesty or want of time forbade him to undertake. Mattheson's knowledge, however, was sufficiently intimate to enable him to supply the necessary details. Later on, in 1761, he brought out a second and distinct Life of the great master, some of the statements in which are difficult to reconcile with the previous Life. This second work was a translation, with additions, of a book by the Rev. John Mainwaring, which for a long series of years remained the only Life of the great musician in the language of the country which he had honoured by making his home.

Another composer, whose reputation was at one time enormous, but who is now almost forgotten, is Hasse (fig. 90). He was born near to Hamburg in 1699, and made his first appearance as a tenor singer at Dresden in 1718, where Keiser, whose acquaintance we made at Hamburg, was conducting the opera. It was not till 1723 that he found the means of producing his first opera, *Antigone*, at Brunswick with success; but he himself recognised that he had much to learn, and, with the object of completing his musical education, he started for Italy in 1724, and having arrived in Naples, he placed himself under Porpora. His ambition was to have lessons

Fig. 90.—Johann Adolph Hasse.

from Alessandro Scarlatti, but he feared that the master's terms would be beyond his modest means. Fortunately the young man had the good luck to meet Scarlatti, and to please him by his skilful performance on the harpsichord, with the result that the veteran proffered his assistance. Several minor works having met with favour, he was entrusted with the composition of an opera, *Sesostrate*, which was performed at the Royal Theatre in 1726. Its success was perfect, and from that day Hasse was known in Italy by no other name than "il caro Sassone."

In 1727 Hasse went to Venice. In this city was performing Faustina Bordoni, a singer endowed with a soprano voice of great beauty and with the most extraordinary skill in the management of it, her execution being truly remarkable; in short, she was one of the greatest singers of that time. This great artist Hasse married, and she continued for many years to take the leading part in the constant succession of operas which he produced for many of the principal cities of Europe. He fixed himself mainly in Dresden. The number of his works was enormous, his operas alone exceeding fifty. He had in contemplation a complete edition of his works, but during the siege of Dresden in 1760 the whole of his manuscripts were destroyed, with other property. The Seven Years' War left the country so impoverished that the court was compelled to discontinue the opera. Hasse and his wife were pensioned, and they settled in Vienna, where he still continued to compose. His last opera was written for Milan, on the marriage of the Archduke Ferdinand. For this occasion also the boy Mozart, then thirteen years of age, wrote his first opera, *Mitridate*. Hasse heard it, and exclaimed, "This child will cause us all to be forgotten." The prophecy has been verified; there is probably no one in the present day who is acquainted with a single air of Hasse, great as was his reputation during his lifetime.

Graun (fig. 91) was more fortunate than Hasse, for one of his works has kept its place in public estimation,

Fig. 91.—Carl Heinrich Graun.

at least, in Germany. He was born near Dresden in 1701, and was the youngest of three brothers, all of whom followed the profession of music. Early in life he had the opportunity of hearing the greatest singers of the day; and as he was the possessor of an excellent tenor voice, he profited by the example, while he was still prosecuting his studies in composition. He was in the service of three successive princes of Brunswick, from the last of whom he was begged by Frederick the Great of Prussia, then only Crown Prince; but when he came to the throne, he confirmed Graun in his musical appointments, which he retained till his death in 1759. He composed no less than thirty operas, but the work by which he is best known is his oratorio *Der Tod Jesu*, which stands in much the same estimation in Germany as Handel's *Messiah* with us, and is frequently performed in churches during Holy Week. A *Te Deum*, with chorus and orchestra, is also well known. His music shows much dramatic power, joined to a grace of melody no doubt owing to the Italian influences of his early life.

The example set by Mattheson of a periodical publication devoted to music soon found imitators. Lorenz Mizler's *Neu-eröffnete Musikalische Bibliothek* was started in 1736 and continued at uncertain intervals till 1754; almost at the same time Scheibe began his *Kritischer Musicus*, which appeared weekly in Hamburg during the years 1737-8. In 1750 the eminent theorist Marpurg brought out the first number of a similar work. As it was published in Berlin, and to distinguish it from the last named, he called it *Der Kritische Musikus an der Spree*, after the muddy river on which that city is situated. As fifty numbers only were published, Marpurg's efforts do not seem to have received the support they deserved. He made another attempt, however, in 1754 with his

Historisch-kritische Beytrage zur aufnahme der Musik, and with this he was more fortunate, as it was continued, although irregularly, till 1762. During the progress of this work he started another weekly periodical, called

Fig 92.—Johann Adam Hiller.

Kritische Briefe über die Tonkunst, which went on from 1759 to 1764. The rarity of the latter numbers of all these works indicates a gradual falling away of the subscribers. J. A. Hiller, of Leipzig (fig. 92), a successor of Bach in the appointment of Cantor of the Thomasschule, of whom we have before spoken, was next in the field; and from that time Germany was never without a paper devoted to musical matters, and in this it was far in advance of any other country.

Marpurg's compositions were not numerous. It is as a theorist that he is best known. His *Handbuch bey dem Generalbasse*, and his *Abhandlung von der Fuge*, both reprinted more than once, and translated into several languages, were looked on as forming the basis of a sound musical education. The mathematical questions involved in the study of music, such as temperament, etc., also engaged his attention, and formed the subject of several of his works.

The golden age of music in Vienna belongs to a later period, and will be treated of in another chapter. The intercourse between that city and Italy had been for a long time intimate. Apostolo Zeno and Metastasio had been successively welcomed as poets-laureate by the Austrian court, and for most of its musicians it depended on the same country. Many names of some celebrity will be found in the list of court musicians, among whom may be mentioned Antonio Draghi, J. B. Buononcini, P. F. Tosi (whose *Treatise on the Florid Song*, originally published in Italian, gives so much information on the science of singing as then practised, and also many interesting particulars of the great singers of those days), Antonio Caldara, and others.

But there was one musician filling the post of Capellmeister at Vienna who deserves a more extended notice, for his celebrity was European. This was Johann Josef Fux, who was court composer from 1698 to 1740, serving under the three emperors Leopold I., Joseph I., and Charles VI. He was born in the year 1660 in Styria, and but little is known of his education beyond the fact that he appears to have travelled in France, Germany and Italy, to increase his knowledge and experience. In 1675 he was already settled in Vienna. All three of the sovereigns whom he served were well versed in music, and testified for him the greatest esteem. He attempted with success all kinds of musical composition: instrumental, sacred and operatic. As an example of the footing on which he stood with the Emperor Charles VI., it is related that, having composed an opera in honour of the birthday of the Archduchess, aunt of the Emperor, the latter was so delighted with the work that, as a special mark of esteem, he himself accompanied it on the harpsichord at the third performance. Fux was placed at the side of the Emperor, and turning over the leaves of the score for him, was so struck with his skill that he exclaimed, " What a pity your Majesty should not be a capellmeister!" "There is no harm done," replied the Emperor; "things are very well as they are!"

On the coronation of Charles VI. at Prague in 1723 as King of Bohemia, Fux wrote an opera, *Costanza e Fortezza*, for the occasion. The whole staff of the Imperial chapel was sent to Prague to unite with the principal musicians of that city and others who came from Italy in the performance of the opera. Fux was unfortunately overcome with an attack of gout. That his presence might not be wanting on so great an occasion, the Emperor had him conveyed the whole way on a litter, and at the performance ordered the composer's chair to be placed at the side of his own. He received the congratulations of the many distinguished people, artists and others, who were gathered together for such an important event, and it was a great triumph for him.

Nearly all his compositions have remained in manuscript, and are now entirely unknown. But every one has heard of the great work of his life, his *Gradus ad Parnassum*. The publication of this treatise formed another opportunity for the Emperor to show his admiration for his capellmeister, as he undertook the entire expense of its publication. The style in which the work is printed shows that no expense was spared to make the externals of the book worthy of its contents. It was published at Vienna in 1725 in the Latin language, but was soon translated into German by Mizler, and subsequently into Italian, French, and English, and for many years it formed the indispensable handbook to the higher branches of a musical education.

The master died in Vienna in the year 1741, at the age of eighty-one years. He was one of the eminent men to whom Mattheson gave a niche in his *Ehrenpforte*, and whom he requested to supply the necessary information. Mattheson had previously criticised some of his theoretical views roughly, as was usual with him, and that in a work which, with a strange want of delicacy, he dedicated to Fux. The latter replied with some dignity that "modesty forbade him to give details how he had received advancement in the offices he held, which would be to sound his own praises. It was sufficient to say that he had been found worthy of being first capellmeister to Charles VI." Thus, unfortunately, most of the particulars of his life are wanting to us.

Up to this time the opera was looked on as a vehicle for the display of the skill of the singers engaged, rather than as a dramatic composition to be developed in musical language. The number of airs and their character were each laid down and ordered according to certain fixed rules. Early in the eighteenth century appeared a musician who could think for himself, and who was destined to sweep away all these arbitrary restrictions. His name was Christopher Willibald Gluck. He was born in the year 1714 in Bohemia. His father was in the service of Prince Lobkowitz, and was in a position to give him a good general as well as musical education. When a young man, he made his way to Vienna, where still lived A. Caldara, J. J. Fux, and other musicians of eminence. While there he had the good fortune to meet, at the house of Prince Lobkowitz, the Prince Melzi, who was so struck with his abilities that he took him back to Milan and then put him under G. B. Sammartini, a composer of merit. He shortly began to compose operas on his own account, which were received with much favour, and caused their author to be looked on as one of the best composers. So great was his reputation that in 1745 he was invited to London to compose two operas for that city. During his residence here, he found time to pay a visit to Paris, in order to hear the operas of Rameau—another musician who thought for himself. After various wanderings in fulfilment of his engagements, he returned to Vienna. He was now forty-four years of age. His reputation had gradually increased; his operas showed an advance in dramatic power, but he was content to work on the same lines as the other dramatic composers of his day. In 1762 he brought out in Vienna his *Orfeo*, in which he made a bound forward; indeed, it is a masterpiece. He had allied himself with Calzabigi, a poet who carried out the composer's views of dramatic treatment. Almost everyone knows the magnificent air *Che faro senza Euridice*, which for depth of feeling is unsurpassed. This opera showed the development of his principles, but in the year 1767 he brought out his *Alcestis*, in which he claimed to revolutionise the art of writing for the theatre. To the score of this work, published in Vienna in 1769, is prefixed a dedicatory epistle, in which he sets out the principles which guided him in its composition. This preface is of such deep interest that we give a translation of the principal passages:—

"When I undertook to set *Alceste* to music, I proposed to myself to avoid all the abuses which the ill-restrained vanity of singers, or the too great compliance of composers, had introduced into Italian opera, which, from being the most dignified and the most splendid of entertainments, had become the most ridiculous and the most tedious. I endeavoured to confine music to its true office of adding force to poetry by the expression and the introduction of melody, without interrupting the action or chilling it by the introduction of useless and superfluous ornament. I thought that it should act in the same way as cheerful colour and the contrast of light and shade do to a well-arranged drawing, that it should animate the design without altering the outline. I had no desire to interrupt an actor in the warmth of a dialogue to listen to a tedious *ritornello*, nor to stop him in the middle of a speech upon a favourite vowel, either for the sake of displaying his fine voice in a long ornamented passage, or to wait while the orchestra gave him time to take breath for a cadenza. I did not believe that the second part of an air should be passed over rapidly when it was the most important, in order to repeat the words, according to rule, four times over, nor to finish the air where the sense did not finish, for the purpose of giving the singer the opportunity of showing, to his own satisfaction, how capriciously he could vary a passage. In short, I endeavoured to restrain all those abuses against which for a long time both good sense and reason had cried out in vain.

"I supposed that the overture should give the spectators a foreshadowing of what was to be presented, and form, so to speak, the argument. . . . I thought also that my great aim should be a noble simplicity; and I have avoided making a show of difficulty at the expense of clearness. I have not sought after novelty which did not arise naturally out of the situation or the sentiment; and there is no customary rule which I have not thought it my duty to sacrifice willingly in favour of effect.

"Such are my principles. . . . Success has justified them, and universal approval in so enlightened a city has shown clearly that simplicity, truth, and natural expression are the great principles in all the productions of art."

The soundness of these principles will be admitted, as well as the dignity and straightforwardness with which they are enforced. It appears, however, that the popular approval was not so complete as he claimed. Many of the public took the opposite view, those who were in entire accord with the composer being the court party, headed by the Emperor, who was a good musician. *Alceste* was followed up by *Paride ed Elena*, in the dedication of which he further developed his views.

He was not, however, completely satisfied with the reception that these works received at the hands of the Viennese public. He formed the idea, possibly from his recollections of the operas of Rameau, that the French stage was more suitable for carrying out his designs. There was at that time (1772) living in Vienna, attached to the French Embassy, the Bailli du Rollet, a man of considerable acquirements. To him Gluck expounded his views, with the result that a libretto was arranged from the *Iphigénie en Aulide* of Racine. The work was at once put in hand, and some preliminary rehearsals of it were gone through.

Du Rollet was much impressed by what he heard, and lost no time in trying to induce the administration of the Opera in Paris to engage Gluck to produce his work in that city. In furtherance of this scheme, he addressed a letter, expounding the new principles, to the *Mercure de France*, which appeared in October, 1772. It proved to be a declaration of war. The administration was strongly opposed to these novelties. Gluck, however, had been the music-master of the Dauphiness Marie Antoinette. She threw her influence into the scale, with the result that Gluck left Vienna for Paris, and the opera was put in rehearsal and produced in 1774. The extraordinary strife which broke out on its production belongs to another chapter. Gluck was now sixty years of age, and he remained in Paris until the end of 1779, when an attack of apoplexy induced him to return to Vienna, and in that city he died in 1787.

Gluck attempted instrumental music, composing several symphonies; but in this style of music he was not so successful. Dramatic situations were requisite to bring out his greatest powers. Instrumental music, however, enjoyed great popularity in Vienna. Among the composers most sought after for such works was Giambattista Sammartini, of Milan (who must not be confounded with Padre Martini, of Bologna, the eminent historian and theorist). So highly was he in fashion, that several amateurs, among whom was Prince Esterhazy, combined in giving a commission to a banker at Milan to buy every symphony he produced at a fixed price. These have now all been forgotten, although many of them have been published at Paris, and some of his compositions in London; but there can be no doubt that they exercised an important influence on the development of that style of music.

BIBLIOGRAPHY.

Forkel, J. W. Ueber Johann Sebastian Bachs Leben, Kunst und Kunstwerke. Leipzig, 1802. 4to (translated London, 1820. 8vo).

Bitter, C. H. Johann Sebastian Bach. Berlin, 1865. 2 vols., 8vo.

Spitta, P. Johann Sebastian Bach. Leipzig, 1873. 2 vols., 8vo (translated by Clara Bell and J. A. Fuller Maitland. London, 1884-5. 3 vols., 8vo).

Bitter, C. H. Carl Philipp Emanuel und Wilhelm Friedemann Bach und deren Brüder, Berlin, 1868. 2 vols., 8vo.

Mattheson, Johann. Grundlage einer Ehren-Pforte. Hamburg, 1742. 4to.

Köchel, Dr. Ludwig Ritter von. Johann Josef Fux. Wien, 1872. 1 vol., 8vo.

Schmid, Anton. Christoph Willibald Ritter von Gluck, dessen Leben und tonkünstlerisches Wirken. Leipzig, 1854. 8vo.

Newman Ernest. Gluck and the Opera. London, 1895. 8vo.

CHAPTER IX.

MUSIC IN ENGLAND AT THE TIME OF THE RESTORATION.

Discouragement of Music during the Commonwealth—The resumption of the Cathedral Service—"Captain" Cooke—Matthew Lock—Pelham Humphrey, Blow, and Wise—The "Verse" Anthem—Jeremiah Clarke and Croft—Henry Purcell—Boyce's "Cathedral Music"—The Progress of Organ-building in England—"Father Smith" and Renatus Harris—The Temple Organ—John Playford, the Music Publisher—Christopher Simpson—Mace's *Musick's Monument*—Tom D'Urfey.

NOTHING could well be more depressing than the outlook of music in England at the time of the Restoration. Cathedral service throughout the land had been abandoned. The choirs had been dispersed, the service books burnt or torn in pieces, and in many cases the organs had been destroyed. Cromwell is believed to have been fond of music, and it is certain that his Latin secretary, Milton, was a good musician, and the friend of Henry Lawes—the "Harry whose tuneful and well-measur'd song" is celebrated in his well-known sonnet, and who in happier times had set the music to the poet's mask of *Comus*. But any appreciation of music was exceptional. The Scriptural injunction, "Is any merry? let him sing psalms," was obeyed implicitly, and no other music was tolerated.

When therefore the King "enjoyed his own again,"

the whole machinery for the decent performance of Divine worship in "quires and places where they sing" had to be reconstructed. Henry Lawes, who during the troubles had managed to support himself by teaching, still survived, and on him devolved the duty of composing the anthem for Charles II.'s coronation.

Among those who had adhered to the Royalist cause was Henry Cooke, formerly a chorister of the Chapel Royal. At the outbreak of the Rebellion his duties ceased, but he followed his royal master in his troubles, and turned soldier, behaving with such bravery that he received a captain's commission. At the Restoration, possibly in reward for his services, he received the appointment of master of the children of the Chapel Royal. He continued to be called Captain Cooke, under which title he is frequently referred to by Pepys in his diary; for instance, under December 21st, 1665: "Captain Cooke and his two boys did sing some Italian songs, which I must in a word say I think was fully the best musique that I ever yet heard in all my life." Pepys was not blind to one of his failings, for he says elsewhere, "A vain coxcomb he is, though he sings so well."

At first it was so difficult to find boys with any musical training whatever, that all sorts of expedients were necessary in order to perform the music at the Chapel Royal. Matthew Lock tells us, "For above a year after the opening of His Majestie's Chappel, the orderers of the musick there were necessitated to supply superior parts of the music with cornets and men's feigned voices, there being not one lad for all that time capable of singing his part readily."

The appointment of Captain Cooke, whatever may have been the motives which prompted it, seems to have been a happy one, as he possessed remarkable skill in the training of boys, and he was, moreover, very fortunate in the material he had to work upon. Of those who first came under his tuition, three—Pelham Humfrey, John Blow, and Michael Wise—soon distinguished themselves. To supply the places of the men was not so difficult. Dr. William Child, Dr. Christopher Gibbons (son of the famous madrigal-writer, Orlando Gibbons), who had both been "children" of the Chapel Royal during the reign of the late King, and Edmund Lowe, formerly of Salisbury, were appointed organists, while twenty men-singers were collected, possessed of some experience. For the coronation, Matthew Lock (well known by name to most people in the present day as the reputed composer of the music to *Macbeth*, although by many it is attributed to Purcell), who had been a choirman at Exeter, was employed to write some triumphal music for performance during the King's progress from the Tower to Whitehall, which was so much appreciated that he was appointed composer-in-ordinary to the King. Lock was a fine example of the musician militant; he was always engaged in controversy. In a service which he wrote for the Chapel Royal, he set each response to the Commandments in a different way. This was of course an innovation, which has not commended itself to subsequent practice, and in those days it was looked on with great disfavour. Lock published his setting, with a preface in which he roundly abused his opponents, under the title "*Modern Church Musick, Pre-accused, Censur'd, and Obstructed in its Performance before His Majesty, April 1st,* 1666. Vindicated by the Author, Matt. Lock, Composer-in-ordinary to His Majesty."

In 1675 he published "*The English Opera: or, The Vocal Musick in 'Psyche,' with the Instrumental Therein Intermix'd.* To which is adjoyned the Instrumental Musick in the *Tempest*," also preceded by an aggressive preface.

He also brought out in 1673 a book called *Melothesia; or, Certain General Rules for Playing upon a Continued Bass.* Becoming a Roman Catholic, he resigned his appointment at the Chapel Royal, and was appointed organist to the Queen at Somerset House.

Anything that savoured of dulness was very distasteful to the King. During his enforced residence in France he had learned to admire the lighter style of Church music which was popular at the court, where Lully had introduced the seductions of instrumental music into the services. To one who had for a long time become accustomed to such variety, the accompaniment of the organ alone seemed monotonous, and the severe and solemn compositions of the older masters tedious. The King determined to form his own chapel on the model of that at Versailles. Twenty-four instrumentalists were engaged, who were first brought into requisition on Sunday, September 14th, 1662. Need it be said that Mr. Pepys was not absent on so important an occasion? He reports as follows:—

"To Whitehall Chapel, when sermon almost done, and I heard Captain Cooke's new musique. This the first of having vialls and other instruments to play a symphony between every verse of the anthems, but the musique more full than it was last Sunday, and very fine it is."

Michael Wise, who was, as we have seen, one of Captain Cooke's early pupils, was born in Salisbury and in 1668 became organist of the cathedral of his native city, being then about twenty years of age. He was in great favour with King Charles, who appointed him his organist. Unfortunately he was a man of hasty temper, which led to his losing his life in a chance medley with a watchman in the streets of Salisbury. He wrote several services and anthems of great beauty and power of expression, which are still sung, especially *The ways of Zion do mourn.*

Pelham Humfrey was probably the most precocious of the three young choristers, for while still singing as a boy in the choir he had already composed several anthems. His quickness, joined to a certain charm of manner, seems to have commended him to the King, who, when his voice broke, sent him to France to have the advantage of studying under Lully. He remained abroad for three years, and returned to find that he had already been appointed a "gentleman of the Chapel Royal." Pepys, who had characterised him as "a pretty boy" before he left England, speaks thus of him on his return:—

"Home, and there find, as I expected, Mr. Cæsar and little Pelham Humfrey, lately returned from France, and is an absolute mosieur, as full of form and confidence and vanity, and disparages everything and everybody's skill but his own. But to hear how he laughs at all the king's music here; at Blagrave and others, that they cannot keep time or tune, nor understand anything; and at Grebus, the Frenchman, the King's master of music, how he understands nothing, nor can play on any instrument, and so cannot compose, and that he will give him a lift out of his place, and that he and the King are mighty great."

"Grebus, the Frenchman," was M. Grabu, who was certainly a dull musician. His only title to fame was the composition, towards the end of Charles II.'s reign, of an opera called *Albion and Albanius*. The words of the piece were by Dryden, and the satire which they contained gave the work an importance which the music alone would never have acquired, except perhaps to the ears of Dryden, who in his preface exalted the composer at the expense of Purcell.

Of the brilliancy of Humfrey's attainments there can be no doubt, and the foreign experience which he had acquired rendered his style peculiarly acceptable to the King, who on the death of Captain Cooke in 1672, appointed him Master of the Children, and soon afterwards composer-in-ordinary for the violin to his Majesty. Several of his sacred compositions are still in use. His secular works, not being readily found in available form, are less known. Unfortunately his career was cut short at the early age of twenty-seven.

Dr. John Blow (fig. 93) was a man of an entirely different

Fig. 93.—Dr. John Blow (from the frontispiece of his *Amphion Anglicus*, drawn and engraved by R. White, 1700).

character. Nothing could exceed his modesty, which actually went so far as to prompt him to resign the post of organist of Westminster Abbey in favour of a pupil whose genius he recognised as exceeding his own; this pupil was Henry Purcell. Blow was without doubt a man of genius. Much of his Church music has come down to us, some of which is still heard, and deserves to continue to be heard. His best-known anthems are, *I beheld, and lo! a great multitude* and *I was in the Spirit*, which in many cathedrals is always sung on Whit-Sunday. He was also the composer of much secular music, a collection of which he made and published under the title of *Amphion Anglicus*, containing songs which could well bear resuscitation. He died in 1608, in his sixtieth year.

To these composers of whom we have been speaking is to be attributed the introduction of the *verse* anthem. Up to the time of the Restoration anthems had consisted entirely of chorus. They were now interspersed with passages written for a single voice to a part. This was called "verse," for what reason is not obvious. The introduction of solos naturally followed.

Another innovation is also due to this period—the introduction of what are now known as "Anglican" chants. On the resumption of the cathedral service, Edward Lowe, originally a chorister of Salisbury, but at that time organist of Christ Church, Oxford, at the request of that university drew up a *Short Direction for the Performance of Cathedral Service*. This was based on the old plain-song. But the more florid style of music which had come into vogue for services and anthems was not in keeping with the severity of the ancient music, and the result was the invention of the well-known Anglican chant, which was soon followed by the double chant.

If Captain Cooke was fortunate in finding three boys of the capacity of Wise, Humfrey, and Blow, the latter, who had been appointed Master of the Children in the year 1674, in succession to Humfrey, was still more so, for he had as pupils Jeremiah Clark, William Croft, and Henry Purcell.

Jeremiah Clark was much esteemed as a composer of Church music, some of his anthems still being in use; but he distinguished himself more by his songs, many of which are to be found in the collections published by Playford and D'Urfey. The circumstances of his death were so romantic that we must give them here. He fórmed a hopeless attachment for a lady of a higher rank in life than himself.. His misfortune induced great despondency; we give the sequel in the words of a contemporary: "Being at the house of a friend in the country, he took an abrupt resolution to return to London; his friend, having observed marks of great dejection, furnished him with a horse and a servant. Riding along a road, a fit of melancholy seized him, upon which he alighted, and giving the servant his horse to hold, went into a field, in the corner whereof was a pond, and also trees, and began to debate with himself whether he should then end his days by hanging or drowning. Not being able to resolve on either, he thought of making what he looked upon as chance the umpire, and drew out of his pocket a piece of money, and tossing it into the air, it came down on its edge, and stuck in the clay. Though the declaration answered not his wish, it was far from ambiguous, as it seemed to forbid both methods of destruction, and would have given unspeakable comfort to a mind less disorganised than his own. Being thus interrupted in his purpose, he returned, and mounting his horse, rode on to London, and in a short time shot himself." This occurred in the year 1707, when Clarke was thirty-eight years of age.

Croft became a chorister at the Chapel Royal in 1685, and in 1699 was appointed organist of St. Anne's, Soho. In 1700 he was admitted a gentleman of the Chapel Royal, as well as to the reversion of the post of organist jointly with Clark, at whose decease he succeeded to the full place. On the death of Blow, in the following year, he was made organist of Westminster Abbey. He wrote many anthems, and some services, which are still much admired; for instance, *God is gone up*, and *We will rejoice*, are frequently heard. The best known of his works, however, is his Funeral Service, the dignity and solemnity of which are in such perfect keeping with its intention that no other music is likely to displace it.

The third of these young men was Henry Purcell, a name which must ever be held in reverence by English musicians, for he was without doubt the greatest of our modern composers.

Henry Purcell (fig. 94) was born in 1658, in a house almost under the shadow of Westminster Abbey, in which his father was a singing-man, in addition to being a gentleman of the Chapel Royal, Master of the Boys at the Abbey and music copyist to that church and a member of the Royal Band, so that the future composer entered on

MUSIC AT THE TIME OF THE RESTORATION. 189

life surrounded by an atmosphere of music. When he was just six years old, his father died; and in proof that

Fig. 94.—Henry Purcell (from the engraving by Zobel after Klosterman's portrait in the possession of the Royal Society of Musicians).

the boy had already acquired some musical knowledge, he was at once admitted a chorister of the Chapel Royal.

He was committed to the charge of his uncle, Thomas Purcell, also an esteemed musician, who honestly did his best by the child.

Captain Cooke was still Master of the Boys, and under him Purcell advanced with rapid strides. On Cooke's death Pelham Humfrey was appointed to his post, and was able to initiate Purcell into the French style of Lully; but he was soon carried off, and Blow was put in his place. Purcell was now sixteen years of age, and must naturally have lost his soprano voice, and have become no longer useful in the choir; it seems, however, that boys who appeared to possess exceptional ability were retained, and this was the case with Purcell. He had already written several works which showed the possession of great talent; and, on the recommendation, as it is believed, of Blow, he was appointed copyist to Westminster Abbey, a post formerly held by his father. It is probable that the music known as Locke's music to *Macbeth* was actually written by Purcell in these early days, and it is certain that he composed music to Dryden's *Aureng-Zebe*, as well as to two plays by Shadwell, in one of which, *The Libertine*, occurs the well-known chorus, *In these delightful pleasant groves.*

At the time of which we are writing there was a minor canon of Canterbury Cathedral, the Rev. John Gosling, who possessed a bass voice of extraordinary depth and power. He was on very intimate terms with the Purcell family, and Henry Purcell wrote more than one anthem specially to show off his lower notes. Of one of these the following story is told. Charles II. was very fond of Gosling, and took him h him on the trial trip of a new yacht. Off the North Foreland a violent storm arose, and the ship was in such great danger that the King and the Duke of York had to work like common sailors in helping to manage the vessel. Fortunately the lives of all on board were saved, but Mr. Gosling was so affected by the dangers they had gone through, and so thankful for their preservation, that he selected from the Psalms the words of an anthem which he requested Purcell to set to music. The result was the well-known *They that go down to the sea in ships*, in which the bass is made to go down to the low D.

In 1680 Dr. Blow performed an extraordinary act of modesty and generosity, in resigning the appointment of organist of Westminster in favour of his pupil Purcell, who was then twenty-two years of age. In the same year Purcell composed his opera, *Dido and Æneas*, which, strange to say, was written for "Mr. Josiah Priest's boarding-school at Chelsey," and "performed by young gentlewomen." It was presumably a fashionable place of education, as the epilogue on the occasion was spoken by "the Lady Dorothy Burk." The book was by Nahum Tate. The music was in advance of the time, for the work was a true opera, not songs interspersed with dialogue, but set to music throughout. The composer seems never to have repeated the experiment.

In 1681 he married, and in 1682 received the further appointment of organist of the Chapel Royal. In the fulfilment of the duties of his Church appointments, he wrote much sacred music, both services and anthems, some with orchestral accompaniments, as his *Te Deum* and

Jubilate, composed for St. Cecilia's Day, 1694, which for many years successively were performed at St. Paul's Cathedral on the occasion of the festival of the "Sons of the Clergy."

But he was equally industrious in secular composition. Although he attempted no other opera, he wrote incidental music to many dramatic pieces. That for *The Tempest* is well known, for it contains *Come unto these yellow sands*, and *Full fathom five*, which are as beautiful as they are familiar. This was followed by *Dioclesian; or, The Prophetess*, adapted by Betterton from Beaumont and Fletcher ; *Amphitryon*, by Dryden, and many others which we cannot mention here. *King Arthur*, however, also by Dryden, cannot be passed over, for in it is the solo for tenor, with chorus, *Come if you dare*, which possesses all the attributes of a patriotic song, and still holds its place. In it is also the celebrated frost scene, now no longer heard, but which used to freeze our ancestors in the days of the "antient concerts," of which we shall have a word to say later. We must also mention *The Indian Queen*, with its *Ye twice ten hundred deities*, and the exquisite song, *I attempt from love's sickness to fly*. Purcell also wrote two sets of sonatas for two violins and bass, which no doubt were the works from which Corelli formed the high opinion he is known to have held of him. It is even said that Corelli proposed to visit England for the express purpose of making the acquaintance of his brother-composer, a decision which he abandoned on hearing of Purcell's death just as he was on the point of starting.

It was an excellent custom in those days for the "friends

of musick" to meet on the feast of St. Cecilia, November 22nd, to celebrate the patron saint of the art they practised —a custom which might well be revived in our own day. The members attended Divine service at St. Bride's Church, in Fleet Street. The service, it need hardly be said, was choral; the anthem was generally composed for the occasion; and a sermon in praise of music was preached, some of which have been published and come down to us. The religious part of the ceremony performed, the members assembled in some public room, where a special ode in praise of music was performed, which, as becomes Englishmen, was followed by a dinner.

There are some reasons for believing that the meetings were instituted earlier than the time of Purcell, but the first recorded celebration took place in 1683, when Purcell set to music three separate odes, two in English and one in Latin; but it seems that one only was performed: certainly only one was published. The ode for 1684 was composed by Blow, as was also that for 1691. The political changes of 1688 interrupted the meetings, and it was not till 1692 that Purcell was again employed. The words of the ode were the production of Nicholas Brady, Tate's associate in the new version of the Psalms. This work met with great success, and was frequently performed, and was published in our own day by the Musical Antiquarian Society. In 1694 the Church service was performed with unusual magnificence, Purcell's *Te Deum* and *Jubilate* in D, with orchestra, of which we have already spoken, being written for the occasion. The intention appears to have been to have repeated its performance at the next festival, but for some unassigned reason this did not take place, a similar work by Dr. Blow being substituted. It will have been seen that this festival was associated with many of Purcell's triumphs. The feast of St. Cecilia in 1695 was a day of mourning for all who had taken part in these celebrations, as well as for all who loved music. On the eve of the festival, within earshot of the Abbey in whose services he had so frequently borne a part, the illustrious composer died, not having completed his thirty-seventh year—an age which has been fatal to several great musicians. He was buried most fittingly in Westminster Abbey, beneath the organ which he had so worthily played, and on a pillar close by may still be read one of those few epitaphs which seem worthy of the occasion :—

"Here lies Henry Purcell, Esq, who left this life, and is gone to that blessed place where only his harmony can be exceeded."

Comparatively a small portion only of his works was published during his lifetime. In fact, he seems to have shown almost an antipathy to printing them. To the best of her powers his widow made it her pious duty to repair this omission. The most important collection was published under the title of "*Orpheus Britannicus*: A Collection of all the choicest Songs for one, two, and three voices, composed by Mr. Henry Purcell"; and this work must have been well received, as a second edition was called for.

His master, Dr. Blow, survived him several years, living

until 1708. Croft was younger than Purcell, and nobly maintained the traditions of sacred music till the year 1727, and in this he was assisted by Weldon, Greene, and Boyce. The latter has further claims on our gratitude for, in addition to his numerous compositions —among which is the well-known *O where shall wisdom be found?* —he published a collection of anthems and services by the most eminent of our Church musicians. The work was originally projected by Greene; but his engagements not allowing him to carry out his design, he bequeathed his materials to Boyce. It was the first attempt to bring out such a collection in score, the only previous work of the kind, Barnard's, having been in parts. The work, which is in three folio volumes, is of the greatest value, and is so much appreciated that it has been twice reprinted in our own days.

These names comprise the greatest among our cathedral composers. Their work was continued by men who were well-instructed and capable musicians. We may mention William Hayes and his son Philip Hayes, who succeeded his father both as organist at Magdalen College, Oxford, and as Professor of Music in the university—each of whom aimed too openly at catching the ear—Charles King, Nares, Travers, Jackson of Exeter—a man of many accomplishments, whose well-known *Te Deum* shows how feeble a man of some talent can be—Dupuis, Benjamin Cooke, and John Battishill, whose greatest triumphs, however, were obtained in secular music.

The destruction of organs during the Civil War had

been so general that there was no lack of work for organ-builders at the Restoration. Among the first builders in the field was Bernard Schmidt, better known in England as "Father Smith," who came over from Germany with two nephews. The first commission given to him was an organ for the Chapel Royal at Whitehall, which was completed in 1660, for evidence of which we appeal again to Mr. Pepys.

"July 8th (Lord's Day.) To Whitchall Chapel, where I got in with ease by going before the Lord Chancellor with Mr. Kipps. Here I heard very good musique, the first time that ever I remember to have heard the organs and singing-men in surplices in my life."

This first effort does not seem to have been entirely satisfactory, but it was built against time. Smith, however, soon had further employment, for in 1662 he built an organ for Westminster Abbey, and subsequently others for St. Giles-in-the-Fields and St. Margaret's, Westminster. He was in great favour with the King, who gave him rooms in Whitehall. The organs he built are very numerous. The quality of tone he produced was very beautiful, but in mechanical arrangements he was not so successful, his touch being bad and the interior work ill arranged.

But he was not allowed to have a monopoly. He had only been a few months in England when Harris, with his son René or Renatus, arrived from France. For some time Smith retained the greater part of the work, but the elder Harris died in 1672, and Renatus turned out to be a man of great ability and resource, proving a formidable rival to his competitor. In one instance this led to a memorable and well-known struggle. At the end of the reign of Charles II., the Societies of the Inner and Middle Temple determined to build for their well-known church the best organ they could obtain. The authorities appear to have been in treaty with Smith on the subject, when some of the Benchers of the Inner Temple brought forward Harris. As a settlement of the matter it was proposed that each of the builders should set up an organ in one of the halls, and that the best should be chosen from the two for erection in the church. After a long and bitter contest the decision was given in favour of Smith. This so added to his reputation that he was at once employed to build the organ for St. Paul's Cathedral, where he was much hampered by the size of the case, which Wren would not allow to exceed certain dimensions, complaining that the building was already spoiled by the "box of whistles."

The most active music-publisher of those times was John Playford. Among the works he brought out was his own *Introduction to the Skill of Music*, which was first published in 1655—a single copy has been found with the date 1654—a book which went through nineteen numbered editions, and four or five to which no number was attached, tending to show that the art of music was assiduously cultivated. The twelfth edition was revised by Purcell, who almost rewrote the part which treats of the art of descant. The later editions claim to be "done on the new Ty'd-Note," *i.e.*, the tails of quavers and smaller notes forming groups were joined, instead of each note being separate. This was a great improvement both in appearance and ease of reading.

Playford had his shop in the Temple, and was a man of great worth, being known as "honest John Playford." At his death his son Henry continued the business. Many important works issued from this establishment, including most of Purcell's, published during the lifetime of the composer: *The Treasury of Musick; The Theater of Musick*, containing airs by Lawes, Purcell, Blow, and others; and *Harmonia Sacra*, consisting of sacred works principally by the same writers.

Another very popular handbook of those days was Christopher Simpson's *Compendium of Practical Musick*, of which nine editions appeared. The author of it was a skilful player on the viol. At the Revolution, his occupation at an end, he served in the army of Charles. After the defeat of the Royalists he found an asylum in the house of Sir Richard Bolles, who, in Simpson's own words, afforded him "a cheerful maintenance, when the Iniquity of the Times had reduced me (with many others in that common calamity) to a condition of needing it." He gives a sad account of the state of music: "That innocent and now distressed muse, driven from her Sacred Habitations and forced to seek a livelihood in Streets and Taverns, where she is exposed and prostituted to all prophaneness, hath, in this her deplorable condition, found a chaste and cheerfull Sanctuary within your Wals." He was charged with the musical education of the son of his protector, who became the most skilful amateur of the day. For his pupil he composed a work entitled *The Division Violist; or, An Introduction to the Playing upon a Ground*, which at that time was the fashionable way of showing the performer's skill. Second and third editions were subsequently brought out, which each contained a Latin translation in parallel columns.

Another very remarkable book was published about this time: *Mace's Musick's Monument; or, A Remembrancer of the Best Practical Musick, Both Divine and Civil, that has ever been known to have been in the world*. The author was chapel clerk of Trinity College, Cambridge, but seems to have given up his post and settled in London to follow his favourite art. The book treats in the first part of music in churches, both parochial and cathedral. The second part gives instructions for playing the lute, with particular directions for executing repairs and keeping it in order, for which purpose he recommends it to be put during the daytime into a bed that is constantly used, between the rug and blanket! The third part contains a scheme for a music-room. But the mere statement of the contents gives a feeble notion of the book. The style is quaint in the highest degree, and must be read to be appreciated. So remarkable is the work that Southey has given long extracts from it in his *Doctor*.

The tastes of Charles II. and his court sanctioned great freedom and licentiousness in the songs of the day, most of the collections of which have now to be kept on the most inaccessible shelves of the library. Among the greatest offenders was Tom D'Urfey, who was said to have been so good a companion that it was considered an honour to have been in his company. He was a great favourite of the King, who, according to the *Guardian*, would lean on his shoulder and hum tunes with him. His *Wit and Mirth; or, Pills to Purge Melancholy*, the well-known collection of his songs, is sufficiently rare and "curious" to have been thought worthy of reprinting in our own time. It is not surprising that this licentiousness should have had the effect of setting the faces of members of the religious world against music and its professors. A similar tendency in France brought forth a treatise "contre les Danses et les Mauvaises Chansons"; here the Rev. Arthur Bedford, of Bristol, but subsequently chaplain of Aske's Hospital in Hoxton, published his *Great Abuse of Musick*, which he dedicated to the Society for Promoting Christian Knowledge, then recently founded. Bedford was himself a great lover of music, and a few years later brought out his *Temple Musick*, the object of which was to prove that the cathedral service was directly derived from that in use in the Temple at Jerusalem. Without doubt his *Great Abuse* was called for, but the intense seriousness of it makes the book very amusing.

BIBLIOGRAPHY.

Barrett, W. A. English Church Composers. London, 1882. 8vo.
Cummings, W. H. Purcell. London, 1881. 8vo.
Hopkins, E. J., and Rimbault, E. F. The Organ, its History and Construction. London, 1870. 8vo.
Macrory, E. A few notes on the Temple Organ. London, s.a. 8vo.
Husk, W. H. An account of the Musical Celebrations on St. Cecilia's Day in the sixteenth, seventeenth, and eighteenth Centuries. London, 1857. 8vo.

CHAPTER X.

THE RISE OF OPERA AND ORATORIO IN ENGLAND.

Early Attempts at English Opera—Celebrated Singers of that Time—Addison's Criticisms—Arrival of Handel in England—His Success in Opera—Story of his "Water Music"—Enters the Service of the Duke of Chandos—His First Oratorio, *Esther*—*Acis and Galatea*—The "Royal Academy of Music"—Buononcini and Ariosti—The Singers Francesca Cuzzoni and Faustina Bordoni—Collapse of the Royal Academy of Music—*The Beggar's Opera*—Handel's Partnership with Heidegger and Resumption of Italian Opera—First Public Performances of Oratorio—Buononcini's Rival Opera—His Disgrace—Heidegger's Perfidy—Handel joins Rich—His Illness—Further Failure of Opera—Handel's Oratorios—*Saul*—*Israel in Egypt*—*The Messiah*—Its success in Dublin—*Samson*—Dettingen *Te Deum*—*Belshazzar*—His Bankruptcy—*Judas Maccabæus*—*Joshua*—*Solomon*—His Blindness and Death.

IT has been seen that music written for the stage in England was rather in the form of incidental music than of regular opera. Among the foreigners attracted to the English court was Cambert, the first to produce opera in France, whom the jealousy of Lully had succeeded in driving from his own country. Charles II. made him his master of the second company of musicians, and, with the assistance of his countryman Grabu, his opera *Ariadne* was arranged for performance in English; but its success was small, and Cambert is supposed to have died of vexation at its failure. It has even been said that he was murdered by assassins employed by

Lully. For this improbable statement there is no evidence whatever; but that it should have been made at all is a proof of the character for vindictiveness which Lully had acquired.

The opera established itself in England very slowly. *Arsinoe, Queen of Cyprus*, an opera then popular in Italy, was translated and set to music by Thomas Clayton, a man of feeble powers, and brought out at Drury Lane Theatre in 1705. This was followed by *Camilla*, which was translated and adapted to the original music by Marc Antonio Buononcini, brother of the more celebrated Giovanni Buononcini. These works were afterwards diversified by the production of *Thomyris, Queen of Scythia*, an opera of the same character.

The favourite female singers were Mrs. Mary Davis, Mrs. Cibber, Mrs. Bracegirdle, and Mrs. Tofts, all Englishwomen; but in 1692 an advertisement appeared in the *Gazette* announcing "the Italian lady that is so famous for singing." This was the celebrated Margherita de l'Epine, who, having acquired a fortune by her singing, afterwards married Dr. Pepusch, of whom we shall have to speak later. The rivalry between the admirers of Mrs. Tofts and Mdlle. de l'Epine divided the world of fashion into two warlike camps, and even produced a disturbance in the theatre.

Mrs. Tofts produced great effect in the character of Camilla. While the piece was running there was a further arrival on our shores of Italian singers. The result was that they received engagements in *Camilla*, performing their own parts in Italian, while the English performers retained the use of their own language. "At length," says Addison in the *Spectator*, "the Audience grew tired of understanding Half the Opera; and therefore, to ease themselves entirely of the Fatigue of thinking, have so ordered it at present that the whole Opera is performed in an unknown Tongue. We no longer understand the Language of our own Stage, insomuch that I have often been afraid, when I have seen our *Italian* Performers chattering in the Vehemence of Action, that they have been calling us Names, and abusing us among themselves; but I hope, since we do put such an entire Confidence in them, they will not talk against us before our Faces, though they may do it with the same Safety as if it were behind our Backs."

There have been people unkind enough to affirm that the strong feeling which Addison shows against Italian opera was caused by his own want of success in writing for the lyric stage. He wrote the libretto for an opera entitled *Rosamund*, on the subject of Queen Eleanor and Fair Rosamund. It is admitted that the poem is pleasing enough, as might be expected from such a master of style; but it was deficient in dramatic power, and the author confided the composition of the music to Clayton, who proved wholly unequal to the task, and the work was received with but little favour. It is only fair, however, to add that when, later, the poem was again set to music by Dr. Arne, the result was much the same; we are thus justified in believing that Addison had miscalculated his powers, which, in spite of the success of his tragedy *Cato*, were not dramatic.

It must be admitted, however, that the opera, whether performed wholly in Italian, or in the ridiculous medley of Italian and English, was a very fair butt for the gentle satire which, in his own transparent style, he heaps upon it from time to time in the pages of the *Spectator*, and in these opinions he was joined by Steele in the *Tatler*. It was, in fact, a period of great dulness; Henry Purcell, the hope of our English school of musicians, had been removed by an early death, and no composer had appeared of sufficient power to lift the opera above the position of a mere fashionable pastime.

But this reproach was to be removed. In 1711, being then in his twenty-seventh year, Handel first landed on these shores, bringing a great reputation with him. Thenceforth for many years the history of music in this country was the history of Handel's life. Great impatience was manifested to hear an opera from his pen, and he was at once engaged by Aaron Hill, director of the Haymarket Theatre (Her Majesty's Theatre of our day), to compose for him an opera on the episode of Rinaldo from Tasso's *Gerusalemme Liberata*, which was translated into English by Hill, and then re-translated into Italian by a poet named Rossi. The work was composed in a race against time between poet and musician, but Handel, always an impetuous composer, was an easy winner. The poor poet was left panting behind, with no opportunity of polishing up his verses, so that he was fain to crave the indulgence of the critics in the following preface to his libretto:—
" Indulgent reader, . . . Herr Handel, the Orpheus of our time, hardly gave me time to write while composing the

music; and I saw with stupor an entire opera set to harmony with the highest degree of perfection in one fortnight. Let this hurried work therefore satisfy you, and, if not deserving of your praise, do not withhold at least your compassion, which indeed will be only justice to the limited time in which it was accomplished."

The new opera took the town by storm, and it was at once seen that a master had appeared. It was put on the stage with great magnificence. In the garden of Armida living birds flew from tree to tree, at which Addison does not fail to make merry. The work was indeed full of beauties—*Cara sposa, Augelletti che cantate, Il tricerbero umiliato*—the march—which were all new. Other numbers had been used in previous works, and among them was the most popular air of them all: *Lascia ch' io pianga.* The Italian opera of the day contained but little concerted music: In *Rinaldo* there are three duets only, The voices required were three sopranos, three altos, and one bass, which unite their forces at the end of the opera, forming the only chorus.

Walsh, who had then become the leading publisher, brought out a volume of songs from *Rinaldo*, by which he is reported to have cleared £1,500, inducing Handel to say to say that Walsh should write the next opera, and that he would sell it.

But his duties as Capellmeister called him to Hanover, from which place, however, he returned as soon as he could obtain leave of absence. In the meantime the directorship of the Opera had passed into the hands of McSwiney. Handel was at once prepared with a new work—*Il Pastor*

Fido—which was produced in November, 1712. Its success

Fig. 95.—George Frederick Handel.

was doubtful. *Teseo*, which was brought out in January, 1713, was more fortunate; but McSwiney, unable to meet his expenses, became bankrupt and absconded. The management now fell into the hands of Heidegger, whose ugliness was his greatest claim to celebrity.

The Peace of Utrecht was celebrated by a solemn service at St. Paul's in July, 1713. For this Handel was commanded to write a *Te Deum* and *Jubilate*. He seems to have taken for model Purcell's *Te Deum*, with orchestra, but it is the first of his works in which he reveals his power of dealing with choral masses. Queen Anne was kept away by illness, but she conferred on the composer a life pension of £200 a year.

In the following year the Queen died, and the Elector, whose Capellmeister Handel was, came to England to be crowned as George I. Handel remembered, only too late, that he had long outstayed his leave of absence. The court were assiduous attendants at the Opera. *Rinaldo* was revived, *Amadigi* was produced, but the King took no notice of his erring Capellmeister. At last a good friend in the person of Count Kielmansegge interfered to put an end to the awkwardness of the situation. At a grand water-party attended by the court he engaged Handel to compose special music for the occasion. This was performed in a boat which followed the royal barge, Handel himself conducting it. The King was pleased with the music, which was new to him, and inquired who was the author. Kielmansegge informed the King, and apologised in Handel's name for his misconduct. The composer was once more taken into favour, and this was the origin of the celebrated *Water Music*. It is only right, however, to say that Handel's most recent biographer, Dr. Chrysander, throws some doubt on this story.

In July, 1716, Handel returned for a time to Hanover in the suite of his royal master, but early in the following year we find him again in England. The favourite *Rinaldo* was once more revived, to be followed by *Amadigi*. But this was the period of wild speculation consequent on the South Sea scheme, which engrossed popular attention, so that the opera languished, and indeed for a time came to a full stop.

At this crisis Handel was fortunate enough to meet with a patron of unexampled magnificence. The Duke of Chandos had just built for himself a palace at Cannons, near Edgware, at an enormous cost, in which he maintained an almost regal state, one of the manifestations of which was a private chapel, for the services in which he kept up a large choir, supported by a band of instruments. Of this magnificence the chapel is the only remaining evidence. No vestiges of the house are to be traced; but the chapel is now the parish church of Whitchurch. The Duke's first musical director was Dr. Pepusch, but in 1718 Handel was appointed in his place. For performance in this chapel he composed a series of twelve anthems, written on a large scale, with instrumental accompaniments, all but one preceded by a regular overture, assuming, in fact, the proportions of a cantata. In addition to these, he composed two separate settings of the *Te Deum*, also with instruments.

But his residence at Cannons had a still more important result. At that place he wrote his first oratorio, *Esther*, which was produced there on August 20th, 1720. The Duke was so delighted with the success of his musical director that he presented him with £1,000. It cannot be doubted that in after years Handel made great advances on his first attempt at this sort of composition, but it is a foretaste of the great works he was to give to us subsequently. The overture was one of the most popular he ever wrote.

Still another form of composition owes its origin to this busy time. At Cannons also he produced his pastoral, *Acis and Galatea*, one of those delightful works which surely can never grow old. Who can forget the charming tenor air, *Love in her eyes sits playing*, or Galatea's *Hush, ye pretty warbling choir*, and *As when the dove*, or Polyphemus's recitative, *I rage, I melt, I burn*, followed by the popular, *O ruddier than the cherry*? Nor are the choruses less delightful; witness *O the pleasure of the plains*, *Wretched lovers*, *Happy we*, and *Galatea, dry thy tears*. The words of this work were supplied by the poet Gay.

While at Cannons he also published his *Suite de Pièces pour le Claveçin*, impelled to do so by the fact that unauthorised persons were circulating incorrect copies. The law of copyright was unsettled in those days, and Handel was a frequent sufferer from its uncertainty. In this set of lessons is the famous composition known as the *Harmonious Blacksmith*, although its author gave it no such title.

During Handel's sojourn at Cannons the public began

to feel the want of an opera in London, and several noblemen and lovers of this form of entertainment united to raise a fund to put the opera on a firm basis.

A capital of £50,000 was raised, the King giving £1,000 a year and his consent that the undertaking should be called "The Royal Academy of Music." A body of directors was to be chosen annually from the contributors, but the virtual manager was Heidegger. Handel, apparently with the consent of the Duke of Chandos, was appointed composer, and was sent abroad to get together a suitable company of singers, among whom was engaged the famous Senesino. The King's Theatre in the Haymarket was opened on April 2nd, 1720, with an opera by Giovanni Porta, entitled *Numitor*, which was only produced to give time for the rehearsals of an opera by Handel. After being postponed by command, *Radamisto* was produced on the 27th of April, amidst a scene of the greatest excitement. The struggle for places was so great that ladies were carried away fainting, and their dresses torn to shreds. Forty shillings were in vain offered for tickets for the gallery, and this excitement was caused purely by a desire to hear the music, for the great singers whom Handel had engaged had not arrived, as they were not yet free from their other engagements. The opera continued to be performed to crowded houses till May 30th, when D. Scarlatti's *Narciso* took its place. It was performed five nights, and a single performance of *Radamisto* and one of *Numitor* closed the season with great success.

With Handel as chief composer had been associated Giovanni Battista Buononcini and Attilio Ariosti. The latter, who had been a Dominican monk, but released from his vows by the Pope, was a respectable composer; the former was something more than respectable. The new season opened with an opera by Buononcini, *Astarto*. The singers engaged by Handel had now arrived, and Senesino, Signora Durastanti and Broschi, with others, took part in it. The directors then announced that they were about to produce a work the joint production of the three composers. The libretto of an opera, *Muzio Scevola*, had been prepared by Paolo Rolli, the poet of the establishment; Ariosti undertook the first act, Buononcini the second, and Handel the third. To ensure fairness as far as possible, each act was to be preceded by an overture. It was an ill-judged scheme, and could not fail to produce unsatisfactory results, but it served to excite the curiosity of the public. Of course, Handel carried off the palm. Ariosti was a man of gentle character, but Buononcini was of a jealous disposition, and this feeling was fomented by his friends, causing the ill-starred rivalry to become the source of much subsequent bitterness.

During 1721 Handel definitely gave up his appointment at Cannons, with the duties of which his operatic pursuits must have greatly interfered. On the 9th of December he brought out his *Floridante*. During the following season one of Handel's most beautiful operas, *Ottone*, was produced for the *début* of the eminent soprano, Francesca Cuzzoni. She was a woman of a difficult temper, and gave much trouble at rehearsal, refusing to sing the beautiful air, *Falsa immagine*. Handel was the last man to brook treatment of this sort. He addressed her thus: "I know, madam, that you are a very she-devil; but I will let you know that I am Beelzebub, the prince of the devils!" Thereupon he took her in his arms, and swore he would throw her out of window. Finding her master, she consented to sing the song, and achieved one of her greatest triumphs in it.

Space does not suffice to give the details of all Handel's operatic successes, which followed each other without a check. We content ourselves with naming *Flavio*, *Giulio Cesare*, *Tamerlano*, *Rodelinda*, and *Scipio*, the march in which is still so popular as the parade march of the Grenadier Guards, in which regiment there is a tradition that it was originally written for them and afterwards introduced into *Scipio*.

This brings us to the season of 1726. Although outside speculators had made large sums by trafficking in tickets, the direction of the Royal Academy had never succeeded in making both ends meet, in spite of the fact that the house was always full. This being the case, it seems remarkable that they should have added largely to their working expenses, and still more to their difficulties, by engaging another soprano of the first rank in addition to Cuzzoni. This course, however, they adopted by the engagement of Signora Faustina Bordoni, afterwards, as we have already related, the wife of the composer Hasse. The new-comer was a woman who possessed great beauty and charm of manner, in addition to a voice clear, sweet, and flexible. As to vocal acquirements Cuzzoni seems to have been her equal, but she was far from beautiful, and did not atone for this deficiency by any charm of manner. To give a notion of the terms which in those days were thought liberal for singers of the first rank, it may be mentioned that each of these ladies received £2,000 per annum. It needs but a slight acquaintance with artistic susceptibility to form a judgment of the difficulties the directors were creating for themselves. When *débutantes*, these rivals had sung in the same piece at Venice, and Handel determined that they should do so again. With this view he composed the opera *Alessandro*, in which neither singer was favoured at the expense of the other. The peculiar style of each was carefully studied. Each in turn had an air which brought out the full beauty of her voice and manner. Each had a duet with Senesino, and in the duet which they sang together the parts were so carefully balanced that neither could claim a victory. Exhibitions of this sort are exhilarating to the audience, but bad blood is engendered, with the result that the public become partisans. The rivalry was continued in *Admeto*, produced on January 31st, 1727, in which the two queens of song were persuaded once more to unite their powers. But Handel, with all his energy, was unable to keep the peace. The admirers of the respective singers waxed uproarious, and from the free use of the legitimate means of showing their opinions proceeded to introduce cat-calls and other noisy methods of enforcing their views, the presence of royalty in the person of the Prince of Wales acting as no restraint. "The town" was divided into two hostile camps, and the season was brought to an abrupt close, amid the lampoons and caricatures of the wits of the day.

Handel had been naturalised in 1726, as a preliminary to receiving the appointment of "Composer of Musick to the Chapel Royal," which could only be held by an Englishman; and he was also nominated composer to the court. In this capacity he was called upon to compose the anthem for the coronation of George II. He interpreted his commission so liberally that he wrote four—*Zadok the Priest, Let thy hand be strengthened, The king shall rejoice*, and *My heart is inditing*—and they were all performed on the occasion.

In October, 1727, peace had been sufficiently patched up between Cuzzoni and Faustina to allow of their united appearance in *Riciardo Primo*, and *Siroe*. But the disgraceful scenes of the last season began to produce their natural results. The more respectable part of the audience stayed away, although the new works presented real attractions. Handel was not to be daunted, but produced his *Tolomeo* in April to diminishing audiences, when an overwhelming attraction elsewhere proved too powerful. The season came to an end. A meeting of the directors was held to consider their position. It appeared that the whole of the £50,000 originally subscribed had been lost in the lavish expenditure of the management; and, in face of so serious a state of affairs, it was decided to abandon the enterprise.

The superior attraction of which we have spoken was the celebrated *Beggar's Opera*, which was produced at Lincoln's Inn Fields in January, 1728. It is said to owe its origin, as reported by Spence in his "Anecdotes," to a remark of Swift to Gay that "a Newgate pastoral might make an odd, pretty kind of thing." Gay acted on the hint. The opera professed to hold up to reprobation highwaymen, thieves, and their associates; but under a thin disguise Walpole and other prominent characters in the world of politics, as well as the frivolities of fashionable life, were satirised. Its success was complete. The upper classes enjoyed the satire; the people were content to look no deeper than the surface of the story. Although professing to have a moral purpose, it really exalted highwaymen into heroes. None of the music was original. It consisted principally of English and Scotch ballads, many of great beauty, selected and arranged by Dr. Pepusch. Even Handel was laid under contribution, his march in *Rinaldo* being set to the words *Let us take the road*. The fickle public, which had been wrangling over the respective merits of Cuzzoni and Faustina, deserted in a body to the new attraction. Walker, the original Macheath, was so courted by the young men of fashion that he fell into habits of dissipation which shortened his days; and the original Polly Peachum, Miss Lavinia Fenton, made a complete conquest of the Duke of Bolton, who ran away with and subsequently married her.

The Academy at an end, Handel was without occupation. But his energy was enormous. He at once entered into partnership for three years with Heidegger, and made a journey to Italy to get another company in order to resume the performance of Italian opera. Among those he engaged was Signora Anna Strada, an excellent soprano, who was always a favourite with him. The theatre opened with *Lotario* in December, 1729, which was handed to the copyist, rehearsed, and produced in the short space of a fortnight. Strada had no pretensions to beauty—in fact, she was commonly called "*the Pig*"—and thus at first made but little way with the public: but she had much capability and willingness, and developed into an excellent artiste.

Partenope followed, but the public gave but a lukewarm support to the undertaking. To revive the interest, Senesino was engaged, for whom *Scipio* was remounted. It was followed by *Poro, Ezio*, and *Orlando*, but the fortunes of the house did not revive.

The success of the *Beggar's Opera* had awakened interest once more in works set to English words. Strange to say, it occurred to Rich to produce at Lincoln's Inn Handel's *Acis and Galatea*. It was a wretched performance; but the same work was given by Arne, father of Dr. Arne, with English singers, the soprano being Miss Arne (afterwards Mrs. Cibber), at the "Little Theatre" in the Haymarket, which had not been long opened. These performances seem to have struck Handel as worthy of imitation, and on June 10th, 1732, he also gave *Acis*, made up of his English composition of that name and partly of an earlier work which he wrote at Naples: *Aci, Galatea e Polifemo*. It was performed by a mixed company of Italian and English singers, each using his or her own language, with scenery and dresses, but without action. Shortly afterwards *Esther* was performed in the concert-room in York buildings, Villars Street, by Bernard Gates,

Master of the Children of the Chapel Royal. It then occurred to Handel that he also might participate in its success, and he therefore brought out a revised version of *Esther* at the King's Theatre on May 2nd, 1732. The advertisement announced, "There will be no acting on the stage, but the house will be fitted up in a decent manner for the audience." The singers were all Italian, Strada and Senesino both appearing, and they sang their parts in Italian.

The success of the performance so greatly surpassed expectation, that Handel was persuaded to renew the attempt, and in March of the following year he brought out his *Deborah*. Several numbers were adaptations from his previous works, while some of the choruses were double. Handel and Heidegger, with whom he was still in partnership, were ill-advised enough to raise the prices, which caused great dissatisfaction; but apart from the ill-feeling thus raised, the work was only moderately successful.

In the meantime the operatic efforts of the partners had been far from flourishing. The season of 1732 opened with an opera by Leonardo Leo—*Catone*—and in January 1733, *Orlando*, by Handel, was produced. This opera contains the last song which Handel wrote for Senesino, who was a man of a scheming disposition. Although receiving an enormous salary, he probably found Handel rather a hard taskmaster. Buononcini, Handel's old rival, had lost no opportunity of making powerful friends, and he found a warm patroness in the person of Lady Henrietta Churchill, daughter of the famous Duke of Marlborough. She had married Earl Godolphin, but on the death of her father, without male issue, the title descended to her, and she became Duchess of Marlborough. She manifested the greatest interest in Buononcini, took him into her house in the Stable Yard, St. James's Palace, and settled on him a pension of £500 a year. When differences arose between Senesino and Handel, she and other partisans started a scheme for the establishment of a new opera at the theatre in Lincoln's Inn Fields, and they succeeded in wiling away all Handel's best singers, with the exception of Strada, who was faithful to the master to whom she owed so much. The assistance of Cuzzoni was also obtained, and Porpora was also engaged to conduct the performances.

As far as the personal triumph of Buononcini was concerned, it was of short duration. Some three years previously he had produced as his own a madrigal entitled *La Vita Caduca*; just at this time a printed volume of music, by the well-known Antonio Lotti, was received in this country, and in it occurred the madrigal *La Vita Caduca*. The music as well as the words, beginning *In una siepe ombrosa*, were identical with the composition brought forward by Buononcini, who asserted in such a positive manner his ownership of the composition that the "Academy of Antient Musick" entered into correspondence with Lotti. The latter produced ample testimony on oath, by a number of gentlemen by whom he was well known, that the music was written by him in the year 1705. The evidence was complete, and Buononcini's misconduct was triumphantly proved. A pamphlet was drawn up embodying the facts, with the result that Buononcini left this country, never to return. He quitted England in company with an adventurer who had persuaded him that he possessed the secret of the philosopher's stone. The spell was of short duration, and he had to revert to music for a livelihood, dying at last at Venice, at an advanced age, in a state of destitution.

The rival opera, arrogating to itself the name of the "Opera of the Nobility," opened its first season at Lincoln's Inn on December 29th, 1733, with an opera on the subject of Ariadne, composed for the occasion and conducted by Porpora. Handel had been beforehand, opening on October 30th, with no great attraction. But he was the last man to fold his hands under the pressure of difficulties, and on December 4th he was prepared with an artist who was in every way competent to take the place of Senesino. This was Giovanni Carestini, who, after a preliminary appearance in a pasticcio, made a great effect in a new opera by Handel, on the same subject as Porpora's. But Handel's troubles were only beginning. His partnership with Heidegger terminated on July 6th, 1734, and the latter was actually mean enough to let the King's Theatre to the rival undertaking. On the 5th of the following October, Handel, in partnership with Rich, opened the Lincoln's Inn Fields Theatre with a reproduction of *Arianna*; on the 29th their opponents opened their season at the King's Theatre with Hasse's *Artaserse*. In addition to the talent already at their command, they had secured the services of the most renowned artificial soprano in Europe, Carlo Broschi, better known as Farinelli.

The odds against Handel were terrible, but he was one of those who do not know when they are beaten. The new theatre of Covent Garden, which also was the property of Rich, was just completed, and to it Handel removed in December. His energy was enormous. Old works were resumed, new ones written and mounted. In this way *Ariodante* and *Alcina* were produced. During Lent performances of oratorio were given. But his efforts were unavailing. Farinelli had monopolised the popular ear. The royal family remained faithful to Handel, but the public stayed away so completely that at one of the oratorios Lord Chesterfield left at the beginning, explaining that he felt it best to do so "lest he should disturb the King in his privacies."

Handel was on the verge of bankruptcy, and at this crisis Carestini, annoyed by the popularity of Farinelli, abandoned the master. His fertility continued, and in 1736-7 *Atalanta, Giustinio, Arminio,* and *Berenice* were put on the stage. In the meantime he had filled up the vacancy caused by Carestini's defection by the engagement of a young soprano, Gioacchino Conti, better known as Gizziello.

With this weight of trouble on his shoulders, he found time to write *Alexander's Feast*, to Dryden's well-known words, which he produced at Covent Garden on February 19th, 1736. To this period also belong his organ concertos, in which he delighted the public by playing the organ part himself. In June 1737, the opposition opera scheme broke down, the deathblow being given by the secession of Farinelli. Its supporters had lost £12,000 and the speculation collapsed completely. Handel's losses were but little less serious. He kept his theatre open for a fortnight longer than his rivals, but the savings of an honourable life—£10,000—had disappeared, and he was obliged to give his creditors bills for part of their claims; it is pleasant to be able to add that these bills were all honourably paid. The only objection to this arrangement proceeded from the husband of Signora Strada, but a benefit arranged by his friends enabled him to surmount it.

There arrives a time, however, when the strongest will and the most vigorous constitution give way. The constant anxiety was beginning to tell both on his body and on his mind. A stroke of paralysis deprived him of the use of his right side. His temper, always easily roused, became ungovernable, but this irritability was varied by fits of torpor, from which he could with difficulty be roused. By the advice of his physicians, he went for a time to Aix-la-Chapelle, where, by a heroic persistence in the use of vapour baths, he was restored to health.

On his return to London he found that Heidegger had once more opened the King's Theatre with opera. The manager made him the offer of £1,000 for two operas, and he at once set to work on the score of *Faramondo*. The work was interrupted by the death of his staunch supporter Queen Caroline. For her funeral he composed the beautiful anthem, *The ways of Zion do mourn*—a worthy tribute of his gratitude. *Faramondo* was followed by four other operas, one of which was a pasticcio. The last was *Deidamia*, in 1740. Heidegger's renewed attempt proved no more successful than its predecessors, and Handel bade a final farewell to a form of composition in the advancement of which he had struggled so manfully and suffered so deeply.

He was now fifty-four years of age, and one is tempted to say that he was only just discovering his true powers. Fine as his operas are, they belong to a style of art which can never be revived. Certain extracts will no doubt continue to delight the musician, but they alone would have been insufficient to place their composer on the pinnacle of fame which he occupies. This position he claims in virtue of that grand series of oratorios which he was now to produce. We have seen that he had already brought out a few such works during his operatic management; and while Heidegger's last ill-starred attempt was in progress on the feast of that saint (November 22nd), the *Ode for St. Cecilia's Day* was performed, with *Alexander's Feast*. The "Ode" contains three magnificent choruses, *The trumpet's loud clangour*, *As from the power*, and *The dead shall live*. This was followed by *L'Allegro, Il Penseroso, ed il Moderato*, with the favourite, *Oft on a plat, Sweet bird*, accompanied by the flute, and the air and chorus, *Haste thee, nymph*, which still retain their charm when performed at a Handel festival. But now began the great series of oratorios. In January, 1739, he took the Opera House for a series of twelve weekly performances of oratorio. He had composed two new oratorios as yet unproduced. *Saul* had occupied him two months and three days; *Israel in Egypt* was written between the 1st and the 28th of October! *Saul* was the first brought out, with very moderate success, although such a chorus as *Envy, eldest-born of Hell*, and the *Dead March* should have secured it. *Israel*, too, was received with coldness. No doubt the succession of choruses was found monotonous, for at the second performance it was announced that "the oratorio will be shortened and intermixed with songs." "Intermixed with songs" it remained for many a long day, and it was only in our own time that it was performed as the composer originally intended. Surely *Israel*, with its magnificent series of double choruses, is one of the most stupendous monuments of choral writing that the world has seen!

This colossal work was followed by one which the universal consent of mankind has considered one of the greatest of musical compositions: his immortal *Messiah*. Handel had been invited to visit Dublin by the Duke of Devonshire, then Lord Lieutenant. Three charitable societies—one for the relief of imprisoned debtors, Mercer's Hospital, and the Charitable Infirmary—had united in requesting him to write a work to be performed on behalf of their funds. He looked on the idea with favour, especially as an excellent violinist, Matthew Dubourg, who was a friend of his, had settled in Dublin and would superintend the necessary musical arrangements. During the late summer of 1741, he set to work on the *Messiah*, the oratorio destined for this purpose. His friend Mr. Charles Jennens made the selection of the words, which were all from the Holy Scriptures, and, it must be added, with judgment. He began the composition on August 22nd. By September 14th the whole work was completed—that is, in twenty-four days! His practice was most methodical, always writing in the date of the beginning and end of each act or part; and as an excellent facsimile of the original score is readily obtainable, those who are interested can almost, as it were, see him at work.

The Charitable Musical Society of Dublin had recently opened an excellent music-room, and in it Handel's performances took place. The *Messiah* was not produced till April 13th, 1742. The advertisements announcing the performance wind up with an appeal to the ladies "not to come with hoops this day," and the gentlemen are desired to come without their swords. The occasion was evidently looked on as important; the work produced abundantly justified the opinion. Handel and the whole of his singers gave their services, the room was crowded, and a sum approaching £400 was available for the purposes of the charities. The oratorio at once took hold of the public, and it has never since lost it. One person alone was not satisfied. This was the compiler of the words. He informs a friend that he will show him "a collection I gave Handel, called *Messiah*, which I value highly. He has made a fine entertainment of it, though not near so good as he might and ought to have done." We will not insult our readers by supposing that they do not know every note of this immortal work—the "sacred oratorio," as Handel always termed it. One of the greatest testimonies to the power of music is the fact that at the first performance of the work in London the whole audience, with George II. at its head, rose with one consent at the Hallelujah Chorus, and the custom survives to the present day.

The work having been originally devoted to the purposes of charity, Handel appears to have considered such a destination of it to have had some claim on him, for after the year 1750 he performed it annually, sometimes more than once, for the benefit of the Foundling Hospital, to which institution he bequeathed copies of the score and parts. For some such sacred purpose it has on numberless occasions been performed since his death; certainly no other work can have produced so large a result in the cause of charity.

Eight days after the completion of the score of the *Messiah*, Handel was at work at *Samson*, the words of which had been arranged for him by Newburgh Hamilton from Milton's *Samson Agonistes*. It contains, among others, the well-known choruses, *Then round about the starry throne*, *Fixed in His everlasting seat*, and *Let their celestial concerts all unite*. The solos are equally fine, for they comprise the broad contralto song, *Return, O God of hosts*, *Total eclipse*, one of his most pathetic airs, and the brilliant *Let the bright seraphim*, with trumpet obligato, which is so effective that it is taken up by many sopranos not otherwise Handelian in their predilections.

Handel's stay in Dublin was extended to nine months. While absent his importance had become more completely recognised and his return was welcomed. Both *Samson* and the *Messiah* were performed, and in 1743 he wrote his well-known *Te Deum* to celebrate the battle of Dettingen. This was followed by *Belshazzar*. He announced a series of twenty-four oratorios, but the attendance was so small that the scheme collapsed at the sixteenth. He had no reserve of capital to fall back upon, and he again became bankrupt. An interval now occurs in his activity, but in the year 1746 he re-appeared with the *Occasional Oratorio*, which was partly a pasticcio. The overture is still a favourite.

Handel now looked more to the general public for support, and abandoned the plan of a subscription. His next work, *Judas Maccabæus*, was fortunate in hitting popular taste, and proved remunerative. It still remains one of his most popular oratorios. This was followed by *Alexander Balus* and *Joshua*, and in 1748 by *Solomon* and *Susanna*. *Solomon* is one of his finest works, and is distinguished by its double choruses, which compare even with those in *Israel*.

In March, 1749, appeared *Theodora*. The work was a favourite with the author, but the song, *Angels ever bright and fair*, alone keeps its place. *Jephtha*, his last oratorio, came out in February, 1752. This contains the recitative, *Deeper and deeper still*, and the song, *Waft her angels*, which have been associated with the names of our great English tenors Braham and Mr. Sims Reeves. But sad affliction was attacking him—strange to say, the same from which his contemporary Bach was also suffering. He was losing his sight. Three times he was operated on without success, and he became totally blind. His spirits gave way for a time, but his marvellous energy re-asserted itself, and he was still able to preside at the organ in the performance of his works. A touching story is told that at such a performance of

Samson, Beard, his favourite tenor, had been singing with great feeling the song—

> "Total eclipse! no sun, no moon;
> All dark amid the blaze of noon!"

The sadness of the old master's fate impressed the hearers so powerfully that many were affected to tears. After a few years his strength visibly failed. On April 6th, 1759, he directed a performance of his masterpiece, the *Messiah*. He returned home to take to his bed, expiring, not, as frequently stated, on Good Friday, April 13th, but on the following day. He was buried in Westminster Abbey. During his last few years fortune had been kinder to him. He had honourably paid off all his liabilities, and had acquired a fortune amounting to £20,000.

BIBLIOGRAPHY.

Mainwaring, Rev. John. Memoirs of the Life of the late George Frederic Handel. London, 1760. 8vo.

Schoelcher, Victor. The Life of Handel. London, 1857. 8vo.

Chrysander, Friedrich. G. F. Handel. Leipzig, 1858. 1860. 1867. 3 vols., 8vo. (The work has not been completed, the first half of the third volume only having been published.)

Rockstro, W. S. The Life of George Frederick Handel. London, 1883. 8vo.

Marshall, Mrs. Julian. Handel. London, 1883. 8vo.

CHAPTER XI.

FURTHER HISTORY OF MUSIC IN ENGLAND.

Dr. Arne—Lampe's *Dragon of Wantley*—Henry Carey—Thomas Britton, "the Musical Small-coal Man"—Ballad Operas—Charles Dibdin—Early Concerts—Foundation of the "Concert of Antient Musick"—Cultivation of Part-singing—Catches—Samuel Webbe and the Glee-writers—The Catch Club and its Secretary, E. T. Warren Horne—The Histories of Burney and Hawkins.

THE death of Handel left a great void in the musical life of England. The most prominent musician was Dr. Arne, a writer with a distinct and charming vein of melody, which, to do English composers justice, is a merit they have generally possessed. Arne was the son of a prosperous cabinet-maker in King Street, Covent Garden, and, like Handel, was destined by his father for the law. Indeed, their early histories have much in common, for the youthful Arne was also compelled to practise secretly on a muffled spinet in a garret. One night his father, being a guest at an entertainment given by a friend, found, to his surprise, his son installed as conductor of the music, and he was at last compelled to acknowledge the uselessness of opposing so strong a predilection. Arne composed a couple of oratorios, but in these he had to contend with a giant, and they have been long forgotten. As a writer of operas he had great success. He composed about thirty. The best known was *Artaxerxes*, now out of date, although for many years it enjoyed great popularity, the overture forming one of the stock pieces of our grandmothers. *Water parted from the sea*, *Where the bee sucks*, *Blow, thou wintry wind*, *Under the greenwood tree*, *The soldier tired*, even now keep their hold on the popular taste, while *Rule Britannia* will last as long as the English nation. His wife was the greatest English singer of the time. As Miss Cecilia Young she had been the pupil of Geminiani, from whom she had received an excellent training.

A sister of Mrs. Arne married J. F. Lampe, a German musician settled in this country, who acquired great celebrity by the composition of an opera called *The Dragon of Wantley*. The libretto was by Henry Carey, and both it and the music were writen in avowed burlesque of the Italian opera, and this was carried out with evident enjoyment by both poet and musician, their aim being to " display in English the beauties of nonsense so prevailing in the Italian operas." It is not surprising, therefore, that the work had enormous success, and the satire is so admirably carried out that it richly deserved it. Henry Carey, who has just been spoken of as writer of the words, was also a musician of some ability. Much obscurity rests on his life; it is supposed that he was a natural son of George Savile, Marquis of Halifax. He composed the music of many songs introduced into the theatrical pieces of the day; these he subsequently collected in a publication called the *Musical Century*. Among them is the charming air, *Sally in our alley*. He was one of those popular men of pleasure who are always behindhand with the world, and at last his circumstances became so desperate that he destroyed himself. The com-

Fig. 96.—Dr. Arne, from a sketch by Bartolozzi.

position of our National Anthem has been claimed for him, apparently on insufficient grounds.

An account of music in England during the eighteenth century would be incomplete without mention of Thomas Britton, the "musical small-coal man," who was indeed a power in the musical world. He carried on his business in Aylesbury Street, Clerkenwell, in a sort of stable, and was to be seen struggling about the neighbourhood daily under the weight of sacks of coal. The loft of his stable he had fitted up as a sort of concert-room, which was resorted to weekly, not only by the most eminent musicians of the day, including Handel himself, but also by many members of the nobility, who paid a yearly subscription of ten shillings. He had acquired an excellent knowledge of music, and had collected a considerable musical library. His end was as curious as his life. A gentleman who was in the habit of attending his concerts one evening brought with him a ventriloquist, who in joke foretold his approaching death. The poor man was so alarmed by what he took for a supernatural announcement that in a few days he died.

Italian opera had been no more than a fashionable amusement in England, and after the death of Handel no original works of the kind were produced in this country. Those which met with success abroad were brought over, and English gold secured a succession of the most eminent performers to support them. Composers of celebrity were sometimes induced to visit this country to superintend the production of their works. Thus Gluck visited England in 1745. Unfortunately the Rebellion had just broken out, and the Lord Chancellor shut up the Opera House, but was persuaded to open it again for Gluck's *Canduta de' Giganti*, a piece specially written in honour of the Duke of Cumberland, who had subdued the rebels. Still later—in 1784—Cherubini came for a similar purpose. His death did not take place till 1842, and his widow survived till 1864! Arne's *Artaxerxes* was an attempt at writing an opera in English on the Italian plan; that is, the whole action was carried on in music, no spoken words being used. This practice, however, was soon abandoned in favour of ballad operas, in which the musical pieces were connected by *spoken* dialogue. These were produced by a succession of facile composers, who aimed rather at immediate effect than at lasting reputation: Linley, whose *Duenna* had a most remarkable success,— the words were by R. B. Sheridan, who had married Linley's beautiful and accomplished daughter,—Dibdin, Shield, and lastly Storace. The latter was the son of an Italian musician settled in England. With his sister, who became a famous dramatic singer, he was sent abroad to complete his musical education; during this time they made the acquaintance of Mozart, who esteemed them both. He wrote fifteen or sixteen operas, among which are *The Haunted Tower*, *The Siege of Belgrade*, and, perhaps the most popular of all, *The Iron Chest*. He was ill during the preparation of the last work, but insisted on being conveyed to the theatre in blankets to superintend the final rehearsals. He thus caught cold and died, at the age of thirty-three, cutting short a career of great promise. The quartet, *Five times by the taper's light*, is still familiar.

Charles Dibdin, whose name we have mentioned, became still more celebrated as a writer of sea songs, the spirit and patriotic feeling of which did much to inspire the bravery of our sailors during the great war. He knew how to be rollicking and how to show real feeling; take, for example, the familiar *Jolly Young Waterman*, and the beautiful and pathetic *Tom Bowling*.

Till the oratorio performances were started by Handel the general public had but few chances of hearing music of a high character; in fact, it was not until the present century that concerts to which the public could obtain admission by payment became general. The first series of concerts on record in England was given by John Banister, a violinist, in his house in Whitefriars. These went on from 1672 to 1678, and the admission was one shilling. This attempt was followed up by Britton, the "small-coal man," of whom we have already spoken. In 1710 a number of noblemen and gentlemen organised a scheme on a broader scale under the title of the Academy of Antient Musick, which was spirited enough to give commissions for the composition of new works, Astorga's *Stabat Mater* having been written for the Society. It does not appear, however, to have received adequate support, in spite of a pamphlet appealing to the public, which ended with the words "Esto perpetua!" and in the year 1776 a new society, under a very similar title—namely, the " Concert of Antient Musick "—was founded. To this Society there can be no doubt that the art was greatly indebted, as it served to perpetuate the traditions of performance of many great works, especially those of Handel, which for some years formed the principal material of its programmes. The Society was exclusively aristocratic. To be a member it was necessary to be " in society "; even to be introduced as a visitor at a concert the name had to be submitted to the directors.

One of the rules provided that no work composed within twenty years could be performed. It may be possible to be too much carried away by novelty, but a rule of this character was obviously absurd in a society whose object was to further art. The noblemen and gentlemen who formed the body of directors took it in turn to select the programme, and on their "night" entertained their brother directors as well as the conductor at dinner before the concert, and this duty kings and royal dukes performed in their turn. The first professional conductor was Joah Bates, and on his death he was succeeded in 1779 by Greatorex. The concerts were up to 1795 held in the "New Rooms, Tottenham Street," on the site which in our days became well known as that of the Prince of Wales's Theatre; after that in the concert-room of the Opera House; and in 1804 they were moved to the Hanover Square Rooms, which had been constructed by Sir John Gallini, a well-known teacher of dancing. Considering that the management was amateur and the expenditure lavish, it is wonderful that the Society continued its work so long. Its existence was continued till the year 1848, but for some time it had been carried on with difficulty; its exclusiveness was no longer in accordance with the spirit of the times; and other societies—notably the Sacred Harmonic Society—had arisen, which were able to perform complete oratorios on a more fitting scale. One of its good actions is still continued. Michael Festing, an esteemed violinist of the last century, having had a case of distress in the family of a professor of music brought under his notice, was instrumental in founding the Royal Society of Musicians, for the benefit of decayed musicians and their families. To support this Society the "Antient Concerts" were in the habit of giving annually a performance of the *Messiah*, at which all gave their services gratis, as stipulated in the performers' engagement for the season. This performance is still kept up for the benefit of a most deserving institution.

The fondness for part-singing had never quite died out in England. The Madrigalian Era, extending from 1588 to the time of the Revolution, was, as we have seen, the golden age of the English school of composition. The love of "social harmony" after the Restoration had been mostly kept alive by means of the "catch," a species of composition consisting of a canon or round for three or four voices, generally so arranged that when sung, the words, by the union of the different voices, acquired a different meaning from that apparent on a simple perusal of them. To quote a familiar example in explanation, the well-known one by Callcott:—

> "Ah! how, Sophia, could you leave
> Your lover, and of hope bereave?
> Go fetch the Indian's borrowed plume," etc.,

where in performance *Ah! how Sophia*, sounds like *Our house on fire*, and *Go fetch the Indian's* like *Go fetch the engines*. It may seem a feeble joke, but the contrivance called forth much musical ability and humour, seldom, it is to be regretted, of so innocent a nature as the one we have quoted. The popularity of such compositions was unbounded in an age which was characterised by no delicacy of feeling. Many clubs were founded for their performance, and many collections of them were published. Out of evil, however, came good, and this was the invention of the "glee," a kind of composition which has been confined exclusively to this country, and which has called forth a large amount of musical genius. A glee may be defined as a composition for three or more voices in harmony, each voice, however, having a separate melody of its own, the lower parts not simply forming an accompaniment, as in a part-song. It comprises two movements at least, which are contrasted in character and is performed with one voice only to a part, whereas the madrigal required several. In some of Playford's publications the term "glee" is attached to certain compositions, but the form was not settled till later. The merit of doing this is mainly to be attributed to Samuel Webbe, a man of very remarkable talents, which were shown in many ways. He was born of English parents in a fair position of life in the island of Minorca in the year 1740. While an infant his father died, leaving his mother in straitened circumstances. She returned to London with her child, and at an early age he was apprenticed to a cabinet-maker. He found opportunities, however, of improving his education, and became eventually an excellent linguist. Chafing at the restraints of a mechanical pursuit, he soon abandoned business, and managed to earn a precarious livelihood by copying music, gradually acquiring at the same time an excellent knowledge of the art.

Among the clubs founded for the performance of vocal music was the " Noblemen and Gentlemen's Catch Club." It first met in 1761, having the support of several members of the nobility, and soon grew into a very fashionable and flourishing institution, most of the royal family becoming members of it. The members consisted of amateur and professional, and the latter comprised all the leading singers of the time.

From the performance of vocal compositions it was a natural step to the offering of prizes for new works. As early as 1763 the Club offered prizes for the two best catches, the two best canons, and the two best glees. The name of Webbe soon appears among those carrying off prizes, for catches as well as for glees, those for the latter with such compositions as *Discord, dire sister*, and *The Mighty Conqueror*. His masterpiece, *When winds breathe soft*, was sent in for competition in 1784, and it is incomprehensible that so noble a composition should not have received a prize. The work is a masterpiece; in the space of a few pages is depicted the gradual rising of the calm sea to a gale which "splits the sturdy mast," "when in an instant He Who rules the floods bids the waters and the winds be still." Nothing can exceed its dramatic power, and the musician who produced it deserves a prominent niche in the Temple of Fame.

If no other writer of glees was the equal of Samuel Webbe in genius, many excellent compositions of this character were produced, and there was no lack of competitors for the prizes which the Club continued to offer. Among these must be mentioned Atterbury, Dr. Alcock, Bellamy, Danby, Lord Mornington, father of the Duke of Wellington, Dr. Cooke, the Paxtons, and John Stafford Smith, whose *Blest pair of sirens*, *While fools their time*, and *Return, blest days*, deserve their popularity. Stafford Smith has also claims on our gratitude as a musical antiquarian, in which capacity, in addition to affording Sir John Hawkins much assistance in his *History of Music*, he also published a well-known collection of ancient music under the title of *Musica Antiqua*. To these succeeded Reginald Spofforth, R. J. S. Stevens, and Dr. Callcott, the last of whom was the cause of an alteration in the rules of the club, for in 1787 he sent in one hundred compositions in competition! The members decided that in future three compositions of each kind only should be accepted.

The first secretary of the Catch Club was E. T. Warren, who subsequently added the name of Horne to his patronymic. He was a man of indefatigable industry, for he copied out with his own hands the whole of the compositions sent in for competition, forming a vast collection, filling thirty-two volumes in oblong folio. But little more than a quarter of the works, which amount to 2269, have been printed. Many of those which have been printed first saw the light in Warren's well-known published collection.

To this country belongs the honour of producing the first History of Music on a scale and completeness at all adequate to the importance of the subject. A work of the same nature had been projected by the eminent Padre Martini, but it was planned on such large dimensions that time was not vouchsafed to the author to complete more than the third volume, which brought his history down to the destruction of the Temple at Jerusalem. Strange to say, two Englishmen attempted the task simultaneously, both of them being members of THE club so well known to readers of Boswell. Of these writers, one was a professor of position, Dr. Burney ; the other was an amateur, Sir John Hawkins, whose work has achieved the greater success of being reprinted in our own time. Both works will be found deficient viewed in the light of the more critical knowledge of our own day, but to both, subsequent writers on musical history have been greatly indebted.

BIBLIOGRAPHY.

Hogarth, Z. Memoirs of the Opera. London, 1851. 2 vols., 8vo.
Barrett, W. A. English Glees and Part Songs. London, 1886. 8vo.

CHAPTER XII.

MUSIC IN FRANCE DURING THE EIGHTEENTH CENTURY.

Rameau as a Theorist and Composer—The "Théâtre de la Foire"—*La Serva Padrona* of Pergolesi in Paris and the "Guerre des Bouffons"—J. J. Rousseau—His Dictionary—Gossec—Monsigny—Gluck in Paris—Piccinni—Grétry—The Philidors—Foundation of the "Concerts Spirituels"—Instrumental Composers—Leclair—Couperin.

SO far as we have as yet traced the history of music in France, that nation had produced no musician of the first rank. To Lully must be conceded the possession of genius, but he was French by naturalisation only; his talent was essentially Italian, and the lustre which he without doubt shed on the French lyric stage, redounded to the credit of that nation only to the extent of showing its power of appreciating excellence when brought under its notice. The successors of Lully, of whom we have spoken, made no advance on the model which he had set before them, and they have long been forgotten.

This reproach, however, was to be removed. On September 25th, 1683, there was born at Dijon, of a family of musicians, Jean Philippe Rameau, who was to make two separate and distinct musical reputations, the first in the capacity of a theorist of originality, the second—and that, strange to say, after middle life—as a composer. As his father was a musician, the child picked up the rudiments of the art as a matter of course, and showed much of the precociousness which so often goes with a musical nature. His parents, knowing how precarious a living music offered, had other wishes for their son, in furtherance of which they placed him at the Jesuits' College in Dijon, with a view of educating him for the law. Such pursuits, however, had no interest for the boy. Music had taken so firm a hold upon him that he paid no attention to his other studies, and finally the fathers requested the elder Rameau to remove his son. Henceforth all his energies were devoted to music; in the pursuit of that study there was no lack of industry; but it is to be regretted that the provincial town in which he lived offered so few advantages for a thorough training in the theory of his art.

A circumstance soon arose which taught him to regret the neglect he had shown for the ordinary branches of education. When only seventeen he fell madly in love with a young widow who lived near. She made him ashamed of the bad spelling of the numerous letters which he addressed to her, and he at once set to work to improve himself. To sever this attachment, his father sent him to make a journey to Italy, in which country, however, he got no further than Milan, and, strange to say, seems to have shown no appreciation of the beauties of Italian music. In that city he made the acquaintance of a theatrical manager, who was projecting a tour through the southern towns of France, and with him young Rameau engaged to travel in the capacity of first violin in his orchestra. The company visited Marseilles, Lyons, Nismes, and other places, and the tour seems to have been of some duration. Occasionally he had the opportunity of giving an organ performance in the towns through which they passed, but from the account which he himself gives it is evident that his theoretical knowledge was as yet only rudimentary. For some time after this the circumstances of his life are involved in doubt, but in 1706 he was unquestionably in Paris, acting as organist of the Jesuits' Church in the Rue St. Jacques, for he then published his first book of pieces for the harpsichord. It is not certain whether it was on this or on a subsequent visit to Paris that he was humiliated by the election of an inferior musician to a vacant organist's place, which injustice determined him to leave that city. He went to Lille first, and soon afterwards to Clermont, as organist, where he remained three or four years, devoting himself to an exhaustive study of the scientific principles of music by means of the treatises of Zarlino, Mersenne, and Descartes. He composed several motets, cantatas, and harpsichord pieces, showing great originality, but the most important result of his studies was the elaboration of a system of harmony, which he embodied in a work entitled *Traité de l'Harmonie réduite à ses Principes Naturels*. The comparative obscurity of a place like Clermont afforded no adequate opportunity for the development of the genius which was striving within him, and he was, moreover, anxious to publish his treatise. He determined therefore to visit Paris once more. This was not so easy as it would appear, for he had made an engagement of long duration with the chapter of the cathedral at Clermont. The latter had not been slow to discover what a fine musician they possessed in their organist, and were by no means disposed to release him from his engagement, and this difficulty was not readily surmounted. At last, however, he found himself in Paris, and in a short time succeeded in persuading Ballard, the famous printer of music, to purchase his treatise, which was published in 1722. It was the first attempt at a rational and scientific explanation of the laws of harmony. The author had already arrived at his thirty-eighth year without achieving the reputation he was so anxious to gain. The success of his book was not immediate, but the novelty of his theories soon began to attract the attention of those who were able to understand the difficulties of the subject, which were not lessened by the obscurity of his style. He lost no time in following up his advantage by publication of other works, the chief of which was his *Nouveau Système de Musique Théorique*, in which he further develops his discovery of the "fundamental bass." His friend D'Alembert, the eminent mathematician, undertook the composition of a short work giving a popular account of his theories, which, if at that time they were more talked about than understood, had at least placed him in the foremost rank of musical theorists. The result of his great reputation was to make him the most famous teacher of the day. Many ladies of the highest birth became his pupils for the harpsichord, on which instrument he was an excellent performer. He also became organist of the Church of Sainte Croix de la Bretonnerie, where his playing became celebrated. But all these successes did not satisfy his ambition. He thirsted to make a name as an operatic composer, a wish which was not fulfilled without some difficulty. His friend Piron was enabled to obtain for him a commission to write the music for one or two of his own pieces, to be performed at the Opéra Comique of the Foire St. Germain. It was not a very dignified position for a man of his attainments, but it served to try his hand. It has been supposed that his reputation as a theorist stood in his way, the notion being common that learning and imagination do not go together. Fortunately he had among his pupils the wife of Lerische de la Popelinière, one of the richest and most influential of the farmers-general, who was an enthusiastic supporter of art. Every one celebrated in the world of music was received in his *salon*. To Rameau he showed the greatest kindness. The composer, no longer a young man, had lately married a lady many years his junior, and the pair passed much of their time in the houses of La Popelinière either in Paris or at Passy. La Popelinière undertook to obtain a suitable poem for the composer, and he was so far successful that he induced no less a man than Voltaire to write the words of an opera to be set to music by Rameau. The work was complete, and on the point of production, when a cabal succeeded in preventing the performance of it on the score of the sacred nature of the subject. Rameau's ambition was for the moment frustrated. The kindness of his protector did not, however, stop. With some difficulty he persuaded the Abbé Pellegrin, at that time a notable character in the world of literature and art, to write a poem for him. Strange to say, an opera on the subject of Jephthah, set to music by Montéclair, the words of which were by the Abbé, had just achieved a great success, although the performance of *Samson* had not been considered decorous. The consent of Pellegrin was not given with great readiness; he stipulated that the composer should give him a bill for five hundred livres as a security against the possible failure of the work. After a short time the libretto was completed; the title of it was *Hippolyte et Aricie*, and it was of course founded on the *Phèdre* of Racine. But little time was lost by Rameau in setting it to music. As soon as it was ready La Popelinière invited his friends, and a trial performance took place. It is only just to the Abbé Pellegrin to say that at the end of the first act he addressed the composer as follows: "Sir, when such music as yours is produced, there is no need for any security," and destroyed the bill before the assembled company. The true test of popularity, a public performance, had still to be gone through. The work was at last produced at the Opera on October 1st, 1733. The first impression produced on the public was that of surprise rather than of complete satisfaction. The composer was disappointed, and almost disposed to renounce the idea of writing for the stage. But in truth the public had been so long habituated to the weary platitudes of the imitators of Lully that they were not prepared for so much vigour. For the previous fifty years Lully and his disciples had held possession of the stage. During that period the character of the audience had altered. The popularity of Lully was ensured by the

Fig. 97.—Rameau (from the portrait of Restout, engraved by Benoist).

personal taste which Louis XIV. had for his music, and the frequenters of the Opera were largely made up of the courtiers who bowed to their sovereign's judgement. On the death of Lully the King's interest in the opera waned, for he could with difficulty be induced to listen to the works of any new composer. The main supporters of the opera were, at the time of which we are writing, the rich financiers and farmers-general, with a large admixture of the *philosophes*, who had become a power, thinking themselves equal to the task of deciding on the merits of any new work either in literature, the drama, or music, and, in fact, almost called on to put their opinion on record, even in spite of an absolute ignorance of the art which they presumed to judge. The immediate result of the production of *Hippolyte* was the bursting forth of one of those curious wars of pamphlets which form so remarkable a feature of the period. Fortunately the arguments of Rameau's supporters prevailed, and he was induced to continue the career of an operatic composer, which he had not entered upon until he had passed his fiftieth year. Other operas followed: *Les Indes Galantes, Castor et Pollux*, which is generally looked on as his masterpiece, *Dardanus*, and many more, to the number of thirty. He gradually conquered, and achieved a position of such respect, that the whole audience made a practice of rising when he entered his box. In person he was tall and gaunt, and in face was considered to resemble Voltaire in a remarkable manner (fig. 97). His disposition was reserved, and his manner abstracted, for he was in the habit of walking through the streets taking no notice whatever of acquaintances he chanced to meet. He lived to the advanced age of eighty-one years, having succeeded by force of character in achieving a great reputation in all the branches of music which he attempted. The principal characteristics of his style were the increased energy, the greater richness of his harmony, and the importance which he gave to the chorus. His instrumentation showed also a wonderful step in advance. The flutes, oboes, and bassoons no longer double the string parts, but are treated independently, as indeed are frequently the brass and drums. We have already drawn attention to the fact that the music of Rameau exercised an important influence on the career of Gluck.

As we have seen, Rameau's first dramatic efforts were made at the Théâtre de la Foire. This was an institution about which a word must be said. During the seventeenth and eighteenth centuries the difficulties of communication gave an importance to fairs, both for business and pleasure, which they have now generally lost. In Paris there were at least two such fairs, one called the "Foire St. Laurent," held in the districts now known as the Faubourg St. Dénis and the Faubourg St. Martin; the other, which was more aristocratic in its aims, was called the "Foire de St. Germain," and was held in the faubourg of that name. Among the attractions of these fairs was a theatre, at which the artistic merit of the performances was much greater than might have been anticipated, and the short pieces represented were frequently the work of esteemed authors,—Le Sage, for example, the author of *Gil Blas*, enjoying great popularity, as did Piron, to one or two of whose works Rameau had been content to set music. These entertainments had not been carried on without a struggle. In 1678 Lully, whose jealousy was soon aroused, had succeeded in obtaining a royal order forbidding singing ont he stage, and confining the orchestra to four violins and a hautboy, while the Comédie Française also insisted on stopping the performance of comedies and farces. The theatre of the fair was in a bad way, but the ingenuity of the managers and the ready wit of the French audiences triumphed. Each performer went through his part in dumb show, but he came on the stage provided with a great placard, on which were written in large letters the words of the songs; and when this was found inconvenient, the placard was lowered from the "flies." The four violins and the hautboy played the tunes, which were generally familiar, so that the audience were able to supply the vocal parts themselves, which they did with great merriment and satisfaction. The keen sense of the ludicrous, which is so strong a characteristic of the French, as may be anticipated, soon triumphed, and a treaty of peace was made between the Academy of Music and Catherine Vanderberg, who at that time was proprietor of the theatre of the Foire St. Laurent. She acquired the privilege of representing dramatic pieces interspersed with songs, dancing, and instrumental interludes, in fact what are now known as *vaudevilles*. In a short time these pieces gained for the theatre of the fair the name of "Opéra Comique," a title it also partly earned from the circumstance that many of the pieces were avowed parodies of the more dignified works performed at the Académie.

In the earliest years of the eighteenth century the discussion of the relative merits of Italian and French music was initiated. It was opened by the Abbé

Raguenet, who, having accompanied the Cardinal de Bouillon to Rome, became an enthusiastic admirer of Italian music. He published his views in a work entitled *Parallèle des Italiens et des Français en ce qui regarde la Musique et les Opéras*, in the year 1602, which was soon afterwards translated into English. The admirers of Lully and the French opera found an advocate in Lecerf de la Vieville. Raguenet replied with a defence of his *Parellèle*, and the strife was continued, but the honours of the fight seem to have been carried off by Raguenet. This discussion, however, had been long forgotten, when in the year 1752 an Italian company, under a director named Bambini, was permitted to appear at the Académie. On August 1st, 1752, *La Serva Padrona* of Pergolesi was produced. It had previously been played at the Comédie Italienne, but the appearance of an Italian work on a stage hitherto devoted exclusively to French opera provoked, as was only natural, a comparison between the two schools of music. The controversy broke out with extraordinary violence, and has become celebrated under the title of the "Guerre" or "Querelle des Bouffons," the name by which the Italian company was designated in France. The theatre at once became a field of battle. The national music received the support of the King and of Madame de Pompadour, and its defenders, ranging themselves under the King's box, were therefore called the "Coin du Roi"; the advocates of Italian music took their places under that of the Queen, and were for that reason designated the "Coin de la Reine." Pamphlet after pamphlet, some witty, all straining after wit, appeared in quick succession, hardly a day passing without an addition to the paper war. Every man who aspired to the character of a wit made his contribution to the literature of the controversy, which counted among its authors many of the leading writers of the day. Among the most prominent were Grimm, D'Holbach, J. J. Rousseau, Cazotte, Travenol, Rameau, and even Frederick the Great of Prussia. The veteran Rameau defended the French school against some of the charges which were so freely brought against it, but it is interesting to know that he appreciated the great beauties of the Italian School also. He said with great sincerity on one occasion to the Abbé Arnaud, "If I were thirty years younger, I would go to Italy. Pergolesi would become my model, and I would make my harmony subordinate to that truth of declamation which should be the only guide of the musician. But when a man has passed sixty years of age, he feels that he must remain where he is; experience points out what would be the right course to adopt: the will refuses to obey."

When there was a lull in the controversy, Jean Jacques Rousseau, who had taken but a small part in it, by way of a judicial winding up of the discussion brought out his *Lettre sur la Musique Française*. The result was very different from his intention: it stirred up the expiring embers, and the flames burst forth with renewed fury. It is not remarkable that this was the case, for Rousseau declares that "the French have no music, and cannot have any, and that if they should succeed in having any, it will be so much the worse for them." The advocates of the national cause were beside themselves with rage, and the band of the Opera hanged and burnt the author in effigy in the courtyard of the theatre. Another storm of pamphlets burst forth, and it was long before the atmosphere again became clear. M. Thoinan has been at the pains of compiling a bibliography of this remarkable controversy, which may be found under the word "Rousseau" in the supplement of Fêtis's *Biographie des Musiciens*; and he brings the number of publications up to sixty-three!

The very remarkable man of whom we have just been speaking came to Paris in the year 1742 with a scheme for a new system of writing music in his pocket, which he succeeded in getting published, under the title of *Project concernant de Nouveau Signes pour la Musique*. His plan was mainly based on the use of numerals to distinguish the notes of the scale, thus, like many others who have endeavoured to simplify the received notation, overlooking the advantage offered by the *pictorial* representation of a musical phrase which the received notation gives. Rousseau made a precarious livelihood in Paris by copying music; and although some of his friends endeavoured to force on him more than the ordinary remuneration for such work, he could never be induced to accept anything beyond the usual terms of payment. His scheme for the improvement of musical notation meeting with but little acceptance, he was next induced to try his skill as a composer, for which his deficient training but ill adapted him. He wrote an opera entitled *Les Muses Galantes*, which was tried at the house of the farmer-general La Popelinière. Rameau, who was present, declared that part appeared to be the work of a skilled artist, while the rest was written by a man ignorant of the first principles of music. Some went so far as to assert that the opera was not the work of Rousseau at all. It was publicly performed in 1747, without success.

Rousseau lived on terms of intimacy with Diderot and D'Alembert, and they therefore chose him as the writer of the articles on music in the *Encyclopédie*. His superficial knowledge of the subject made the attempt a very unwise one; and although he devoted himself to some serious study, the time at his disposal was short, and the result unsatisfactory. Rameau had been induced to suppose that the work would have been entrusted to him, and unquestionably that great musician and theorist was the fittest person to have undertaken it; but differences had arisen between him and D'Alembert, and his claims were in consequence passed by. It would have been more than human for one so fond of controversy to allow the occasion to pass by unnoticed, and he was soon in the field with a pamphlet exposing the errors in a work which had laid claim to be a model of accuracy. Rousseau himself recognised his deficiencies, and determined to correct and amend them. This was the origin of his famous *Dictionnaire de Musique*, published at Geneva in the year 1767, which has since appeared in numerous editions and in many languages. Its success was enormous, although the work was very far from perfect. Its great deficiencies are in the theoretical portions; the author was by temperament

MUSIC IN FRANCE IN EIGHTEENTH CENTURY. 255

and education unfitted to cope with such subjects, which require the training of a mathematician. The critical portions show the taste which he undoubtedly possessed, and the charm of his style makes the book of great interest.

A few months after the production of *La Serva Padrona* at the Académie, and shortly after the appearance of his articles in the *Encyclopédie*, Rousseau succeeded in obtaining a hearing for his little opera *Le Devin du Village* before the court at Fontainebleau. The music was so simple and natural, that it was received with enthusiasm, and early in the following year—in March, 1783—it was transferred to the stage of the Opera, where it gave equal pleasure. Its popularity was unbounded. The deficiency of ordinary musicianship was still apparent, but the work was full of charm—a quality in which many compositions of much greater learning have been wanting —and the result was that it kept the stage for more than sixty years, and went the round of nearly all the theatres in France. Even in this instance his enemies grudged him his success, and he was accused of passing off the work of another as his own. An obscure musician of Lyons, named Granet, was brought forward as the real composer, but there seems no ground for doubting that the work was actually by Rousseau. The last performance in Paris took place in 1829. On that occasion a large peruke descended on the stage; there was some suspicion that it was launched by Berlioz, but it is only fair to say that he denies it in his autobiography. This proved its deathblow in the capital, although it was still to be heard occasionally in the provinces. After the death of Rousseau, a collection of a hundred songs was published under the title of *Les Consolations des Misères de ma Vie*, which show much the same touching simplicity as the melodies of *Le Devin du Village*.

Among the lesser lights of the musical world in France we must mention Gossec, who, having been brought up in the choir of the cathedral at Antwerp, found his way to Paris, and became conductor of the music at the house of La Popelinière, where he had the advantage of profiting greatly by the advice of Rameau. His early inclinations led him to cultivate instrumental music, and he was the first who attempted the composition of a symphony in France. He afterwards passed into the service of the Prince de Conti, employing the greater leisure which this position offered him in compositions of very varied character, among which some string quartets met with great success. In 1764 his career as a dramatic composer began with the opera *Le faux Lord*. He followed up his success with *Les Pêcheurs*, achieving even greater popularity, which was shared by several other operas of his composition. Many of the operas of Dezède enjoyed great appreciation, and Monsigny also is deserving of notice. Born of a good family, but thrown by the death of his father on his own resources, after some other employments he entered the service of the Duc d'Orléans. He had only followed music as an amateur, but a hearing of *La Serva Padrona*, then first produced in Paris, filled him with so strong an impulse to attempt composition that he began to

MUSIC IN FRANCE IN EIGHTEENTH CENTURY. 257

study the art with greater seriousness, and after a short time succeeded in bringing out an opera: *Les Aveux*

Fig. 98.—Gluck (after Auguste de St. Aubin, 1781).

Indiscrets. Its reception encouraged him to continue, and in 1760 he produced *Le Cadi dupé*, the comic force of which ensured it a great success. Several other works followed, the best known of which was *Le Déserteur*, his masterpiece, and long a favourite on the French stage. His last opera was written in 1777; and although he lived for forty years afterwards, he made no further attempt at composition, declaring that music was as though dead to him.

In 1774 a musician of a very different calibre arrived in Paris. This was the renowned Gluck (fig. 98). In a former chapter we have recounted the action of Du Rollet which led to this visit. The personal influence of the Dauphiness, Marie Antoinette, who had been the pupil of the great musician, was necessary to surmount the difficulties which stood in the way of Gluck's engagement; but these were at last overcome, and the *Iphigénie en Aulide* was produced for the first time on April 19th, 1774, the composer having arrived at the ripe age of sixty. This performance was an epoch in the history of opera in France; no work of such breadth and loftiness of style had as yet been heard in that country, and it was at first but little understood. The rehearsals had given the composer infinite trouble, for all the performers had to be educated in their parts, and there was no great show of good feeling on the part of many of them, as it was looked on almost as a reproach that a foreigner should presume to set to music the work of one of their greatest poets. The composer, however, was the last man to be turned aside by any manifestations of unwillingness. The public at once recognised that they were face to face with a new departure; the dramatic truth and the consistent earnestness of the new opera was a revelation. In August of the same year *Orphée* was arranged for the French stage. Owing to the want of a contralto (a voice which is rare in France), the principal part had to be transposed, which somewhat detracted from its effect; but it was nevertheless hailed with enthusiasm, as was also *Alceste*, brought out in 1776.

There were some, however, who were unable to appreciate the superior merits of the great master. At their instance an Italian composer of merit and celebrity, Piccinni, who had made a reputation in Naples, Rome, and other parts of Italy, was invited. He arrived in Paris at the end of 1776, and at once set to work to compose an opera for the French stage. But his ignorance of the language was complete, so that Marmontel, who was entrusted with the task of compiling the libretto from Quinault, was compelled to go through it word by word with the composer to explain not only the meaning, but also the prosody. In this laborious manner *Roland* was at last written, but a whole year was occupied in the process, and the work was not produced till January, 1778. The votaries of the rival composer had not been idle, and all sorts of difficulties had been created during the progress of the rehearsals, to such a point that the composer had come to the opinion that its failure was inevitable, and his family was in despair. Contrary to his expectation, its success was complete. This was the signal for the breaking out of another of those paper wars which seemed inevitable at that time on the arrival of each new canditate for fame on the stage of the French opera. Many of those who had taken part in the war of the *bouffons* still survived, and rushed into the fray like ancient war-horses. Suard and the Abbé Arnaud were at the head of the *Gluckistes*; Marmontel, the well-known critic La Harpe, Ginguené, and D'Alembert took the side of Piccinni. The discussion was continued till 1780, when Gluck returned to Vienna. It may be interesting to mention that the correspondence of the rival factions was collected and published in a volume by the Abbé Leblond, under the title of *Mémoires pour servir à l'Histoire de la Revolution operée dans la Musique par M. le Chevalier Gluck*, in the year 1781, from the frontispiece of which work our portrait of the great composer is taken.

While Piccinni was engaged in the composition of *Roland*, Gluck had brought out his opera *Armide*. Its composer was not wanting in self-appreciation; he addressed a letter to Du Rollet in which he declared that it nearly approached perfection, and when the Queen inquired one day if the opera was nearly complete, he replied, "Madam, that opera will soon be finished, and in truth it will be superb!" Authors, however, are frequently mistaken in their estimates of their own works, or at least the public judgment is not always in accord. The opera was received with coldness, although after a time it made its way.

It had been the original intention that *Roland* should be set to music simultaneously by Gluck and Piccinni; but when the former found that his rival was also to be entrusted with the libretto, he tore up what he had written, and declined to proceed with the work. This disinclination to enter into a trial of skill was afterwards got over, and both composers were induced to write an opera, *Iphigénie en Tauride*, although the words were written by different authors. That of Gluck, it will be readily believed, was the first completed. It was produced at the Académie in May, 1779, and was a crowning victory for the composer and his supporters. The work was a masterpiece. Some one remarking that there were five pieces in the opera, Arnaud, his great admirer, declared, "There is but one." "Which is that?" "The entire work," replied Arnaud. Piccinni's opera was not brought out until January, 1781; and although very melodious, it was completely overshadowed by the recollection of the work of his rival. Gluck's *Echo et Narcisse*, produced at the end of the same year, met with only moderate success. The great composer was now sixty-five years of age. He had undertaken to set to music the *Danaides*, the poem of which was in part by his friend Du Rollet; but an attack of apoplexy warned him of the necessity for rest. He returned to Vienna, handed over the libretto to Salieri, his friend and pupil, and, it is supposed, indicated to the latter his general ideas of the treatment of the subject. The opera, which had great success, was for the first few representations given under the name of the better-known composer, although it is not certain that he was privy to the deception. After a few years of retirement a second attack of apoplexy carried him off on November 25th, 1787.

Piccinni, who was an amiable and worthy man, remained

for a time in Paris, having some success at the Théâtre Italien; but his life seemed destined to be one of strife and trouble, for no sooner had his great rival returned to Vienna than Sacchini arrived in Paris to dispute his position. In 1791 the latter returned to Italy, the close of his life being clouded by pecuniary troubles, caused by the outbreak of the French Revolution. He was a most voluminous composer; the names of eighty of his operas are given by Fétis, and it is believed that this large number does not include the whole.

By that geographical comprehensiveness which is so marked a feature of the French nation, Grétry (fig 99) is always claimed as a native of that country, although he was born in the year 1741 at Liége, which at the time formed no part of that kingdom. Grétry at a very early age showed a disposition for music, and was educated in the choir of one of the churches in his native city, his beautiful voice attracting great notice. The arrival of a company of Italian singers in Liége, who performed Pergolesi's *Serva Padrona*, at once confirmed him in his wish to become a composer. His ambition was so great that he could hardly be persuaded of the importance of theoretical study. Some of his symphonies having been performed with success, one of the canons of the cathedral suggested to him the idea of a journey to Rome. His parents were poor, but the chapter came to his aid, and he actually performed the whole journey on foot. On his arrival he studied counterpoint with an esteemed master for some months, but he never arrived at the possession of great ease in the use of harmony, his taste being in the direction of expressive melody. His stay in Italy was extended to nine years; in that country his music was well received, but his desire was to write for the French stage. On his return he visited Voltaire at Geneva, hoping to obtain from

Fig. 99.—Grétry at his pianoforte (after the picture by Isabey).

him the poem of a comic-opera. He received vague promises only, but the presence of a French operatic company in that city enabled him to try his hand at that style of composition. His *Isabelle et Gertrude* had some success, and obtained for him a number of pupils, who provided him with the means of life. But he was now twenty-eight years of age, and had made no reputation. Voltaire counselled him to go at once to Paris. It is no easy thing for an unknown man to get a hearing, or even a libretto to set to music. At last, after two years of fruitless efforts he succeeded in obtaining one from an obscure poet named Du Rozoy. The title of the work was *Les Mariages Samnites*. The opera was written and rehearsed, but the judgment of those who were invited to hear it was unfavourable, and the work was withdrawn, to be produced some years later, when the reputation of the composer was established. One of the hearers did not agree with the general verdict; this was the Comte de Creutz, the Swedish envoy, and at his suggestion Marmontel was induced to entrust to the composer his comedy *Le Huron*. It was produced in August, 1768, at the Théâtre Italien, and formed the beginning of a long series of triumphs. Space fails to give a complete list of the whole of these; we must be content to mention *Le Tableau Parlant, Zémire et Azor, La Fausse Magie,* and *Richard Cœur de Lion,* containing the airs *O Richard! ô mon roi!* and *Une fièvre brûlante.* Grétry also claimed the suffrages of the public as an author, having written a series of *Essais,* the main interest of which consists in the autobiographical account of his life, which is not diminished by a pleasant vein of self-satisfaction which pervades the work.

During the reign of Louis XIII., there arrived in Paris a hautboy-player of the name of Danican. He had the good fortune to please the King, who asserted that his performance recalled that of an Italian named Filidori.

On the strength of the King's remark, Danican added the name of Philidor to his own, and he became the ancestor of a numerous family of musicians—so numerous that to distinguish them it has become customary to *number* the different members, as in the case of a line of kings. Several of them achieved eminence as composers and performers, but one rendered great service to the history of music, for, having been appointed to the charge of the court musical library, he succeeded in getting together an excellent collection—which still bears his name—of the greatest interest to those engaged in the investigation of the history of music in France. Another member of the family, François André Danican Philidor, in addition to a reputation based on a series of operas, which achieved a brilliant success, was still more celebrated as the greatest chess-player of the day, and in the latter capacity made several visits to this country, where his society was much sought. To still another member—Anne Danican Philidor—Paris is indebted for the foundation of the famous "Concerts Spirituels," which were the first public concerts given in France. As the opera was closed on the festivals of the Church, including Holy Week and a fortnight at Easter, Philidor proposed to make use of the enforced holiday, and to find employment for the musicians by a series of concerts during that period, at which the music performed should be suitable for the holy season; hence the name of "Concerts Spirituels." He acquired the privilege on the condition of paying to the Opera a yearly contribution of six thousand livres. The first of these performances took place on March 18th, 1725, in one of the halls of the Tuileries, and they were continued almost without interruption till 1791. It is hardly necessary to add that the company was a fashionable one; in fact, the concerts were as exclusive as our own "Antient Concerts." To make an appearance at them was the honourable ambition of every artist; Mozart's heart-burnings over his negotiations with the director of these concerts will be remembered by those who have read his life.

During the eighteenth century instrumental music was much cultivated in France. Among the greatest changes was the gradual but definite abandonment of the viol family, in which the finger-board was *fretted*, in favour of that of the violins. The most famous player on the violin during this period in France was Leclair, born in Lyons in 1697, who, in addition to being an excellent performer, also wrote admirably for his instrument, some of his sonatas having survived even to our own day. His end was a sad one, for he was assassinated at his own door on the night of October 22nd, 1764, and his murderer was never discovered. Jean Pierre Guignon was also a fine violinist; and Gaviniés, an excellent performer and also a successful teacher, may be considered the founder of the French School of violin-playing.

We have seen that in the case of the family of the Philidors nearly every member was distinguished as a musician. In another family of French musicians this also happened. Their name was Couperin, and they nearly all acquired some celebrity as organists or players on the harpsichord. One member of the family, however

François, excelled the rest so completely that he acquired the title of "Couperin le Grand." He became organist of St. Gervais, and was the only French organist whose treatment of the instrument was at all worthy of its capabilities. He is perhaps better known as a writer for the harpsichord, for which he composed several collections of pieces, a testimony to the merit of which is that they have been thought worthy of republication in Germany within the last few years.

It cannot be claimed for the French school of music that it was very fruitful in the production of singers of eminence. Among the most eminent was Mademoiselle Chantilly, who afterwards became Madame Favart. She appeared at the Opéra Comique, where she delighted the public by the charm of her singing, as well as by the grace of her dancing. Sophie Arnould is remembered for her wit and her waywardness better perhaps than for her powers as a singer. At the time of which we are writing prima donnas were not allowed in France to indulge their caprices with impunity, and any serious breach of engagement received the punishment of a few days' seclusion. Madame Saint-Huberty was a singer of great dramatic power, which Gluck did not fail to discover. For a long time she filled the leading parts, and ultimately married the Comte d'Entraignes, with whom she settled in England, where both she and her husband were assassinated by a servant, for reasons which have never been explained, although it is believed that they were political. Of men singers the only one who need be mentioned here is Jélyotte.

BIBLIOGRAPHY.

Poisot, Charles. Notice biographique sur Jean Philippe Rameau. Dijon, 1864. 16mo.

Pougin, Arthur. Rameau, essai sur sa vie et ses œuvres. Paris, 1876. 32mo.

(*Contant D'Orville.*) Histoire de l'opéra bouffon. Amsterdam and Paris, 1768. 12mo.

Rousseau, J. J. Lettre sur la Musique française S.L. (Paris), 1753. 8vo. (A complete list of the pamphlets called forth by the "Querelle des Bouffons" may be found in Pougin's supplement to Fetis' "Biographie Universelle." Vol. II., p. 449.)

(*Gluck.*) Mémoires pour servir à l'histoire de la révolution opérée dans la Musique par M. le Chevalier Gluck. Naples (?) and Paris, 1781. (Collected by the Abbé Leblond.)

Grétry, A. E. M. Mémoires, ou essais sur la Musique. Paris. Pluviose, an V. 3 vols., 8vo. (Contain his autobiography.)

CHAPTER XIII.

MUSIC IN VIENNA.

Franz Josef Haydn—His Early Years—Influence of Emmanuel Bach's Sonatas—Makes the Acquaintance of Porpora—Engagement with Prince Esterhazy—His two Visits to London—His Symphonies—His Quartets—His Oratorio *The Creation*—Mozart—His Early Years and Travels—His Rupture with the Archbishop of Salzburg—*Idomeneo*—*Entführung aus dem Serail*—His Marriage—*La Nozze di Figaro*—*Don Giovanni*—*Cosi fan tutte*—*Zauberflöte*—*Requiem*—His Death—His Instrumental Music—Beethoven—Leaves Bonn and Settles in Vienna—His three Periods—*Fidelio*—His Deafness—Relations with his Nephew—Estimate of his Works—Schubert—His Songs—His Posthumous Fame—Ignaz Plezel—J. N. Hummel—Ferdinand Ries—Karl Czerny—J. Mayseder.

WE must now carry our readers to Vienna, which for a long time became the home of all that was greatest in music—for in it Gluck, Haydn, Mozart, Beethoven, and Schubert lived and worked.

The career of Gluck we have already traced. We have now to speak of Haydn, the father of modern music.

Franz Josef Haydn was born in the year 1732, the son of a poor wheelwright in Rohrau, a village on the confines of Austria and Hungary. Music was the family relaxation, and the child soon developed a correct ear and a voice of great beauty, which led to an engagement as chorister in the cathedral of St. Stephen at Vienna, where he was shortly joined by his brother Michael, afterwards to achieve some reputation as a composer of Church music. No provision was made for the boys when their voices broke, so when this took place, about the year 1748, the youth found himself adrift in the world.

Fortunately he found good friends and a few pupils, and thus was able to save enough to buy a few theoretical works, among them the *Gradus ad Parnassum* of Fux, which he afterwards used in his own teaching, as well as the first set of Emmanuel Bach's Sonatas, which without doubt exercised a great influence on his future style.

Chance led him to a lodging in the same house as Metastasio, and through the poet Haydn formed the acquaintance of the great master of singing, Porpora, who offered him the post of accompanist. This employment gave him the opportunity of studying the Italian method of writing for the voice, and in return for many menial services the master gave him lessons in composition.

The Countess Thun having been struck with a clavier sonata by Haydn, which she chanced to meet with, sought his acquaintance and became his pupil. He also became intimate with Karl Josef von Fürnberg, a wealthy amateur, who encouraged him to write string quartets —a branch of art in which he subsequently made a great reputation. Through Fürnberg's interest he was, in 1759, appointed music director by Count Morzin; this gave him the command of a small but excellent orchestra, for which he composed his first symphony—the first of a long series which alone would have sufficed to make his name famous. He now considered his position so assured—rejoicing in a salary of two hundred florins—say twenty pounds—with board and lodging!—that he ventured on marrying, a step which resulted in much

Fig. 100.—Franz Josef Haydn.

discomfort, for his wife was a shrew, and they soon separated.

Count Morzin having been compelled to break up his orchestra, Prince Paul Anton Esterhazy at once secured the services of Haydn as second capellmeister under Werner. In 1761 he entered on his new duties at the Prince's seat at Eisenstadt in Hungary. In less than a year the Prince died, but the Esterhazy family were devoted to music, and Prince Nicolaus, who succeeded, was an excellent performer on the *baryton*, or *viola di bardone*, an instrument of the violin family no longer in use. For this instrument Haydn composed no fewer than a hundred and seventy-five works. In 1766 Werner died, and Haydn became sole director of the music. The orchestra, which was at his daily disposal, was gradually enlarged, and in a short time the prince built a summer residence on a scale of the greatest splendour, called Esterhàz, containing a theatre for operas and comedies, and a second for marionettes. For both these Haydn composed the music, nearly all his operas having been written for Esterhàz, where the greater part of the year was passed, varied by an occasional visit to Vienna, when the Prince's musical establishment frequently delighted the court. The Prince and his capellmeister were on terms of great intimacy, and the life at Esterhàz was most congenial to our composer, who was a man of the most regular habits. He rose early, dressed himself with care, and at once sat down to compose till his dinner hour, and this practice he continued daily. It is not, therefore, wonderful that the number of his works should be so great. The only disadvantage of his position was its comparative obscurity; but in spite of that his fame extended, and we find that as early as 1766 some of his compositions were published in Leipzig, Paris, and London. Thus his life flowed on smoothly and happily. Cramer, the violinist, who was living in London, had vainly endeavoured to induce the composer to visit this country. Salomon, another violinist, also a resident here, was not more successful. In 1790 the Prince died, leaving his capellmeister a pension of one thousand florins, which his successor increased; but the orchestra was dismissed, and Haydn's office became a sinecure. He thereupon fixed his residence in Vienna, and felt free to accept the offer which Salomon renewed, and he arrived in this country in January 1791, meeting with a reception worthy of his genius. He had undertaken to compose six symphonies for Salomon. His visit extended to eighteen months, and, in fulfilment of a further engagement, he came to this country again in 1794. To these two visits we are indebted for the twelve symphonies known as the Salomon set—probably his masterpieces in that form of composition. It was during his stay in England also that he wrote his favourite canzonets. He returned in the autumn of 1795 with an enhanced reputation, and with such an addition to his means as to place him in a position of comfort. His fame was still more extended by the production of his oratorio, the *Creation*, which he brought out in 1798. Its effect was remarkable, and as soon as the score could be engraved, it was performed everywhere. It was followed after a short interval by the *Seasons*, which was received with equal enthusiasm, although it has not maintained its ground so well as the earlier work. The last days of the composer were clouded by the misfortunes of his country. In 1809 the French bombarded Vienna; the first shot fell near his residence, and while the enemy were in occupation of the city, on May 31st, 1809, he died, at the age of seventy-seven.

His industry, as we have already said, was prodigious. There exists a catalogue of his works drawn up by his own hand, but from memory, and therefore not claiming to be complete, which brings the number of his works up to nearly eight hundred, comprising one hundred and eleven symphonies, nineteen masses, twenty-two operas, and eighty-three string quartets.

By his admirers (and who is not among these?) he is lovingly called *Papa* Haydn, and without doubt he is entitled to be considered the father of instrumental music. Very early in his career he gave the sonata form that final development which he adopted as a basis of his symphonies and quartets. It is in the latter, perhaps, that his genius is most fully manifested—in fact, he was the true creator of the string quartet, that admirably balanced arrangement of instruments which since his time the greatest composers have reserved for their most serious efforts. The symphony is equally indebted to him, especially for that independent treatment of the wind instruments which till his day was unknown. In dramatic power he was deficient ; it was in fact foreign to that easy cheerfulness of his character which makes itself felt throughout his works. From this cause none of his operas have made any permanent mark, and are, indeed, forgotten His deep and real religious feeling shows itself in his sacred music, especially in the *Seven Last Words*, and in his masses, which still remain in constant use, although the severer taste of the present day may consider their style, however beautiful as music, not the most suitable for public worship. The *Creation* has given the greatest

Fig. 101.—Wolfgang Amadeus Mozart.

delight to several generations of musicians. We cannot claim for it a place beside the sublimer work of Handel, but it is so melodious, so full of charm of instrumentation, that it is as great as pleasure to the performer as to the listener.

An even greater musician was his contemporary, Johann Chrysostom Wolfgang Amadeus Mozart—born in 1756 at Salzburg, when Haydn was already twenty-four years of age; died in 1791, eighteen years before the elder musician, to the eternal loss of musical art. At the very earliest age the child showed his marvellous capacity, and fortunately his father, a man of sense and a good musician, was well able to direct his studies, which, indeed, wanted but little direction. The elder Mozart was court musician, and afterwards vice-capellmeister at the court of the Prince Archbishop of Salzburg. He distinguished himself by publishing in 1756 an excellent method for the violin, which passed through many editions in several languages, but he was also an excellent composer both of secular and church music. Although the pay was scanty, living was cheap, and several esteemed musicians, for instance Eberlin and Michael Haydn, both distinguished for their church music, were attracted to the Archbishop's service. Of a numerous family two only grew up, Nannerl (Maria Ann), born in 1751, and the great composer, in 1756. Both children showed great musical ability, but the genius of the little Wolfgang was most precocious. At the age of three he would pick out thirds on the harpsichord, and try to imitate what his sister played. In his fifth year he began to compose little pieces, which his father wrote down in a book fortunately preserved. In addition to the harpsichord, he learned the violin, and the progress of both children was so rapid that their father decided on taking them on a tour. In January, 1762, they arrived in Vienna. The boy was most engaging, both in appearance and manner, and remained perfectly natural and unspoiled. The tour was a brilliant success. Everywhere they were received with delight, especially by the Imperial family, and both the Empress Maria Theresa and her husband Francis I. were excellent musicians. In June, 1763, Leopold Mozart with difficulty again got leave of absence and started with his children for Paris, visiting the German courts on the road. Paris was not reached till November 18th. Grimm, the well-known *littérateur*, was their good friend, arranging concerts and introducing them at Court, where the children were received with the greatest kindness and admiration. Here the boy's first work was published, four sonatas for harpsichord and violin, "*par J. C. Wolfgang Mozart de Salzburg agé de sept ans.*" It was decided to continue the journey to London, where they arrived on April 23rd, 1764. In a few days they were summoned to Buckingham House, and had no reason to be dissatisfied with their reception. "We have met with extraordinary politeness at every Court, but what we have experienced here surpasses all the rest," writes the father. Among all classes the acquirements of the children, and especially those of the boy, excited the greatest enthusiasm, and the Hon. Daines Barrington, a well-known lawyer and man of science, having verified the date of his birth, put him to the most careful examination, the results of which he contributed to the Royal Society.

Space fails to give particulars of all the travels of this

remarkable family. The year 1768 found them again in Vienna, where at the Emperor's suggestion Wolfgang wrote his first opera *La Finta Semplice*. Owing to intrigues it was not performed there, but was brought out the following year at Salzburg at the instance of the Archbishop, who appointed the young composer concertmeister. Meanwhile Mozart's studies continued, Fux's *Gradus* forming his text-book. But a visit to Italy was looked on as a part of the education of every musician, and in December, 1769, Leopold Mozart and his son set forth. It was a triumphal progress. At Bologna he was received with open arms by the Padre Martini, a prodigy of musical learning, who put him through every test, and subsequently he was made a *compositore* of the Accademia Filarmonica of that city. They reached Rome in Holy Week, and at once went to the Sistine Chapel to hear the famous *Miserere* of Allegri, the music of which was held in such esteem that the Papal singers were forbidden to take any copy out of the Chapel under pain of excommunication. This elaborate work, as we have already mentioned, the boy of fourteen wrote out entirely from memory, taking his copy on Good Friday, that he might correct it by a second hearing. For Milan he wrote an opera, *Mitridate*, produced in December, 1770, with the greatest success.

In March, 1772, the Archbishop of Salzburg died. He was succeeded by Hieronymus, Count Colleredo, who appears to have done all he could to vex and offend his young concert-meister, whose transcendent abilities he was incapable of appreciating. This studied neglect made him endeavour to obtain a position elsewhere. Successes achieved by his operas both in Milan and Munich served only to set the Archbishop still more against him. The circumstances of the Mozart family were straitened, and the greatest composer of the age was asking only for such a modest position as would enable him to bring to a hearing the works which he knew were floating in his brain. There was no other course than to resume his career of travelling virtuoso, and he started once again for Paris, this time accompanied by his mother. The journey was the cause of much unhappiness. During his stay in Paris his mother died. At Mannheim he made the acquaintance of the Weber family, and with the eldest daughter Aloysia, a young singer of great beauty and ability, he fell in love. The attachment was mutual, but on his return he found that her feelings for him had changed. She subsequently married the actor Lange. An air which Mozart wrote for her shows how great a singer she must have been. During his absence he had been appointed organist to the Archbishop, and in deference to his father's wishes he returned to take up his appointment; but his position soon became unbearable, and a complete rupture took place. His ruffled feelings were soothed by the reception of his opera *Idomeneo* at Munich, in 1781. With this opera began the splendour of Mozart's career. He here meets Gluck on his own ground, and fears no comparison. Such tendernesss joined to such vigour had never before been heard, and the work was, of course, received with the greatest enthusiasm.

The break with the Archbishop occurred in Vienna, whither he had repaired to congratulate the Emperor Joseph on his succession. It was necessary for Mozart at once to find lodgings. Madame Weber, now a widow, was living in Vienna in needy circumstances, drawn there by the engagement of her eldest daughter Aloysia, now Madame Lange, as principal singer at the National Theatre. With the Weber family Mozart took up his abode. Leopold Mozart at once took fright, and desired him to find other lodgings, in spite of his protests that matrimony was the farthest thing from his thoughts. During the early part of his residence in Vienna he was principally known as a pianist. The Emperor Joseph received him with great cordiality, but his sympathies were with the Italian musicians, who had obtained a strong footing at the Austrian Court. He was in much request as a teacher, and among others the Baroness Waldstätten and Countess Thun, who had also studied with Haydn, became his pupils. By the musicians he was received with jealousy, except by Haydn, who always showed an unaffected admiration for his genius. At last he received the libretto of an opera, the *Entführung aus dem Serail*, but owing to the cabals of his rivals—principally Salieri— it was not produced till July 16th, 1782. The success of the work was triumphant, although the Emperor expressed the opinion that it was "too fine for our ears, my dear Mozart,—too many notes!" to which the composer replied " Exactly as many notes as are necessary, your Majesty." During the progress of the opera his intimacy with the Webers had been ripening, and it ended in a mutual attachment between Mozart and the youngest daughter Constance. The elder Mozart withheld his consent, nor was the attitude taken by Madame Weber much more propitious, while her ill-temper made Constance's life almost unbearable. A friend appeared in the person of Baroness Waldstätten, who took the girl into her own house, and by her good offices the lovers were united on August 4th, 1782. To complete Mozart's happiness a letter of consent from his father arrived the following day. To Constance, Mozart was sincerely attached, and continued to be so. She played the pianoforte fairly well and was a good singer, especially at sight. Unfortunately she soon became delicate, and although not extravagant, did not shine as a domestic manager, so that household cares weighed heavily on Mozart for the rest of his life.

And now he entered on a period of the greatest activity as a composer. In the year 1784 Mozart began to keep a catalogue of his compositions as they were produced. It is a catalogue of masterpieces. In the early part of 1786 we find the music to the comedy *Der Schauspiel Director* followed in April of the same year by *Le Nozze di Figaro*. What musician is unacquainted with this charming work—perhaps the most individual of all his operas? To particularise its beauties would be to give a list of all the numbers of which it consists! Strange to say, the effect produced by this masterpiece was comparatively small, and it was only when brought out at Prague in the following year that it was received with the enthusiasm it deserved. So pleased was the composer at this result that he exclaimed, "The Bohemians understand me so well I must write an opera for them!" The result was his masterpiece, *Don Giovanni*. In September, 1787, he repaired to Prague, accompanied by his wife, with a view to composing his opera on the spot. The whole was laid out in his mind, but as yet not a note committed to paper. The work was carried on in a garden house in the suburbs belonging to his friend Duschek, a musician. It was much frequented by his acquaintances, who were in the habit of enjoying a game of bowls in the garden. Amid this scene of merriment the work was carried on, the composer frequently breaking off to take his turn in the game. The opera was produced on October 29th, 1787. On the previous evening the overture had not been written. At his request his wife made him a glass of punch, and told him fairy tales to keep him awake while he composed his overture. As soon as she stopped talking he became drowsy, and she therefore persuaded him to take some rest, awaking him at five o'clock. He had ordered the copyists to come at seven, and by that time the overture was finished. The parts were copied during the day, and the overture played without rehearsal at night amid a scene of tumultuous applause, which continued as number after number added to the delight of the audience. Prague once again showed its thorough appreciation of the master. At Vienna its reception was less enthusiastic —the Viennese found the music too learned for their taste, but even there its beauties gradually made their way. The dramatic power of the music, its wealth of melody, form the delight of all who have an ear for "sweet sounds," while the learned contrivance displayed is the wonder and admiration of the musician.

Following the order of the catalogue, in the year 1788 we find that marvellous trio of symphonies, known wherever orchestral works are appreciated, those in E flat, G minor, and C, the last known as the *Jupiter*, the finale of which is the wonder of musicians. The year 1790 saw the production of the opera *Cosi fan tutte*, the libretto of which was not to his taste, so that the work hardly rises to his standard of excellence.

We now come to the last year of the great musician's life. To help his friend Schickaneder, director of a theatre in Vienna, out of a pecuniary difficulty, he undertook to write for him a German opera, *Der Zauberflöte*. Schickaneder himself contrived the libretto, and a strange incomprehensible jumble was the result. The music itself is delightful.

The health of Mozart was now giving way. During the composition of the opera he received the visit of a mysterious stranger, who handed him an anonymous letter asking the sum he would require for the composition of a requiem, and the time necessary to execute the commission. It is now ascertained that the mysterious stranger was the steward of Count Franz von Walsegg, that the requiem was for his wife, and that he was desirous of passing himself off as the composer, as he had done before with other works similarly commissioned. But Mozart was weakened by illness, and could not rid himself of the idea that the messenger was supernatural, and the requiem intended for his own death. In the meantime he was called on to compose an opera, *La Clemenza di Tito*, by the Bohemian nobles, to celebrate the coronation of the Emperor Leopold II. Well disposed as the inhabitants of Prague were to Mozart, the work, written against time, was received with coldness, and he returned to Vienna, sick in mind and body, to set to work again on *Der Zauberflöte* and the requiem. The opera was brought out with unbounded success, and established the fortunes of Schickaneder. He now set to work on the requiem, more than ever confirmed in the idea that it was for himself. Full of gloomy fancies, he became convinced that he was poisoned. On November 21st he took to his bed, from which he never rose again. The requiem lay constantly on his bed, and his young friend Süssmayer, who had assisted him in the composition of *La Clemenza*, received his instructions as to the filling up of the score. At two o'clock on the 4th December, some friends who were visiting him sang through the score, he himself being able to to take the alto part. On arriving at the "*Lacrymosa*" he burst into tears and laid down the music. Towards evening it was evident that death was near, and at one o'clock in the morning of December 5th the great musician ceased to breathe. Then only did the Viennese find out what a loss they had sustained.

He had barely completed his thirty-sixth year, but the number of his compositions was enormous. The excellent catalogue drawn up by Von Köchel contains six hundred and twenty-six works, in addition to those which were unfinished. Among so large a number many will, of course, be found trivial, being written for a particular purpose, or to oblige a friend, in which he was

Fig. 102.—Ludwig van Beethoven.

most generous. But among them are many works of the highest genius. Perhaps his greatness was most fully shown in his dramatic work, but in all forms of composition he excelled. Nothing can be more delightful than his symphonies, or his later string quartets. His sacred music conformed to the fashion of the time, but is full of charm—for example, the well-known *Ave Verum*. Towards the end of his career he appears to have soared to greater heights, and we cannot cease to regret that his life should have been cut off so prematurely. Among his contemporaries he seems to have been appreciated at his true worth by Haydn alone, who, born twenty-four years earlier, survived him for eighteen years. Although he gave advice to many, two only are known as his pupils, the pianist and composer Hummel, and our own Attwood, for whom he had great regard.

And now we come to the greatest master of modern times—Ludwig van Beethoven—who, although not a native of Vienna, made that city the home of his adoption, and shed on it the lustre of his surpassing genius. Beethoven was born in Bonn on the Rhine, on December 16th or 17th, 1770, the son of a somewhat disreputable singer in the chapel of the Elector Archbishop of Cologne, whose court was at Bonn. He soon began to show that precocity which is so frequently the accompaniment of musical genius. His father at once looked to his son's abilities as a possible addition to his scanty means, and all the time when the boy was not at school was passed in the constant effort to force his musical talent. In this he was assisted by his friend Pfeiffer, a tenor singer at the opera, who lived in the same house. That the boy was not disgusted with music altogether only shows how great was the force of genius. In this way he was made to study both the pianoforte and the violin, as well as the organ, receiving lessons from C. G. Neefe, a capable musician and court organist, whose duties he was soon able to perform. When only twelve years and four months old he was appointed harpsichord-player to the opera—a post which involved the ability to play accompaniments from score during rehearsals. In the year 1787 he was enabled to make a long-wished-for visit to Vienna, and had the good fortune to become acquainted with Mozart, who predicted his future greatness. The visit was brought to a sudden end by the death of his mother. To keep the household together it was necessary for Beethoven to add to its resources by giving lessons. Among his pupils were two members of a cultivated family of good position named Von Breuning. The introduction soon ripened into intimacy, and in Madame von Breuning he almost found a second mother, who exercised a most happy influence over his wayward and irritable character, while the intercourse helped to improve his somewhat neglected education. He found another good friend in Count Waldstein, an excellent amateur, who presented him with a pianoforte, and also rendered him pecuniary help in so delicate a manner that his susceptibilities were not wounded. It was probably owing to his good offices with the Elector, and perhaps with some assistance from himself, that Beethoven was enabled in 1792 to pay another visit to Vienna. He had made the acquaintance of Haydn in a visit the latter made to Bonn, and it was his intention to place himself under the old master, who set him to work on the *Gradus ad Parnassum* of Fux. The respective characters of master and pupil were but ill adapted to each other. Beethoven always maintained that he learned nothing of Haydn, and it was with small regret on the part of the former that the intercourse was brought to an end by the visit of Haydn to England. But he was still anxious to ground himself thoroughly in counterpoint, and with this view placed himself under Albrechtsberger, a very learned but dry musician, while at the same time he studied with Salieri the art of writing for the voice.

His musical ability, as well as the real worth concealed under a rough exterior, seem to have been soon recognised by the leaders of musical society in Vienna. Baron vou Swieten, the friend both of Haydn and of Mozart, gladly welcomed him to his Sunday concerts, and Prince Lichnowsky and his beautiful wife, formerly Countess von Thun, almost adopted him as a son, and he was soon installed as an inmate of their house. His wayward and eccentric habits rendered the arrangement somewhat difficult. Beethoven could not be brought to conform to fixed hours for meals, nor to the ordinary habits of costume common in good society. The Countess, however, while doing her best to correct his faults, treated him with remarkable consideration and judgment, and the arrangement seems to have lasted for six years. One of the great advantages he enjoyed there was the celebrated quartet party, which met at the palace every Friday, consisting of Schuppanzigh, Sina, Weiss and Kraft, which led his thoughts to that kind of composition.

Among other members of the aristocracy, the Archduke Rudolph became his pupil. At a large party at Prince Lichnowsky's were first performed the three pianoforte trios, Op. 1, Haydn being present. The veteran master approved of the first two, but tried to dissuade Beethoven from publishing the last—the one in C minor. It was the composer's favourite, and Haydn's judgment led to a final rupture, although Beethoven dedicated his set of pianoforte sonatas, Op. 2, to his old master.

He was at first recognised rather as a virtuoso than as a composer, and was especially distinguished as an improviser. Anything like display, however, was hateful to him, and on many occasions it was with the greatest difficulty that he could be induced to perform. His public appearances were, however, few, and generally for some charitable object—for instance, he played one of Mozart's concertos at a performance organised for the benefit of the great composer's widow, and it is not surprising to learn that the effect of his playing was produced rather by intense feeling than by excellence of mechanism. Up to the time when he settled in Vienna, his publications had been few and unimportant, but now began that period of productiveness which ceased only with his death. His earliest compositions show an obvious imitation of the style of Haydn, and even more of Mozart, although abounding in many signs of originality. To this period must be referred the first two symphonies, the septet, the six quartets, Op. 18, the early sonatas for the pianoforte, among which we may specially notice the *Pathétique*, Op. 13, and the one in C sharp minor, Op. 27, known as the *Moonlight*—the string quintet, Op. 29, the *adagio* of which is surely one of the most beautiful movements ever written for stringed instruments—the pianoforte and violin sonatas, including the *Kreutzer*, Op. 47, and the song, *Adelaida*.

It occurred to a Russian amateur, named Lenz, that the works of Beethoven might be divided into three periods, and to support his theory he wrote a book entitled, *Beethoven et ses trois styles*. Such arbitrary divisions are generally fanciful, and development of genius is in most cases a gradual process rather than a sudden abandonment of previous methods. There can be little doubt, however, that with his third symphony, Op. 55, known as the *Eroica*, composed in the year 1804, at about the same time as the great sonata for pianoforte dedicated to Count Waldstein, Op. 53, the master stands revealed in the full splendour of his genius. The work is absolutely Beethoven, owing no obligation to any previous composer, It is well known that the work had its origin in Beethoven's admiration for Napoleon, whom he supposed to be a model of Republican virtue. His design was to call it the *Bonaparte Symphony*, when the news came that the First Consul had made himself Emperor. The dedication was destroyed in a rage, to be replaced by the following title :—" *Sinfonia eroica per festeggiare il sovvenire d'un grand uomo.*"

To this second period belong the symphonies in B flat, Op. 60, that in C minor, Op. 67—generally looked on as his finest orchestral composition, and that is equivalent to calling it the finest that had ever been written—the pastoral symphony, Op. 68,—the three magnificent quartets, Op. 59, known as the *Rasoumoffsky*—the violin concerto,—the first mass in C,—the pianoforte concerto in G, and several of his finest piano sonatas. During this time also he wrote his only oratorio, *The Mount of Olives*, which, in spite of much beauty, scarcely ranks among his greatest works.

In the year 1803, Schickaneder, whom we have known as the friend of Mozart, proposed to Beethoven to write an opera for the Theatre An der Wien. The negotiation fell through, to be resumed later, in 1805. The *libretto* chosen was taken from the French of Bouilly—" *Leonora; ou, l'amour conjugale,*" and had already been twice set to music. Beethoven, as his habit was, retired to the country to be uninterrupted while composing, returning in time to superintend the rehearsals. Singers and orchestras alike gave him infinite trouble, and the opera was produced at a most unfortunate time, when the French army had just made its entry into Vienna. Four performances only were given, to empty benches. The opera was afterwards reduced from three to two acts, and brought out again in 1806 under the title of *Fidelio*, with but little more success, and it was only gradually that it made its way with the public. The part of the heroine demands a great actress, and it was not till Madame Schröder Devrient took it up that the popularity of the opera was assured. It is well known that *Fidelio* enjoys the unique distinction of having had four overtures written for it.

In 1801 Beethoven was overtaken with the beginning

of that malady which embittered the remainder of his existence—deafness—a calamity especially terrible to a musician. Nor was his life made pleasant by the settlement in Vienna of his two brothers, who caused him much annoyance by officious meddling in his concerns. Still worse trouble followed, for in 1815 the younger brother died, leaving Beethoven the guardian of his only son Carl, then in his ninth year. The widow resented the arrangement, and the result was a lawsuit which dragged on for four years, when it was decided that the mother was unfit to be entrusted with the education of the boy. With the best intentions Beethoven took his nephew to live with him, but he was utterly unfit to manage the practical affairs of life, and the plan ended in failure. As he grew up Carl tried several careers, succeeding in none, and at last attempted suicide. The devotion of Beethoven to so unworthy an object is most touching, and to the end of his life he continued to work and to save with a view of providing for his ungrateful and worthless nephew.

About the year 1808 Jerome Bonaparte, King of Westphalia, offered Beethoven the post of capellmeister at Cassel. The salary was to be about £300. To induce him to remain in Vienna the Archduke Rudolph, Prince Lobhowitz, and Prince Kinsky agreed to make him a yearly allowance of 4000 florins. This well-meant arrangement was a source of much worry, for the value of Austrian money depreciated rapidly, and after a time Prince Kinsky became bankrupt. Beethoven's wants were moderate: He was now making a fair income by the sale of his compositions, and it does not appear that actual pecuniary trouble was added to his other miseries.

It was during this period, worn and solitary from his increasing deafness, worried by the escapades of his troublesome nephew, that he composed those remarkable works which are considered to embody his third style. Among those the most prominent are the *Pianoforte Sonatas* Op. 101, 106, 109, and 111, the later string quartets, the *Great Mass* in D, and the colossal *Choral Symphony* Op. 125, with its *Ode to Joy* for solo voices and chorus. All these works contain much that is difficult to understand—some critics have even gone so far as to maintain that they are the aberrations of a man who was precluded from judging the effects of the music which he had written. Certainly it is impossible to guess at their intent by once or twice hearing them, but with increased familiarity their great beauties gradually develop.

Towards the end of his life Beethoven manifested an unwonted keenness in money matters—not on his own account but in the interests of his unworthy nephew. He succeeded in disposing of several of his works, the proceeds of which were found untouched at his death. An unsuccessful attempt was made by our Philharmonic Society to induce him to pay a visit to England. At the end of 1826 his health gave way, and he was seized with inflammation of the lungs, followed by dropsy. He had quarrelled with several physicians of eminence, and it was not till after some delay, owing to his nephew's neglect, that any doctor attended him, and then an inferior practitioner. At last Dr. Malfatti, whom he had also dismissed without ceremony on a previous occasion, was induced to overlook old grievances. Under his treatment hopes revived. The great composer, unable to work, conceiving himself debared from touching the sum laid aside for his nephew, lay on his sick-bed in great straits. In his trouble he thought of the offer of the Philharmonic Society, which at once sent him £100 on account of a concert which they proposed to give for his benefit; and thus he lingered on till March 26th, 1827, when at five in the afternoon, during a thunderstorm, the great master passed away, in his fifty-seventh year.

Although he was granted a much longer span of life than Mozart, the number of his compositions was much smaller. His method of working was entirely different. With Mozart, music seemed to flow from his pen. Beethoven's composition were the result of long-continued study. Fortunately several of his notebooks have been preserved, and have been published by the care of Nottebohm, to whom we are also indebted for a thematic catalogue of his works. From these we are able to trace the gradual development of many of his most important works. Musical ideas are jotted down in Beethoven's almost incomprehensible handwriting, to be produced, frequently after a long interval of time, and with the most complete appearance of spontaneousness. In him the critical faculty seems to have been as powerful as the creative, and thus it is that he published so little that has not stood the test of time, or that can be considered trivial. He attempted almost every known form of composition, and with success. It has been often objected that he used the voice cruelly, and that is indeed the case in his later compositions, but the composer of *Adelaide* and *Ah! Perfido* had shown that he could make his music grateful to the singer. In his symphonies, his quartets, and his pianoforte sonatas he has never been approached.

The *scherzo* may be looked on as a creation of his own, but it is probably in his slow movements that he is at his greatest. Such a depth of feeling had never been touched before.

One more great musician adds to the lustre of Vienna —Franz Schubert—whose genius, hardly appreciated at all during his lifetime, may be said to have received its full recognition only during our own days.

Franz Peter Schubert was born January 31st, 1797, at Lichtenthal, a suburb of Vienna, of which his father was parish schoolmaster. The whole family was musical; the talent was manifested in Franz at a very early age, and he was also the possessor of a fine voice, which gained his admission to the parish choir. So fine was his voice that in 1808 he became a candidate for admission to the Imperial Chapel, and was at once admitted. This secured for him an education in the "Stadtconvict," where his musical education was left to chance; but he had the advantage of taking part as violinist in the school orchestra, and thus became acquainted with the symphonies of Haydn, Mozart, and Beethoven. He began to compose at a very early age, his attempts being limited only by his want of money to buy music paper; but this want was supplied by one of his schoolfellows, Joseph Spaun, whose circumstances were more easy. One of his youthful compositions having attracted the attention of Salieri, he for some years gave him instruction and advice; and this really appears to have been all the musical education he received. Among his other works while at the "Convict" was an orchestral symphony which was performed by the school band. Music was his passion, and the other branches of education he seems to have neglected.

In October, 1813, his voice broke, and he left the "Convict" for the uncongenial duty of helping in his father's school. All his spare time—and probably some that should have been otherwise occupied—was devoted to composition. A *Mass in F* which he wrote had the good fortune to be sung at the centenary of the parish church of Lichtenthal, and was repeated at St. Augustine's. This is one of his finest masses, and received the warm admiration of Salieri. Composition after composition flowed from his pen. The list for 1815 contains two symphonies, two masses, a Stabat Mater, six operas or operettas, much part music, and one hundred and thirty-eight songs! And on this vast scale he continued to produce, still continuing his duties at his father's school. In 1816 he composed *Der Erlkönig* and *Der Wanderer*, the former of which first made him famous, although it was not till five years later that it became known beyond his immediate circle. It was characteristic of Schubert that, while careless of public recognition, he was always surrounded by a group of affectionate admirers. Among

Fig. 103.—Franz Schubert.

these was Franz von Schober, a student of the Vienna University, who, having been interested in some of his songs, sought the acquaintance of the composer. The friendship ripened so rapidly that Schober persuaded Schubert to forsake the drudgery of a schoolmaster and to live with him, so that he might pursue his art. As to the means of subsistence at Schubert's disposal at this time, we are absolutely ignorant. The friendship was interrupted only by the death of the composer. This intimacy led to others, notably to one with Johann Michael Vogl, a baritone singer of great eminence and a good musician, who was the first to sing his songs in public. In 1818, Count Johann Esterhazy, requiring a music master for his three young children, made an arrangement with Schubert to reside in his family, in winter in Vienna, in summer at Zelesz, his country seat. The Esterhazys were a musical family, and the arrangement was a pleasant one, but, for unknown reasons, not of long duration; although, some years after, the visit to Zelesz was repeated, and it is even said that on this occasion he conceived a hopeless passion for Caroline Esterhazy, the youngest daughter of the Count.

It was not till 1819 that any song of his was sung in public, and not till 1821 that any composition was published. In that year Leopold von Sonnleithner, a distinguished amateur, and Schubert's warm admirer, offered the *Erlkönig* successively to Diabelli and to Haslinger, who both refused it. It was then determined, with the help of three other friends, to publish it by subscription through Diabelli. The result was encouraging. The song sold well, and Schubert was enabled to pay off what few debts he had, leaving something over.

Eighteen other songs, among them *Gretchen am Spinnrade* and the *Wanderer*, were published under the same arrangement, when Diabelli woke up to the fact that the works of the unknown composer had a certain marketable value. And now Schubert was fairly launched on his course of life. Song after song was composed—sometimes six in a morning—to be sold to Diabelli for what he would give, and that was never too much. The result barely sufficed to keep soul and body together. On rare occasions he succeeded in disposing of some compositions for the pianoforte. His attempts at dramatic compositions met with but scant success, partly owing to the feebleness of the librettos with which he was entrusted.

His income at no time exceeded a hundred pounds a year. He was shy and retiring, and received but little encouragement from the public; and yet, supported only by the admiration of a few intimate friends, he contrived to pour forth a continued stream, not only of songs, but of masses, symphonies, and chamber music, most of which not only remained unpublished, but can never have been so much as heard by the composer.

In November 1828 he died, aged thirty-one years. Gradually his songs came into vogue, and he acquired a certain celebrity from them.

It was reserved for another generation to discover how great a musician had been lost. Schubert's brother Ferdinand, also a musician, had treasured up the unappreciated works, and in 1838 Schumann, during a visit to Vienna, examined this collection, which filled him with admiration. He carried off the score of the great

Symphony in C, and it was performed under Mendelssohn's direction at the Gewandhaus concerts, to the delight of the audience. Other works followed, and Schubert's true position as a composer was gradually established. This good work has been greatly helped on by the researches of Sir George Grove and Sir Arthur Sullivan, who succeeded in discovering and bringing to light many compositions which lay mouldering and forgotten. Now the great *Symphony in C*, the beautiful unfinished *Symphony in B minor*, the masses, the string quartets and quintet, the two pianoforte trios, the pianoforte quintet the octet for strings and wind, are familiar to all musicians, and never cease to give delight.

Of course the presence of the great musicians whose lives we have been tracing attracted a large number of men of less note to Vienna. Among the pupils of Haydn must be mentioned Ignaz Pleyel, an instrumental composer, once of great popularity, but now almost forgotten. In the latter years of his life he founded a music-publishing business in Paris, as well as a manufactory of pianofortes, still carried on. Another pupil of Haydn, Sigismund Neukomm, was an accomplished musician, and at one time well known in this country, where two of his oratorios were produced. The only pupils of Mozart were our own Attwood, and J. N. Hummel, who attained to great celebrity as a pianist, especially as a very remarkable extempore player, and also as a composer, his pianoforte concertos having held their own to a comparatively recent date. His masses and offertories are still in use.

Ferdinand Ries, although a native of Bonn, may here

find a place, as he was for several years the pupil and friend of Beethoven. He was a fine pianist, and a composer of all styles of music. After a long career as a travelling virtuoso he settled in England, where he became the leading teacher. Nor must we omit to mention Carl Czerny, distinguished as a teacher, who had for pupils Liszt, Thalberg, and Madame Oury. He must have been one of the most industrious of men, for although giving lessons for twelve hours a day, he contrived to write upwards of nine hundred works for the pianoforte, and this does not include arrangements, nor other works of a larger scale, such as twenty-four masses, symphonies, etc. By the irony of fate he is best known in our day by his *Études de la Vélocité*. Josef Mayseder was an excellent violinist, and an agreeable writer for his instrument.

It would be too much to say that the Viennese appreciated adequately their musical privileges. They are an easy and pleasure-loving people, and were readily carried away by the charms of Italian opera, which had already gained a footing in that city. Salieri (1750-1825) had for a long time made it his home, and had produced a constant succession of operas, of which the most famous were *Tarrare* and *Les Danaides*. When the operas of Rossini reached Vienna no other music was listened to. One other kind of music, for which Vienna has acquired a reputation, must be mentioned, even in a serious history of music—the delightful waltzes and other dance music which Lanner and the Strausses knew how to make so piquant.

BIBLIOGRAPHY.

Carpani, Giuseppe. Le Haydine, ovvero lettere su la vita e le opere del celebre Maestro Giuseppe Haydn. Milano, 1812. 8vo. (A French translation, brought out as his own, by M. H. Beyle. Paris, 1814. 8vo.)

Pohl, C. F. Joseph Haydn. Berlin, 1875. 8vo. (Not completed.)

Von Nissen, Georg Nikolaus. Biographie W. A. Mozart's. Nach Originalbriefen. Leipzig, 1828. 8vo. (Nissen married Mozart's widow.)

Holmes, Edward. The Life of Mozart, including his correspondence. London, 1845. 8vo. (Based on Nissen.)

Jahn, Otto. W. A. Mozart. Leipzig, 1856. 2nd edition, 1867. 4 vols., 8vo. (Translated by Pauline D. Townsend. London, 1882. 3 vols., 8vo.)

Wegeler, F. G., and Ries, F. Biographische Notizen über Ludwig van Beethoven. Coblenz, 1838. 8vo.

Schindler, Anton. Biographie von Ludwig van Beethoven. Münster, 1845 (2nd edition.) 8vo.

Moscheles, Ignace. The Life of Beethoven. London, 1841. 2 vols., 8vo. (Mainly a translation of the previous work.)

Marx, A. B. Ludwig van Beethoven, Leben und Schaffen. Berlin, 1859. 2 vols., 8vo.

Nohl, Ludwig. Beethoven's Leben. Wien, 1864. 4 vols., 8vo.

Thayer, A. W. Ludwig van Beethoven's Leben. Berlin, 1866, etc. 3 vols., 8vo.

Kreissle von Hellborn, H. Franz Schubert. Wien, 1865. 8vo. (Translated by E. Wilberforce, London, 1866. 8vo, and by A. D. Coleridge, London, 1869. 2 vols., 8vo.)

Frost, H. F. Schubert. (The Great Musicians.) London, 1881. 8vo.

CHAPTER XIV.

THE MODERN ITALIAN OPERA.

Popularity of the Opera in Italy—Sarti—Sacchini—Paisiello—Cimarosa—His *Matrimonio Segreto*—Salieri—Cherubini—Settles in Paris—His Sacred Music—Simone Mayr -F. Paer—Rossini—His Career in Italy—Settles in Paris—*Guillaume Tell*—his *Stabat Mater*—Donizetti—Bellini—Mercadante—The great Italian Singers—Spontini—Verdi—His Operas—His *Requiem*—Arrigo Boito — Mascagni — Leoncavallo — Puccini — Gordigiani — Boccherini—Paganini.

WITH the death of Jomelli, in 1774, the great school of Church music in Italy may be said to have come to an end. Paolucci, Sabbatini and Mattei for a time kept alive the theoretical teaching of their great master, G. B. Martini, but henceforward the stage monopolised the musical genius of the "land of song."

The opera had become a necessity among the Italian people, although it was looked on as little more than an agreeable way of passing an evening, and the social enjoyment was more valued than the artistic. "A woman," says Beyle, "is always surrounded in her box with five or six people; it is a *salon* in which she receives, and where her friends look in as soon as they see her arrive with her admirer. . . . At a first performance people are quiet; at the following only when they come to the fine piece." With such influence is it wonderful that Italian opera seldom entirely avoids a certain triviality, in spite of the genius it so often shows?

Taking the Italian operatic composers chronologically, we have first to mention G. Sarti (1729-1802), who passed much of his life in Denmark and Russia. He appears to have written forty-two operas—all now forgotten. The main facts of the life of Piccinni have already been given at p. 259. Sacchini (1734-1786), his fellow-pupil under Durante, had great success both in Italy and in France: his most famous works were *Œdipe in Colone* and *Il grand Cid*, produced originally in Rome, subsequently in London, and afterwards in Paris under the title of *Climène*. Paisiello (1741-1815), a graceful writer, composed ninety-four operas, among which the most esteemed were *Nina* and *La Molinara*. Of all these works one air alone survives—*Nel cor più non mi sento*, embalmed in a set of variations by Beethoven, and known in England as *Hope told a flattering tale*. Paisiello was the favourite composer of the Emperor Napoleon, who begged his services of the King of Naples in order to set him up as a rival to Cherubini, whom he did not like.

In Domenico Cimarosa (1749[1754?]-1801), we have a man of more original genius. Left an orphan at the age of seven years, he was admitted a pupil at the Conservatoire of Santa Maria di Loreto at Naples. His ability soon declared itself, and on leaving the Conservatoire he was at once engaged to compose an opera for the Teatro dei Fiorentini in Naples. In 1775 he was called to Rome, and returning to Naples continued to produce a succession of operas, among which *Il*

Fanatico per gli antichi Romani, written in 1777, was the first to contain trios and quintets carrying on the dramatic action. His genius was everywhere in demand, and 1789 he was induced to visit St. Petersburg. The rigours of the Russian climate proved too great for him, and in 1792 he arrived in Vienna, where he was most warmly received by the Emperor, who wished to attach him to his court. It was there that he produced his masterpiece, *Il Matrimonio Segreto*. Its success was triumphant. One unique honour it received : the whole opera was encored! The Emperor was so delighted with the first performance that he had the whole company to supper, at the conclusion of which the work was at once repeated. It is a masterpiece of comic opera, and would surely bear reviving. The ladies' trio, *Le faccio un' inchino* is still sometimes heard. Cimarosa died in Venice in 1801.

Salieri (1750-1825), as we have seen, settled in Vienna, where he was the leader of the Italian party. His reputation rests mainly on his operas *Les Danaides* and *Tarare*, both written for Paris. Cherubini (1760-1842), who takes rank among the greatest of Italian musicians of this period, was born in Florence. He was the son of a musician, and soon gave evidence of his ability by writing a mass when only thirteen years of age. The Grand Duke Leopold II., struck by this and other compositions of the boy, granted him a pension to enable him to study under Sarti, then living at Bologna ; in addition to strict theoretical studies, the master employed him in writing airs for the less important characters in his operas, and under this guidance he learned all that a master could teach. His first opera, *Quinto Fabio*, was composed in 1780, and had but moderate success; but his reputation gradually increased, and in 1784 he was invited to London, where he remained two years. In 1786 he settled in Paris, and produced his *Demophoon*,

Fig. 104.—Cherubini.

Lodoiska, *Les deux Journées*, and *Anacréon*. These exhibited more science and more musical effect than the Parisians were used to. Unfortunately, with the exception of *Les deux Journées*, they were handicapped by uninteresting libretti, so that the latter is the only one which keeps the stage; but they are all distinguished by a great nobility of style, and led up to the modern grand opera. In 1806 he brought out his *Faniska* at Vienna, which caused him to be pronounced, both by Haydn and Beethoven, the first dramatic composer of his time.

As we have already said, Napoleon had an antipathy to Cherubini. The manner of the composer was cold and reserved, and probably he may not have shown that respect for the First Consul which he conceived to be his due. Certain it is, however, that no adequate provision was made for the great composer; an inspectorship of the Conservatoire was the only post given to him. Probably this neglect weighed on his mind, for, on his return to Vienna, he ceased altogether to occupy himself in composition. By the persuasion of his friends, he was induced to write an opera, *Pimmalione*, for the theatre of the Tuileries, which wrung a tribute of admiration even from Napoleon. But after this effort he again forsook his art, devoting himself entirely to the study of botany. While on a visit to Prince de Chimay, a local musical society was anxious to celebrate St. Cecilia's Day. The president and leading members of the society waited on Cherubini with the request that he would write them a mass. Cherubini replied with coldness that it was impossible, and the deputation retired in dismay. It was observed, however, that the composer took his walk alone in the park, with an air of pre-occupation, and that he was not botanising, as was his usual habit. Madame de Chimay advised that no notice should be taken, but was wise enough to leave plenty of music paper on his table. In a few days the Kyrie and Gloria were completed, in time for the Saint's feast. The rest of the work was subsequently written in Paris, and performed at the house of Prince de Chimay. It was a noble work, and the forerunner of much beautiful church music, distinguished by a lofty severity of style.

After the events of 1815 the Conservatoire was abolished. To indemnify Cherubini for the loss of his position, he was appointed superintendent of the King's chapel, and in that capacity produced much of the church music of which we have just spoken. On the resumption of the Conservatoire, he was appointed Professor of Composition, and in 1821 became Director. He lived till March 1842, a power in the musical world, and was buried with every testimony of respect, to the beautiful music of his own requiem. In him the more serious aims of the classic period of Italian music seem to have been revived.

Simone Mayr (1763-1845), Bavarian by birth, but Italian by education, and Ferdinand Paer (1771[74?]-1839), are little more than names to the present generation. They were both distinguished composers in their day, the latter passing much of his life in Paris, where his opera *Agnèse* enjoyed a great reputation, keeping the boards for many years.

But the most famous and the most brilliant of the modern Italian school was undoubtedly Gioacchino Rossini, born at Pesaro in 1792. His father was a horn-player—and inspector of slaughter-houses! while his mother was a sufficiently good singer to take an occasional engagement in a travelling operatic company.

The boy was soon introduced to the stage, and when

only seven years old took a child's part in Paer's *Camilla*. It is on record that nothing could be more tender or more touching than his voice and action in this small part. His father taught him the horn, so that before he was twelve years old he was able to play second to his father in the tours which the family took. In course of time he became a pupil of Mattei, at the Liceo of Bologna. Such drudgery did not suit this lively youngster, and he asked his master if he had not acquired sufficient knowledge to compose. Mattei replied that for the strict church style much more thorough study was required, but that in the free style he might pass muster. "You mean, then, that I know enough to write operas?—that is all I want"; and his lessons were brought to an end. But he continued to work on his own account, his studies taking the form of putting the symphonies and quartets of Haydn and Mozart into score. His first work was a cantata, *Il Pianto d'Armonia*, which was performed at Bologna in 1808; but he also wrote a symphony, as well as several quartets, which have been since published. He returned to Pesaro in 1810, and by the help of friends in that city was engaged to write the opera *La Cambiale di Matrimonio* for Venice. From that time he never wanted occupation. In 1813, the first of those works which made his name famous, *Tancredi*, was brought out at the Fenice in Venice, and *L'Italiana in Algieri* at the San Benedetto, in the same city. At once he was hailed as the foremost composer of Italy. The pedants objected, but the Italian audiences were mad with delight, and in four years *Tancredi* had made the tour of Europe. All the principal theatres were clamorous for operas from his pen. He could only be brought to work under pressure, but he contrived to send forth a continual stream of operas at the rate of three or four a year. Among these the best known are *Elisabetta, Torvaldo, Il*

Fig. 105.—Rossini.

Barbiere di Seviglia, Otello, Cenerentola, La gazza Ladra, Mose, La Donna del Lago, Maometto, and *Semiramide.*

The life of Rossini is not complete without mention of Barbaja, impresario, and proprietor of the gambling saloon attached to the San Carlo theatre in Naples. He had been waiter in this establishment, but contrived to become lessee not only of this theatre, as well as of the Teatro del Fondo in that city, but also of La Scala in Milan and of the opera-house in Vienna. In this capacity he had most of the leading vocalists in his employ. The success of *Tancredi* at once induced him to offer an engagement to Rossini, who signed an agreement for several years with him. He was to receive two hundred ducats a month (£40)—with a share in the profits of the gaming rooms. For this he was to write two operas annually, and to arrange any old works which might be mounted. Barbaja was a man of great ignorance, but a good judge of what music would suit the public. Under this engagement it was that most of Rossini's works mentioned above were written.

The *prima donna* at Naples was Mademoiselle Colbran, a fine dramatic singer. Rossini soon conceived a passion for this lady, and some of his best parts were written to display her voice and style. In 1822 she became his wife. His contract with Barbaja allowed him to accept other offers, and *Il Barbiere* was written for Rome. Beaumarchais' comedy had been already set to music by Paisiello, and probably owing to the opposition of the friends of the latter composer, and partly owing to a series of those accidents which sometimes attend a first night, it was received with great disfavour. The second performance, however, served to open the public ears to its merits, and it has ever since taken that place which charming melody and delightful comedy entitle it to.

Semiramide was written for the Fenice at Venice, for the carnival of 1823. It was composed in too broad and elevated a style for the Venetians, and was received coldly. This indifference decided Rossini to write no more for Italy, and he at once set out with his wife for Paris and London. Up to this time he had made but a modest income. On arriving in England, he was received with open arms by the Prince Regent and the *élite* of society, and was overwhelmed with engagements for his wife as singer with himself as accompanist, for which he fixed the fee at £50. It is said that by these engagements and lessons, with two benefit concerts, he made no less than £10,000 during his five months' visit. In the autumn he returned to Paris, where he had arranged to become director of the Théâtre Italien with a salary of 20,000 francs. In this capacity he produced *Le Siége de Corinth* —a rearrangement of *Maometto*—*Moïse*, and *Le Comte Ory*, which also contained much old material.

But his admirers were anxious that he should write an entirely new work for the French opera. For several years, ending with 1819, Spontini, of whom we shall have to speak again, had been resident in Paris, where his operas had habituated the Parisians to a passion and energy which became the characteristics of the French school. We cannot help thinking that these considerations weighed with Rossini in the composition of *Guillaume Tell*, in which his previous style was abandoned and he at once became the greatest composer of the French school.

Tell was produced in 1829. The composer was only thirty-seven years of age, and seemed to be entering on a new career. It was his masterpiece. Suddenly he decided to write no more for the stage. The reason has been much debated; he is reported to have said, "Another success would add nothing to my reputation; a failure might damage it. I have no need for the one, and do not choose to subject myself to the other!"

The directorship of the opera was not a congenial post for a man of his self-indulgent habits. Under his management it soon drifted into difficulties, and it became necessary to appoint a more vigorous substitute. He was, however, made inspector-general of singing in France—a sinecure office, with his original salary and a pension if his duties should cease! The post was of course made for him, hoping that he would be induced to continue to write for the opera. The Revolution of 1830 abolished the office, and after much litigation he substantiated his claim to the pension. This lawsuit detained him in Paris till 1836, when he determined to revisit Italy. In the year 1832 he had written some movements of a *Stabat Mater* for a rich Spanish amateur. In 1841 Troupenas the publisher prevailed on him to complete this work—in order to prevent the missing portions from being supplied by another hand. This is the origin of the well-known, and it must be added beautiful, *Stabat Mater*. Special concerts were got up for its performance, and copies could not be supplied fast enough to satisfy the demand. It is said that Rossini did not intend it for church use, for which its style is most inappropriate. This the Church has failed to recognise, and continues to use it whenever a large congregation is to be attracted. In ridicule of its secular style, the late J. W. Davison, the well-known critic, arranged it in the form of a set of quadrilles!

Political events in 1853 forced him once more back to Paris, which became his home for the rest of his life. In 1845 his wife, Madame Colbran, died, and he subsequently married Mdlle. Olympe Pelissier, also a singer, who survived him. A wit and a *bon-vivant*, he made his house a centre of attraction to all who were eminent in the musical world. His advice was always at the disposal of artists, both young and old. He amused himself from time to time with composition, mostly for the pianoforte, although the only work of any importance was a mass which he characteristically described as *Ni Bach ni Offenbach*! He died in 1868.

It is the fashion of the present day to look down on the works of Rossini as simply vehicles for the display of singing, and as deficient in seriousness of purpose. Certainly any such aim was foreign to his nature. He wrote to please—and succeeded. For a whole generation he continued to give such delight that other composers with difficulty obtained a hearing. One must grant a certain cheapness of effect to the well-known Rossini *crescendo*, but at least it never misses its intention. How beautiful are his melodies, and how elegant the *fioriture* with which he embroiders them! Let us be grateful to the man who can give us such an evening's pleasure as the *Barber of Seville*.

The immediate successors to Rossini in popularity were Donizetti and Bellini. The former, born at Bergamo, and living only to the age of fifty years (1798-

1848), composed no fewer than sixty-four operas! Of this number many for a long time formed the staple of the Italian opera-houses : *Anna Bolena, L'Elisir d'Amore, Lucrezia Borgia, Lucia di Lammermoor, Belisario, La Figlia del Reggimento, Linda di Chamounix, Don Pasquale,* some of which still keep the stage, and are full of taking melody and dramatic power. Bellini, who died still younger (1802-1835) was a Sicilian and a pupil of Zingarelli (1752-1837), at Naples, a pedantic teacher to whom he owed little. *La Sonnambula, Norma,* and *I Puritani* are the works which best preserve his reputation. They display much elegance, although a little wanting in power and variety of instrumentation.

Mercadante (1795-1870) was also a pupil of Zingarelli, who expelled him from the Conservatoire at Naples for the heinous crime of—putting Mozart's quartets into score! He also was a voluminous composer, although two only of his operas, *Elisa e Claudio* and *Il Giuramento,* are remembered. In the year 1840 he was chosen head of the Conservatoire from which he had been so ignominiously driven when a boy. He was an excellent conductor, and for the last years of his life was blind. Pacini (1796-1867), also a very popular composer, was melodious, but unoriginal.

The success of these composers was much heightened by the perfect way by which their works were interpreted by a marvellous group of Italian singers, who have probably never been equalled. The mention of the names of Catalana, Camporese, Pasta, Grisi, Persiani, among the women ; Rubini, Mario, Lablache, Tamburini, among the men, suffices. Strange to say, Italy has quite ceased in our own day to produce fine voices, and the rarer gift of perfect vocalisation appears likely to become a thing of the past.

We have mentioned Spontini as exercising great influence on French taste. In 1803 he made Paris his residence, and there brought out, among other works, *La Vestale, Fernand Cortez,* and *Olympie,* all distinguished by largeness of style and great scenic splendour. The King of Prussia, Frederick William III., was so impressed with the merits of the composer, that he resolved to attach him to his court as director-general of music, in spite of the opposition of Count Brühl, the *intendant* of the Royal Theatre. Spontini neither spoke nor understood German, and his temper was known to be imperious, so that the opposition was not altogether ill-founded, as the result proved. The King, however, stood by him, and there is no doubt that he raised the standard of performance at the Berlin Opera to a high pitch of excellence. His works were well received, the opera *Nourmahal,* among others, being specially written for that theatre. But his duties were carried on under much opposition, and he made many enemies, the foremost of whom was the critic Rellstab, who suffered some months' imprisonment for a libellous attack on him.

The career of Bellini had been closed by his untimely death, and that of Donizetti was drawing to an end, when an operatic composer of greater vigour and dramatic power appeared in the person of Giuseppe Verdi. Born

THE MODERN ITALIAN OPERA.

in 1813, at Le Roncole, a village in the Duchy of Parma, at the foot of the Apennines, where his father supported his family on the profits of the village inn, and of a

Fig. 106.—Verdi.

general shop, the child showed that early capacity for music so frequently met with in the history of eminent musicians. At the age of ten he succeeded to the post of village organist, rendered vacant by the retirement of his instructor Baistrocchi, a post he held for seven years, during which his general education was not neglected, and he appears to have been of a grave and studious disposition, making the best use of such sources of instruction as came in his way. When his schooldays were ended his father persuaded Antonio Barezzi, a merchant of the neighbouring town of Busseto, from whom he was in the habit of buying wines and other goods for the supply of his inn and shop, to take the boy into his warehouse. This proved a fortunate arrangement, for Barezzi was an enthusiastic amateur of music, and the Philharmonic Society of Busseto, of which he was president, met at his house. From this time the career of Verdi may be looked on as fortunate. Provesi, the conductor of the society, and a good musician, soon discovered his ability and gave him lessons. A Canon of the Cathedral also volunteered to teach him Latin, and tried to persuade him, fortunately without success, to abandon all ideas of a musical career for that of a priest. His talent developed so rapidly that both Provesi and Barezzi felt that he must be sent to Milan for further training. A small endowment for deserving scholars, added to the generosity of Barezzi, fortunately rendered this possible, and in June 1832 Verdi found himself in Milan, where however, he failed to gain admission to the Conservatoire, of which Basily, a pedantic musician, was principal. The reason of his exclusion has not been adequately explained, but it is said that Basily laid great weight on physiognomy, and failed to discover genius in the expression of his countenance! However this may have been, the result was probably not unfortunate, for

Verdi was led to seek the instruction of Lavigna, the accompanist at La Scala, and an operatic composer of some merit. A fortunate chance led to the production of his opera *Oberto di San Bonifacio* at La Scala, and from that time the young *maestro* was never in want of commissions. His second opera, *Un giorno di Regno*, written while he was plunged in grief at the loss of his wife—the daughter of Barezzi,—and of both his children, failed, and it was with difficulty that he was persuaded to attempt composition again. At last *Nabucodonosor* appeared, and this work served to introduce him both to the Paris and London audiences. Each successive year saw a new opera from his pen, many of which are now virtually forgotten, the only one which may be said to keep the stage being *Ernani*. They differ but little from the works of Donizetti except in the adoption of a more boisterous orchestration, and in the exhibition of greater dramatic power. It is in *Rigoletto*, brought out in Venice in 1851, that his true power first manifests itself. The libretto is based on Victor Hugo's drama *Le Roi s'amuse*, and in it Verdi found those lurid contrasts which at that period of his career were so congenial to him. Although by no means deficient in melody, the music shows a great advance in declamatory power which lifts it far above the current Italian style of the period. *Il Trovatore*, which succeeded it after an unusual interval of two years, was brought out at Rome in 1853. It is in every respect inferior to its predecessor, yet in spite of its noisy vulgarity it remains one of the most popular of operas in every country in Europe. His next work, of a much more delicate fibre, *La Traviata*, which contains much beautiful music, ran a narrow risk of failure. The consumptive heroine, who expires on the stage, was represented by a *prima donna* of extraordinary stoutness, so that the scene was received with shouts of laughter. The work, however, survived the ordeal, and still remains a favourite both with *prima donnas* and the public. *Les Vêpres Siciliennes*, written for Paris, owed its success to the dramatic singing of Sophie Cruvelli. *Simone Boccanegra* was weighed down by the badness of the libretto, but in *Un Ballo in Maschera* he scored a success. *La Forza del Destino*, written for St. Petersburg, and *Don Carlos* for Paris have neither of them kept the stage.

In the year 1869, the Khedive, Ismail Pacha, opened his new opera house in Cairo, and was anxious to have represented an opera, specially written for it, on an Egyptian subject, by the leading composer of the day. Verdi accepted the commission, but the production of the new work was delayed, as the scenery and costumes were shut up in Paris during the siege. At last *Aida* was produced, with every advantage of scenic splendour, and well-chosen caste. It proved a triumphant success. While equally dramatic, it was characterised by much greater refinement and delicacy than any of his former works.

On the death of Rossini (Nov. 13th, 1868) a suggestion was made by Verdi that a Requiem should be written by the co-operation of the leading Italian composers. The idea was carried out, but as might have been expected, the work was found unsatisfactory from the diversity of style. The last movement (*Libera me*) was from the pen of Verdi, and it was proposed to him that he should write a complete requiem. The death of Manzoni soon afterwards prompted him to fall in with the idea, and the result was the *Requiem*, which was received with general enthusiasm by the public. To most critics the work appeared too dramatic, and suggestive of the opera, but it must be borne in mind that modern Italy views sacred music from its own standpoint.

For several years after this it seemed that the career of Verdi was closed. He retired to his estate, Sant' Agata, and devoted himself to its cultivation. From time to time it was rumoured that he was engaged on an opera based on Shakspere's *Othello*, and on February 5th, 1887, it was produced at La Scala, amid a scene of indescribable enthusiasm. The composer was now seventy-four years of age, but his years appeared only to have mellowed his talents, and the work proved altogether admirable. As librettist, he had the co-operation of the poet and musician Arrigo Boito, who performed his task with remarkable skill and judgment. Six years afterwards, in February, 1893, the musical world was once more surprised and delighted by the production of another Shaksperian opera, *Falstaff*, in which the veteran composer, now eighty years of age, also had the advantage of Boito's help as author of the libretto. The master has lost none of his skill, and while all his previous operas, with the exception of his unfortunate *Un giorno di Regno*, have been tragic, it shows a marvellous versatility for a man of his years to attempt, and to attempt successfully, an entirely different style.

For a long time Arrigo Boito was looked on as the

Fig. 107. — Pietro Mascagni.

coming man, but to the disappointment of his admirers he appears to be content with his one success, *Mefistofele*, and to have definitely abandoned music for literature. This opera was originally brought out at La Scala, in

1868, and the highest anticipations were formed of its success. These were doomed to complete disappointment: the first performance ended in something like a riot between a compact body of his admirers and the rest of the audience, and the composer was chased from the theatre. In truth, the work stood in need of compression, and in an amended form it was reproduced at Bologna, in 1875. While Gounod's *Faust* presents the episode of Margaret only, Boito, who was his own librettist, follows much more closely the poem of Goethe. The work is so full of beauties, that it is a matter of regret that the composer has not followed up his success by another effort, especially as it is generally reported that he has a finished opera, *Nerone*, in his portfolio.

Pietro Mascagni (fig. 107) has scored a wonderful—and it must be said, deserved—success in *La Cavalleria Rusticana*, which he has failed to maintain in his subsequent works. *I Pagliacci*, of Leoncavallo (fig. 108), has also greatly pleased the public, in large measure owing to its vigorous and dramatic plot, and its piquant orchestration. Giacomo Puccini, one of a family of musicians, has extended his reputation beyond his native country by his *Manon Lescaut* —a reputation which his opera *La Bohème*, recently produced by the Carl Rosa Company, seems likely to confirm.

Luigi Gordigiani (1806-1860) began his career as a writer of operas—*that* an Italian composer could hardly avoid—but he acquired a great reputation as a writer of songs, to which their charm, elegance, and vocal qualities certainly entitle him.

324 THE HISTORY OF MUSIC.

Instrumental music was but little cultivated in Italy at this period. Luigi Boccherini (1740-1805) belongs to a somewhat earlier time, but must be mentioned here. This

Fig. 108.—Leoncavallo.

charming composer—alas! now but little known—settled in Madrid, under the protection of Don Louis, Infante of Spain. He here produced a large quantity of chamber music—trios, quartets, but mainly quintets, in which two violoncellos are employed. They display great originality, if somewhat wanting in that force which is now so much sought for. He has been called the "wife of Haydn," and the designation very happily characterises his music.

One supreme virtuoso Italy can claim—probably the greatest that ever existed—Niccolo Paganini (1782 [1784?] -1840). He was born at Genoa, and at an early age learned the violin, mostly under obscure professors, his only master of any eminence having been Rolla. His natural aptitude was marvellous, and he soon began to occupy himself in the discovery of those effects on which his reputation depended. These were the use of "harmonics" to an extent not then thought of; *pizzicato* with the left hand while sustaining bowed notes with the right; a marvellous suppleness of bowing, so that *staccato* passages and a great variety of accent were produced in a manner then perfectly new; a fine quality and a marvellous variety of tone; a certainty in stopping intervals, however distant; alterations in the manner of tuning the violin. All these resources he had completely under control, and in his hands they became the means of enhancing that deep musical sentiment which he undoubtedly possessed. The wonder which his performances created was increased by his remarkable personal appearance. He was tall and cadaverous, with long black hair, and was always surrounded by a certain air of mystery which he was far from discouraging, although he did find it desirable to disclaim any league with his satanic majesty. It must be added that he was grasping and avaricious, and not altogether free from the charge of charlatanry.

The excitement which his appearances caused throughout Europe is a matter of common knowledge.

Antonio Bazzini (1818-1897) began his career as a successful virtuoso on the violin, but later in life he became Professor of Composition, and subsequently Director of the Conservatoire of Milan, for which post he was admirably fitted. His compositions are numerous, and in nearly all styles; they possess great merit, but are wanting in that impress of genius necessary to prevent them passing into oblivion.

Giovanni Sgambati, the son of an Italian father and an English mother, is well known both in Rome and London as a pianist of no mean powers, having enjoyed the advantage of much advice from Liszt, with whom he was intimate. He has also attained some eminence as a composer, principally of chamber music.

BIBLIOGRAPHY.

Edwards, H. Sutherland. History of the Opera. London, 1862. 2 vols., 8vo.

Bottée de Toulmon, A. Notice des Manuscrits Autographes de la Musique composée par feu M. L. C. Z. S. Cherubini. Paris, 1845. 8vo.

Bellasis, Edward. Cherubini: Memorials illustrative of his Life. London, 1874. 8vo.

Crowest, F. J. Cherubini (The Great Musicians). London, 1890. 8vo.

De Stendhal (Beyle, M. H.). Vie de Rossini. Paris, 1824. 8vo.

Azevedo, A. G. Rossini, sa Vie et ses Œuvres. Paris, 1864. 8vo.

Edwards, H. Sutherland. The Life of Rossini. London, 1869. 8vo. *Ibid.*, Rossini and his School (The Great Musicians). London, 1881. 8vo.

Pougin, Arthur. Bellini, sa Vie, ses Œuvres. Paris, 1868. 12mo.

Grove, Sir G. Dictionary of Music and Musicians: Article Spontini (by Dr. P. Spitta).

Picquot, L. Notice sur la Vie et les Œuvres de Luigi Boccherini, suivie du Catalogue raisonné de toutes ses Œuvres. Paris, 1851. 8vo.

Conestabile, Giancarlo. Vita di Niccolo Paganini. Perugia, 1851. 8vo.

Fétis, F. J. Notice biographique sur Niccolo Paganini suivie de l'Analyse de ses Ouvrages. Paris, 1851. 8vo. (Translated by Wellington Guernsey: London, 1852.)

CHAPTER XV.

FURTHER HISTORY OF MUSIC IN GERMANY AND IN NORTHERN EUROPE.

The Abbé Vogler and his Pupils—C. M. von Weber—Settles in Prague—Becomes Capellmeister at Dresden—*Der Freyschütz*—*Euryanthe*—His Visit to England—*Oberon*—His Death—Early Career of Meyerbeer—Louis Spohr—Settles in Cassel—His *Faust*—*Jessonda*—The *Last Judgment*—His Works for Violin—Mendelssohn—His Early Years—*Midsummer Night's Dream* and *Fingal's Cave* Overtures—Visits to England—Settles in Leipzig—His Engagement in Berlin—His Symphonies—*St. Paul*—*Lobgesang*—*Elijah*—R. Schumann—Founds the *Neue Zeitschrift für Musik*—His Pianoforte Works—Songs—Symphonies—*Genoveva*—His Chamber Music—Dussek—Steibelt—A. and B. Romberg—Thalberg—Franz Liszt—Richard Wagner—His Youth—*Rienzi*—*Der Fliegende Holländer*—*Tannhäuser*—Settles in Dresden—Is banished—His Intercourse with Liszt—*Lohengrin*—*Der Ring des Nibelungen*—*Tannhäuser* in Paris—King Ludwig II.—*Der Meistersinger*—The Bayreuth Theatre—*Parsifal*—His Musical Principles—Johannes Brahms—R. Franz—Dvorák—Max Bruch—Goldwark—Rheinberger—Reinscke—Goetz—Humperdinck—Russian Music—Bortniansky—Glinka—Rubinstein—Tschaikowsky—César Cui—Rimsky Korsakow—Lvoff—Scandinavian Music—Gade—Grieg.

AMONG the strangest figures in the musical world at the end of the eighteenth century was the Abbé Vogler—a man of original views on almost every subject, with perfect faith in his own opinions (a gift which is common enough), but with an exceptional capacity for impressing them on others.

Born at Würzburg in 1749, he soon found a patron

in the Elector of Mannheim, who sent him to study counterpoint with the renowned Padre Martini. But the ordinary roads to knowledge were too long for him. The connection with Martini lasted only six weeks. Vogler found his system much too deliberate. He then placed himself under the instruction of Valotti, with no happier results. His impatience caused his master to exclaim that his pupil wanted to learn in a moment all that it had taken him fifty years to acquire. We next find him in Rome, where he was ordained priest; and returning to Mannheim, he established a school for instruction in music, promising to lead his disciples by a royal road into the mysteries of composition.

Space fails to follow the details of the life of this restless and extraordinary man. He was always travelling; visiting Spain, Portugal, Greece, Africa, America, and even Greenland, though for what musical purpose it is impossible to conceive. Probably in 1783, certainly in 1790, he was in London, where he made a great impression by his performance at the Pantheon on the organ. There can be no doubt that on that instrument he was a remarkable performer, although frequently devoting his talents to a style of music but little removed from claptrap. He wrote operas, gave concerts, advocated a new system of organ-building which has still its adherents, introduced the free reed, the use of which was in after years to develop into the harmonium, wrote numerous books to advance his musical theories, contributed freely to the musical press, and travelled as constantly as the Wandering Jew.

For three periods only in his life did he settle down for any time: namely, at Mannheim, at Stockholm, and at Darmstadt. In each place he founded a school for instruction in composition, and it is on account of the remarkable pupils which he turned out that he more especially claims mention here. Among them were Peter von Winter (1755-1825), a copious writer both for the church and the theatre,—whose opera *Das unterbrochene Opferfest* kept the stage down to our own times; Knecht, the famous organist; B. A. Weber, capellmeister to the King of Prussia; Gänsbacher, famous both for his military services and also as organist of St. Stephen's at Vienna; Gottfried Weber, the well-known theoretical writer, and founder of the musical journal *Cæcilia*; and Madame Lange (Aloysia Weber, Mozart's first love), the great singer, who owed her position to his instruction. To this long list must be added the two famous musicians Carl Maria von Weber and Meyerbeer, who were also his pupils. A man who produced so many pupils of eminence must have had remarkable gifts for imparting knowledge, and he also appears to have been much loved by them all.

The father of Carl Maria von Weber, was in his way as eccentric as the Abbé Vogler. Franz Anton, Baron von Weber, had been lieutenant in the Guard of the Elector of the Palatinate, at whose court both he and his brother Fridolin, the father of Mozart's wife, were famous as musical amateurs. Franz Anton, being probably the most unsuitable man to be found, was made

Financial Counsellor and District Judge to the Bishop of Lübeck and Eutin. He married a lady of some fortune, which he devoted himself to squandering,

Fig. 109.—Carl Maria von Weber.

breaking his wife's heart in the process. A change of bishops having occurred, the Financial Counsellor was pensioned, and for want of a better occupation became director of a strolling company of players. At the age of fifty he married Genovefa von Brenner, a delicate girl of sixteen, and from this union, on December 18th, 1716, was born the famous composer Carl Maria von Weber—a weak, sickly child, with a disease of the hip which made him permanently lame.

It was the ambition of the elder Weber to be the father of a prodigy who should rival his nephew Mozart. He had done all in his power to develop the abilities of his elder children, with but moderate result. His youngest son showed more promise, and this promise was forced by all the means at his father's disposal; but the latter possessed neither the sound knowledge nor the good sense of the elder Mozart, so that the boy's education was unsystematic, especially as the dramatic company was constantly moving from town to town. His mother died of consumption before her son reached the age of twelve. When only fourteen he had composed an opera *Das Waldmädchen*. One advantage the boy gained from the life he led—a thorough knowledge of the stage and all its requirements. He was able to paint scenes, to design costumes, and to undertake the duties of stage manager; all of which gifts helped to make him the perfect director of an opera which he subsequently became. For a time he studied with Michael Haydn, and wrote a comic opera, *Peter Schmoll*, produced at Augsburg in 1803, but with no effect. His father then placed him under the Abbé Vogler, through whose influence Weber obtained the post of conductor of the Opera at Breslau, being then only eighteen years of age. During this time he worked hard at the pianoforte, on which he became a remarkable performer. An unfortunate accident, which incapacitated him for some months, led to his resigning this appointment at the end of two years. While at Breslau he composed several numbers of an opera, *Rübezahl*, of which but little survives, with the exception of the overture, now known as *The Ruler of the Spirits*.

Circumstances led to his accepting the office of secretary to Duke Louis of Würtemburg, at Stuttgart, a dissipated young man, who employed his secretary principally in raising loans from the king for the purposes of his debauches. It was a bad school for Weber, but it enabled him to make many pleasant acquaintances, among whom were Spohr, Dannecker the sculptor, Matthison the poet, and Danzi, conductor of the opera, a worthy man who did all in his power to keep the young secretary in the right path. His youthful opera *Das Waldmädchen* was remodelled, with the assistance of a brilliant young friend of the musician, who led him into all sorts of extravagances, under the name of *Sylvana*. The opera was in rehearsal when it was discovered that his worthless father had appropriated a sum of money entrusted by the Duke to his secretary. The son was entirely innocent of any complicity in his father's crime, but both were sent across the frontier and banished for ever.

This circumstance was really the making of the composer. The exiles made their way to Mannheim, where Carl Maria found a home for his father and resolved to devote himself to serious study. He resumed his intercourse with Vogler, and at his house made the acquaintance of Meyerbeer, the son of a wealthy banker in Berlin, who devoted himself entirely to music, and although only seventeen was already one of the first pianists of the day. Under this impulse Weber composed much music for the pianoforte, and also his operetta *Abu Hassan*. In the autumn of 1810 his opera *Sylvana*, the performance of which had been so rudely interrupted, was brought out at Frankfort, but the ascent of a female aëronaut had superior attractions for the public, and the work obtained but very moderate success. In one respect the performance was noticeable: the leading part was taken by a charming young singer, Caroline Brandt, who subsequently became Weber's wife. In the following year he. began a long tour through Germany and Switzerland as a pianist, in part of which he was accompanied by his friend Baermann, the eminent clarinettist—a connection which had the result of adding several fine compositions, including two concertos, to the *répertoire* of that instrument. While at Munich the operetta *Abu Hassan* was performed with the greatest success, and at once made its way to the principal theatres in Germany. In 1813 he became musical director of the theatre at Prague, where his youthful experiences proved most useful to him. The opera in that city wanted a thorough reform. He got together an excellent company, including the charming Caroline Brandt, and at once put Spontini's *Fernand Cortez* into rehearsal. His energy inspired the whole company; a magnificent performance was the result, and it was followed up by the production of other works selected from various schools. At this period Prussia had succeeded in throwing off the yoke of Napoleon, and the whole country was in a state of patriotic excitement consequent on the victorious battle of Leipzig. This feeling found vent with Weber in the famous part-songs *Lützow's Wild Hunt* and the *Sword Song*, which soon spread over the length and breadth of the land, and did much to extend his fame.

At Christmas 1816 he received the appointment of Capellmeister to the King of Saxony, with the object of organising a national German Opera in Dresden. Morlacchi (an Italian composer of respectable acquirements, but of an intriguing spirit) was already installed as director of the Italian opera, and the King's preference was for Italian music. Weber's life, therefore, was not altogether a bed of roses; he seems to have taken a lofty view of his mission to regenerate the music of his country, and moreover he defended his views with much literary ability and vigour in the journals, which had a tendency to increase the rancour of his opponents. One consolation he possessed in his union with Caroline Brandt.

At the suggestion of Count Brühl, the *intendant* at Berlin, Weber was employed to compose the incidental music to *Preciosa*, a work which he completed with the happiest results; but the subject of *The Hunter's Bride*, subsequently known as *Der Freyschütz*, had long been floating in his mind. A libretto was at last arranged by Kind, and it was produced for the opening of the new opera house in Berlin on June 18th, 1821. His friends were afraid that the great popularity of Spontini's works in that city would interfere with his success, but the new opera was received with the greatest enthusiasm.

At Vienna the excitement it created was even greater. It soon made its way all over Europe—unfortunately often in garbled versions, as was the case both in Paris and in London, where it was running simultaneously at Covent Garden and the Lyceum. The Huntsman's Chorus was heard everywhere, and the composer was overwhelmed with offers of commissions. Unfortunately his choice of a librettist fell on a certain sentimental lady poet, Helmina von Chezy, who concocted an absurd drama, *Euryanthe*, which he composed for Vienna. The music was beautiful, some say his masterpiece, but it was weighed down by the libretto, and was not successful.

And now we come to the sad ending of Weber's life. The success of *Der Freyschütz* prompted Charles Kemble, then lessee of Covent Garden Theatre, to induce the composer to write an opera for that theatre, and to visit England to produce it. Planché was employed to write a *libretto* based on Wieland's *Oberon*. The composer was already in the last stage of consumption, and was warned by his doctor that the visit would probably end fatally, but the desire to provide for his family was too powerful. His friend Fürstenau, a distinguished flute-player in the Dresden orchestra, offered to accompany him, for he was wholly unfit to travel alone. He found a comfortable home and kind attention in the house of Sir George Smart, and was enabled to superintend the rehearsals of the new opera and to conduct selections from *Der Freyschütz* in those curious entertainments called oratorios held in the theatres during Lent. On April 12th, 1826, *Oberon* was produced. The composer was received with indescribable enthusiasm. He had undertaken to conduct twelve performances, and was enabled to do so, but with great difficulty. He then proceeded to arrange his benefit concert, from which he had great expectations. By unaccountable oversight this was fixed for the Epsom week, and the weather was disastrous, so that the results were a disappointment. He had just strength enough to accompany Miss Stephens (the late Countess of Essex) in a song specially written for the occasion, and he was taken home. His great anxiety was to get back to his family at once; his kind friends humoured his intention, but saw that it was impossible. On the evening of June 4th, Moscheles and Göschen, father of the present First Lord of the Admiralty, came to wish him farewell, and at ten o'clock Sir G. Smart and Fürstenau prevailed on him to retire to bed; the latter was anxious to sit up with him, but the offer was refused. In the morning, Sir G. Smart's servant knocked at the door as usual. The only sound was the ticking of his watch. At last the door was forced open, and the master was found as if in a peaceful sleep, but quite dead—far away from the wife and children he loved so well. He was buried on June 17th with every mark of respect in the church of St. Mary, Moorfields, to the solemn strains of Mozart's Requiem, sung by Miss Stephens, Miss Paton, Braham, and Lablache. Many years after—in 1844—his body was removed to Dresden, in great measure at the instigation of Richard Wagner.

The reputation of Weber rests, no doubt, mainly on his operatic music—especially on *Der Freyschütz*, which inaugurated the school of "romantic" opera so ably continued by Meyerbeer, Marschner and Wagner. The overtures to *Freyschütz*, *Euryanthe* and *Oberon* were a new departure in construction, and have been called "programme overtures"—that is, they were based on subjects used in the opera so woven together as to give almost an epitome of the work. The practice has been objected to, but there can be no doubt that in Weber's hands the results were some of the most exciting works in the whole range of music. He was the first to insist on the national element in music which afterwards so strongly influenced Wagner. Of his pianoforte music much is truly admirable, showing an advance in brilliancy over his predecessors. His *Invitation to the Waltz*, and his *Concert-Stück* still remain favourites with pianists.

Heinrich Marschner (1795-1861), although he can hardly be claimed as an actual pupil of Weber, had the advantage of the master's advice both at Prague and afterwards at Dresden, where he became assistant director both of the Italian and German Operas, forfeiting some of Weber's good opinion by the admiration, which he could not conceal, for the works of Rossini. He wrote many operas, but his fame rests upon *Der Vampyr*, *Der Templer und die Jüdin*, and *Hans Heiling*, which all keep the stage in Germany. In 1830 Marschner settled in Hanover as capellmeister, and in that city he ended his days.

Meyerbeer (1791[94 ?]-1864), Vogler's other famous pupil and Weber's intimate friend, was the son of a rich Jewish banker at Berlin. His actual name was Jacob Meyer Beer, which he changed into the more euphonious Giacomo Meyerbeer. Although rich, his father decided that the great talent for music which his son showed should be cultivated professionally. At a very early age the boy acquired a reputation as a virtuoso on the pianoforte, but this was soon overshadowed by his success as a composer. His earliest efforts were in oratorio, but he produced his first opera, *Ahimeleck*, at Vienna, in 1813, with little effect. During a visit to Venice he heard Rossini's *Tancredi*, which filled him with admiration. He at once adopted the Italian style, and composed several works which had great success. The most famous of these were *Emma di Risburgo* and *Il Crociato*. It is not surprising that his friend Weber, whose national feeling was so strong, should have made an appeal to his musical principles. He did not live to witness the result, but after several years it bore fruit in the succession of works written for the Paris Opera, of which we shall have to speak later.

Among the operatic composers of the second rank in Germany we must mention Himmel (1765-1814), best remembered by his *Fanchon*, and Lindpainter (1791-1856), not one of whose thirty-one operas has survived. The latter visited England in 1855 to conduct the concerts of the Philharmonic Society, and produced his oratorios *Abraham* and *The Widow of Nain*; but his greatest popularity was created by a vigorous song, *The Standard Bearer*. Lortzing

(1803-1852) was early in life a tenor singer, but afterwards conductor at Leipzig and Berlin; his name still lives in the opera *Czar und Zimmermann*. Franz Lachner (1804-

Fig. 110.—Lachner.

1890) (fig. 110), capellmeister at Stuttgart, produced *Catherina Cornaro*, which had some success. But he was also favourably known by many chamber and orchestral works, including several symphonies. Otto Nicolai (1810-

MUSIC IN GERMANY AND NORTHERN EUROPE. 341

1849), distinguished also as a pianist, died a few days after the production of his best opera, *Die lustigen Weiber von Windsor*, the tuneful overture to which is so universally popular; and Flotow (1812-1883), whose *Martha*, introducing the well-known "Last Rose of Summer," is played by every operatic company.

A much more important figure was Louis Spohr (1784-1859) (fig. 111), celebrated both as a great violinist and as a composer. He was born at Brunswick, but his father soon afterwards settled as a physician at Seesen. At an early age he taught his son those accurate, methodical habits which became so characteristic of the composer. He soon showed his musical ability, and by the persuasion of a French *émigré* was sent to Brunswick to continue his musical studies, attending also the grammar school. At a school concert he played a concerto of his own composition, and so great was his success that he was called on to repeat it at a concert given by the Duke's band. At the early age of fourteen he started, by his father's desire, on a musical tour to Hamburg, armed with a few letters of introduction. But it was summer; all the leading inhabitants were in the country, and he was compelled to leave without gaining so much as a hearing. He returned to Brunswick with his means exhausted. The happy inspiration suddenly struck him of applying to the Duke, asking for the means to continue his studies and for a post in his orchestra. The Duke looked favourably on the petition, gave him the desired post, and subsequently placed him with Franz Eck, an able violinist who was then travelling about Europe as a virtuoso. With him

Spohr visited St. Petersburg, and profited greatly by his instruction. On his return to Brunswick he had the good fortune to hear Rode, the famous French violinist, whose

Fig. 111.—Spohr.

playing greatly influenced his style. He now began a series of musical tours, in which his performance was always received with marked favour. In 1805 he settled in Gotha as leader of the band, and in that city married his first wife, Dorette Scheidler, an excellent harpist, for whom he wrote both solos, and duets with the violin, which they played together on their numerous tours. His earliest compositions were for the violin, but he soon began to try works on a more extended scale, his first symphony appearing in 1809. His earliest and one of his best operas, *Faust*, first performed at Frankfort in 1818, at once achieved success, and made its way everywhere, keeping the boards for many years, and in 1852 it was adapted for Covent Garden Theatre by the composer, with recitatives instead of the spoken dialogue. For a projected tour in Italy he wrote the beautiful concerto for violin, No. 8, with the charming *Scena cantate* which is so well known. *Faust* was followed by *Zemire and Azor*, one air in which, " Rose softly blooming," is still popular. In 1820 he was in London, having been invited by the Philharmonic Society, and it is worthy of notice that he was the first to conduct with the baton in this country. While here he produced two symphonies and his beautiful Nonetto for strings and wind. On his return, well pleased with his reception in England, and with the splendid playing of the Philharmonic Band, he stayed in Paris, making the acquaintance of Cherubini, who was so interested in Spohr's compositions that he made him play one of his quartets three times.

Spohr now settled in Dresden, gaining the esteem of Weber, who, when he was offered the post of capellmeister at Cassel, not wishing to leave Dresden, suggested Spohr as suitable for the office. Cassel thus became his home for the rest of his life. He was an excellent conductor, and under him the performances at the Opera acquired a great reputation. There he produced his *Jessonda* with great enthusiasm. The year 1826 is memorable for the first performance of *The Last Judgment*, at the Rhine Festival in Dusseldorf, a work which still preserves its popularity in this country. In 1831 his famous *Violin-School* was published, which has remained a text-book and is known to every violinist.

In 1832, owing to political difficulties, the performances at the Opera were suspended. Spohr availed himself of this enforced inactivity to write his well-known and beautiful symphony *Die Weihe der Töne*, known in this country as *The Power of Sound*, although it should correctly be called *The Consecration of Sound*. It may be mentioned that Spohr was an advanced Liberal in politics, and expressed his sympathies a little too freely, which had the effect of embittering the relations between Elector and Capellmeister. At this period also he wrote his oratorio *Des Heiland's letzte Stunden (Calvary)*, which soon after it was produced at Cassel found a place in the programme of the Norwich Festival of 1839, at the instance of the late Mr. Edward Taylor, Gresham Professor of Music, a great admirer of the composer, who induced him to write another oratorio, *The Fall of Babylon*, for the next Festival. One of the most noticeable features of his rule at Cassel was the production of Wagner's *Der fliegende Holländer* in 1842, the music of which would not have seemed likely to commend itself to his tastes. Is it possible that political sympathy may have been a factor in this result? After much opposition from the Elector, he succeeded in following this up by *Tannhäuser*, although he describes some of the music as "truly frightful"; but on *Lohengrin* the Elector put an absolute veto. In 1853 he was again in England, where he conducted his symphony *The Earthly and the Heavenly in Man's Nature* for a double orchestra at the New Philharmonic Concerts, as well as other works. In 1857 age was making inroads on his vigorous constitution, and, sorely against his will, he was pensioned. He died at Cassel on October 16th, 1859, greatly esteemed by all who knew him.

As a violinist his playing was in the first rank. His tone was broad and of fine quality, not falling off in rapid passages. His *singing* on the instrument has never been excelled, and he possessed great and refined powers of expression. In this, as in all he did, his love of system is very apparent, but it does not appear to have interfered with the freedom and spontaneousness of his performance, in the way which has been frequently apparent in that of his pupils and followers; and while equal to any difficulties, he never introduced them for the sake of display.

As a composer he was, without doubt, mannered. All his works show a charming grace of melody, but he was so given to chromatic progressions that although the listener is at first struck with admiration at the extreme beauty of his music, a certain sense of monotony is apt to steal over him. He was very fond of novel combinations—as, for instance, the symphony for double orchestra which we have just mentioned, and his double quartets. Nothing can exceed the beauty of his violin concertos, nor the admirable way in which they are written for the instrument of which he was so great a master. His string quartets have also great charm, although the interest is apt to be concentrated too much in the first violin part. Some of them are avowedly "solo" quartets, which of course assume in a great measure the form of a concerto. His oratorios are so well known and appreciated in this country, especially the *Last Judgment*, that it is unnecessary to say more about them here.

Excellent and worthy man as he was, he had but little sympathy with the compositions of his contemporaries. Weber he was quite unable to appreciate; and he considered that "Beethoven was wanting in æsthetic culture and sense of beauty"! In fact, there was one musician alone who conformed to his ideal, and that was Louis Spohr. It is this conviction which helps to make his Autobiography such delightful reading.

Among his pupils may be mentioned Moritz Hauptmann (1794-1868), who became *Cantor* of the Thomasschule at Leipzig, a post formerly held by the great Sebastian Bach, of whose works he became editor. He was probably the most learned theorist of modern times. The eminent violinist Ferdinand David, the intimate friend of Mendelssohn, who for a long time was leader of the Gewandhaus Concerts in Leipzig, was also his pupil. He became celebrated not only as a solo player, but also as an instructor, reckoning among his pupils both Joachim and Wilhelmj.

MUSIC IN GERMANY AND NORTHERN EUROPE.

And now we have to speak of one whose name is a household word wherever music is held in honour—Felix Mendelssohn Bartholdy, who was born in Hamburg in

Fig. 112.—Felix Mendelssohn Bartholdy.

1809. He was one of a Jewish family, all of whom were possessed of considerable cultivation. His grandfather, Moses Mendelssohn, was the friend of Lessing, and a distinguished philosophical writer; so that the father of the musician was in the habit of saying that he began life as the son of his father, and that later he became the father of his son. At the time of the birth of Felix his father was in easy circumstances; and when the boy was three years old, he moved to Berlin with his brother to found the banking house now so well known. No pains were spared in the education of the children, and any gift of intellect which they showed was carefully cultivated. Music was the delight of the house; and both Fanny, the eldest daughter, and Felix were systematically taught, in the first place by their mother, and later, during a visit made to Paris, by Madame Bigot, who was an excellent teacher. On their return to Berlin both children were placed under Ludwig Berger for the pianoforte, studying composition with Zelter, the well-known composer and friend of Goethe. When a little over nine years of age Felix made his first appearance as a pianist in public; and in his twelfth year began seriously to compose. In 1822 his first published work was written—a pianoforte quartet. It was the practice of the family to have Sunday concerts in the large dining-room of their house, with a small band, and he thus had the opportunity of hearing his compositions performed. The pianoforte on these occasions was usually taken by himself or Fanny, and he always acted as conductor.

Under such fostering circumstances his powers grew apace. In 1824 his first published symphony in C minor (Op. 11) was written. At this time Moscheles was passing through Berlin, where he enjoyed the intimacy of the Mendelssohn family, of whom he writes: "A family such as I have never known before,—Felix a mature artist, as yet but fifteen ; Fanny extraordinarily gifted—in fact, a thorough musician." With much hesitation Moscheles was induced to give Felix pianoforte lessons, and thus was begun a friendship which lasted to the end of Mendelssohn's life. In 1825 his father took Felix with him to Paris, where he made the acquaintance of all the musicians in that city—Cherubini, Onslow, Hummel, Herz, Halévy, Rossini, Meyerbeer, and others—who were all astonished at the boy's acquirements. The visit was in part undertaken with a view to obtain Cherubini's advice as to the boy's future, his father not being able to reconcile himself to making a musician of him, and still wishing to put him to business.

In the summer of 1825 the Mendelssohn family moved to a large house, then almost in the suburbs of Berlin, with spacious grounds, in which was a music room separated from the house, and capable of holding several hundred people, the site of which is now occupied by the Herrenhaus of the German Government. This naturally gave a greater importance to the Sunday concerts, and was not without its influence on the young composer. He now wrote his well-known octet for strings, a marvellous composition for a boy of sixteen. He also occupied himself with an opera, *Camacho's Wedding*, which Spontini produced in 1827, after it had experienced some obstruction. It had but one performance, owing to the illness of the tenor ; but in the two years which had passed since its composition, Mendelssohn had made great strides, and was not sorry to allow it to pass into oblivion. In 1826 he brought out that charming inspiration, the overture to the *Midsummer Night's Dream*. It was first played by an orchestra in the garden-house, to the delight of a crowded audience, and has never lost its freshness. In 1828 he wrote his overture to Goethe's *Calm Sea and Prosperous Voyage*.

As early as the winter of 1827 Mendelssohn was attracted to the great St. Matthew's *Passion* of Bach. With a view to studying the work, he formed a choir of sixteen voices, who met every Saturday to practise it. The members of the little society became so enthusiastic in their admiration, that they were anxious to have a public performance of it with the help of the Sing-Akademie, under Mendelssohn's direction. Zelter, the conductor of this society, was not a person to be reckoned with easily. A few of the more enthusiastic members, however, had the courage to approach him on the subject; and after some opposition his consent was gained. His young pupil at once began the rehearsals, and on March 11th, 1829, the performance took place —the first that had been given since the death of the great composer. Mendelssohn had feared that the public would prove apathetic, and that the concert would be a failure; but so far from this being the case, hundreds of people were turned away, and a second performance was given on March 21st—Bach's birthday.

In April 1829 Mendelssohn started on his first visit to England, as part of a comprehensive scheme of travel arranged by his father to give him a knowledge of the world, and the opportunity of trying his wings as a musician by profession. He was received by his friend Moscheles, then established in London, and Klingemann, secretary to the Hanse Towns legation, with whom he had been intimate. He made his first public performance in this country at a Philharmonic Concert, on Monday, May 25th, conducting his C minor Symphony, which he published with a dedication to the Philharmonic Society. He appeared at several other concerts; both in public and in private society his reception in England was from the first enthusiastic, and it is certain that he retained a warm affection for this country to the end of his days. At the conclusion of the musical season, Mendelssohn, accompanied by his friend Klingemann, started on a Scotch tour, visiting Fingal's Cave. In a letter describing his visit, he writes down a passage of music to "show how the place affected him," which became the subject of his wonderful *Hebrides* or *Fingal's Cave Overture*. On this tour, also, his "Scotch" symphony was sketched in his head, although not committed to paper.

An accident, caused by a fall from a gig, detained him in London for two months longer than he intended; but he returned in time to celebrate his parents' silver wedding by the performance of his operetta *Heimkehr aus der Fremde*, known here as *Son and Stranger*. It was not till May of the following year that his projected tour was resumed. It began with a visit to Weimar, where he enjoyed much intimacy with Goethe; and was continued through Munich and Vienna to Venice, Rome, and Naples. He was fully alive to all the charms of Italy, but never lost sight of the main object of his journey. During this time he completed his *Hebrides* overture; the *Walpurgis Nacht*, the result of his intercourse with Goethe; made great progress with the Italian and Scotch symphonies, and at the same time cultivated the society of the most eminent musicians and artists then living in Rome. On his return through Munich, he played for the first time his G minor Pianoforte Concerto, which has since become so popular. Here also he received a commission to compose an opera, fixing on *The Tempest* as a subject; but the scheme was never carried out owing to his disappointment with the libretto.

In 1832 he was again in England, and in the autumn of that year the Philharmonic Society requested him to compose a symphony, an overture, and a vocal piece. The symphony was the "Italian," produced on May 13th of the following year. He had engaged to conduct the Lower Rhine Festival at Düsseldorf. The principal work was *Israel in Egypt*, and under his management the festival was so successful that the inhabitants begged him to undertake the entire musical arrangements of the town. He accepted the invitation, and settled in Düsseldorf, where his enthusiasm greatly advanced the cause of music. But the superintendence of the opera was distasteful to him, and in 1835 he received the offer of the post of conductor of the Gewandhaus Concerts in Leipzig, which we need hardly say are the most important in Germany. This offer he accepted. Ferdinand David was induced by his persuasion to become leader of the band, and the concerts were raised to a pitch of the highest excellence, among the events of the first season being a performance of Beethoven's Choral Symphony. His engagement at Leipzig left him free to undertake the conductorship of the Cäcilien-Verein at Frankfort, and there he met his future wife, Cécile Jeanrenaud, a young lady of great beauty, the daughter of a Protestant clergyman who had been dead for some years. The composition of his oratorio *St. Paul* had occupied his attention for some time past; and it was first produced at the Lower Rhine Festival at Düsseldorf in May 1836, with the greatest enthusiasm. He had undertaken to conduct his oratorio at the Birmingham Festival of 1837, and it was received with equal enthusiasm both there and in London when performed by the Sacred Harmonic Society. His engagement with the Birmingham Festival Committee did not allow him to conduct the performance in London; but the Society had the advantage of his assistance at the rehearsals, and it is interesting to know that he expressed himself as delighted to have his work "performed in so beautiful a manner" by that excellent body. During this and subsequent visits to England he gave great pleasure to many musicians by his organ performances at St. Paul's Cathedral, at Christ Church, Newgate Street, and elsewhere.

During 1840 he composed his *Lobgesang* or *Hymn of Praise*, to celebrate the 400th anniversary of the invention of printing,—a beautiful work, consisting of an orchestral symphony in three movements, followed by a cantata.

This also had been secured for the Birmingham Festival, and Mendelssohn made his sixth journey to England to conduct it.

Mendelssohn's position in Leipzig was entirely congenial to him. He was constantly producing new or forgotten works at the Gewandhaus, so that the programmes were of the greatest interest to musicians, and the performances unsurpassed in excellence. In 1841, however, he received an offer which, although very flattering to his abilities and character, was productive of much worry and unhappiness. Frederick William IV., a prince of great culture, had just succeeded to the throne of Prussia. He was fired with the idea of forming an Academy of Art in Berlin, and fixed on Mendelssohn as the head of the musical department, in which capacity he was to be director of musical studies, and also to organise a series of concerts in which works of importance were to be performed by the Royal orchestra and the opera company. The details of the scheme entailed a long and weary correspondence, and he had no faith in the working of it. He was conscious that at Leipzig he was carrying on a great work, and had made that town the most important musical centre in Germany; he had trained an orchestra which had perfect confidence in its conductor; and he dreaded the official trammels of the court at Berlin. The pressure brought to bear on him was, however, too great, and it was strengthened by that of his family, who were naturally delighted to have him back in Berlin. He undertook his new duties for a year only, and found his position most uncongenial.

He therefore sought an interview with the King, who agreed to Mendelssohn's proposition that he should accept half the salary and be at liberty to live where he chose. At this interview the King, for whom personally Mendelssohn had great regard, conferred on him the office of general music-director of a choir of picked singers, to be called the Dom-chor; and to this connection we owe the composition of his beautiful psalms. At the King's request he wrote the music to Racine's *Athalie*, several new numbers to the *Midsummer Night's Dream*, *Antigone*, and *Œdipus Coloneus*. The composer led a sort of double life, partly in Berlin and partly in Leipzig. At the latter place a legacy had been left to the town, which Mendelssohn persuaded the King of Saxony to apply to the foundation of a conservatorium, which shortly became famous. It opened in June 1843, with Mendelssohn, Hauptmann, Ferdinand David, C. F. Becker, and Schumann as professors; and in 1846 he persuaded his friend Moscheles, at a sacrifice of income, to leave England and become principal teacher of the pianoforte.

In 1844 he was again in England, having accepted the offer of the Philharmonic Society to become conductor of their concerts. The oratorio of *Elijah* had been occupying much of his attention from time to time, and it was completed for the Birmingham Festival of 1846. It is unnecessary to say how impressed the English people at once were with this masterpiece. The rehearsals were fatiguing, and it was observed that Mendelssohn appeared much worn on his arrival from

England. His return, however, brought him no rest. He at once began to make important alterations in his oratorio before sending it to the engravers; and soon afterwards began a third oratorio, *Christus*, fragments of which only were completed. One more visit to England—his tenth—was made in 1847, mainly to conduct three performances of *Elijah* for the Sacred Harmonic Society. To his friends he appeared prematurely aged, and a few days after his return home his favourite sister, Fanny Hensel, died quite suddenly, on May 14th. The shock was so great that he remained for some time insensible. Accompanied by his family, he visited Baden-Baden during the summer; but his usual cheerfulness was long in returning. The sight of his sister's room during a visit to Berlin brought on a return of depression. He was attacked with shivering and severe headache on October 9th, but on the application of leeches he became better, and on the 28th was able to take a walk with his wife. But the improvement was only temporary: on November 3rd he was again attacked, and, having never recovered consciousness, died at Leipzig on the evening of November 4th, 1847. Public feeling in Leipzig was intense; bulletins were issued, and when the fatal end was announced the town was hushed as if by some public calamity. In England, the country in which he had felt so much at home, the feeling was scarcely less remarkable. The character of the man was so sunny and winning, that every one with whom he had come in contact felt as if he had lost a personal friend.

For a long period Mendelssohn and Spohr were the most prominent musicians of Germany, if not of Europe ; and it must be admitted that Mendelssohn's reputation has much more successfully withstood the lapse of time. In Germany it has perhaps been somewhat obscured by that of Schumann, of whom we shall have to speak presently ; but in this country his music has taken hold of the public taste in a way which that of no other composer has done since the days of Handel. In the popular mind *Elijah* occupies a position almost on a level with the *Messiah*, and the two works are considered essential at every musical festival. Mendelssohn tried all forms of composition, but his oratorios *St. Paul* and *Elijah* will probably be considered his masterpieces. The former is the favourite in Germany : in it the influence of Sebastian Bach is more strongly exhibited ; *Elijah*, according to English opinion, is characterised by greater freedom of style, and is in the noblest sense dramatic without a trace of the theatrical, and the music is invariably worthy of the subject. It was always Mendelssohn's wish to write an opera, but he never succeeded in finding a libretto to his mind. The *Loreley* finale is sufficient to show what we have missed. His overtures (and *Melusina* and *Ruy Blas* must be added to those already mentioned) are poetic and delightful in the highest degree, as are his symphonies, the *Italian*, the *Scotch*, and that to the *Hymn of Praise*. His string quartets, with all their beauty, are perhaps too orchestral in treatment ; they have been happily described as " little whirlwinds." His Psalms are noble works, happily well known, as are many of his part songs and songs for solo voice. Of his pianoforte music, the most fortunate in securing popularity have been his *Songs without Words*, many of which have great charm. The form was of his own invention, and it supplied a want for short pieces of poetical character suitable for performance on occasions when a sonata would be inadmissible. It must be added that he was a man of great general accomplishments, sketching with something more than the ability of an amateur. The two volumes of his correspondence show how delightful he was as a letter-writer.

The reputation of his contemporary Robert Schumann (fig. 113) was of somewhat slow growth, and in this country almost posthumous. He was born at Zwickau in Saxony on June 8th, 1810, and was thus little more than a year younger than Mendelssohn. His father was a bookseller, who, although not a musician, was a man of culture, and anxious to encourage his son's early leanings to that art. With this view he endeavoured to place him with C. M. von Weber, but the negotiation broke down. His father unfortunately died in 1826, and his mother would lend no countenance to music as a profession. He therefore entered the University of Leipzig as a student of law; but the study of Jean Paul seems to have had much greater attractions for him than that of the faculty chosen for him. His love for music, however, soon broke forth again, and he made the acquaintance of Wieck, an eminent teacher, the father of his future wife, and of him he took some pianoforte lessons. He there made the acquaintance of other musical students, who joined him in meeting together for the practice of

Fig. 113.—Robert Schumann.

chamber music. In 1828 he tried his hand at composition and began a systematic study of the works of Bach. In 1829 Schumann, with a friend, migrated to the University of Heidelberg. It is probable that they were attracted there by the lectures of Thibaut, the celebrated jurist, who was also the author of a well-known treatise on *Purity in Musical Art*, which has gone through many editions and had much influence on musical taste. If the better study of law was the ostensible reason for the change, in reality the only study carried on was that of music. At the end of three years he was no more reconciled to the law, and he endeavoured to persuade his mother to consent to his abandonment of it in favour of his beloved art. The decision was at last referred to Wieck, and in the end he became free to follow the bent of his inclination. He proposed to study the pianoforte with a view to public performance, and placed himself again under Wieck. He threw himself into his work with great energy, and in order to make way as quickly as possible invented a contrivance for drawing back the third finger while the others were free of practise exercises. The result was a strain of the tendons of the third finger, which destroyed all hope of becoming a virtuoso. For a long time the right hand was wholly useless, but at last he was able to play again, although the third finger never recovered its power. It shows great confidence in his genius that he still continued the intention of making music his profession. His whole energy was of necessity now devoted to composition, which he studied with Dorn, while still living on terms of intimacy with Wieck. He was fortunately possessed of a small income, which placed him out of the reach of actual difficulties. At this period he produced a few works, including a symphony, none of which seem to have had much success.

While at Leipzig Schumann was in the habit of passing his evenings with a small circle of friends at a restaurant called the "Kaffeebaum." Musical criticism in Germany was at that time very superficial, and it occurred to these young men that it was their mission to combat the light and frivolous tastes of the day by starting a musical paper animated by serious and lofty aims. The *Neue Zeitschrift für Musik* was the result, the first number of which appeared on April 3rd, 1834. Schumann possessed in large measure the golden gift of silence; but he handled the pen with skill. He became the principal editor, assisted by Wieck, Ludwig Schunke, a young and gifted pianist who died at the early age of twenty-four, and Julius Knorr. In the course of the first year Schumann became sole editor and proprietor. He had not studied Jean Paul for nothing, and a certain air of mysticism animated his contributions. His articles appeared under various signatures, sometimes with a number in which the figure 2 always appears, sometimes with a name such as Florestan and Eusebius, which are explained as representing different phases of his mind, Florestan being the stormy and vehement, Eusebius the gentle and poetic side of his nature. Many references are made to the Davidsbündler,—an association, it need hardly be said, entirely imaginary,—which was supposed to wage war against the Philistines in the kingdom of Music. It was an entirely new departure in musical criticism; the paper soon gained a large circulation, and the influence it exercised was important, having mainly for its object the development of an advanced school of music founded on the romanticism of Beethoven and Schubert. The paper contained many enthusiastic and appreciative criticisms, from the pen of Schumann, of new works by Mendelssohn, Chopin, Hiller, Heller, Sterndale Bennett, Gade, Franz, and Brahms. Many of these contributions were collected towards the close of his life, and are thus readily available in the original German, and in an English translation.

These journalistic occupations no doubt interrupted composition, but while thus engaged he found time to compose several works for the pianoforte; among which are the *Carnaval*, Op. 9, the Études symphoniques, Op. 13, the *Fantasie*, Op. 17, a Sonata, Op. 14, first published under the title of *Concerto without Orchestra*, and sundry smaller works, such as the *Novelletten*, *Kreisleriana*, and the delightful *Kinderscenen*. During his intimacy with Wieck he had been much impressed with the abilities of his youthful daughter Clara. The feeling soon deepened into mutual affection. Wieck, however, was opposed to the union, thinking probably that Schumann's prospects were not sufficiently certain to warrant such a step. To gain a position, the latter determined on settling in Vienna, proposing to publish his paper in that city. This intention was frustrated by the regulations of the Austrian censorship, and at the end of six months he returned to Leipzig. The only good result from this visit was the examination he was able to make of Schubert's manuscripts in the possession of his brother

Ferdinand, among which he found the great C major symphony, the score of which he was enabled to send to Leipzig, and to have it performed at the Gewandhaus concerts under the direction of Mendelssohn, with whom he enjoyed much intimacy.

Wieck's objection to his daughter's marriage grew even stronger, and it became necessary to appeal to the legal rights of the young couple, who were married on September 12th, 1840. Schumann was by nature shy and unsociable, and the result of his marriage, an eminently happy one, was to withdraw him even more from general society, while it had the effect of greatly increasing his musical productiveness. Till this time, with the exception of his youthful symphony, the whole of his compositions had been for the pianoforte. He now suddenly broke out into song, pouring forth during the year 1840 vocal compositions with a profusion worthy of Schubert. The way in which he devoted himself for a time to one style of composition is very remarkable. In the following year he took up orchestra writing with equal energy, writing two symphonies and an overture, Scherzo and Finale, Op. 52. In 1842 he gave his attention to chamber music, resulting in three string quartets, the pianoforte quintet, the pianoforte quartet, and the Phantasie-stücke for pianoforte, violin, and violoncello. The year 1843 saw the production of a work on a larger scale—*Paradise and the Peri*, for solo voices, chorus and orchestra. The success of this work was immediate, and established his reputation, encouraging him to set to work on scenes from Goethe's

Faust, which, however, was not completed till the year 1853. The quiet of his life was broken from time to time by musical tours with his wife, who lost no opportunity of extending her husband's fame by playing his compositions. These journeys included one to St. Petersburg, where he found his old friend Henselt, a pianist of the first rank, who did all he could to hide away his own marvellous gifts in the northern city. In 1846 they visited Vienna, where neither his B flat Symphony nor his beautiful Pianoforte Concerto in A minor was appreciated. In Berlin *Paradise and the Peri* met with but little better reception; but in Prague his compositions were greeted with enthusiasm.

In 1844 he gave up the editorship of the *Neue Zeitschrift*. He had, in 1843, at Mendelssohn's instance, become Professor of Pianoforte-playing and Composition in the new Conservatorium, although his shyness and reserve ill qualified him for the position of teacher. But overwork was beginning to tell upon his excitable nature, and he already began to show that nervous depression which afterwards developed so acutely. His doctor insisted on an abstinence from continued musical excitement, to ensure which he decided to remove to Dresden, where he was able to live in comparative seclusion. It was long before he was able to resume work, but in 1846 His C major Symphony was completed and produced at the Gewandhaus. It had long been his wish to write a German opera. The usual difficulty of a suitable subject stood in his way. He at last decided on the legend of St. Geneviève, which had been treated dramatically both by Tieck and Hebbel. The poet Reinick was persuaded to undertake the duty of arranging from these materials a book suitable for operatic treatment. The result did not commend itself to Schumann, and he undertook himself the work of librettist. The music was completed in August 1848, but it was not till June 25th, 1850, after the usual vexations inherent in matters theatrical, that the opera was produced at Leipzig under the title of *Genoveva*. The reputation of the composer ensured a crowded house at the first performance, but the work was only a *succès d'estime*. To the composer this was a great disappointment, some solace for which he found in the reception given to his *Faust* music, which was performed at Dresden, Leipzig and Weimar, to celebrate the hundredth anniversary of Goethe's birth.

Schumann continued in Dresden till 1850, during the latter part of the time capable of much work. His music to Byron's *Manfred* belongs to this period. But he also occupied himself as conductor, succeeding Ferdinand Hiller, who left Dresden to become Director of Music at Düsseldorf, in the charge of a male choir, for which he wrote a few works. He also conducted a mixed choir, which was much more to his taste. Finding that he was more successful in that capacity than he anticipated, he aspired to the conductorship of the Gewandhaus, which, since the death of Mendelssohn, had been occupied by Julius Rietz. The latter, however, remained in Leipzig, and the vacancy did not occur. But in 1850 Hiller left Düsseldorf to become Capellmeister at Cologne, and Schumann succeeded to his position. He proved wholly wanting in the gifts of a conductor, and this incapacity increased as time went on and his health failed, so that attempts were made in 1853 to induce him to allow Julius Tausch to conduct for a time. The suggestion was distasteful to him, but from that time he ceased to act as conductor.

If the appointment thus became a source of heart-burning, his residence in Düsseldorf was fruitful in original work. During this time he wrote his great Symphony in E flat, known as the Rhenish, the overtures to the *Braut von Messina* and to Goethe's *Hermann und Dorothea*, also a cantata *Der Rose Pilgerfahrt*, and, strange to say, both a Mass and a Requiem. But his mind gradually became unhinged. He fancied that he heard the constant sounding of a particular note, and even that he was visited by the spirits of Schubert and Mendelssohn, who brought him musical subjects; and he insisted on rising from his bed to note them down. On February 27th, 1854, while engaged in conversation with friends, he suddenly left the house and threw himself from the bridge into the Rhine. He was with difficulty rescued by some boatmen; but his intellect had completely given way, and it was necessary to place him in an asylum, where he died on July 29th, 1856.

At his death his music at once became popular in Germany. In England his reputation was of slow growth. The public mind was filled with the works of Mendelssohn; and there can be no doubt that the perfection of construction which the latter always show appears more congenial to the English taste than the dreamy formlessness which characterises Schumann. Gradually this is being remedied, and many of his works, for pianoforte solo, and with instruments, especially the Quintet, Op. 44, and the Quartet, Op. 47, both in the key of E flat, as well as his three string quartets, have become favourites. The opportunities of hearing his symphonies are of course fewer, and they are thus not so familiar. Many of his songs are well known, and it must be admitted that they open up a depth of power and feeling which Mendelssohn did not attain to in works of the same kind. His wife, a pianist of the first rank, whose playing was characterised by a complete absence of personal display, made it the business of her life to familiarise the public with the compositions of her husband. Her touching devotion to his memory was crowned with the success it deserved; she died in June 1896, enjoying the respect—one may say the affection—of all musicians—having survived her husband for forty years, during which, in addition to her public performances, she trained several successful pupils, among whom may be mentioned Miss Fanny Davis and Mr. Leonard Borwick.

We must now go back for a few years to mention several musicians, who, though not of the first rank, occupied prominent positions in the musical world during their lives, but are now in a measure forgotten. The first of these is J. L. Dussek, who attained to great eminence both as a pianist and as a composer, mainly for his own instrument. He was born at Czaslau, in Bohemia, in 1761, received a liberal education, and was anxious to join the Cistercian order—a desire fortunately frustrated. His father, a musician, taught him the pianoforte at an early age. His wandering life began early, and we find him organist of several churches in Belgium and Holland. His fine performance on the pianoforte soon attracted notice, and was received with enthusiasm at most of the principal cities of Europe which he visited. His stay in London was extended to twelve years, for he married the daughter of Domenico Corri, an excellent singer settled there, and entered into partnership with his father-in-law as a music publisher. The business, however, was not successful, and Dussek left this country to avoid his creditors. In 1803 he made the acquaintance of Prince Louis Ferdinand of Prussia, who showed such excellence, both as a composer and a pianist, that Beethoven preferred his playing to that of Himmel, and complimented him on "not playing at all like a prince." The Prince was kind and generous, but a free liver, and Dussek became his boon companion, passing much of his time in making music with his patron. The Prince met his death at the battle of Saalfeld, in October 1806. Dussek subsequently entered the service of Talleyrand, who treated him with great distinction. He gave occasional lessons to Talleyrand's adopted daughter, but the greater part of his time was at his own disposal; the arrangement was only broken by the death of Dussek, in 1812. There can be no doubt, from the universal testimony of contemporary musicians, that as a performer Dussek was in the first rank, excelling not only in finish of execution and beauty of tone, but also in fineness of style, especially in *cantabile* passages. His published compositions are all for the pianoforte, many with accompaniments, and are admirably written for the instrument, fertile in invention, very graceful, but, according to present views, deficient in seriousness of purpose,—in fact, he seems to have possessed a fatal facility. Among his finest works is the Sonata called *L'Invocation*. The *Plus ultra* Sonata was written in avowed rivalry as to difficulty of execution with the *Ne plus ultra* Sonata of Woelfl, a pianist of prodigious power, a native of Salzburg, who ended his days at an early age in England.

Daniel Steibelt is another musician of much the same calibre as Dussek. He was born in Berlin, where his father was an esteemed maker of harpsichords and pianofortes. Having attracted the notice of the Crown Prince of Prussia, afterwards Frederick William II., he was placed by him under Kirnberger, better known as a theorist than as a performer or composer. No traces of his influence are discoverable in the pupil. Steibelt joined the army; but after a time he appeared in Paris as a pianist, with great success. During his residence in that city he was induced to compose an opera, *Romeo and Juliet*, which, although rejected by the Académie, was produced at the Théâtre Feydeau with great success. Both as a pianist and as a teacher he became very popular in Paris; but he damaged his reputation by palming off on a publisher, as new, works which he had already printed elsewhere, and owing to this and other laxities he was compelled to leave that city. He now visited England, and although Clementi, Dussek, and Cramer were already in the field, contrived to make a great impression, especially with his Concerto containing the "Storm Rondo," which became very popular. Here he remained three years, and then revisited his native country, where his style of playing does not seem to have been so much appreciated. But so great a reputation had preceded him in Vienna that the friends of Beethoven felt some apprehension; a trial of strength, however, left the honours with Beethoven. We next find him in Paris, producing Haydn's *Creation*. While making that city his headquarters, he spent much of his time in London, where he still maintained his reputation. Pecuniary difficulties again made residence in Paris impossible; he therefore started for St. Petersburg, giving concerts on his journey; and in the northern capital he died in 1823. His style of playing was neat and brilliant in quick movements; but slow movements he seldom attempted. In his sonatas the slow movement is either altogether wanting, or is reduced to the proportions of a mere introduction to the finale. He was extravagant in his habits, and always in difficulties; so that much of his music was written hurriedly, for the mere purpose of obtaining money. At his best he was capable of really fine writing; but his work is very uneven, and a sonata, which opens in a way that promises grandeur, often falls off into triviality.

Of other pianists we must mention J. P. Pixis (1788-1875); Kalkbrenner (1784?-1849), who was for a time resident in England, and enjoyed great vogue both as a performer and composer for his instrument, as well as for his method of instruction; and Ferdinand Hiller (1811-1885), who was deservedly esteemed both for his personal character and as an executant. He is favourably known as a composer in all departments of music, and as a critic, and also as director of music in Cologne, where he always maintained the high character of the music performed at the Gürzenich Concerts. Nor must we omit to mention Stephen Heller (1814-1888), the writer of much poetic and graceful music for the pianoforte, on which instrument his retiring disposition alone prevented him from being known as a great virtuoso.

The cousins Andreas and Bernhard Romberg, the former of whom was an excellent violinist, the latter a violoncellist of the first rank, were both known as composers. The works of Bernhard Romberg were mainly for his own instrument, and include several quartets in which the violoncello takes an unusually prominent part. Andreas Romberg was more catholic in his aims, and wrote several cantatas, among which *The Lay of the Bell* and *The Harmony of the Spheres* still form part of the *répertoire* of country choral societies. Reissiger, a man of refined taste and an excellent musician, tried all forms of composition, through which there runs an agreeable vein of melody which makes his music pleasing, if not very profound. He is perhaps best known to amateurs by his pianoforte trios and quartets. In much the same category may be mentioned F. W. Kücken (1810-1882) and Franz Abt (1819-1885), both writers of pleasing and tuneful songs. C. F. Curschmann (1805-1841) lives in the popular trio *Ti prego*. J. W. Kalliwoda (1800-1866), an excellent violinist, was the writer of several symphonies and overtures; and H. W. Ernst (1814-1865) was one of the most poetic performers on the violin, as well as the writer of much refined and beautiful music for that instrument, among which his *Elégie* is the best known.

We need hardly say that in the land of Sebastian Bach there was no dearth of good organists. The nature of their duties stands in the way of any wide-spread reputation; but among those who are well known beyond their immediate neighbourhood, we must mention J. C. H. Rinck (1770-1846), whose *Practical Organ School* is a standard book; J. G. Schneider (1789-1864), organist successively at Leipzig and Dresden; and A. F. Hesse (1809-1863), born in Breslau, in which city he passed his life.

Space fails to give the names even of all the German musicians who have achieved eminence. But there are two pianists of the first rank, both probably among the greatest executants of any age, of whom we must speak. These are Sigismund Thalberg (1812-1871) and Franz Liszt, (fig. 114) (1811-1886). The former has been called the greatest singer on the pianoforte that ever existed; his power of sustaining the tone and of legato playing was unrivalled. He composed many works for his own use, aiming mainly at effect, which are seldom successful in other hands. Liszt, the greatest virtuoso of his time on the pianoforte, was born in Hungary, and at an early age was taken by his father to Paris, with a view of entering the Conservatoire, but as a foreigner Cherubini refused him admission, and he therefore studied under Reicha. His father devoted himself entirely to the cultivation of his son's talents, and he soon acquired prodigious powers of execution. His tours were triumphal progresses. In 1827 his father died, and he was thrown on his own resources. He fixed his residence in Paris with his mother, and became acquainted with many of the most prominent men of letters. It is said that he became affected by the doctrines of St. Simon, but these were abandoned for a desire to enter the priesthood—a wish to be renewed and gratified later in life. The effect of his playing must have been extraordinary. He seemed to transform himself for the time into the very composer he was interpreting. For him difficulties of execution did not exist, so that his whole mind was free to devote itself to the intentions of the composition. At last he became weary of the wandering life of a virtuoso, and accepted the post of conductor of the Court Theatre at Weimar, with the avowed object of producing works of genius which were unable to obtain a hearing elsewhere. His residence in Weimar made it a rallying place for earnest musicians, and for those who were anxious to become his pupils. Among those attracted by his influence was Joachim Raff (1822-1882), who was enabled by Liszt's kindness to produce his opera *King Alfred*; and this laid the foundation of that reputation which was maintained by many compositions, which, however, vary strangely in excellence; among the most important are the symphonies, *Im Wald* and *Lenore*. Liszt now began to occupy himself seriously with composition, his previous works having been principally solos for his own use. Among his larger works are the oratorio *The Legend of St. Elizabeth*, the great Mass written for the consecration of the Cathedral at Gran, the *Faust* and the *Dante* symphonies, and the *Symphonic Poems*. In 1859 he gave up his appointment at Weimar,

Fig. 114.—Franz Liszt.

although still continuing to live there in turn with Rome and Pesth. Dwell where he might, he was from early life surrounded by a little court of adorers and disciples of both sexes. Such homage had become a necessity to him. He loved to keep himself before the public, and in his latter years, after a somewhat stormy life, surprised his friends by the announcement that he had become a priest, and was from that time known as the Abbé Liszt. There are those who find his compositions admirable; to the majority of musicians they appear noisy and pretentious—frequently positively repulsive. His reputation, we think, will rest more on his extraordinary powers as an interpreter of the works of others, whether as performer or conductor. His personal fascination was irresistible; his character one of great nobility and generosity. It is well known that the greater part of the funds necessary for the Beethoven monument at Bonn was provided by him; and the ultimate triumph of the extraordinary man whose career we proceed to notice was largely due to his support.

It is hardly necessary to say that we are speaking of Richard Wagner (fig. 115), whose genius and strong personality have occupied so much of the musical attention of latter times. He was born at Leipzig on May 22nd, 1813, and was the youngest child of a government official, who filled the office of clerk to the city police courts. Five months after the birth of the child the father died, leaving his widow in great straits, the eldest son being only fourteen; in 1815 she was married again to Ludwig Geyer, an actor, writer of plays, and painter of portraits, and the family removed to Dresden, where Geyer had an engagement. Wagner always spoke of him with affection, and he seems to have done his duty by the boy, superintending his studies, and attempting to make a painter of him. Wagner's triumphs were to be in another direction, and he soon began to learn to play on the pianoforte, but never to the end of his life succeeded in becoming an even passable performer. His taste for literature soon showed itself, and at the age of fourteen he began a tragedy. "Forty-two persons," he tells us, "died in the course of the piece, and the want of living characters compelled me to let most of them appear as ghosts in the last act." For this tragedy he thought it necessary to have incidental music, such as that supplied by Beethoven to Goethe's *Egmont*, and he was thus led to undertake a more serious study of the art of composition. The engagement of his eldest sister at the Leipzig theatre led the family back again to his native place, where he had some regular instruction in music from Gottlieb Müller, and afterwards, when he had entered at the University of Leipzig, from Weinling, Cantor of the Thomas-schule, to whose training Wagner always expressed his obligations. Then follows the old story of other subjects neglected in favour of that which filled his whole being. Beethoven became his idol, and Dorn expresses a doubt whether there was ever a young musician who knew Beethoven's works so thoroughly as Wagner in his eighteenth year. The immediate outcome of this study was a pianoforte arrangement of Beethoven's choral symphony, a sonata for the pianoforte, and one or two other works for the same instrument.

In the year 1833 Wagner's brother Albert was engaged as tenor singer, actor, and stage manager at the Würzburg theatre, and Richard took the place of chorus master at a salary of ten florins a month! It gave him theatrical experience, and he wrote an opera, *Die Feen*, which was never performed till after the composer's death. In 1834 Madame Schröder-Devrient was in Leipzig, and she became his ideal actress; with a view to her performance in it, he composed another opera, *Das Liebesverbot*, a hope in which he was disappointed. This engagement he relinquished to become music director of the Magdeburg theatre, where his opera was performed unsuccessfully. He was burdened with debts, and visited Königsberg in the hope of obtaining an engagement. At last he received the promise of the conductorship, and on the strength of it he married Wilhelmina Planer, an actress at the theatre at Königsberg, who had formed one of the company at Magdeburg. His desire was to compose an opera for Paris, which he rightly looked on as the headquarters of dramatic music at that time. He even went so far as to send the sketch of an opera to Scribe, but, as was natural, the successful librettist took no notice of the application of an unknown correspondent. In the meantime the lessee of the Königsberg theatre became bankrupt, and Wagner was again without occupation. Fortunately an opening was found at the theatre at Riga, of which he became conductor, both his wife and her sister receiving engagements also. He now began the composition of *Rienzi*, the libretto of which was written by himself on the basis of Lytton's novel. The opera was composed with a distinct intention for the Paris Opera. At the conclusion of his engagement at Riga two acts were completed, and he determined to visit Paris, to see how far personal effort would ensure the acceptance of his opera. To reach Paris he started from Pillau, the port of Königsberg, in a sailing vessel bound for London, accompanied by his wife and a big Newfoundland dog. The voyage was an eventful one: three times they were nearly wrecked;

Fig. 115.—Richard Wagner.

they had to seek shelter in a Norwegian port, and it was only after three weeks and a half that they reached London. The scenes of this boisterous voyage made a great impression on his imagination, and suggested to him the treatment of the legend of the Flying Dutchman. He arrived in Paris in September 1839, at the age of twenty-six, and the visit was extended to the spring of 1842. As far as his plans were concerned, it was fruitless. At Boulogne he had made the acquaintance of Meyerbeer, who furnished him with letters of introduction to several of the leaders of the musical world in Paris. They received him with kindness, but were unable to further his wishes. Wagner was reduced to the direst straits, being glad to do hackwork for the music shops for a miserable pittance. As was perhaps natural, success in others embittered his feelings towards them: thus he failed completely at that time to appreciate Liszt, to whom he was afterwards to become so greatly indebted; and it was doubtless this feeling which led him always to speak so slightingly of Meyerbeer and Mendelssohn, who were both lifted by circumstances above any pecuniary difficulties. During this period he contributed several articles to the *Gazette Musicale*, one of which, entitled "A Visit to Beethoven," attracted the attention of Berlioz. With the exception of his overture *Columbus*, produced by the publisher Schlesinger at the annual concert to which he invited the subscribers to the *Gazette Musicale*, no work by Wagner was performed in Paris during this visit. But *The Flying Dutchman* had been acquiring shape, and on Meyerbeer's advice it was offered to the lessee of the Opera, who showed a disposition to avail himself of the story, without employing Wagner to write the music for it. The dispute was settled by a payment of £20 for the use of the libretto, and Wagner at once set to work to complete his own opera.

In the meantime *Rienzi* had been accepted at the Opera at Dresden, and Wagner left Paris to superintend the rehearsal. The opera was produced on October 20th, 1842, Madame Schröder-Devrient taking the part of Adriano, and Tichatschek that of Rienzi. Reissiger conducted, there was a good band, and the whole company were well disposed towards the composer. The result was triumphant. Two other performances took place during the next ten days to crowded houses, and Wagner enjoyed all the delights of success, which was so complete that the managers were anxious to produce *The Flying Dutchman*. In later years Wagner came to look on *Rienzi* as unworthy of him. No doubt it conforms too completely to the style of the French grand opera, as indeed was the aim of the composer when writing it. In *The Flying Dutchman* he gave freer play to his original genius, and strove to break loose from the ordinary operatic trammels. The opera was produced at Dresden on January 2nd, 1843, with Madame Schröder-Devrient as Senta. It was in advance of the musical public of the day, and its reception was doubtful, the audience being partly impressed and partly failing to understand it

A vacancy having arisen, Wagner was appointed to the post of music director with the salary of 1200 thalers, but was soon promoted to that of Capellmeister with 1500 thalers per annum. In that capacity he conducted a large number of the principal operas, and at the subscription concerts among other works, the symphonies of Beethoven, including the Choral, and his reading of these works attracted great attention. In 1844, mainly at his instance, the body of Weber, his predecessor at Dresden, was removed from London and reinterred in that city.

Even before he left Paris the story of Tannhäuser had attracted his notice, and he had been much struck with its suitability for operatic treatment. He traced the legend back to its earliest form, and on this he based his libretto. The opera was completed in 1844, and the first performance was given at Dresden October 19th, 1845. It had at first but a modified success. Even the singers were puzzled by it; Madame Schröder-Devrient pronounced parts of it "Such eccentric stuff, it is hardly possible to sing it." The opera was a work of genius, but the public were not educated up to it, although the march, and Wolfram's song, "*O du mein holder Abend-Stern,*" could not fail to delight even the groundlings. The opera, however, soon made its way to the principal theatres in Germany. Wagner was again suffering from pecuniary troubles, mainly brought on by the expense incurred in printing the scores of his operas, which were not sold with the rapidity he had anticipated. He was unfortunately led to mix himself up with politics, mainly, his friends assert, with the hope of advancing the cause of music! In May 1849 the Court of Saxony had to seek safety in flight, and Prussian troops were sent to quell the riots in the streets of Dresden. He learnt that a warrant had been issued for his arrest, and succeeded in reaching Weimar in safety. Further news reached him that even there he was not safe, and with the assistance of Liszt he was enabled to make his way to Paris. In this he was more fortunate than his friend and colleague Roeckel, who was arrested and remained in prison for no less than fourteen years. His second visit to Paris was a short one; at the end of a month he moved to Zurich, where he was joined by his wife and by several friends who were victims of the same misfortune as himself. The earlier years of his residence there were much occupied with literary work, contributing, among other things, his *Das Judenthum in der Musik* anonymously to the *Neue Zeitschrift für Musik*, to the editorship of which Brendel had succeeded on the resignation of Schumann. The excitement caused by this attack on the influence of the Jews in music was so great that eleven professors at the Leipzig Conservatoire, where Brendel was lecturer on musical history, called on him to resign his post or to give up the name of the writer. He also made a separate and bitter attack on Meyerbeer in his *Oper und Drama*, in spite of the assistance Meyerbeer had tried to render him in past years.

On Wagner's first visit to Paris he had made the acquaintance of Liszt. Wagner was in the depths of despair at his failure to obtain a hearing,—Liszt was then, as ever, the spoiled child of society. Wagner therefore looked on him with suspicion, and the acquaintance did not, at that time, proceed further. Wagner's feelings were reported to Liszt, who was surprised to find himself so misjudged. By his initiative the misconception was at last removed, and when Wagner passed through Weimar he found Liszt engaged in rehearsing *Tannhäuser*, and, as he says, "was astonished to find my second self in his achievement. What I had felt in inventing this music, he felt in performing it; what I wanted to express in writing it down, he proclaimed in making it sound. Strange to say, through the love of this rarest friend, I gained, at the moment of becoming homeless, the real home for my art." With the encouragement of Liszt, the finishing touches were given to *Lohengrin*, on which he had been for some time occupied. It was produced at Weimar under Liszt's direction on August 28th, 1850, before an audience comprising most of the eminent musicians in Europe, whom Liszt had invited to be present. As with *Tannhäuser*, the work was received with mixed feelings. It was too far removed from ordinary standards to be accepted at once. The correspondence of Wagner and Liszt has lately been brought out in Germany, and a translation of it, by the late Dr. Hueffer, by the publishers of this volume. It is of great interest for this period of Wagner's history, and gives an excellent insight into the generosity of Liszt's character.

Wagner found occupation at Zurich, among other things superintending a production of *Tannhäuser*. But he was mainly engaged with his great work *Der Ring der Nibelungen*, consisting of four operas to be played on successive days, *Das Rheingold*, *Die Walküre*, *Siegfried* and *Götterdämmerung*, the composition of which went on apace. This occupation was interrupted by an invitation to visit London as conductor of the Philharmonic Concerts, which he accepted, conducting during the season of 1855, but the engagement was not repeated.

It soon became evident that a work on the vast scale of the *Nibelungen* was unlikely to come to performance, and he had, while at work on it, become impressed with the legends of Tristan and Isolde, and of Parsifal. With a view, therefore, of being provided with something more available, he set to work on *Tristan*. Part of this was written at Venice, whither he had removed with the consent of the Austrian Government. He had long been trying to obtain permission to return to Dresden without success, although his efforts were supported by the Grand Dukes of Weimar and Baden. It was not till 1862 that the desired permission was granted him.

In 1859 he visited Paris again, with the hope of either producing *Tristan*, or, at least, *Tannhäuser* or *Lohengrin*. He there found an unexpected friend in Princess Metternich, at whose instance the Emperor ordered the mounting of *Tannhäuser*. This was done on a scale of extraordinary magnificence. No expense nor trouble was spared. Wagner was allowed to choose his own singers, and one hundred and sixty-four rehearsals actually took place! The total cost of the production approached £8,000! But a cabal was formed to prevent the success of the work, organised by the Paris Jockey Club, mainly for the reason that there was no ballet, and after three performances the opera was withdrawn.

The treatment he had received in Paris created a

strong reaction in his favour in Germany. His operas became popular, but the pecuniary returns were insufficient to afford him a living. At last he succeeded in getting *Tristan* accepted at Vienna, but after fifty-seven rehearsals it was abandoned owing to the incompetence of the tenor. During this visit he heard *Lohengrin* for the first time.

With a view of retrieving his position, he organised a series of concerts. They were but moderately successful, and broken down in health and spirits he determined to retire to Switzerland. He had published the poem of the *Ring der Nibelungen*, stating that he could hardly expect to complete the music, and that he had abandoned all hope of seeing it performed. This fell into the hands of the young King Ludwig II. of Bavaria. He sent a private secretary to try to find Wagner, and to bid him come to Munich and finish his work. After much trouble the secretary found him in Stuttgart. Wagner readily accepted the invitation. The King allowed him a yearly pension of £100 and a small house as a residence. The King's enthusiasm—we had almost said infatuation—for the composer rapidly increased, to such an extent that a strong opposition grew up against him, and he found it impossible to continue to reside in Munich. He was formally engaged to complete the *Nibelungen*; his pension was raised; and in 1865 *Tristan* was produced under the direction of Hans von Bülow. At the end of that year he removed to Triebschen, near Lucerne, where he completed his comic opera *Die Meistersinger*, which was performed at Munich in June 1868.

In 1866 his wife died, and in 1870 he married Cosima von Bülow, Liszt's daughter. It had long been the desire of the composer to build a theatre specially adapted for the production of his works. It was the King's wish to fix it at Munich, but it was thought advisable to abandon this intention, and Bayreuth was fixed on as the Mecca of the Wagnerian faith. Wagnerism had become a cult. Societies were founded throughout Germany to collect funds for the purpose, with branches in all the principal cities of Europe—and even in Cairo and New York. Concerts were given in support of the cause, and the theatre was completed in 1876. One of the principal innovations was the entire concealment of the orchestra and conductor. The house before the curtain was constructed to hold fifteen hundred people, all facing the stage, and each row so raised that every one had an uninterrupted view. There were no side boxes. One hundred of the seats were appropriated to those who had subscribed to the building; the rest were to be distributed gratis to those thought worthy of being present. In August of 1876 the *Ring der Nibelungen* was performed three times, each performance occupying four days. The result was artistically most satisfactory; pecuniarily there was a deficit of £7500, in spite of the sacrifices made by the artistes engaged. For this sum Wagner was personally liable. With a view of helping to clear off this debt, it was thought that a series of concerts in London, with "the Master" as conductor, would be well received. They were given on a large scale in the Albert Hall, but the result was insignificant in proportion to the trouble incurred.

His last opera, *Parsifal*, was begun in 1878, when Wagner was in his sixty-fifth year. It was completed in 1882, and sixteen performances were given under his superintendence. In the winter of 1882 he had taken up his residence in Venice, but his health was giving way; and on February 13th, 1883, he died. His body was taken to Bayreuth, and interred in a vault which he had already prepared in the garden of his house there.

All our readers know how great has been the controversy which has gathered round the name of Wagner. In the first place, he appears before us as a reformer. In his hands the opera is no longer a succession of separate airs, duets, and finales, strung together by a thread of recitative. The music arises out of the dramatic situation, and most of the cherished forms are destroyed. The aria, at least as a vehicle of display, disappears. Assuredly the singer must be well qualified, both physically and vocally, to render the music at all; but it is rather by dramatic power than by the art of the vocalist that success will be attained. In this Wagner appears as a nineteenth-century follower of the principles enunciated by Gluck in his famous dedication of *Alcestis*. But he is very careful to point out that his operas were composed on no theories previously laid down, and that the form they have assumed is in all cases the natural outcome of his feeling of the dramatic situation. It is often asserted that he thought slightingly of melody; and his characterising of Mozart as "the greatest of absolute musicians" is often quoted against him, as though he were speaking disparagingly of that great composer. Nothing can be more untrue or more unfair. As a matter of fact, his own operas overflow with a wealth of melody, only it is not of a kind that can be divorced from its surroundings. The ordinary operatic air can be performed on the platform, and lose but little in the process.

In this he was no doubt an innovator; but one of his most prominent characteristics is the use he makes of the *Leit-motif*, or *leading theme*; that is, a musical phrase appropriated to each character, and even to particular shades of feeling, for we have the *Love-motive*, the *Fear-motive*, and many others. The skill he shows in combining these is almost as wonderful as that of the construction of a fugue of Bach. It need hardly be said that the influence of Wagner has been enormous—it may almost be considered paramount; and it would be difficult to mention a modern composition which is not impressed with it.

The discussion of the value of these principles has occupied the musical world ever since their enunciation. It has been carried on with much bitterness on both sides. Wagner himself was a skilful controversialist; doubt had no place in his mind. A long period of struggle with the world had helped to accentuate the cynicism of his character, and he never hesitated to express his opinion of those who differed from him. The literature of the subject has assumed enormous dimensions; the *Querelle des Bouffons* sinks into insignificance by the side of it.

An enthusiastic bibliographer, Herr Oesterlein, has compiled a catalogue of a Wagner library, of which four large

Fig. 116.—Johannes Brahms.

octavo volumes have already been published. But it is still increasing, and hardly a week passes without some addition. Among the most amusing of the works called forth is Tappert's Lexicon of the "uncourteous" things which have been written about the master. It would not be difficult to compile a *Wörterbuch der Unhöflichkeit* on the other side of the question, which would be at least as racy.

In April 1897 the world was called on to mourn the death of Johannes Brahms (fig. 116), a musician assuredly a head and shoulders above his fellows. Born in Strasburg on May 7th, 1833, the son of a musician, he received a careful education, and first appeared before the public as a pianist. In this capacity he accompanied the violinist Remenyi on a concert tour, and on one occasion, finding that the pianoforte was a semitone flat, he actually transposed Beethoven's Kreutzer sonata from A to B flat! By good fortune Joachim chanced to be in the audience, with the result that he gave the young artist an introduction to Schumann. The latter found him to be a musician after his own heart, and received him with enthusiasm, writing of him in the *Neue Zeitschrift*, " He has come, this chosen youth, over whose cradle the Graces and Heroes seem to have kept watch. . . . His mere outward appearance assures us that he is one of the elect. Seated at the piano he disclosed wondrous regions." It is not surprising that these ecstatic utterances were received with some hesitation, but time has certainly justified them, and by many it is claimed that on him the mantle of Beethoven has fallen.

The career of a virtuoso was soon dropped, and indeed it seems that his *technique* was not sufficient to place him in the first rank of performers, and public appearances were distasteful to him. After some stay in his native city and in Switzerland, he finally settled in Vienna—that home of musicians—in 1862, from that time devoting himself almost exclusively to composition. With the

Fig. 117.—Robert Franz.

exception of opera, he attempted every form of work, composing for the orchestra four symphonies, overtures, and concertos for the pianoforte and other solo instruments. In the department of chamber music will be found three string quartets, two quintets, one of which is for clarionet, two sextets which have become popular, while in conjunction with the pianoforte are five trios (in one of which the horn replaces the violoncello, and in another the clarionet the violin), three quartets and a quintet. In vocal music his two sets of *Liebeslieder Walzer* and some of his songs, which are characterised by deep expression, are the works by which he has become best known—at least in this country. In sacred music his *Deutsches Requiem*, which at once secured his fame, and the *Schicksalslied* are both works of the most elevated character. The catalogue of his works comprises 119 numbers, in addition to a few without opera numbers. To criticise these in detail is impossible here, but it may be said that Brahms is emphatically a composer for musicians. No attempt is made to tickle the popular ear. One of his characteristics is a fondness for strange rhythms and for displacing the accent. It must be admitted that at times he shows a disregard—one is tempted to say a contempt —for actual beauty.

The reputation of the late Robert Franz (1815-1892) (fig. 117), which has been of somewhat slow growth, is based on his songs, which are worthy to be placed on a level with those of Schubert and Schumann. Of these he has published over 250. Unfortunately he was early in life attacked by deafness and a nervous complaint which for a long time rendered all work impossible. In this trouble Liszt, Joachim, and other friends came to the rescue, and by means of concerts raised a sum sufficient to place him above pecuniary difficulty. His deafness is said to have been aggravated by the screech of a locomotive engine.

MUSIC IN GERMANY AND NORTHERN EUROPE. 393

In later life he came somewhat prominently before the public as a writer of additional accompaniments to several of the works of Handel, Bach, and others of the earlier

Fig. 118.—A. Dvořák.

writers. They are written with reverence for the original composers, but of course have excited the hostility of those who look on all such attempts as sacrilege.

Of the living musicians of Germany the foremost place

is probably occupied by Antonin Dvořák (fig. 118), who was born in 1841 at Mühlhausen, in Bohemia. His career is an example of triumph over uncongenial conditions. His father was the butcher and innkeeper of the place and it was his intention to bring up his son to his own calling. He was at last persuaded to allow his son to go to Prague and study music. After a long period of hardship as violin-player in a theatrical band, and as organist, he succeeded at last, in his thirty-second year, in obtaining a public performance of one of his compositions—a cantata —*Die Erben des weissen Berges*. The production of several other works followed, including his opera *Der König und der Köhler*. His fame now reached Vienna, with the result that he received a pension of £50 a year from the Kultus-ministerium, the amount of which was subsequently increased. This circumstance procured him the friendship of Brahms, and his position became assured, enabling him to produce a constant succession of new works, which served to increase his reputation. Among these the *Stabat Mater*, brought out in 1881, one of the most beautiful choral works of modern times, at once ensured his popularity in this country. Its success procured him the commission to write a cantata, *The Spectre's Bride*, also a masterpiece, for the Birmingham Festival of 1885, and for the Leeds Festival of the following year an oratorio *St. Ludmilla*, being in both cases invited to conduct the work. These were followed by a setting of the *Te Deum*; but his labours have been by no means confined to choral composition, as we have several symphonies and much chamber music from his pen, including a pianoforte quintet of exceptional beauty.

A few years back Dvořák was induced to accept the direction of the Musical Society, New York, but the post did not prove congenial and he returned to Europe after a short absence.

A leading characteristic of Dvořák's music is its employment of national forms of melody, especially the *dumka*, a sort of dirge, which he introduces in the slow movements of many of his works, as well as the *furiant*, a most exciting form of scherzo. While brimful of originality, he appears to be very susceptible to external influences. The *Stabat Mater* has very strong traces of Italian feeling, while his visit to America has borne fruit in the shape of a symphony and a quartet, both based on plantation melodies, somewhat to the sacrifice of the dignity looked for in serious compositions.

Max Bruch, born at Cologne in 1838, and a pupil of Ferdinand Hiller, is well known in England, having lived in this country for some time as conductor of the Liverpool Philharmonic Society. His most important work is the cantata, *Odysseus*, but the best known is probably his Violin Concerto in G minor, written for Joachim, which is among the most beautiful works we possess of that kind. A second concerto was written for Sarasate, somewhat more brilliant in style. His arrangement of the pathetic Hebrew wail, *Kol Nidrei*, is well known.

The reputation of Karl Goldmark (born 1830), rests mainly on his opera, *Die Königen von Saba*, a work the production of which is rendered impossible in this country by its biblical libretto. Goldmark, who is avowedly Wagnerian, has produced another opera, *Merlin*. He has also written some successful orchestral and chamber music. Josef Rheinberger (born 1839), is known in England almost exclusively by a pianoforte quintet in E flat, but he is in fact a voluminous composer, his published works running to 175. For a long time an organist of distinction in Munich, much of his writing was for that instrument, including seventeen organ sonatas. He has also produced several masses, and other service music. Karl Reinecke (born 1827), who in 1860 succeeded Julius Rietz as conductor of the Gewandhaus Concerts, is deservedly respected as a fine virtuoso on the pianoforte, devoid of all affectation, and as a musician, thoroughly master of every detail of his art; as a composer he has been most prolific, and most of his music is excellent, but apparently just misses that touch of genius which ensures abiding fame. Hermann Goetz, who died at the age of thirty-six (1840-76), lived long enough to witness the success of his opera, *Der Widerspänstigen Zähmung* (The Taming of the Shrew), the one work by which he is remembered; while in the last few years we have all been delighted by the charming and delicate fairy opera, *Hansel und Gretel*, of Humperdinck (fig. 119), which makes us anxious to hear his subsequent work, *The Royal Children*, described as equally delightful.

It would be easy to add to the above list of German musicians. The country swarms with well instructed artists, most of them aspiring to become composers.

MUSIC IN GERMANY AND NORTHERN EUROPE. 397

They produce works in large quantity absolutely correct, but absolutely uninteresting. It is a German who has applied to these compositions the term "*Kapellmeister Musick.*"

Fig. 119—Engelbert Humperdinck.

A few words must be said on the music of the northern nations. The main interest of the History of Music in Russia centres in that of the Church. It is well known that the Eastern ritual allows of the employment of no instrumental music whatever. In its original purity the service was entirely in unison, differing in no essential particular from that of the Western Church. It is said to owe its introduction to St. John Damascene, but we are unable to give authority for the tradition. The absence of the organ may possibly have led to the introduction of harmony, which was introduced for the first time in the reign of the Czar Theodore Alexeisvitch (1676-1682.) We have previously mentioned that Galuppi was induced to visit Russia on the invitation of the Empress Catherine II. While there, he found an apt pupil in Dimitri Bortniansky (1752-1828) (his actual name was Bartnansky), who followed him to Venice on the termination of Galuppi's visit to the northern capital. To him the Russian Church is indebted for the arrangement of the beautiful music which forms so prominent a feature of the religious services in that country; and this has gained for him the title of the Russian Palestrina. Those who have visited St. Petersburg must be acquainted with the beautiful manner in which this entirely unaccompanied music is sung, the marvellous training of the choir, and the magnificent quality of the bass voices, which are equalled in no other country. In the ancient service-books neums were employed. The origin and development of this music is a subject of great interest, which awaits elucidation.

While showing the influence of their national melody and rhythm, manifested by an underlying melancholy and by a fondness for $\frac{5}{4}$ time, nearly all the northern composers are German by training. Among the most popular in his own country has been the Russian Glinka (1803-1857), whose most successful opera *La vie pour le Czar*, has, from the patriotic nature of the libretto, been accepted as an embodiment of national feeling to be performed on

Fig. 120.—Anton Rubinstein.

every display of popular loyalty. The work, although pleasing, has not travelled beyond its home. His second opera, *Roulstan and Ludmila*, is almost unknown, although said to be more musically interesting.

The foremost Russian musician has undoubtedly been Anton Rubinstein (1830-1895) (fig. 120), who probably owes his fame rather to his almost unrivalled power as a pianist than to his compositions, which embrace every department of music. His gift of melody is striking, and this makes his songs and smaller compositions most effective; but in his more extended works his want of skill in development is disappointing. His works comprise six symphonies, at least a dozen operas, among which may be mentioned *Paradise Lost, The Tower of Babel, The Demon, Feramors, The Maccabees, Nero, Moses*, several of which it will be seen are on sacred subjects, which fact in itself militates against their performance; and indeed none of them have achieved popularity, and now that the composer is no more may be considered as virtually shelved. In addition to these larger works he published much chamber music in nearly every known form, as well as numerous works for his own instrument. In the later years of his life he abandoned public performance, refusing immense sums for a series of concerts in America, and devoted himself with great energy to the development of the Conservatoire of Music in St. Petersburg.

The career of Peter Tschaikowsky (born 1840) (fig. 121) was brought to an end by his death in 1893. His works have been gaining in appreciation, and his Pathetic Symphony, which is instinct with the melancholy which underlies Russian national music, has become actually popular. His opera, *Eugen Onegin*, has not met with success. César Cui, a professor of fortification, and Alesander

MUSIC IN GERMANY AND NORTHERN EUROPE. 401

Borodin (1834-1887), a chemist of some eminence, both devoted themselves with enthusiasm to music; but their compositions are unknown outside their own country. Rimsky-Korzakow, at one time an officer of marines (it

Fig. 121.—P. Tschaikowsky.

is strange how many Russian composers have taken up music as a second career), became professor of composition at the St. Petersburg Conservatoire. He is also a voluminous composer, and has done good service by

26

a collection of a hundred national melodies. To the violinist Alexis Lvoff (1799-1870) Russia is indebted for a National Hymn of great vigour and beauty.

Of the other northern countries, Denmark claims Niels W. Gade (1817-1890). Early in life his works created an interest both in Mendelssohn and Schumann. His best known compositions are the cantatas, *Comala*, *The Erl King's Daughter*, and *The Crusaders*. His works have great delicacy and refinement, as well as skill in orchestration, with a strong national feeling. He has also written seven symphonies, some chamber music and solos for the pianoforte, as well as vocal music. It must perhaps be admitted that his early reputation has scarcely been maintained; possibly too much was claimed for him by Schumann.

The hopes of Norway centre in Edvard Grieg (born 1843), who is both a composer and pianist. His work is strongly Scandinavian in character. Many of his songs have become popular; his larger works comprise a concerto for pianoforte, an orchestral suite, *Aus Holberg's Zeit*, and the somewhat noisy incidental music to *Peer Gynt*, which is a great favourite with popular audiences.

BIBLIOGRAPHY.

(*Vogler, G. J.*) Article by Rev. J. H. Mee in Grove's Dictionary of Music and Musicians.

Weber, Max Maria von. Carl Maria von Weber. Ein Lebensbild. Leipzig, 1864-1866. 3 vols., 8vo. (Translated by J. Palgrave Simpson. London, 1865. 2 vols., 8vo.)

Benedict, Sir Julius. Weber. (The Great Musicians.) London, 1881. 8vo.

Pougin, Arthur. Meyerbeer, Notes biographiques. Paris, 1864. 12mo.

Blaze de Bury, Henri. Meyerbeer et son temps. Paris, 1865. 8vo.

Spohr, Louis. Selbstbiographie. Cassel, 1860-1861. 2 vols., 8vo. (An English translation. London, 1865. 8vo.)

Hensel, S. Die Familie Mendelssohn, 1729-1847. Eighth Edition. Berlin, 1897. 2 vols., 8vo. (An English translation by C. Klingemann. London, 1881. 2 vols., 8vo.)

Reissmann, August. Felix Mendelssohn-Bartholdy. Sein Leben und seine Werke. Berlin, 1867. 8vo.

Mendelssohn-Bartholdy, F. Reisebriefe aus den Jahren, 1830 bis 1832. Leipzig, 1861. 8vo. Briefe aus den Jahren, 1833 bis 1847. Leipzig, 1863. 8vo. (Both series translated by Lady Wallace. London, 1862-1863. 2 vols., 8vo.)

Schumann, Robert. Gesammelte Schriften über Musik und Musiker. Leipzig, 1854. 4 vols., 8vo. Second Edition, 1871. 2 vols., 8vo.

Wasielewski, J. W. von. Robert Schumann. Eine Biographie. Dresden, 1858. 8vo. Third Edition. Bonn, 1880. 8vo.

Reissmann, August. Robert Schumann, sein Leben und seine Werke. Berlin, 1865.

Ramann, Lina. Franz Liszt, als Künstler und Mensch. Leipzig, 1881. 2 vols., 8vo. (Translated by Miss E. Cowdery. London, 1882. 2 vols., 8vo.)

Wagner, Richard. Gesammelte Schriften und Dichtungen. Leipzig, 1871-1885. 10 vols., 8vo.

Glasenapp, C. F., and Stein, H. von. Wagner Lexicon. Stuttgart, 1883. 8vo.

Glasenapp, C. F. Richard Wagner's Leben und Werken. Leipzig, 1896. 2 vols., 8vo. Third Edition.

Hueffer, Franz. Richard Wagner and the Music of the Future. History and Æsthetics. London, 1874. 8vo.

Hueffer, Franz. Wagner. (The Great Musicians.) London, 1881. 8vo.

Jullien, Adolphe. Richard Wagner, sa vie et ses œuvres. Ouvrage orné de quatorze lithographies originales par M. Fantin-Latour, de quinze portraits de Richard Wagner, de quatre eaux-fortes et de 120 gravures, scènes d'opéras, caricatures, vues de théâtres, autographes, etc. Paris, 1886. 4to.

Briefwechsel zwischen Wagner und Liszt. Leipzig, 1887. 2 vols., 8vo. (Translated by F. Hueffer. London, 1888.)

Briefe an Theodor Uhlig, etc. Leipzig, 1888. 8vo. (Translated by J. S. Shedlock. London, 1890.)

Finck, H. T. Wagner and his Works. London, 1893. 2 vols., 8vo.

CHAPTER XVI.

MUSIC IN FRANCE AND ENGLAND DURING THE PRESENT CENTURY.

Operatic Composers in France — Dalayrac — Méhul — Lesueur — Berton — Isouard ("Nicolo") — Boieldieu — *Le Calife de Bagdad* — Visits St. Petersburg—*La Dame Blanche*—Auber—His *Masaniello*—His Death— Hérold's *Zampa*—Meyerbeer's French Career—*Robert le Diable*—*Les Huguenots* — *Le Prophète* — His Later Operas — Halévy — *La Juive*— Adolphe Adam—Offenbach—Hector Berlioz, his Career and Works— Onslow—Félicien David—Bizet— Ambroise Thomas — Gounod — Saint Saëns—Massenet—César Franck—Lalo—Reyer—Chopin—His Arrival in Paris—His Works—The French School of the Violin—Choron—La Fage—F. J. Fétis—Music in England—Clementi—J. B. Cramer—Field —Sir H. R. Bishop—Balfe—Vincent Wallace—Macfarren—Benedict— Costa—Sterndale Bennett—English Organists—H. H. Pierson — A. Goring Thomas—Sir Arthur Sullivan—Sir A. Mackenzie—C. Hubert H. Parry—C. Villiers Stanford—Sir John Stainer—F. H. Cowen—The Philharmonic and Sacred Harmonic Societies—The Monday Popular Concerts—Cheap Music—Educational Institutions.

MUSICAL activity in France continued to occupy itself mainly in writing for the stage. To the composers mentioned in Chapter XII. must be added the name of Dalayrac, a facile and agreeable writer, who caught the ear of the public by the elegant, if somewhat trivial airs and romances, so plentifully scattered among his fifty operas, the very names of which would now call up no recollections. Méhul was a composer of high aspirations. He was the son of a cook, and owed his success rather to his own genius than to the modest education his father was able to afford him. His early instruction in music was from a blind organist, and at ten years of age he was sufficiently advanced to take the organ at the church of the Récollets in his native place, Givet in the Ardennes. By the kindness of the abbot of a neighbouring monastery the boy was given some better instruction, by which he profited so well that he was appointed organist. He had already become a novice, and was qualifying for a monk, which was the highest ambition of his parents. But this was not to be. The colonel of a regiment quartered in the neighbourhood, who was a good musician, having heard him play, foresaw his future excellence, and persuaded the young man to accompany him to Paris. There he was present at the first performance of Gluck's *Iphigénie en Tauride*, and was so much impressed by it that he sought the acquaintance of the great master, who received him with kindness and superintended his further studies. His opera *Alonzo et Cora* was accepted by the Opéra, but six years of weary waiting passed before it was produced. Much annoyed at this delay, he offered *Euphrosine et Coradin* to the Opéra Comique. It was brought out in 1790, and at once made him famous. It is needless to say that no more time was lost in mounting *Alonzo*. It had but moderate success; but his next venture, *Stratonice*, confirmed his position. In 1797 appeared his *Chasse du Jeune Henri*, the overture to which had extraordinary success. His masterpiece, *Joseph*, was produced in 1807. The touching romance from it, "*A peine au sortir de l'Enfance,"* is known to every one. In addition to his numerous operas, many of which are distinguished by great dramatic power, he wrote several symphonies, which will not hold a place by the side of those of Haydn and Mozart, and have thus been forgotten. He was also the composer of much patriotic music, among which was the *Chant du Départ*. Personally Méhul was a man of much disinterestedness of character. Napoleon proposed to appoint him his *maître de chapelle*, but when he spoke to him on the subject, Méhul suggested that he should share the post with Cherubini. The Emperor replied, "Don't speak to me of that man," and gave the place to Lesueur, a musician who, having been *maître de chapelle* of several cathedrals in France, had acquired a great reputation by his sacred music, although he misjudged the principles of church music so completely as to aim at making it dramatic and descriptive. He also wrote several operas, among which are *Les Bardes* and *La Mort d'Adam*. He was a man who passed his life in an atmosphere of controversy, carried on with great bitterness. His score of *La Mort d'Adam* is a most remarkable production, for every page bristles with notes, partly in French, partly in Italian, advocating his peculiar views.

Marie Montan Berton, whose father Pierre Montan Berton had also acquired some reputation both as a composer and as a conductor, is best remembered by his *chef-d'œuvre, Montano et Stephanie*, although his operas amount to over fifty. For a long time he was Professor of Harmony at the Conservatoire, and was also conductor at the Italian Opera. Nicolo Isouard, always known in France as "Nicolo," was born of French parents in Malta. He was very popular as a composer of operas, of which *Cendrillon* became a favourite. But the reputation of neither of these two composers extended beyond France. The name of Boieldieu is more widely known, and his opera *La Dame Blanche* still keeps the stage, not only in his native country, but also in Germany. Boieldieu was born in 1775 at Rouen, where his father was secretary to the Archbishop. The boy obtained his musical education from the organist of the cathedral, and produced a couple of operas with success in his native city. A local reputation, of course, failed to satisfy him, and he made his way to Paris, where he became acquainted with Cherubini and other musicians. His opera *La Famille Suisse* was produced at the Théâtre Feydeau, and meeting with success, was followed by several others, culminating in *Le Calife de Bagdad*. He was a man of great modesty, and always bent on self-improvement in his art. It is said that after a performance of *Le Calife*, in which the composer had been overwhelmed with applause, Cherubini met him in the theatre and addressed him with the words, "Malheureux! are you not ashamed of such undeserved success?" Boieldieu replied with a request for further instruction. There was an interval of three years before he produced his next opera, *Ma Tante Aurore*.

In 1803, for reasons which have not been explained, Boieldieu left Paris and took up his residence in St. Petersburg, where he remained eight years, filling the post of conductor at the opera, but writing nothing of sufficient importance to add to his reputation. In 1811 he returned. Some of his former operas were revived, and he produced his *Jean de Paris*, which showed a great advance on his previous efforts. To this succeeded several operas now forgotten, with the exception of *Le petit Chaperon rouge*. It almost seemed as though his powers had failed him, when in 1825 *La Dame Blanche* burst upon the musical world. Its success was unprecedented. It was based on what is little better than a "jumble" of Scott's *Monastery* and *Guy Mannering*, but the music is delightful, full of piquancy, and of that feeling for rhythm which is so characteristic of French music. Strange to say, the very popular overture was in reality written by his pupil Adolphe Adam. It is sad to have to report that the latter years of the composer's life were clouded both by illness and by straitened circumstances, caused by the bankruptcy of the Opéra Comique and by the expulsion of Charles X., who had allowed him a pension, which after a time was restored to him by Louis Philippe.

Even better known to the present generation is Auber (fig. 122), whose long career enabled him to add a large number of sparkling and delightful works to the *répertoire* of the French stage. He was born at Caen in 1782, and died in Paris during the horrors of the Commune in the year 1871. Like so many musicians, he was intended for a commercial career, in the pursuit of which he passed some months in London. For a time he practised music as an amateur, and his first opera was written for private performance. Among the audience Cherubini chanced to be; he at once detected promise in the work and offered to superintend the young composer's studies. One or two operas were unsuccessful, but at last he caught the public ear with *La Bergère Châtelaine*. He

Fig. 122.—D. F. E. Auber.

now became allied with Scribe, the most skilful librettist of modern times, who provided him with a succession of libretti, to which Auber composed the most graceful and piquant music conceivable, nearly all of which met with unbounded success. Among his most popular operas are *Leicester, Le Maçon, Fra Diavolo, Gustave III., Lestocq, Le Cheval de Bronze, Le Domino Noir, Les Diamants de la Couronne, La Part du Diable, L'Enfant prodigue, Manon Lescaut, La Fiancée,* and *Le Premier Jour de Bonheur.* In this list, which contains a few only of Auber's works, we have not mentioned his masterpiece *La Muette de Portici*, better known in England as *Masaniello*, which differs entirely from his other works, exhibiting a much larger style and greater dramatic power, together with more boldness of orchestration, which give it a foremost place in the French "Grand Opera." A performance of this work was the immediate cause of the rising in Brussels in 1830, which resulted in the formation of the kingdom of Belgium, a circumstance which caused it to be looked on with disfavour by several of the Governments of Europe.

It remains only to add that he became principal of the Conservatoire, and received many tokens of distinction. He was a man of quiet and kindly habits, a true Parisian, with a reputation for wit. It is said that he never could bring himself to be present at a performance of his own works, asserting that if he broke through this rule he should never venture to write another note of music. His death was accelerated by the terrors of the Commune. His remains were concealed for a time in the crypt of the Church of La Trinité, and were interred at Montmartre in July 1871.

Hérold, the son of a musician, received his education in the Paris Conservatoire, and carried off the "grand prix de Rome." At first it seemed as if he were to become a writer of instrumental music, for he achieved some success both by his quartets and also by his symphonies. But the attractions of the stage prevailed. Fortunately Boieldieu invited him to write the latter part of *Charles de France*, which served as an introduction to the public, and caused him to be entrusted with a succession of libretti, which he set to music with varying success. Any work he was ready to accept. For seven years he was accompanist at the Opéra Italien; he then became chorus-master at the Académie; he wrote ballets, and turned out an immense quantity of pianoforte music for the publishers, but through all this hack-work always aimed at success in opera. It came at last. *Zampa* was brought out in May 1831, and at once secured his reputation, having kept its place in the *répertoire* ever since, in spite of an indifferent libretto. The work, which has been seldom performed in England, abounds in beautiful melody, and the music rises to the level of the dramatic situations. The brilliant overture, founded on subjects used in the course of the opera, is known everywhere. His reputation was maintained, or even enhanced, by his *Pré aux Clercs*, brought out in 1832; but he had been long suffering from consumption, and was carried off at the early age of forty-two, a month only after the production of the opera which the French consider his *chef-d'œuvre*.

During the period of which we have been writing, the "Grand Opera," as it is called, had been represented by the works of Cherubini and Spontini, as we have already pointed out in a previous chapter. We have also seen the marvellous way in which Rossini adapted himself to French tastes in his *Guillaume Tell*, produced in 1829. A change of style no less remarkable was manifested by Meyerbeer (fig. 123). Up to this time his success had been gained by operas written in the Italian manner. On November 21st, 1831, his *Robert le Diable* was brought out at the Académie; the libretto, by Scribe and Casimir Delavigne, offered opportunities for the exhibition of great dramatic effect, and Meyerbeer rose to the occasion. The opera was full of originality and power. He appears at once to have acquired, with even greater intensity, that strong feeling for marked rhythm which is so prominent a characteristic of the French school. The orchestration, sonorous, original and varied, always strengthens the dramatic situation. It is not therefore wonderful that this weird and powerful work at once took hold of the public taste. The composer followed up this success with another, equally brilliant and even more lasting, in *The Huguenots*, produced in 1836. It possessed all the merits of *Robert le Diable* in even a larger measure. Nothing can be more delightful than the variety and piquancy of the orchestration; and, adequately rendered, the finale of the fourth act is among the most dramatic in the whole range of operatic music. His third work, written for the Académie, *Le Prophète*, exhibits the same powers, but the plot is uniformly sombre and gloomy, for which reason, probably, it has not been so popular.

With that adaptability which was so remarkable a feature of his character, he now invaded the peculiar domain of the French composers in his opera brought out at the Opéra Comique, in 1854, *L'Etoile du Nord*, some numbers of which he transferred from his *Feldlager in*

Fig. 123.—Giacomo Meyerbeer.

Sch lesien, an opera written for Berlin ten years previously, the success of which had been greatly helped by the marvellous singing of Jenny Lind, whom he then introduced for the first time to a German audience. He had made her acquaintance in Paris, and charged himself with the success of her career. At the same theatre he also produced in 1859 *Le Pardon de Ploermel*, known in England as *Dinorah*, grounded on a Breton legend. It is still played, the well-known "Shadow Song" affording an excellent opportunity for distinction to the prima donna; but his style was not idyllic, and it cannot be reckoned among his successes.

As many years back as 1838 he had received the libretto of *L'Africaine* from Scribe. But Meyerbeer was peculiarly anxious and fidgety about every detail connected with his compositions, and suggested so many alterations in the book that Scribe lost patience and withdrew it. Meyerbeer afterwards took it up again, and worked at it for several years. It was at last completed (at least so far as an opera by Meyerbeer ever was completed till the final rehearsal had taken place), but his fastidiousness extended to the choice of a suitable cast, and death overtook him in April 1863, before he had satisfied himself. Two years later it was brought out at the Académie. The opera as the composer left it would have occupied six or seven hours, so that the pruning knife had to be vigorously employed. The performance was delayed for several months by the construction of the vessel on which part of the action takes place. The music is beautiful; much of it had been composed during the period which produced *The Huguenots* and *Le Prophète*. Among the most famous passages is the celebrated *morceau d'unisson*, the effect of which is electrical.

Of the same musically favoured race as Meyerbeer, Halévy, who was born in Paris in 1799, entered the Conservatoire at an early age, and in 1819 succeeded in carrying off the " prix de Rome." On his return he had long to wait before he obtained a hearing, but at last some of his works were produced and received with favour. It was not, however, till 1835 that he astonished the world with his opera *La Juive,* a work of the most intense dramatic interest, which at once made him famous. In the same year he produced *L'Eclair,* a lyric drama of an entirely different character, distinguished by the delicacy and grace of its music. Several other works, among which may be mentioned *Guido et Genevra, La Reine de Chypre,* and *Le Val d'Andorre,* followed in quick succession, but he never repeated the great success of *La Juive* and *L'Eclair.* His opera *La Tempesta* was written for Her Majesty's Theatre to the libretto originally intended for Mendelssohn, and created great excitement in 1850, both on account of the music and partly in consequence of the appearance in it of Madame Sontag on her return to the stage.

Adolphe Adam's greatest triumph has been *Le Postillon de Longjumeau,* the rollicking gaiety of which still keeps it on the stage. But he wrote other operas—for instance, *Le Chalet* and *Le Brasseur de Preston*—which were well received; and he also made considerable reputation by his ballets, for which his piquant and melodious style well qualified him. There is no doubt that the boisterous fun of some of Adam's operas paved the way for the reception of Jacques Offenbach, a native of Cologne, but Parisian by education. Having begun life as a violoncello player, he acquired great vogue during the days of the Second Empire by his *operas bouffes*, produced at the little theatre Les Bouffes Parisiens, of which he was the proprietor. He was possessed of ample cleverness, and certainly succeeded in being amusing. But his best-known works, such as *La Grande Duchesse de Gérolstein*, *L'Orphée aux Enfers*, and *La Belle Hélène*, depend more on their bustle and extravagance than on their musical merits, which is proved by the fact that when interpreted by actors having no pretensions as singers their success was in no way diminished.

We have only space just to mention the names of Niedermeyer (1803-1861), a native of Geneva settled in Paris, who was also a composer of sacred music; Reber (1807-1880) who, in addition to operas, produced chamber music, and was also Professor of Composition and Harmony at the Conservatoire, having in that capacity written an excellent work on Harmony; Clapisson (1808-1866), a prolific composer of operas, and Grisar (1808-1867), an elegant writer of operas and romances, somewhat wanting in backbone.

This was not the character of Hector Berlioz (fig. 124), whose defiant self-assertion has made him one of the most prominent musicians of modern times. He was born in 1803, near Grenoble, and was the son of a physician, who proposed to bring him up to follow his own profession. With this view he sent him to Paris to study medicine; but the dissecting-room was too much for him; and after a violent quarrel with his father he entered the

Conservatoire, earning a precarious living by singing in the chorus of a theatre. At the Conservatoire he was the despair of the professors, and Cherubini positively hated both him and his compositions. His overture *Les Francs Juges* and the *Symphonie fantastique* were both written while he was a pupil at the Conservatoire, and after several unsuccessful attempts he was at last somewhat grudgingly accorded the "prix de Rome." On his return he found it impossible to get his works performed; he therefore began the career of musical critic. For twenty years he furnished the musical article for the *Journal des Débats*, written in a style of great brilliancy, which earned him the position of the most capable critic of the day. He had the misfortune to fall violently in love with Miss Smithson, an Irish actress of great beauty, who made much sensation in Paris in the characters of Ophelia and Juliet. They were married, but the union was not happy, and she finally died in a madhouse. His compositions were brought to a hearing with great difficulty, and during his life were never popular even in France. It will thus be seen that the circumstances of his life offered but a small share of happiness.

His most important works consist of three operas, the first of which, *Benvenuto Cellini*, was produced at the Académie in 1831, but the public would not listen to it. In 1851 it was given at Covent Garden with the same results. *Les Troyens* was produced in 1863, in spite of much opposition, said to be organised, and had a run of twenty-one nights. His other opera, *Beatrice et Benedict*, was his one operatic success, but that was obtained in Baden, and not in his native country. His orchestral works are his most remarkable compositions. Among these are his symphonies *Episode de la Vie d'un*

Fig. 124.—Hector Berlioz.

Artiste, with its continuation *Lélio; ou, le Retour à la Vie*. In the former of these, one of the movements endeavours to depict the feelings of a man who dreams that he is being led to execution ; this is followed by a witches'

Sabbath. It will be seen, therefore, that he was an advocate of "programme music," to which he attempts to impart more meaning than it is able to convey, and it is only by consulting his programme that the listener is able to ascertain the intention of the composer. In the same style are his other symphonies, *Harold in Italy*, which has an obbligato part for the viola, and *Romeo and Juliet*, in which he employs solo voices and chorus. Berlioz was a master of orchestration, and these works contain many beautiful passages; but his writing frequently degenerates into a noisy vulgarity which it is difficult to qualify with the name of music. In addition to the works mentioned, he wrote an oratorio, *L'Enfance du Christ*, a comparatively sane work, and also a sort of cantata, *La Damnation de Faust*, in which he indulges in his peculiar style to the full extent. Much of Berlioz's time was occupied in getting up concerts for the performance of his own works, to which end he travelled through Germany and Russia. As a critic he was clearsighted, if somewhat bitter in expression, and his writings on music are of great interest. As we have said, his knowledge of the orchestra was remarkable; he had studied the qualities and peculiarities of every instrument, and this he embodied in his well-known and excellent treatise on orchestration.

During his life he was neglected, not to put it more strongly, in his native country. He died in 1869. At once, with that strange habit of mixing up their artistic tastes with their political feelings, the French public seized on his works as a counterpoise to those of the hated

Wagner, and no praise could be sufficiently strong for them.

George Onslow, born in France of English parentage on his father's side, was rich, and under no obligation to practise music as a profession. His operas were never successful, and are now forgotten, although the overture to *Le Colporteur* was long popular. He is best remembered in these days by his chamber music, of which his quintets, with contrabasso, are without doubt the best, some of them being works of much grace and beauty.

If the life of Félicien David should come to be narrated fully, it would prove a work of great interest. He was born in 1810, and at an early age showed the bent of his talent. He received his musical education at the Conservatoire. In 1831, having embraced the doctrines of St. Simon, he went to live in a kind of convent belonging to the society at Ménilmontant; near to Paris, and became the composer of the music used in their worship. The body having been dispersed by order of the Government, the leading supporters of the cause separated into groups, with the intention of still advocating the tenets of the order. David and his companions decided on visiting the East, which after many adventures they reached. At the end of three years he had returned, and was again in Paris, where he published a volume of Oriental melodies which he had collected in his travels. In addition to this he wrote and published many works of different kinds, but failed to get recognition. It was not till 1844 that he produced his so-called ode-symphony, *Le Désert*. It at once obtained marvellous success, for the work was of great originality, and remarkable for its local colour. This remains his masterpiece. He wrote another descriptive symphony, *Christophe*

Fig. 125.—Ambroise Thomas.

Colomb, which failed to please, although his operas, *La Perle du Brésil*, *Herculaneum*, and *Lalla Roukh* had a certain amount of success.

We must not omit to mention Georges Bizet, whose

opera *Carmen* has become so great a favourite. He was a pupil of Halévy, and married his daughter. Unfortunately he had but a short enjoyment of the sweets of success, for he died three months only after the production of this opera.

Born a year after Félicien David, Ambroise Thomas (fig. 125) passed the greater part of his life in just missing absolute success with a series of operas the very names of which call up no memories, with the exception of *La Caïd* (1849) and *Le Songe d'une Nuit d'Été* (1850). Fame at last came to him with *Mignon* in 1866, a work of much grace and beauty, although neither librettist nor composer are the ideal interpreters of Goethe's original. This success was followed up by *Hamlet* in 1868. The esteem in which he was held, both for his musical acquirements and for his personal character, at once pointed him out for the successor of Auber as Principal of the Conservatoire, where his rule was one of marked success. Doubtless the claims of his official position left him but little time for composition. He died in 1896.

The best known name of modern musicians is that of Charles Gounod (fig. 126) (1818-1893). The son of a painter who died in his early childhood, his education was carefully watched over by his mother, herself an excellent musician, who had the wisdom not to force the boy's musical abilities at the expense of the other branches of a liberal education. Having graduated as *Bachelier-ès-lettres*, he entered the Conservatoire in 1836, and in 1839 carried off the "grand prix de Rome."

Ingres was at that time principal of the Villa Medici, and the young pupil was half inclined to abandon the pursuit of music for that of painting, for which he showed some ability. His musical studies were chiefly

Fig. 126.—Charles Gounod.

the works of Palestrina and his school, and those of Bach, and these no doubt served to develop that technical skill which is so prominent in his compositions. He had the further good fortune while in Rome to make the acquaintance of Mendelssohn and of his sister Fanny Hensel, who were both admirers of the young man's ability and seriousness of purpose. On his return to Paris he became organist of the "Missions étrangères," and while holding this office embarked on a course of theological study with such ardour that he was nearly landed in the priesthood. While at Rome he had manifested much religious exaltation, and this feeling had great influence on him throughout his life. His first opera, *Sapho*, owed its appearance to the good offices of Madame Viardot, who herself took the leading character. It was not successful, nor was his second operatic venture *La Nonne sanglante* (1854). He had in the meantime become conductor of the Orphéon de Paris, an office which he held for eight years, gaining great experience in the management of large bodies of voices. For them he wrote several choruses, as well as two masses for male voices.

The subject of Faust had long occupied his thoughts, but it was set aside, at the suggestion of M. Carvallo, in favour of a libretto arranged by Messrs. Carré and Barbier, *Le Médecin malgré lui* of Molière. It was produced in 1858 at the Théâtre Lyrique and may be considered Gounod's first real success. *Faust* was at last completed and produced, also at the Lyrique in March 1859. We need hardly say with what enthusiasm it was received, and that it has remained his masterpiece. Its beauties are so familiar to all that no description of the work can be necessary; it is probably the most popular work that has appeared in our own day.

Philémon et Baucis, La Reine de Saba, Mirelle, La Colombe succeeded it, but none of them repeated the success of *Faust*. *Romeo et Juliette* was brought out in 1867, and in this he once more appears in his full powers, and although it has never captivated the public so completely there are those who place it on the same level as *Faust*. After this effort his dramatic works show a gradual declension. *Cinq Mars, Polyeucte, Le Tribut de Zamora* have been successively shelved.

On the breaking out of the Franco-German war Gounod took refuge in England. While here he wrote many songs which had great success, and also much sacred music, including his noble work *Gallia*, for soprano solo, chorus and orchestra—a lament for the sorrows of his native country. His visit to this country had a great, and in the writer's opinion an unfortunate, influence on many of our native church composers, in whose works it may be readily traced. His great reputation caused him to be invited to write a work on a large scale for the Birmingham Festival of 1882. The result was *The Redemption*, which at once achieved a great success, not a little favoured by very skilful business management. The work has remained popular, although much of the music is somewhat tawdry where it is not dull. *Mors et Vita*, also commissioned for the Birmingham Festival of 1885, is inscribed by the author, "*Opus vitæ meæ.*" This opinion has not been shared by the public; *Mors et Vita* is shelved, *Faust* retains its popularity; surely we may forgive the composer such an error of self-judgment, partly the result of the religious feeling of which we have already spoken, in consideration of the delight which the earlier work continues to give. Many of his songs are most delicate and delightful, while some of his work—for example the ballet music of *La Reine de Saba*, has a voluptuous beauty which has never been exceeded in music. Gounod died in 1893.

Of living French musicians the most eminent, without doubt, is Camille Saint-Saëns (fig. 127), who unites in his own person the qualities of a great pianist, a well read musician, a fine composer, and an excellent critic. He was born in Paris in 1835, began to study the pianoforte at an early age, entered the Conservatoire, but in spite of his brilliant acquirements was unsuccessful, after two trials, in securing the "prix de Rome." He composed his first symphony when only sixteen, and in 1858 became organist of the Madeleine, a post he resigned in 1877. His works in all departments of composition are exceedingly numerous and have met with much success. They include four pianoforte concertos, four *poèmes symphoniques*, a form of composition adopted from Liszt, *Le Rouet d'Omphale*, *Danse Macabre*, *Phaeton*, and *La Jeunesse d'Hercule* (the first two of which are well known in this country), and much chamber music, including a septet for the pianoforte, with five strings and trumpet. His earlier operas were unsuccessful, and *Samson and Delila* (first performed at Weimar in 1877, under Liszt's auspices) after achieving success in the provinces was not heard in Paris till 1892. Owing to the nature of the libretto it has been heard in England as an oratorio only, and in that form has become popular. In the meantime his opera *Henri VIII.* had been produced in Paris during the year 1883, and had shown him to be a composer of

Fig. 127.—C. Saint-Saëns.

great dramatic power. *Proserpine* was brought out at the Opéra Comique in 1887, but the run of the piece was brought to a close by the burning of that theatre. *Ascanio,* of which Benvenuto Cellini is the hero, appeared at the Grand Opera in 1890, and seems to have been somewhat disappointing. At the first performance the public were much mystified by the sudden disappearance of the composer, who was discovered some weeks later in the Canary Islands under an assumed name! Saint-Saëns has visited this country in the capacities both of pianist and conductor.

Jules Massenet (fig. 128) (born 1842) laid the foundation of his fame on the incidental music to Lecomte de Lisle's drama, *Les Erinnyes*, but his best known work is *Le Roi de Lahore*, which went the round of Europe before it was received at its full value in the composer's native country. He has since composed several operas, the best known of which are *Hérodiade*, and *Manon* (the Abbé Prévost's heroine), but he has scarcely maintained his reputation.

César Franck (born 1822 at Liége, but naturalised as a Frenchman) is well known as an organist, and as professor of that instrument at the Conservatoire. A man of noble aims and an excellent musician, he has had great influence over a large number of pupils, but it cannot be claimed that his compositions have met with extended success. His best known work is an oratorio, *Ruth*, written in 1845 and re-cast in 1868, since which it has been more than once revived.

Edouard Victor Antoine Lalo (born 1823) is most distinguished as an orchestral and concert-room composer, having written a very successful violin concerto, and a so-called *symphonie espagnole* for violin and orchestra, both for the eminent performer Sarasate, besides other orchestral works. His reputation as a writer of symphonies has rather militated against him with the Parisian public as a composer of operas, although *Le Roi d'Ys*

Fig. 128.—Jules Massenet.

was well received. We must content ourselves with the bare mention of Ernest Reyer, Alfred Bruneau, Widor and Godard, while the labours of MM. Pasdeloup,

Lameureux, and Colonne in popularising music of the best kind in Paris must not be passed over in silence.

In the second quarter of the present century Paris became a rendezvous for pianists of many nationalities; among whom were to be found Liszt, Hiller, Kalkbrenner G. A. Osborne and several others. The circle was joined in 1831 by a young virtuoso who was destined to exercise a vast influence on the art of pianoforte playing—François Frédéric Chopin (1809-1849), a native of Poland, but the son of a French father, a teacher of his own language, who had settled in that country and married a Polish lady. At an early age he played a concerto of Gyrowetz in public. He learned all he knew from two masters— Zwyny, a Bohemian, and Elsner, a German resident in Warsaw, whose best claims to fame rest on having turned out such a pupil as Chopin. At the age of nineteen he had become a remarkable performer, and had written several works for the pianoforte, including two concertos. He then started for Paris, staying to give concerts at Vienna and Munich on the way, and making the acquaintance of the principal musicians in those cities. At last he arrived in Paris, and was at once received with open arms by the colony of Poles settled there, and in that city the greater part of his life was spent. His playing was distinguished by great lightness, refinement, and grace; it was, in fact, almost too delicate for a large room, and could be heard to perfection only in a drawing-room. From time to time he gave public concerts, but such appearances were distasteful to him, and he seldom did himself justice, and it has been said that he appeared at his best when playing to an audience of beautiful women. To the fascinations of female beauty and intellect he was very susceptible, and this led him into an unfortunate *liaison* with Mme. Georges Sand. In 1838 weakness of the lungs had already declared itself, and together they visited Majorca, in the hope that the climate would restore him to health. The hope was fallacious, and his life continued to be a struggle with disease, although he was able to continue his profession, numbering many of the aristocracy among his pupils. Of this number was Miss Stirling, a Scotch lady, and mainly at her instance he was induced to visit England and Scotland, where he played a few times in public. But the hand of death was upon him. His last days were soothed by the kindness of Miss Stirling and many other admiring friends. On the news of his serious illness the Countess Delphine Potocka hastened to Paris. Chopin begged that she would once again let him hear her beautiful voice. With difficulty she suppressed her sobs and did as he wished. Two days afterwards, on the morning of October 17th, 1849, he died.

By far the larger part of the works of Chopin is for the pianoforte alone. In writing for the orchestra he was not at ease, and the accompaniments to his two pianoforte concertos, the solo parts of which are very fine, are generally used in a re-scored version. His solo works are brimful of originality, having nothing in common with those of any other composer. It is not saying too much to assert that they show a more thorough appreciation of the resources of the instrument than the works of any other writer. Classical forms were irksome to him, and although he wrote three solo sonatas, and one with violoncello for his friend Franchomme, the most characteristic part of his writings consists of études, preludes, nocturnes, mazurkas, polonaises and waltzes, in most of which the influence of Polish national music is strongly marked. Of the mazurkas alone there are fifty-two, and it is remarkable that a single well-defined rhythmic form should lend itself to such variety of treatment. To play Chopin requires a peculiar organisation, and of the many who in the present day attempt it few approach success.

Paris, from the earliest years of this century, has boasted a fine school of the violin, the leaders of which Rode, Baillot and Kreutzer (who, although of German parentage, was born at Versailles), were professors at the Conservatoire, and in that capacity compiled the *Méthode de Violon*, still in use. Among the pupils of Baillot, himself a player of very sterling acquirements, Habeneck had a great reputation as a teacher, and still greater as a conducter, in which capacity he was the first to produce Beethoven's symphonies in France. The characteristics of the French style of playing, as compared with that of Germany, as exemplified by Spohr and his successors, are greater vigour and brilliancy. The Belgian violinists, De Beriot and Vieuxtemps, virtually drew their training from the same source. The former was a voluminous writer for his instrument, his works, while excellently written for the violin, being very showy and brilliant. It is well known that he married the celebrated and delightful singer, Malibran. The best traditions of the school are at present most ably maintained by Señor Sarasate, who, although of Spanish birth, owes his training to the Conservatoire of Paris.

As organists we must mention the names of Lefébure-Wély and Baptiste, who both acquired great reputation. But the French organists appear to aim at a greater brilliancy than, either in England or Germany, is considered to suit the character of the instrument. An Englishman named Barker applied himself to the invention of a method for lightening the touch of the organ, which resulted in what is known as the *pneumatic lever*. Finding no organ builder in his native country willing to take it up, he induced Cavaillé-Col, a famous French builder, to adopt it. This invention, or a development of it, is now in universal use for organs of any size, and there is no doubt that its adoption is gradually modifying the character of organ music in the same way that the improvement of the pianoforte action has affected the style of music written for that instrument. The music of Chopin would be an impossibility on the pianoforte of the days of Mozart.

The name of Choron (1771-1834) deserves mention for the excellent influence he had in the cause of musical education in France, not only by the school which he founded for instruction in classical and religious music, but also by his didactic works, which placed the best traditions of Italian music within reach of his fellow-countrymen. In this he was assisted by Adrian de la Fage (1801-1862), a very learned musician with a wide knowledge of the early Italian writers. Among La

Fage's works the best known are *Histoire générale de la Musique* (Paris, 1844, 2 vols., 8vo, and a vol. of plates), which is only a fragment; and his *Cours complet de Plain Chant* (Paris, 1855-56, 2 vols., 8vo). The restoration of the true traditions of Plain-Song occupied much attention in France at the time of which we are writing. The labours of F. Danjou (1812-1866) towards this object deserve mention. To further the cause he founded the *Revue de la Musique Réligieuse*, in which he was assisted, among others, by a very remarkable man, to whom all who are interested in music are under great obligations —F. J. Fétis (1784-1871), a scholar whose mental activity reached to every corner of musical knowledge. He is best known by his *Biographie Universelle des Musiciens* (1st edition, Paris and Brussels, 1834-44; 2nd edition, Paris, 1860-65, both in 8 vols., 8vo), a work of marvellous knowledge and erudition. Faults there are in it, without doubt—errors of date, inadequate treatment of English musicians, a tendency to ignore the labours of others, and a frequent exhibition of a dogmatic spirit—for Fétis was a man troubled with no doubts: he *knew* he was right, and had but little charity for those who ventured to differ from him. But with these drawbacks it remains a noble monument of industry and research, for which no other work will serve as a substitute. For a quarter of a century the writer has had occasion to consult it almost daily; the occasions are rare on which he has failed to find the information he sought, and he is very glad of this opportunity of placing his gratitude on record. It should be added that the second edition is the one to possess, as much more correct, although the first has a certain value from the *Résumé philosophique* prefixed to it. An excellent supplement in two volumes has been compiled by M. Arthur Pougin, assisted by musical writers of eminence. Among his other works, the mere titles of which would fill more space than we can afford, the most important is his *Histoire générale de la Musique*, which unfortunately he lived to bring down no further than the fifteenth century. *La Musique mise à la Portée de tout le Monde*, a most useful little book, went through numerous editions, and was translated into nearly every European language. His noble musical library, the most remarkable that has ever been collected, was purchased at his death by the Belgian Government, and an excellent catalogue of it was published. He was a native of Mons, in Belgium, and since 1833 had filled the office of Director of the Conservatoire in Brussels. To a distinguished lawyer, M. C. E. H. de Coussemaker, a native of French Flanders, we are also indebted for many important additions to the early history of music, among which is the series of mediæval writers on music in continuation of that issued by the Abbé Gerbert.

It remains to say a few words on the history of music in England during the present century. It must be admitted that the record is not very flattering to our vanity. If, however, we produced but few musicians whose names acquired any great reputation beyond our own country, we have been always ready to welcome foreign professors to our shores. Among those we have already mentioned Dussek and Steibelt; but before their arrival here, Muzio Clementi had already made England his dwelling-place, for he was brought to this country from Rome, his native city, by an English gentleman, Mr. Beckford, who was much struck with his ability. In his house in Dorsetshire he remained for some time, pursuing his general studies and perfecting himself as a performer on the pianoforte. He then appeared in London, and at once took the foremost place in the profession. He made occasional tours on the Continent, in one of which he had a trial of skill with Mozart; but his home was in England, where he was in great request both as a performer and as a teacher. By these means he acquired a large fortune and became, in conjunction with Mr. Collard, the founder of the well-known firm of pianoforte makers. He was an admirable writer for the pianoforte, having left no fewer than one hundred sonatas for that instrument; but the work by which he is probably best known is his *Gradus ad Parnassum*, a series of studies of the highest value. Among his pupils the most famous was J. B. Cramer (1771-1858), the son of the violinist Wilhelm Cramer (1745-1799 or 1800), who settled in England when the child was only a year old, so that by education he was entirely English. He was a fine pianist and writer for his instrument, best known in our own time by his celebrated studies, which are excellent for cultivating that even power in the two hands which was so distinguishing a feature of his own playing. John Field (1782-1837), known as

"Russian Field," a native of Dublin, was also a pupil of Clementi, who took him to Russia, where he settled and died. His nocturnes are charming little compositions, and Chopin is said to owe much, both as a player and as a composer, to the study of his style and works. For a long time—from 1826 to 1846—the great pianist Ignaz Moscheles made London, which he had previously visited more than once as a virtuoso, his dwelling-place, to the great advantage of sound music in England; but in the latter year, as we have already stated, he was induced by his friend Mendelssohn to become a professor in the Leipzig Conservatorium.

Among the foremost English musicians of the earlier part of the century was Sir Henry R. Bishop (1786-1855), who principally devoted himself to dramatic composition for the English Opera at Covent Garden Theatre, of which he was musical director. He was possessed of an inexhaustible fund of melody, and although his operas have long been laid on the shelf, much of the beautiful music they contain still retains its popularity. Among the best known airs is the touching and simple *Home, sweet home!* from the opera of *Clari*. *Should he upbraid, Bid me discourse, The Pilgrim of Love, My pretty Jane,* are other examples of his gift of tune. His glees, such as *Mynheer van Dunck, Sleep, gentle Lady, The Chough and Crow,* and many other well-known favourites, first saw the light in his operas. It is to be regretted that, in conformity with the practice of the day, he "arranged" several foreign operas—even *Don Giovanni* and *Figaro*—for the English stage in a way little short of barbarous.

The career of Balfe (1808-1870), violinist, singer and composer, belongs as much to the Continent as to England. He was born in Dublin, and received his first instruction from O'Rourke, a musician who afterwards removed to London, and under the name of Rooke produced at Covent Garden in 1837 an opera, *Amilie; or, the Love Test*, which had some success. Balfe's first triumphs were obtained at an early age as a violinist; but in 1825 he went to Italy, and on his way back made the acquaintance of Rossini in Paris, under whose advice he appeared as a baritone singer in Mozart's *Figaro*, under the name of Signor Balfo! Other engagements followed in Italy, where he also produced several operas, now forgotten. He returned to England in 1835, and brought out his first English opera, *The Siege of Rochelle*, which at once established his fame. *The Maid of Artois* succeeded it, and had the advantage of Malibran's charming singing. In 1837 his Italian opera *Falstaff* was brought out at Her Majesty's Theatre. He next gave, at the Opéra Comique in Paris, *Le Puits d'Amour* and *Les Quatre Fils d'Aymon*. But in 1843 he produced his masterpiece, *The Bohemian Girl*, which took the public by storm, not only in England, but throughout the Continent. From the secession of Costa, in 1846, to the collapse of Mr. Lumley, he was conductor of the Italian Opera at Her Majesty's Theatre. Several other operas from his pen were produced at Continental theatres, and for the Pyne and Harrison English Opera Company, at the Lyceum, he wrote *The Rose of Castile* and *Satanella*, both of which were very popular. In 1864 he retired from active life and devoted himself to farming. His music is tuneful and spontaneous.

His countryman, W. Vincent Wallace (1814-1865), whose life was one of romance and adventure, also made his first appearance as a violinist in Dublin. But he soon longed for a wider field of action, and having married in 1835, left Ireland with his wife and her sister. On the voyage his wife considered that he was too attentive to her sister, and when it was at an end they parted never to meet again! He was next to be found in the Bush, near Sydney, where by mere accident his musical acquirements were discovered. At the instigation of the Governor, Sir John Burke, he was induced to give a concert, the Governor paying for his seats with one hundred sheep! He then wandered about Tasmania and New Zealand, on one occasion only escaping death at the hands of the natives by the intervention of the chief's daughter. He next started on a whaling voyage on a ship called *The Good Intent*; but, in spite of the happy omen of the name, the crew mutinied, and Wallace and three others only escaped. We cannot follow all his wanderings; but he visited India, where he was splendidly rewarded by the Queen of Oude, sailed to Valparaiso, crossed the Andes on a mule, travelled to Havana, Mexico, and New Orleans, and finally turned up one evening in 1845 in a complete suit of nankeen, with a broad-brimmed white hat, in a private box at a London theatre. A friend who recognised him took him off to the "poet" Fitzball, who was discovered with the libretto of *Maritana* before him, the ink of which was still wet! Fitzball was soon satisfied that Wallace might be entrusted with it, and in the autumn of the same year this opera, which still keeps the stage, was produced at Drury Lane with the greatest success. Wallace now went to Germany, and occupied himself in writing for the pianoforte. There he remained fourteen years—a long time for so restless a spirit. He was invited to write a work for the Paris Opera, but his eyesight failed, and he started off once again on his travels, visiting both North and South America, making much money by concerts, being nearly blown up in a steamboat, making a fortune, and losing it by the failure of a pianoforte factory in New York into which he had placed his savings. He returned to London in 1853, and in 1860 *Lurline* was produced at Covent Garden. It brimmed over with melody, and delighted the public even more than *Maritana*. The *Amber Witch* and some other works followed; but his health was breaking, and he died in the Pyrenees in October 1865. All this reads like romance, but we believe that it is an accurate outline of this remarkable man's life.

John Barnett (1802-1890) made one great success with his *Mountain Sylph*, which showed much dramatic power, and is still remembered on account of the trio *This Magic-wove Scarf*. We must also mention *The Night Dancers* of E. J. Loder, and *Don Quixote* of G. A. Macfarren. The latter was an esteemed and learned musician, who took an earnest view of his art, which he practised under great difficulties, for at a comparatively early age he became quite blind. He tried all forms of composition; among his best works is the oratorio *St. John the Baptist*.

He succeeded Sir W. Sterndale Bennett, of whom we shall write shortly, both as Professor of Music at the University of Cambridge and as Principal of the Royal Academy of Music, and received the honour of knighthood.

Sir Julius Benedict (1804-1885) was a musician who had lived so long among us as to have become almost an Englishman. He was born at Stuttgart, and having studied under Hummel, became a pupil of Weber. After some Continental experience he settled in England in 1835, his only long absence having been with Jenny Lind in America, in 1850. He produced in 1838 his first English opera, *The Gipsy's Warning*, which contains the vigorous bass song *Rage, thou angry Storm!* This was followed by *The Brides of Venice*, *The Crusaders*, and some years afterwards by *The Lily of Killarney*, a tuneful and charming work which still gives delight. His oratorios *St. Cecilia* and *St. Peter* were produced with success at Norwich and Birmingham Festivals. To many he will be best known by the admirable way in which he accompanied the vocal music at the Monday Popular Concerts. He was an excellent musician, with extraordinary powers of work, and after a long day's toil he would steal time from the night to keep up correspondence with all the principal musicians of Europe.

Another prominent foreign musician long resident in England was Sir Michael Costa (1810-1884). In 1829 he was sent to England by Zingarelli, of Naples, whose pupil he was, to direct the performance of a composition which he had written for the Birmingham Festival. This the arrangements did not allow him to do, but he sang the tenor part in it. In the following year he was appointed accompanist at the King's Theatre, and in 1833 he was engaged as conductor. His marvellous qualifications for the post at once justified the choice. In 1846, Lumley, then lessee, had contrived to alienate his best singers, as well as his conductor and band, who went over in a body to the rival opera under Mr. Gye at Covent Garden. Here Costa had a free hand, and he succeeded in raising the performances to a pitch of excellence unknown in London. There has been no such band in England, either before or since, as that enlisted under Costa's command. All the members, both string and wind, were the best obtainable, and their instruments were of a quality but seldom found in Continental orchestras. The result was a quality and vigour of tone which has never been heard since. Costa was also conductor for several years of the Philharmonic Concerts, as well as of the Sacred Harmonic Society and the Birmingham Festival. Where he went his band went. In conducting rehearsals he was always considerate, always punctual, business-like, and methodical; a man with whom no one would think of taking a liberty, and who succeeded in inspiring his band with a loyalty and *esprit de corps* which have not existed since he ceased to conduct. As a composer he wrote several ballets, and two operas, *Malek-Adhel* and *Don Carlos.* His oratorios *Eli* and *Naaman* contain much beautiful music, which, however, seems in a fair way of being forgotten.

Of the many other foreign musicians living and working

among us, Mr. Silas has never attained to the position which the excellence of his compositions entitle him, while Mr. Randegger has allowed the claims of his pupils to interrupt the career of a composer which his operetta *The Rival Beauties*, and the cantata *Fridolin*—a work of great dramatic power—led us to hope would be fruitful.

We have yet to speak of our greatest modern musician. Sir W. Sterndale Bennett (1816-1875), the son and the grandson of musicians, was born at Sheffield, but having at an early age lost his father, he was sent to Cambridge, where his grandfather was a lay clerk at King's, Trinity and St. John's Colleges. When eight years of age he followed in the same steps by becoming a singing boy at King's, from which, on account of the talent he showed, he was soon removed to the Royal Academy of Music. He became an excellent pianist, and as a student produced several works which at once attracted notice. Among these were the delightful *Naiades* overture, and a pianoforte concerto, the excellences of which induced Messrs. Broadwood, with the liberality they have so constantly shown, to offer to send him for a year to Leipzig, to benefit by the advice of Mendelssohn. There he met with an enthusiastic reception, both as a performer and as a composer; one of his warmest admirers being Robert Schumann, who spoke of him in the highest terms in the *Neue Zeitschrift*. On his return to England he was much before the public as a player. In 1853 he was offered the conductorship of the Gewandhaus Concerts, a testimony to the esteem in which he was held in Germany. This he did not feel at liberty to accept, but in 1856 he became conductor of the Philharmonic Society, which he resigned in 1866 on becoming principal of the Royal Academy of Music. In 1856 he had also become Professor of Music at Cambridge, in succession to Dr. Walmisley. Of his larger works the most important are his cantata *The May Queen* and his oratorio *The Woman of Samaria*. He also wrote the overtures *The Wood Nymphs* and *Paradise and the Peri*, as well as a symphony, many works for the pianoforte, and two books of exquisite songs. It is to be regretted that his works are so few; but he was a man of great modesty, which restrained him from rushing into print, and unfortunately too much of his time was devoted to the drudgery of teaching. His style is one of peculiar delicacy and refinement, although of marked individuality, but no doubt somewhat deficient in vigour.

The needs of cathedrals and large churches have kept up a succession of excellent organists in England. At St. Paul's Cathedral, Thomas Attwood, the favourite pupil of Mozart and familiar friend of Mendelssohn, was organist from 1796 to his death in 1838, and acquired much reputation, beyond his ecclesiastical duties, by his glees and other secular compositions. To him succeeded John Goss (afterwards Sir John Goss), an admirable composer both of church music and glees. Thomas Adams (1785-1858), was well known as an organist of exceptional skill, who possessed remarkable powers of extemporising, and was constantly chosen by organ builders to exhibit new instruments before leaving their factories, when he never failed to draw large audiences. Samuel Wesley (1766-1837), a nephew of the celebrated Rev. John Wesley, was one of our greatest organists, and a composer of great ability and learning—as witness, among other works, his motet *In Exitu Israel.* But he had further claims to gratitude as having been, in conjunction with C. F. Horn and Benjamin Jacob, the organist of the Rev. Rowland Hill's Chapel, the first to introduce the works of Sebastian Bach to the English public. His son, Samuel Sebastian Wesley (1810-1876), was also a great player, and inherited his father's genius for composition. From his father also he inherited a certain amount of eccentricity. His compositions are few, but admirable,—his anthems *Ascribe unto the Lord* and *The Wilderness* are equal to anything that has been written in that style. He was probably the last organist of eminence who advocated unequal temperament, and the G keyboard, against which the late Dr. Gauntlett made it the business of his life to fight.

The English nation seems to have never recognised the remarkable genius it possessed in the person of Henry Hugo Pearson or Pierson (as he preferred to spell his name) (1815-1873). The son of Dr. Pearson, of St. John's College, Oxford, afterwards Dean of Salisbury, he was sent to Harrow, and proceeded to Trinity College, Cambridge, with the intention of taking up medicine as a career. But the attractions of music were too strong, and after studying with Attwood and Arthur Corfe, he went to Germany in 1839 and sought the instruction of Rink, Tomaschek and Reissiger. For a short time he held the Reid Professorship of Music at Edinburgh, to which he was elected on the death of Sir Henry Bishop, but soon afterwards he married a German lady and made his home in that country, where his abilities were more readily acknowledged than in his native land. He produced the opera *Leila* at Hamburg in 1848, but his masterpiece was the oratorio *Jerusalem*, written for the Norwich Festival of 1852, and performed again in London in the following year. It seems to have been more warmly received by musicians than by the general public. In 1854 his music to the second part of *Faust* was performed many times in Hamburg, and it has continued to be played at several places in Germany in yearly commemoration of Goethe's birthday. The work added greatly to his reputation in his adopted country. A selection from his second oratorio, *Hezekiah*, was produced at Norwich in 1869, but the work was never completed. His last composition, the opera *Contarini*, appeared at Hamburg in 1892. A large number of his works remain in manuscript, and while in Germany he is appreciated at his true value, in the land of his birth he is known only as the writer of a part song, *Ye mariners of England*.

The career of the late Arthur Goring Thomas was unfortunately cut off prematurely. Mainly French by training, he produced his opera *Esmeralda* in 1883; it was at once hailed with enthusiasm, and its success was followed up by that of *Nadeshda* in 1885. He has also written songs showing great refinement.

The most popular of English musicians is, without doubt, Sir Arthur Sullivan (born 1842). His father was a professor at Kneller Hall, the School of Military Music, so that the young musician was brought up in an atmosphere of art. At twelve years of age he entered the Chapel Royal, being endowed with a voice of great beauty, which he used with much taste. While still one of the "Children of the Chapel Royal," in the year 1856 he became the first holder of the Mendelssohn Scholarship, and became a pupil of the Royal Academy.

It is curious, and one cannot help looking at it as somewhat disappointing, that with such a start in life his reputation with the public should rest mainly on a series of comic operas, brilliant though they are. The first of these, suggested by a private performance of *Les deux aveugles* of Offenbach, was the delightful *Cox and Box*, originally performed by amateurs for the benefit of the family of a late member of the staff of *Punch*. This was followed by *The Contrabandista*. In *Trial by Jury* he had the co-operation of Mr. W. S. Gilbert, and with it began a series of well known works in which the wit of the librettist and the piquant music of the composer are most happily blended. It is hardly necessary to mention *The Sorcerer*, *H.M.S. Pinafore*, *The Pirates of Penzance*, *Patience*, *Iolanthe*, *Princess Ida*, *The Mikado*, *Ruddigore*, *The Yeomen of the Guard*, for they are known to every one capable of appreciating frank and wholesome mirth. For the ill-starred English Opera House, now the Palace Theatre, he wrote his one serious opera, *Ivanhoe*.

Works of a light and airy nature appeal to a much wider public than those of higher aim. It is for this reason that Sir Arthur Sullivan's more serious efforts have been somewhat overshadowed by his popularity in the former direction. But musicians will appreciate much excellent work shown in his oratorios, *The Prodigal Son, The Light of the World, The Martyr of Antioch,* and the most popular of all, *The Golden Legend,* as well as in his incidental music to several of Shakspere's plays, in his overtures, especially his *In Memoriam,* written on the death of his father. Much of his vocal music is also very popular.

Sir Alexander Mackenzie (born 1847), the present principal of the Royal Academy of Music, is the son of a much esteemed musician in Edinburgh. A musician of great earnestness of purpose, he has produced two operas, *Colomba* and *The Troubadour,* an oratorio, *The Rose of Sharon,* besides lesser works.

Charles Hubert Hastings Parry (born 1848), the brilliant son of an accomplished father, was educated at Winchester and at Eton, and while still at school passed his examination for the degree of Mus. Bac., and entered at Exeter College, Oxford. While at Winchester, he received some instruction from Dr. S. S. Wesley, and at Eton took some lessons in harmony from Dr., afterwards Sir George Elvey. At the conclusion of his University course he studied with H. H. Pierson at Stuttgart, and also with the late Sir G. Macfarren, and Mr. Dannreuther. In spite of the obvious bent of his abilities, it was his father's wish that he should become a man of business, and therefore, when he had taken his degree, he entered the office of an underwriter, and for seven years tried to reconcile the claims of Lloyds' with those of his favourite art. Music at last triumphed, and now Mr. Parry is the well-known and popular principal of the Royal College of Music, a position adorned by his abilities. His largest work is the oratorio *Judith*, composed for the Birmingham Festival of 1888, and he has, in addition, written several symphonies, the music for a performance at Cambridge of *The Birds*, of Aristophanes, as well as the choral odes, *The Glories of our Blood and State*, Milton's *Blest Pair of Sirens*, and *An Ode for St. Cecilia's Day*. Dr. Parry is also favourably known as a critic on music; some of the most valuable articles in Grove's "Dictionary" were contributed by him, and he has also published an admirable work, *The Art of Music* (London, 1874, 8vo, with subsequent editions). It is a masterly history of the development of musical form.

Dr. Charles Villiers Stanford (born 1852) is of Irish birth, a fact well vouched for by his favourite symphony, *The Irish*, and by his most recent opera. He is known as the composer of four operas, *The Veiled Prophet of Khorassin*, produced at Hanover in 1881, *Savonarola*, at Hamburg in 1884, *The Canterbury Pilgrims*, written for the Carl Rosa Company, and produced also in 1884, while *Shamus O'Brien* has recently been brought out by the same company. Dr. Stanford has written much chamber music of great interest. It has been well said that he should be appointed composer to the Admiralty, for his choral ballads, *The Revenge* and *The Battle of the Baltic*, breathe the true British sea-dog spirit. He has done much excellent work as Conductor of the Musical Society of Cambridge, of which University he is now Professor of Music, in succession to the late Sir G. A. Macfarren; he is also Professor of Composition at the Royal College.

Sir John Stainer, the Professor of the sister University, was brought up in the choir of St. Paul's Cathedral, where he succeeded Sir John Goss as organist in 1872, having in the meantime held the like office at Sir F. A. Gore Ouseley's College at Tenbury, at Magdalen College, Oxford, and to the University of Oxford. He raised the choir of St. Paul's to the high pitch of excellence which it still maintains under Sir G. Martin, but in 1888, threatened blindness compelled him to resign the office. He had, however, succeeded Mr. John Hullah as Government Inspector of Music in Elementary Schools, an office which he still holds, together with his professorship. As a composer, he has produced an oratorio, *Gideon*, a cantata, *The Daughter of Jairus*, and much service music.

We must not conclude these notices without mentioning Mr. F. H. Cowen (born 1852), a composer of much grace and delicacy, with remarkable skill in orchestration, as witness his charming orchestral suite, *The Language of Flowers*. His opera *Pauline* was brought out by the Carl Rosa Company, and had but a short run; his operatic ventures have not been fortunate, owing, perhaps, to a certain want of vigour.

Among the younger musicians of promise may be mentioned Messrs. Hamish McCunn, E. German, and Arthur Somervell.

A few words must be said on one or two of those societies which have done so much to advance the cause of music in England. And first we must place the Philharmonic Society, founded in 1813 at the suggestion of J. B. Cramer, Corri, and Dance, which, having passed through occasional times of trouble, is still vigorous. The main object of the Society is the adequate performance of orchestral music, and this aim is kept well in view.

The Sacred Harmonic Society—now, alas! a thing of the past—rose from the most humble beginnings, —the meetings of a few amateurs at Gate Street Chapel, Lincoln's Inn, for the practice of oratorios, in the year 1832. In 1834 it had gained strength enough to move to Exeter Hall, where it gave its concerts in the minor hall. It was not till 1836 that it ventured on taking the large hall for a charity performance, which was so successful that it continued to give its concerts in it. The Society was conducted by Mr. Surman, a man of great zeal, but with insufficient qualifications for the wants of such a body; and in 1848 Mr. Costa consented to become its conductor. The change at once produced the most happy results. All the principal oratorios were given in an adequate manner, with the assistance of the best vocalists obtainable. The Society gained additional glory by its management of the Handel Festivals at the Crystal Palace. In 1880 Exeter Hall became no longer available, and the Society was compelled to migrate to St. James's Hall, which afforded inadequate accommodation for performance on the accustomed scale. The fortunes of the Society gradually drooped, and it finally was decided to dissolve it, after an existence of fifty years, during which it had done a noble work in popularising the finest compositions of the greatest masters.

Among the most successful undertakings have been the Monday Popular Concerts, which have been the means of enabling the public to become acquainted with chamber music in a way which was previously impossible. The only opportunities for hearing such music were the Musical Union of the late Mr. Ella, the subscription to which was to most people prohibitory, and the occasional performances of artists who ventured on giving a series of quartet concerts. St. James's Hall is crowded twice a week during the winter by an audience which follows the performance with the deepest interest, while a constant succession of orchestral concerts of a high character is given in the spacious and admirably arranged Queen's Hall, which has been recently added to the concert rooms of London.

A great help to the advance of music has been the greatly reduced prices at which the best works are now obtainable. The pioneers in this movement were Messrs. Novello, whose octavo oratorios have had a marvellous sale. Their example has been followed on the Continent by Messrs. Peters and Messrs. Litolff, who publish most of the classics at prices within the reach of all.

Musical education in its higher walks has been well provided for. The Royal Academy of Music, founded in 1822, has turned out the majority of our orchestral players and many excellent singers. The Royal College of Music at South Kensington is doing a good work, while the Corporation of the City of London has founded a music school of its own with a large number of pupils. A vast number of chorus singers owed their training to the classes of the late Mr. John Hullah, who adopted the Wilhelm system of teaching. But among the most extraordinary movements has been the Tonic Sol-fa, which owes its success to the energy of the Rev. J. Curwen and his son Mr. J. S. Curwen, and counts its pupils by hundreds of thousands. So much activity belies the often repeated assertion that the English are not a musical nation, and it is certain that in no other country is so sound a musical training placed within the reach of every one, and in no other capital in the world can an adequate reading of the masterpieces, orchestral and otherwise, of the great composers be so frequently heard, and nowhere can be found more attentive and discriminating audiences.

BIBLIOGRAPHY.

Pougin, Arthur. Méhul, sa Vie, son Génie, son Caractère. Paris, 1889. 8vo.

——— Boieldieu, sa Vie, ses Œuvres, son Caractère. Paris, 1885. 12mo.

——— Auber, ses Commencements, les Origines de sa Carrière. Paris, 1873. 12mo.

Jouvin, B. D. F. E. Auber, sa Vie et ses Œuvres. Paris, 1864. 8vo.

——— Hérold, sa Vie et ses Œuvres. Paris, 1868. 8vo. (For *Meyerbeer* see last chapter.)

Pougin, A. F. Halévy, écrivain. Paris, 1865. 8vo.

Halévy, Léon. F. Halévy, sa Vie et ses Œuvres. Paris, 1863. 8vo.

Pougin, A. Adolphe Adam, sa Vie, sa Carrière, ses Mémoires. Paris, 1877. 12mo.

Martinet, André. Offenbach, sa Vie et ses Œuvres. Paris, 1877. 12mo.

(Berlioz, Hector.) Mémoires de Hector Berlioz. Paris, 1878. 2 vols., 12mo.

——— Correspondance inédite de. Paris, 1878. 12mo.

——— Lettres intimes. Paris, 1882. 12mo.

——— (Life and Letters of Berlioz, translated by H. M. Dunstan. London, 1882. 2 vols., 8vo.)

Jullien, Adolphe. Hector Berlioz, sa Vie et ses Œuvres. Ouvrage orné de quatorze lithographies originales par M. Fantin-Latour, de douze portraits . . . caricatures, etc. Paris, 1888. 4to.

Azevedo, Alexis. Félicien David, sa Vie et son Œuvre. Paris, 1863. 8vo.

Pigot, Charles. Georges Bizet et son Œuvre. Paris, 1886. 12mo.

Karasowski, Moritz. Friedrich Chopin, sein Leben, seine Werke und Briefe. Dresden, 1877. 2 vols., 8vo. (Translated by Emily Hill, London, 1879. 2 vols., 8vo.)

Niecks, Frederick. Frederick Chopin as a Man and Musician. London, 1881. 2 vols., 8vo.

Audley, Mdme. A. Fréderic Chopin, sa Vie et ses Œuvres. Paris, 1880. 12mo.

Barrett, Wm. Alexander. Balfe: His Life and Work. London, 1882. 8vo.

Pougin, Arthur. William Vincent Wallace: Étude biographique et critique. Paris, 1866. 8vo.

Hogarth, George. The Philharmonic Society of London; from its foundation in 1813 to its fiftieth year, 1862. London, 1862. 8vo.

Bowley, R. K. The Sacred Harmonic Society: a Thirty-five years' Retrospect, from its commencement in 1832 to its five hundredth concert in Exeter Hall, 13th December, 1867. London (privately printed), 1867. 8vo.

Sacred Harmonic Society. Annual Reports.

Cazalet, Rev. W. W. The History of the Royal Academy of Music, compiled from authentic sources. London, 1854. 8vo.

Willeby, Charles. Masters of English Music. London, 1893. 8vo.

INDEX.

Abhandlung von der Fuge, by Marpurg, 170.
Abraham, oratorio by Lindpainter, 339.
Abt, Franz (1819—1885), 371.
Abu Hassan, operetta by Weber, 334.
Academy of Antient Musick, 234.
Accompaniments, additional, by Franz, 393.
Acis and Galatea, cantata by Handel, 210, 217.
Adam, Adolphe (1803—1856), 409, 416.
Adam and Eve, opera by Theile, 154.
Adam de la Halle. See "Halle, Adam de la."
Adams, Thomas (1785—1858), 445.
Addison, remarks in the *Spectator* on Italian opera, 204; his opera *Rosamund*, *ib.*
Adelaide, song by Beethoven, 290, 295.
Admeto, opera by Handel, 214.
Africaine, opera by Meyerbeer, 415.
Agnese, opera by Paer, 308.
Agricola, J. F. (1720—1774), 151.
Agrippina, opera by Handel, 160.
Ah! how, Sophia, Callcott's catch, 236.
Ah! perfido, scena by Beethoven, 295.
Ahimelek, opera by Meyerbeer, 339.
Aichinger, Gregoir (1565—), 73.
Aida, opera by Verdi, 320.
Albert V. of Bavaria, Duke, his friendship for Orlando di Lassus, 63.
Alberti (1685—), 106.

Albinoni, T. (1674—1745), 106.
Albion and Albanius, opera by Grabu, 184.
Albrechtsberger, J. G. (1736—1809), 288.
Alceste; ou, Le Triomphe d'Alcide, opera by Lully, 125.
Alcestis, opera by Gluck, 174, 259, 387.
Alcina, opera by Handel, 221.
Alcock, Dr. John (1715—1805), 239.
Alessandro, opera by Handel, 214.
Alexander Balus, Handel's oratorio, 227.
Alexander's Feast, cantata by Handel, 221, 223.
Allegri, Gregorio (1560—1652), 70, 278.
Allison, Richard (1565[?]—), 90.
Almira, opera by Handel, 159, 160.
Alonzo et Cora, opera by Méhul, 406.
Altnikol, J. C., 151.
Amadigi, opera by Handel, 208, 209.
Amati, Andreas (—1577[?]), 54.
Amber Witch, opera by W. V. Wallace, 441.
Amilie; or, The Love Test, opera by Rooke, 439.
Ambrose, St. (340—397), collects the ancient Church melodies, 2; his reforms in Church Music, *ib.*
Amour Médecin, incidental music to, by Lully, 122.
Amphion Anglicus, collection of songs by Dr. Blow, 186.
Amphitryon, Dryden's, incidental music by Purcell, 192.
Anacreon, opera by Cherubini, 306.

INDEX.

Ancient Christian melodies, corruption of, 2.
Ancient music, exaggerated appreciation of, at the Renaissance, 92.
Andromeda, words by Corneille, music by D'Assoucy, 118.
Anerio, Felice (1560—   ), 70.
Anerio, Francesco (1567—   ), 70.
Angels ever Bright and Fair, song from Handel's *Theodora*, 227.
"Anglican" chant, introduction of, 186.
Animuccia, Giovanni (1505—1571), 70, 98.
Anjou, Count of, 14.
Anna Bolena, opera by Donizetti, 315.
"Antient Concerts," 192, 234.
Antigone, opera by Hasse, 165.
—— music to, by Mendelssohn, 355.
Antiphonarium of St. Gregory, 3, 4.
A peine au sortir de l'enfance, air from Méhul's *Joseph*, 406.
Arcadelt, Jacques (1490[?]—1575[?]), 61.
Archlute, 48.
Ariana, opera by Monteverde, 95.
Ariane; ou, Le Mariage de Bacchus, opera by Cambert, 119, 201.
Arianna, opera by Handel, 220.
Ariodante, opera by Handel, 221.
Ariosti, Attilio (1660—   ), 157, 211.
Arkwright, G. E. P., his editions of madrigals, etc., 86.
Arles, sculpture at, 31.
Armide, opera by Gluck, 260.
—— opera by Lully, 126, 129.
Arminio, opera by Handel, 221.
Arnaud, Abbé, (1721—1784), 252, 260, 261.
Arne, Thomas Augustine, Mus. Doc. (1710—1778), 204, 229; his *Artaxerxes*, 204, 230, 233.
Arne, Miss (Mrs. Cibber), singer (1714—1766), 217.
Arne, Mrs. (Cecilia Young) (—1795), singer, 230.
Arnould, Sophie (1744—1802), singer, 267.

Aron Pietro (1490[?]—   ), 72.
Ars Canendi of Sebaldus Heyden, 78.
Arsinoe, Queen of Cyprus, opera by Clayton, 203.
Art of Music, The, by C. H. H. Parry, 450.
Artaserse, opera by Hasse, 220.
Artaxerxes, opera by Dr. Arne, 230, 233.
Artusi, G. M. (1554—   ), 97.
Ascanio, opera by Saint-Saëns, 428.
Ascribe unto the Lord, anthem by S. S. Wesley, 446.
As from the power, chorus from Handel's *Ode for St. Cecilia's Day*, 223.
Astarto, opera by G. B. Buononcini, 212.
Astorga, Baron E. (1681—1736), 234.
As when the dove, air in Handel's *Acis and Galatea*, 210.
Atalanta, opera by Handel, 221.
Athalie, music to, by Mendelssohn, 355.
Atterbury, L. (c. 1740—1796), 239.
Attwood, Thos. (1767—1838), 286, 303, 445.
Atys, opera by Lully, 127.
Auber, D. F. E. (1782—1871), 409.
Augelletti che cantate, air from Handel's *Rinaldo*, 206.
Aureng-Zebe, Dryden's, music for, composed by Purcell, 190.
Aus Holberg's Zeit, suite by Grieg, 402.
Ave Verum, by Mozart, 286.
Aveux Indiscrets, Les, opera by Monsigny, 257.
Avison, Charles (1710—1770), 103.

BACH, Carl Philipp Emmanuel (1714—1788), 144, 150, 270.
Bach family, the, 138.
Bach, Johann Christian (1735—1782), 150.
Bach, Johann Sebastian (1685—1750), 140; appointed organist at Arnstadt, *ib.*; at Mühlhausen, 141; and at Weimar, 142; enters

INDEX. 459

service of the Prince of Anhalt-Coethen, *ib.*; appointed "Cantor" of the Thomas-schule, Leipzig, 143; visit to Potsdam, 144; his death, 146; his works, *ib.*; the B minor mass, 147; his writings for the harpsichord, *ib.*; his pupils, 151;—162; his *St. Matthew's Passion* produced by Mendelssohn, 350.
Bach, Wilhelm Friedemann (1710—1784), 150, 162.
Baermann, H. J., clarinettist (1784—1847), 334.
Bagpipes, 29; Calabrian, 29, 30; Scotch, *ib.*; Irish and Lowland Scotch, *ib.*
Baillot, P. M., F. de S. (1771—1842), 433.
Balfe, M. W. (1808—1870), 439.
Ballad operas, English, 233.
Ballet Comique de la Royne, 113.
Ballets, popularity of, 114.
Ballo in Maschera, opera by Verdi, 320.
Banister, John (1630—1679), his concerts, 234.
Barbaja, D., impresario (1778—1841), 310.
Barbiere di Seviglia, opera by Paisiello, 311.
—— Rossini, 310, 311.
Bardes, Les, opera by Lesueur, 407.
Barker, C. S., inventor of pneumatic action for organ (1806—1879), 433.
Barnard, Rev. John, his collection of *Church Musick*, 88, 195.
Barnett, John (1802—1890), 441.
Barrington, Hon. Daines, his account of Mozart, 277.
Basilius, opera by Keiser, 154.
Bassani, G. B. (1657[?]—1716), 104.
Bassoon, 37.
Bates, Joah (1740—1799), 235.
Bateson, Thomas (1575[?]—), 84.
Batiste, A. E. (1820—1876), 434.
Battishill, Jonathan (1738—1801), 195.
Battle of the Baltic, Choral Ballad by Stanford, 450.

Bauderon, Antoine, his *Lettre de Clément Maroi*, 128.
Bayreuth, Theatre at, 386.
Bazzini, Antonio (1818—1897), 326.
Beatrice et Benedict, opera by Berlioz, 418.
Beaujoyeulx, Baltasar de, 114.
Beaulieu (living 1582), 114.
Bedford, Rev. Arthur, his *Great Abuse of Musick*, 200; *Temple Musick*, *ib.*
Beethoven, L. van: his birth and education, 286; first visit to Vienna, 287; the Breunings and Count Waldstein, *ib.*; second visit to Vienna, *ib.*; fixes his residence there, 288; the Schuppanzigh quartet, *ib.*; his pianoforte playing, 289; his three styles, 290; his symphonies, 303; the Rasoumoffsky quartet, 291; *Mount of Olives, ib.*; his opera *Fidelio, ib.*; his deafness, *ib.*; relations with his nephew, 292; his third manner, 293; his method of working, 294; Spohr's opinion of, 346; Monument at Bonn, 375; —— 304, 353, 379.
Beggar's Opera, The, 215.
Belisario, opera by Donizetti, 315.
Bellamy, Richard (1745[?]—1813), 239.
Belle Hélène, La, opera by Offenbach, 417.
Belleville, 116.
Bellini, Vincenzo (1802—1835), 314, 315.
Bells, 24.
Belshazzar, Handel's oratorio, 226.
—— oratorio by Carissimi, 99.
Benedict, Sir Julius (1804—1885), 442.
Bennett, Sir W. Sterndale (1816—1875), 362, 442.
Benvenuto Cellini, opera by Berlioz, 418.
Berg, Adam, *Patrocinium Musices* of, 65.
Berger, Ludwig (1777—1838), 348.
Bergère Châtelaine, La, opera by Auber, 410.

Berenice, opera by Handel, 221.
Beriot, C. A. de (1802—1870), 433.
Berlin Dom-Chor, 355.
Berlioz, Hector (1803—1869), his education, 417; early works, 418; becomes musical critic, *ib.*; marriage, *ib.*; his operas, *ib.*; symphonies, 419; *L'Enfance du Christ*, 420; *La Damnation de Faust*, *ib.*——379.
Bertolazzi, Margarita, singer, 117.
Berton, H. M. (1767—1842), 407.
Beyle, H., on opera in Italy, 303.
Beza, Theodore, completes Marot's translation of the Psalms, 112.
Bid me discourse, song by Bishop, 438.
Bigot, Madame M. (1786—1820), 348.
Binchois, Egidius (1400—1465), 56, 59.
Biographie des Musiciens of Fétis, 253, 435.
Birds, The, of Aristophanes. Music by C. H. H. Parry, 450.
Birmingham Musical Festival, 353.
Bishop, Sir H. R. (1786—1855), 438.
Bizet, Georges (1838—1875), 422.
Blest pair of sirens, glee by J. Stafford Smith, 239.
Blondeau de Nesle, 15.
Blow, Dr. John (1648—1708), 181, 184, 188, 190, 191, 193, 198.
Blow, thou wintry wind, air by Dr. Arne, 230.
Boccherini, Luigi (1740—1805), 323.
Boethius (455—526), author of first Latin treatise on music, 11, 72.
Bohème, La, opera by Puccini, 323.
Bohemian Girl, The, opera by Balfe, 439.
Boieldieu, F. A. (1775—1834), 408.
Boito, Arrigo, 321, 322.
Bonanni, his *Gabinetto Armonico*, 21.
Bonaparte, Jerome, King of Westphalia, 292.
Booke, The, of Common Praier Noted, 81.

Borjon, C. E., his *Traité de la Musette*, 134.
Borodin, Alesander (1834—1887), 401.
Borromeo, Cardinal, 68.
Bortniansky, D. (1752—1828), 398.
Boscherville, bas-relief of concert at, 50, 51.
"Bouffons," "Guerre des," 251, 388.
Bourgeois Gentilhomme, Le, incidental music to, by Lully, 122.
Boyce, Dr. William (1710—1779), 195; his *Cathedral Music, ib.*
Brabant, Duke of, 14.
Bracegirdle, Mrs., singer (1663—1748), 203.
Brady and Tate, their "New Version" of the Psalms, 90.
Braham, John (1774—1856), 227, 337.
Brahms, Johannes, 362, 390.
Brasseur de Preston, Le, opera by A. Adam, 416.
Braut von Messina, overture by Schumann, 366.
Breitkopf and Härtel, their edition of Palestrina's works, 70.
Breuning, von, family of, 287.
Brides of Venice, opera by Benedict, 442.
Britton, Thomas, "the musical small-coal man" (1651—1714), 231, 234.
Broschi, C., 212, 220.
Brouncker, Lord, his translation of Descartes' *Compendium Musicæ*, 134.
Bruch, Max, 395.
Brumel, Antonio (1460[?]—15—), 61.
Bruneau, Alfred, 430.
Bull, Dr. John (1563[?]—1628), 86, 87.
Buononcini, G. B. (1665[?]—1750), 157, 170, 212, 218——M. A. (1655—1726), 203.
Burney, Dr. (1726—1814), his edition of music for Holy Week sung in the Sistine Chapel, 70 his *History of Music*, 240.

INDEX. 461

Buxtehude, Dietrich (1637—1707), 137, 140, 158.
Byrd, Thomas, 88.
—— William (1537[?]—1623), 82; his patent for printing music with Tallis, *ib.*

CACCINI, Giulio (1558[?]—1640), 94.
Cadi Dupé, Le, opera by Monsigny, 257.
Cadmus, opera by Lully, 126.
Caduta de' Giganti, opera by Gluck, 232.
Cæcilia, Musical Journal, 330.
Cäcilien-Verein at Frankfurt, 353.
Caffiarelli, G. M. (1703—1783), 104.
Caïd, La, opera by Amb. Thomas, 423.
Caldara, Antonio (1678—1763), 170, 173.
Calife de Bagdad, Le, opera by Boieldieu, 408.
Callcott, Dr. J. W. (1766—1821), 236, 239.
Calm Sea and Prosperous Voyage, overture of Mendelssohn, 350.
Calvary, oratorio of Spohr, 344.
Calvin on sacred music, 112.
Calzabigi, poet, writes Gluck's libretti, 174.
Camacho's Wedding, opera by Mendelssohn, 349.
Cambert, Robert (1628—1677), 118; his opera, *La Pastorale,* 119; his *Ariane; ou, Le Mariage de Bacchus, ib.*; his *Pomona,* 120; supplanted by Lully, 124, 128, 201.
Cambiale di Matrimonio, opera by Rossini, 309.
Camilla, opera by M. A. Buononcini, 203.
—— opera by Paer, 321.
Campanile, 24.
Campra, André (1660—1744), 132.
Canterbury Pilgrims, The, opera by C. V. Stanford, 450.
Cantiones Sacræ, by Tallis and Byrd, 82.
Capistrum, or mouth bandage, 27.

Cara sposa, air from Handel's *Rinaldo,* 206.
Carestini, Giovanni, singer (1705—1763), 220, 221.
Carey, Henry (1685[?]—1743), 230.
Carillon, 25.
Carissimi, Giacomo (1604[?]—1674), 99.
Carmen, opera by Bizet, 423.
Castor et Pollux, opera by Rameau, 248.
Catch Club, Noblemen and Gentlemen's, 238.
Catch that catch can, 88.
Catch, the, 236.
Cathedral music, Boyce's collection of, 195.
Cathedral Service, Short Direction for the Performance of, by E. Lowe, 186.
Catherina Cornaro, opera by Lachner, 340.
Catone, opera by Leonardo Leo, 218.
Caurroy, Eustache de (1549—1609), 116.
Cavaliere, Emilio del (1550[?]—1598[?]), 94, 95, 99.
Cavaillé-Col, organ-builder, 433.
Cavalleria rusticana, La, opera by Mascagni, 323.
Cavalli, P. Francesco (1599[?]—1676), 98.
Cazotte, Jacques (1720—1793), 252.
Cecilia, St., Cologne, bell at, 25.
Cecilia's (St.) Day, 193, 194.
Cecilia's Day, Ode for St., Handel's, 223.
Cendrillon, opera by Isouard, 408.
Cenerentola, opera by Rossini, 310.
Cesti, Marco Antonio (1620—1675), 98.
Chalet Le, opera by Adolphe Adam, 416.
Chalumeau, 37.
Champeron finances the opera founded by Perrin and Cambert, 119.
Chandos *Anthems* and *Te Deums,* Handel's, 209.
—— Duke of, 209.

Change-ringing, 26.
Chant du Départ, by Méhul, 406.
Chant sur le Livre, 14.
Chanterelle, 47.
Chantilly, Mademoiselle, singer (Madame Favart), 277.
Chapel Royal, London, at the Restoration, choir of, 179; introduction of instrumental music in, 182.
Chappell, Mr. W., his *Popular Music of the Olden Time*, facsimile of *Sumer is icumen in*, 79.
Charlemagne endeavours to introduce uniformity of ritual, 4; receives an organ from Haroun Alraschid, 32.
Charles II. of England, music at his court, 199.
—— VI., Emperor of Austria, 171.
—— VII., of France, 59.
—— VIII., of France, 59.
—— IX. of France, 111.
Charles de France, opera by Boieldieu and Hérold, 412.
Charmante Gabrielle, the air, 116.
Chasse du jeune Henri, Le, opera by Méhul, 406.
Che faro senza Euridice, from Gluck's *Orfeo*, 174.
Chelys. See "*Division Violist*, Simpson's."
Cherubini, M. L C. Z. S. (1760—1842), 305; settles in Paris, 306; relations with Napoleon, 307; his sacred music, *ib.*; his death, 308.
—— 232, 349, 372, 407, 408, 410, 412, 418.
Chest of Viols, 52.
Cheval de Bronze, Le, opera by Auber, 411.
Child, Dr. William (1606—1697), 181.
Chimay, Prince de, 307.
Chimes, 25.
Chittarone, 48, 95.
Choir-schools, established by St. Gregory, 4.
Chopin, F. (1809—1849), his career and works, 431; —— 362.

Chorales, introduction of, 73.
Choral symphony of Beethoven, 293.
Choron, A. E. (1771—1834), 434.
"Chorus" (musical instrument), 28.
Chough and Crow, The, glee by Bishop, 438.
Christian religion, effect of on music, 2.
Christophe Colomb, symphony by Félicien David, 422.
Christus, fragment of oratorio by Mendelssohn, 356.
Chrysander, Dr. F., his edition of Carissimi's oratorios, 99; Life of Handel, 209.
Cibber, Mrs., singer (1714—1766), 203.
Cimarosa, Domenico (1749—1801), 304.
Cinq Mars, opera by Gounod, 426.
Cithara, Hebrew, 22; described by Gerbert, 39.
Clapisson, A. L. (1808—1866), 417.
Clarionet, 37.
Clark, Dr. Jeremiah (1668[?]—1707), 187.
Clavichord, 44.
Clavicytherium, 44.
Clayton, Thomas (1665[?]—), 203, 204.
Clemens non Papa (first half 16th century), 61.
Clementi, Muzio (1752—1832), 370, 437.
Clemenza di Tito, opera by Mozart, 284.
Cleopatra, opera by Mattheson, 158.
Climène, opera by Sacchini, 304.
Clovis, baptism of, 3; treaty with Theodoric, *ib.*
"Coin du Roi," "Coin de la Reine," 251.
Colasse, Pascal (1639[?]—1709), 130.
Colbran, Isabella A. (1785—1845), (Madame Rossini), 311.
Cologne, bell at, 25.
Colporteur, Le, opera by Onslow, 421.
Colomba, opera by Mackenzie, 449.

INDEX. 463

Colombe, La, opera by Gounod, 426.
Columbus, overture by Wagner, 379.
Comala, cantata by Gade, 402.
Come if you dare, from Purcell's *King Arthur*, 192.
Come unto these yellow sands, from Purcell's *Tempest*, 192.
Commandments, Matthew Lock's responses to, 181.
Compendium of Practical Musick, Simpson's, 198.
Comte Ory, Le, opera by Rossini, 312.
"Concert of Antient Musick," 234.
Concertos, organ, by Handel, 225.
Concert-Stück of Weber, 338.
Concerts, early, in England, 234.
Concerts spirituels, founded by A. D. Philidor, 265.
Consolations des Misères de ma Vie, songs by J. J. Rousseau, 256.
Constantine, Christian worship under, 2.
Constantine Copronymus sends an organ to Pépin, 32.
Contarini, opera by Pierson, 447.
Contrabasso introduced into French orchestra by Montéclair, 134.
Contralto voice, rarity of, in France, 259.
Contrapunto a mente, 14.
Cooke, "Captain" Henry (1610[?] —1672), 180, 181, 183, 184, 187.
Cooke, Dr. Benjamin (1732[?]— 1793), 195, 239.
Corelli, Arcangelo (1653—1713), 104, 161, 192.
Corneille, P., writes words of the opera *Andromeda*, 118.
Cornemuse, or bagpipes, 29, 30.
Coronation anthems by Handel, 215.
Cosi fan tutte, opera by Mozart, 283.
Costa, Sir Michael (1810—1884), 442, 452.
Costanza e Fortezza, opera by Fux, 171.
Cotton, John (11th century), his explanation of *organum*, 13.

Coucy, Châtelain de (—1192), 14.
Couperin, family of the, 266.
Coussemaker, C. E. H. de (1805— 1876), on early harmony, 12; his collection of the works of Adam de la Halle, 16, and of liturgical dramas, 17; on manuscript of *Sumer is icumen in*, 80.— 436.
Cowen, F. H., 451.
Cramer, J. B., pianist (1771—1858), 369, 437, 452.
—— William, violinist (1745—1799), 273, 439.
Creation, oratorio by Haydn, 273, 275, 370.
Cremona violins, 54.
Crétin, Déploration sur le Trépas de feu Okeghem, 59.
Cristofali, Bartolomeo (1651—1731), inventor of pianoforte, 46.
Critica Musica, Mattheson's, 163.
Croce, Giovanni della (1550[?]— 1609), 72.
Crociato, Il, opera by Meyerbeer, 339.
Croft, Dr. William (1677—1727), 187, 188, 195.
Cromwell, 179.
Crotala, 24.
Crusaders, The, opera by Benedict, 442.
—— cantata by Gade, 402.
Crwth, 48.
Cui, César, 400.
Curschmann, C. F. (1805—1841), 371.
Curwen, Rev. J., 454.
Cuzzoni, Francesca, singer (1700— 1770), 212, 213, 215, 219.
Cymbals, 24.
Czar und Zimmermann, opera by Lortzing, 340.
Czerny, Carl (1791—1857), 300.

Dafne, by Jacopo Peri, 94.
Dalayrac, N. (1753—1809), 405.
D'Alembert, J. Le R. (1717—1783), 244, 254, 260.
Damasus, Pope, introduces chanting the Psalms, 3.

Dame Blanche, La, opera by Boieldieu, 408, 409.
Damnation de Faust, cantata by Berlioz, 420.
Danaides, Les, opera by Salieri, 261, 301, 305.
Danby, John (1757—1798), 239.
Danican. See "Philidor."
Danjou, F. (1812—1866), 435.
Danse Macabre, Poème Symphonique by Saint-Saëns, 427.
Dante Symphony, by Liszt, 374.
Dardanus, opera by Rameau, 248.
D'Assoucy, C. Coypeau (1604—1679), 118.
Daughter of Jairus, The, cantata by Stainer, 451.
David, Félicien (1810—1876), 241.
—— Ferdinand (1810—1873), 346, 352, 355.
Davidsbündler, the, 361.
Davis, Mrs. Mary, singer, 203.
Deborah, oratorio by Handel, 218.
Deeper and deeper still, recitative from Handel's *Jephtha*, 227.
Deidamia, opera by Handel, 222.
De la Rue, Pierre (second half 15th century), 61.
Délivrance de Renaud, ballet of, 116.
Demon, The, opera by Rubinstein, 400.
Demophoon, opera of Cherubini, 306.
Descartes, René (1596—1650), his *Compendium Musicæ*, 134.
Désert, Le, ode-symphony of Félicien David, 421.
Déserteur, Le, opera by Monsigny, 258.
Desmarets, Henri (1662—1741), 130.
Destouches, A. C. (1672—1749), 132.
Dettingen *Te Deum*, Handel's, 226.
Deuteromelia, by T. Ravenscroft, 88.
Deutsches Requiem, by Brahms, 392.
Deux Journées, Les, opera by Cherubini, 306.
Devin du Village, Le, opera by J. J. Rousseau, 255.

Dezède (1740—1793), 256.
Diabelli, the publisher, 298.
Diamants de la Couronne, opera by Auber, 411.
Diaphony, or *organum*, 12.
Dibdin, Charles (1745—1814), 233.
Dictionary Musical, of Tinctoris, 60.
Dictionnaire de Musique, by J. J. Rousseau, 254.
Diderot, D. (1712—1784), 254.
Dido and Æneas, opera by Purcell, 191.
Dinorah (Pardon de Ploermel), opera by Meyerbeer, 415.
Diocletian; or, The Prophetess, incidental music by Purcell, 192.
Discant, introduction of the, 13.
Discord, dire sister, glee by S. Webbe, 238.
Division Violist, Simpson's, 199.
Dodecachordon of Glareanus, 57.
Doles, J. F. (1715—1797), 152.
Dom-Chor in Berlin, 355.
Domino Noir, Le, opera by Auber, 411.
Don Carlos, opera by Costa, 443.
Don Carlos, opera by Verdi, 320.
Don Giovanni, opera by Mozart, 282.
Don Pasquale, opera by Donizetti, 315.
Don Quixote, opera by G. A. Macfarren, 441.
Donizetti, Gaetano (1798—1848), 314.
Donna del Lago, La, opera by Rossini, 310.
Douland, John (1562—1626), 90.
Draghi, Antonio (1642—1707), 170.
Dragon of Wantley, burlesque opera by J. F. Lampe, 230.
Drums, 23. See also "Kettledrums."
Dryden, John, poet, 184, 190, 192, 221.
Dublin, Handel's visit to, 224.
Duenna, The, opera by Linley, 233.
Dufay, Guillaume (1350—1432), 56.
Duiffoprugcar, Gaspar (first half 16th century), 54.
Dulcimer or psaltery, 43, 46.

INDEX. 465

Dunstable, John of (c. 1400—1458), 56, 80.
Dupuis, Dr. T. S. (1733—1796), 195.
Durante, Francesco (1684—1755), 100, 304.
Durastanti, Signora, singer (18th century), 212.
D'Urfey, Thomas (—1723), 187; his *Wit and Mirth; or, Pills to Purge Melancholy*, 200.
Dussek, J. L. (1761—1812), 367.
Dvorák, Antonin, 394.

EARLY history of music, 1.
Early secular music, 14.
Earthly and Heavenly in Man's Nature, symphony by Spohr, 345.
Eberlin, J. E. (1702—1762), 276.
Echo et Narcisse, opera by Gluck, 261.
Eclair, L', opera by Halévy, 416.
Edward VI., Reformed Prayerbook of, 80.
Edwards, Richard (1523—1566), 81.
Ehrenpforte Grundlage einer, by Mattheson, 164, 172.
Ein' feste Burg, the chorale, 73.
Elégie of Ernst, for violin, 372.
Eli, oratorio by Costa, 443.
Elijah, oratorio by Mendelssohn, 355, 356, 357.
Elisabetta, opera by Rossini, 310.
Elisa e Claudio, opera by Mercadante, 315.
Elisir d' Amore, L', opera by Donizetti, 315.
Elizabeth, Queen, her fondness for the virginal, 44; celebrated in the *Triumphs of Oriana*, 85.
Ella, J., his "Musical Union," 453.
Emma di Risburgo, opera by Meyerbeer, 339.
Encyclopédie, L', J. J. Rousseau's articles in, 254.
Enfance du Christ, L', oratorio by Berlioz, 420.
Enfant prodigue, L', opera by Auber, 411.
Engel, Carl, catalogue of musical instruments in the South Kensington Museum, 21.

Entführung aus dem Serail, opera by Mozart, 280.
Envy, eldest-born of Hell, chorus from Handel's *Saul*, 224.
Epine, Margherita de l' (—1746), 203.
Episode de la Vie d'un Artiste, symphony by Berlioz, 419.
Equal temperament advocated by Bach, 148.
Erasmus, Desiderius, 57.
Ercole d'Este, Duke of Ferrara, 60.
Erinnyes, Les, opera by Massenet, 429.
Erl King's Daughter, The, cantata by Gade, 402.
Erlkönig, Der, song by Schubert, 296, 298.
Ernani, opera by Verdi, 319.
Ernst, H. W. (1814—1865), 372.
Escobedo, Bartolomeo (1510—), 70.
Esmeralda, opera by A. Goring Thomas, 447.
Essais sur la Musique, by Grétry, 264.
Esther, Handel's oratorio, 210, 217.
Est's *Psalms*, 90.
Etoile du Nord, L', opera by Meyerbeer, 414.
Eugen Onegin, opera by Tschaikowsky, 400.
Euphrosine et Coradin, opera of Méhul, 406.
Euridice, by Rinuccini, set to music both by Peri and Caccini, 94.
Euryanthe, opera by Weber, 336, 338.
Eusebius and Florestan, 361.
Ezio, opera by Handel, 217.

FAIRFAX, Dr. Robert (second half 15th century), 80.
Fall of Babylon, oratorio by Spohr, 344.
Falstaff, opera by Balfe, 439.
—— opera by Verdi, 321.
Famille Suisse, La, opera by Boieldieu, 408.
Fanatico per gli antichi Romani, opera by Cimarosa, 304.

30

INDEX.

Fanchon, opera by Himmel, 339.
Faniska, opera by Cherubini, 307.
Faramondo, opera by Handel, 222.
Farinelli (Carlo Broschi called) (1705—1782), 104, 220, 221.
Farmer, John (1565[?]—), 90.
Farnaby, Giles (1560—), 90.
Farrant, Richard (1530[?]—1581), 82.
Fausse Magie, La, opera by Grétry, 264.
Faust, cantata, by Schumann, 364, 365.
—— opera by Gounod, 323, 425.
—— opera by Spohr, 343.
—— symphony by Liszt, 374.
—— music to second part of, by Pierson, 447.
Faustina Bordoni, wife of Hasse (1700—1783), 166, 213.
Faux Lord, Le, opera by Gossec, 256.
Favart, Madame, singer and dancer (1727—1772), 267.
Favorita, La, opera by Donizetti, 315.
Feen, Die, opera by Wagner, 376.
Feldlager in Schlesien, opera by Meyerbeer, 414.
Fenton, Lavinia (Duchess of Bolton) (18th century), 216.
Feramors, opera by Rubinstein, 400.
Fernand Cortez, opera by Spontini, 316, 334.
Ferrari, Benedetto (—1681), 98.
Festes de l' Eté, opera by Montéclair, 134.
Fêtes de l'Amour et de Bacchus, opera by Lully, 124.
Fétis, F. J. (1784—1871), remarks on Guido d'Arezzo, 10; ——253, 435.
Fiancée, La, opera by Auber, 411.
Fidelio, opera by Beethoven, 291.
Field, John (1782—1837), 437.
Figlia del Reggimento, La, opera by Donizetti, 315.
Fingal's Cave, overture by Mendelssohn, 351.

Finta Pazza, La, performed in Paris, 1645, 117.
Finta Semplice, La, opera by Mozart, 278.
Five times by the taper's light, quartet by Storace, 233.
Fixed in His everlasting seat, chorus in Handel's *Samson*, 226.
Flageolet, 23, 28.
Flavio, opera by Handel, 213.
Fliegende Holländer, Der, opera by Wagner, 344, 379, 380.
Flores Musicæ, by Hugo von Reutlingen, 75.
Florestan and Eusebius, 361.
Floridante, opera by Handel, 212.
Florid Song, Treatise on the, by Tosi, 170.
Flotow, F. F. A. von (1812—1883), 341.
Flute, the, 22, 27; double, 27; horizontal or "German," 28; à-bec, *ib.*
Foire, Théâtre de la, 249.
Foolish Virgins, song of the, 18.
Forza del destino, La, opera by Verdi, 320.
Foundling Hospital, Handel's interest in the, 226.
Four-line staff introduced, 9.
Fournival, Richard de (13th century), 14.
Fra Diavolo, opera by Auber, 411.
Franc, Guillaume (16th century), his music to Marot's *Psalms*, 112.
Francis I. of France, 111.
Franck, César, 429.
Francs Juges, Les, overture by Berlioz, 418.
Franz, R. (1815—1892), 362, 392.
Frederick the Great of Prussia, 144, 179, 252.
Frederick William IV. of Prussia, 354.
French and Italian music, comparison between, 251.
French singers, 267.
Frescobaldi, Girolamo (1587—1654), 108.
Freyschütz, Der, opera by Weber, 335, 336, 338.

INDEX. 467

Froberger, J. J. (1615—1667), 137.
Froissart, figure of monochord from MS. copy of, 54.
Frost scene in Purcell's *King Arthur*, 192.
Fürstenau, A. B. (1792—1852), 336, 337.
Full fathom five, from Purcell's *Tempest*, 192.
Funeral service by Dr. Croft, 188.
Fux, Johann Josef (1660—1741), 170, 173, 271, 278, 288.

Gabinetto Armonico, of Bonanni, 21.
Gabrieli, Andrea (1510—1586), 72, 107.
—— Giovanni (1557—1613), 72, 107.
Gade, Niels (1817—1890), 362, 402.
Gaforius (or Gaffurius) (1451—1522), writer on theory of music, 72.
Galatea, dry thy tears, chorus from *Acis and Galatea*, 210.
Galilei, Vincenzo (1533[?]—), his dialogue on the music of the ancients, 93.
Gallia, by Gounod, 426.
Galuppi, Baldassare (1701 [1706?]—1785), 101.
Gänsbacher, J. (1778—1844), 330.
Gardano, Antonio (16th century), music printer, 62.
Gardiner, Bishop, 81.
Garth, John, 103.
Gaspar di Salo (end of 16th century), 54.
Gastoldi, Giangiacomo (1532—1598), 72.
Gates, Bernard (1686—1773), 217.
Gauntlett, Dr. (1806—1876), 446.
Gaviniés, Pierre (1728—1800), 266.
Gavotte of Louis XIII., 114.
Gazza Ladra, La, opera by Rossini, 310.
Geminiani, F. (1680—1762), 106, 230.
Genoveva, opera by Schumann, 365.
Gerbert, Martin (1720—1793) (prince abbot of St. Blaise, in the Black Forest), 7, 39, 52.

Germany, early history of music in, 73.
Gewandhaus concerts, 152, 352.
Gheyn, Matthias van den (1721—1785), 25.
Gibbons, Christopher (1615—1676), 181.
—— Ellis (1580[?]—1650), 85.
—— Orlando (1583—1625), his madrigals, 84; his *Fantasies in three parts*, 86.
Gideon, oratorio by Stainer, 451.
Gilbert, Gabriel, writes poem of *Les Peines et les Plaisirs d'Amour*, opera by Cambert, 121.
Ginguené, P. L. (1748—1816), 260.
Giorno di Regno, Un, opera by Verdi, 319, 321.
Giulio Cesare, opera by Handel, 213.
Giuramento, Il, opera by Mercadante, 315.
Giustiniani's *Psalms* set to music by Marcello, 102.
Giustinio, opera by Handel, 221.
Gizziello (Gioacchino Conti called) (1714—1761), singer, 221.
Glareanus, Henricus Loritus (1488—1563), 57, 59, 73, 76.
Glee, introduction of the, 237; definition of, *ib*.
Glinka, M. I. (1803—1857), 399.
Gluck, Christopher Willibald (1714—1787), 173; his *Orfeo*, 174; *Alcestis*, *ib.*; principles of dramatic composition, *ib.*; *Paride ed Elena*, 176; *Iphigénie en Aulide*, *ib.*; visits Paris, *ib.* 177, 258; visits London, 232; *Iphigénie en Aulide* in Paris, 258; *Orphée*, 259; *Alceste, ib.*; rivalry with Piccinni, *ib.*; *Armide*, 260; *Iphigénie en Tauride*, 261; his death, *ib.*; —— 267, 387.
Gluckistes and Piccinnistes, controversy of the, 259.
God is gone up, anthem by Dr. Croft, 188.
Godard, Benjamin, 430.
Goetz, Hermann (1840—1876), 396.
Götterdämmerung, opera by Wagner, 383.

Golden Legend, The, oratorio by Sullivan, 449.
Goldmark, Karl, 395.
Gombert, Nicolas (1495—1570[?]), 61.
Gordigiani, L. (1806—1860), 323.
Gosling, Rev. John (1652—1733), 191.
Goss, Sir John (1800—1880), 445.
Gossec, E. J. (1733—1829), 256.
Goudimel, Claude (1510—1572), 61, 69.
Gounod, Charles (1815—1893); childhood, 423; sojourn in Rome, 424; his *Faust*, 425; visit to England, 426; his operas, *ib*.
Grabu, Louis (living 1685), 184.
Gradus ad Parnassum, by Clementi, 437.
—— by Fux, 172, 270.
Grand Cid, Il, opera by Sacchini, 304.
Grande Duchesse de Gérolstein, La, opera bouffe by Offenbach, 417.
Graner Mass of Liszt, 374.
Graun, C. H. (1701—1759), 167.
Great Abuse of Musick, Rev. A. Bedford's, 200.
Greatorex, Thomas (1758—1831), 235.
Greece, musicians in Rome from that country, 1; musical instruments of, 22.
Greene, Dr. Maurice (1696[?]—1755, 195).
"Gregorian" music, 4.
Gregory, St., the great (542—604), his services to Church music, 3; his method of notation, 4; his claim to the invention of neums, *ib*.
Gregory, St., of Tours, 3.
Gresham, Sir Thomas, his college, 87.
Gretchen am Spinnrade, song by Schubert, 299.
Grétry, A. E. M. (1741—1813), 262.
Grieg, Edward, 402.
Grimm, F. M. Baron (1723—1807), 252, 277.
Grisar, Albert (1808—1869), 417.

Groppo Antonio, his catalogue of *drammi in musica* played in Venice, 97.
Grove, Sir G., his *Dictionary of Music*, facsimile of *Sumer is icumen in*, 79; —— 312.
Guarnerius, Joseph (1683—1745), 55.
Guerrero, Francesco (1518—1599), 70.
Guesdron, 116.
Guido d'Arezzo (c. 990—1070), his invention of *solfeggio*, 9.
Guido et Genevra, opera by Halévy, 416.
Guignon, J. P. (1702—1775), 266.
Guildhall School of Music, 454.
Guillaume Tell, opera by Rossini, 312.
Guitar, 48.
Gumpelzhaimer, Adam (1560—), 137.
Gürzenich Concerts, 371.
Gustave III., opera by Auber, 411.
Gypsy's Warning, The, opera by Benedict, 442.

HABENECK, F. A. (1781—1849), 433.
Händl, Jakob (1550—1591), 73.
Halévy, J. F. F. E. (1799—1862), 349, 416.
Halle, Adam de la (13th century), 15; his compositions, 16.
Hallelujah Chorus in Handel's *Messiah*, 225.
Hamburg, first public performance of opera given in, 154;
Hamlet, opera by Amb. Thomas, 423.
Handbuch bey dem Generalbasse, by Marpurg, 170.
Handel, George Frederic (1685—1759), his youth, 156; settles in Hamburg, 157; relations with Mattheson, *ib*.; his opera *Almira*, 159; and *Nero*, *ib*.; visits Italy, 160; appointed Capellmeister at Hanover, 162; his arrival in England, 205; operatic career, *ib*.; Utrecht *Te Deum* and *Jubilate*, 208; "Water Music," *ib*.;

INDEX.   469

enters service of the Duke of Chandos, 209; production of his first oratorio, *Esther*, 210; foundation of the Royal Academy of Music, 211; coronation anthems, 215; collapse of the Royal Academy, *ib.*; partnership with Heidegger, 216; production of *Acis and Galatea* and *Deborah*, 217; partnership with Rich, 220; his bankruptcy and illness, 222; his oratorios, 223; *The Messiah*, 224; his visit to Dublin, 225; his second bankruptcy, 227; his blindness, 227; and death, 228.
Handel, Life of, by Mattheson, 164.
Handel's fondness for the trumpet, 37.
Hannibal, opera by Keiser, 155.
Hansel und Gretel, opera by Humperdinck, 396.
Hans Heiling, opera by Marschner, 338.
Happy we, chorus from Handel's *Acis and Galatea*, 210.
Harmonia Sacra, Playford's, 198.
Harmonie Universelle, by Mersenne, 135.
Harmonious Blacksmith, Handel's, 210.
Harmony, early attempts at, 12.
Harmony of the Spheres, cantata by A. Romberg, 371.
Harold en Italie, symphony by Berlioz, 420.
Haroun Alraschid sends an organ to Charlemagne, 32.
Harp, the, 40; of O'Brien, *ib.*; Welsh triple, *ib.*; pedal, 42; Erard's improvements, 43.
Harpsichord, 45.
Harris, Renatus, organ-builder (1725), 196.
Hasse, John Adolph (1699—1783), 100, 164, 220.
Hassler, Hans Leo (1564—1612), 72.
Haste thee, nymph, air and chorus from Handel's *L'Allegro*, 223.
Haunted Tower, The, opera by Storace, 233.

Hauptmann, M. (1794—1868), 346, 355.
Hawkins, Sir John, his *History of Music*, 240.
Haydn, Franz Josef (1732—1809), his youth, 269; becomes accompanist to Porpora, 270; acquaintance with Countess Thun and Count Morzin, *ib.*; enters service of Prince Esterhazy, 271; residence in Vienna, 273; visits to England, *ib.*, his *Creation, ib.*; *Seasons, ib.*; his death, 274; his symphonies and quartets, *ib.*; *The Seven Last Words, ib.*; his admiration for Mozart, 280; Beethoven becomes his pupil, 287, 289.
Haydn, Johann Michael (1737—1806), 269, 276.
Hayes, Dr. Philip (1738—1797), 195.
—— Dr. William (1707—1777), 195.
Hebrides, overture by Mendelssohn, 351.
Heidegger, James, 208, 211, 216, 218, 220, 222.
Heilands Letzte Stunden, Das, oratorio by Spohr, 344.
Heimkehr aus der Fremde, operetta by Mendelssohn, 351.
Heller, Stephen (1815—1888), 362, 371.
Henri II. of France, 111.
Henri VIII., opera by Saint-Saëns, 428.
Henry VIII. of England, 63.
Hensel, Fanny (1805—1847), 348, 356.
Henselt, Adolph (1814—   ), 364.
Herculaneum, opera of Féln. David, 422.
Hermann und Dorothea, overture of Schumann, 366.
Hérodiade, opera by Massenet, 429.
Hérold, L. J. F. (1791—1833), 411.
Hesse, A. J. (1809—1863), 372.
Heyden, Sebaldus (1498—1561), his *Ars Canendi*, 76.

Hezekiah, oratorio by Pierson, 487.
Hiller, Johann Adam (1728—1804), 152, 169.
—— Ferdinand (1811—1885), 362, 365, 371, 431.
Hilton, John (1575[?]—1657), 82; his *Catch that catch can*, 88.
Himmel, F. H. (1765—1814), 339.
Hippolyte et Aricie, opera by Rameau, 246.
Histoire de la Révolution Operée dans la Musique par M. le Chevalier Gluck of Leblond, 260.
Historisch-kritische Beytrage zur Aufnahme der Musik, Marpurg's, 169.
Histrio-Mastix, Prynne's, 116.
Hobrecht (1430[?]—1507), 57, 58.
Holbach, P. Thyry, Baron d' (1723—1789), 252.
Holy Week, music for, in Sistine Chapel, 70.
Home, sweet home! air by Bishop, 438.
Hope told a flattering tale (Nel cor più), air by Paisiello, 304.
Horn, C. F. (1762—1830), 446.
Hucbald (840[?]—930), his treatise *Musica Enchiriadis*, 12.
Hugo von Reutlingen (14th century), his *Flores Musicæ*, 75.
Huguenots, Les, opera by Meyerbeer, 413.
Hullah, John (1812—1884), 454.
Humfrey, Pelham (1647—1674), 181, 183, 190.
Hummel, J. N. (1778—1837), 286, 300, 349.
Huntsman's Chorus, in *Der Freyschütz*, by Weber, 336.
Huron, Le, opera by Grétry, 264.
Hush, ye pretty, warbling choir, air in Handel's *Acis and Galatea*, 210.
Hymn of Praise (Lobgesang), by Mendelssohn, 353, 357.

I attempt from love's sickness to fly, from Purcell's *Indian Queen*, 192.
I beheld, and lo! a great multitude, anthem by Dr. Blow, 186.
Idomeneo, opera by Mozart, 279.
Il tricerbero umiliato, air from Handel's *Rinaldo*, 206.
Im Wald, symphony by J. Raff, 373.
Indes Galantes, opera by Rameau, 248.
Indian Queen, Purcell's, 192.
In Exitu Israel, motet by Samuel Wesley, 446.
In going to my naked bed, madrigal by R. Edwards, 81.
In memoriam, overture by Sullivan, 449.
Instrumental music, early, 86; in France, 134, 266.
Instruments, musical, history of, 20.
In these delightful pleasant groves, chorus from Purcell's *Libertine*, 190.
Introduction to the Skill of Musick, Playford's, 197.
In una siepe ombrosa, madrigal by Lotti, 101, 219.
Invitation to the Waltz, by Weber, 338.
Invocation, L', sonata by Dussek, 369.
Iphigénie en Aulide, opera by Gluck, 176, 258.
Iphigénie en Tauride, opera by Gluck, 261, 406.
I rage, I melt, I burn, recitative in Handel's *Acis and Galatea*, 210.
Iron Chest, The, opera by Storace, 233.
Isaak, Heinrich (1445[?]—1518[?]), 73.
Isabelle et Gertrude, opera by Grétry, 263.
Isidore, St., Bishop of Seville, (c. 570—636), on the use of neums, 8.
Isouard, Nicolo (1775—1818), 408.
Israel in Egypt, Handel's oratorio, 223, 352.

INDEX. 471

Issé, opera by Destouches, 132.
Italiana in Algieri, opera by Rossini, 309.
Italian and French music, comparison between, 251.
Italian singers introduced into France by Cardinal Mazarin, 116.
Italian Symphony, by Mendelssohn, 352, 357.
Italy, early history of music in, 67.
Ivanhoe, opera by Sullivan, 448.
I was in the Spirit, anthem by Dr. Blow, 186.

"JACK," action in keyed stringed instruments, 44.
Jackson, William, of Exeter (1730—1803), 195.
Jacob, Benjamin (1778—1829), 446.
Jannequin, Clément (c. 1480—), 61.
Jean de Paris, opera by Boieldieu, 409.
Jélyotte, Pierre, singer (1711—1782), 267.
Jennens, Charles, selects the words of Handel's *Messiah*, 224, 225.
Jephtha, Handel's oratorio, 227.
—— oratorio by Carissimi, 99.
Jerome, St. (331—420), his letter on musical instruments, 22.
Jerusalem, oratorio by Pierson, 447.
Jessonda, opera by Spohr, 344.
Jeunesse d'Hercule, La, poème symphonique by Saint-Saëns, 427.
Jewish influence on early Christian music, 2.
Jolly Young Waterman, song by Dibdin, 234.
Jomelli, Nicolo (1714—1774), 101, 303.
Jonah, oratorio by Carissimi, 99.
Jongleurs, 15.
Joseph, opera by Méhul, 406.
Joshua, Handel's oratorio, 227.
Josquin de Près (1450[?]—1521), 59, 60, 67, 73, 111.
Jubilate, by Purcell, 192, 193.
—— by Handel, 208.

Judas Maccabæus, Handel's oratorio, 227.
Judenthum in der Musik, Das, by Wagner, 382.
Judgment of Solomon, oratorio by Carissimi, 99.
Judith, oratorio by Parry, 450.
Juive, La, opera by Halévy, 416.
Julius III., Pope, appoints Palestrina a singer in the Sistine Chapel, 69.

KALKBRENNER, F. W. M. (1788—1849), 370, 431.
Kalliwoda, J. W. (1800—1866), 371.
Keiser, Reinhard (1673—1739), 154, 160, 164.
Kettledrums, orchestral, 24.
Kielmansegge, Baron, 162, 208.
King Arthur, Dryden's, incidental music by Purcell, 192.
King, Charles (1687—1748), 195.
Kinsky, Prince, 292.
Kirkman, maker of harpsichords, 46.
Kirnberger, J. P. (1721—1783), 151, 369.
Knecht, J. H. (1752—1817), 330.
Knorr, Julius (1807—1861), 361.
Köchel, L. von, his Mozart catalogue, 284.
Königen von Saba, opera by Goldmark, 395.
Krebs, J. Ludwig (1713—1780), 151.
Kreutzer, Rodolphe (1766—1831), 433.
Kritische Briefe über die Tonkunst, Marpurg's, 169.
Kritischer Musicus of Scheibe, 168.
Kritischer Musikus an der Spree, Marpurg's, 168.
Kücken, F. W. (1810—1882), 371.

LABLACHE, Luigi (1794—1858), 337.
Lachner, Franz (1804—1890), 340.
La Fage, Adrien de (1801—1862), 434.
La Harpe, F. J. de (1739—1803), 260.

Lalla Roukh, opera by Félicien David, 422.
L'Allegro, Il Penseroso, ed Il Moderato, Handel's cantata, 223.
Lalo, E. V. A., 429.
Lalouette, J. F. (1651—1728), 128.
Lambillotte, Père (1797—1855), 6.
Lamentabatur Jacob, motet by Cristoforo Morales, 70.
Lamoureux, 430.
Lampe, J. F. (1692[?]—1751), 230.
Lange, Madame (Aloysia Weber), 279, 280, 330.
Language of Flowers, The, suite by Cowen, 451.
Lascia ch'io pianga, air from Handel's *Rinaldo*, 159, 206.
Lassus, Orlando di (1520[?]—1594), 62, 67, 94; collection of his works at Munich, 65.
Last Judgment, oratorio by Spohr, 344, 346, 348.
Lateran, St. John, Church of, Palestrina made director of the music at, 69.
Lattre, Roland de. See "Lassus, Orlando di."
Laudi Spirituali, 98.
Lawes, Henry (1595—1662), 90, 179, 180, 198.
Lay of the Bell, cantata by A. Romberg, 371.
Leblond, Abbé (1738—1809), 260.
Lecerf de la Vieville, J. L. (1647—1710), 251.
Leclair, J. M. (1697—1764), 266.
Le faccio un' inchino, trio from Cimarosa's *Matrimonio Segreto*, 305.
Lefébure-Wély (1817—1869), 434.
Legend of St. Elizabeth, oratorio by Liszt, 374.
Leicester, opera by Auber, 411.
Leila, opera by Pierson, 447.
Leipzig Conservatorium, foundation of, 355, 364.
Leit-motif of Wagner, 388.
Le Jeune, Claude (1528[?]—1606 [?]), 61, 116.
Lélio; ou, le Retour à la Vie, symphony by Berlioz, 419.

Lenore, symphony by J. Raff, 373.
Lenten oratorios given by Handel, 221.
Lenz, W. von, his *Beethoven et ses trois styles*, 290.
Leo, Leonardo (1694—1746), 100, 218.
Leoncavallo, 323.
Leonora, opera by Beethoven, 291.
Leroy, Adrian (16th century), 114.
Lestocq, opera by Auber, 411.
Lesueur, J. F. (1763—1837), 407.
Let the bright seraphim, air from Handel's *Samson*, 226.
Let their celestial concerts all unite, chorus in Handel's *Samson*, 226.
Let thy hand be strengthened, coronation anthem by Handel, 215.
Lettre sur la MusiqueFrançaise, by J. J. Rousseau, 252.
Let us take the road, song in the *Beggar's Opera*, 216.
L'Homme Armé, the air, 17, 67.
Libertine, The, Purcell's music to, 190.
Lichnowsky, Prince, 288.
Liebeslieder Walzer, by Brahms, 392.
Liebesverbot, Das, opera by Wagner, 377.
Lieder ohne Wörter, by Mendelssohn, 358.
Light of the World, oratorio by Sullivan, 449.
Li Gieus de Robin et de Marion, by Adam de la Halle, 16.
Lily of Killarney, opera by Benedict, 442.
Lind, Jenny (1820—1887), 414.
Linda di Chamounix, opera by Donizetti, 315.
Lindpainter, Peter Joseph (1791—1856), 339.
Linley, Thomas (1725—1795), 233.
Liszt, Franz (1811—1886), 301, 372, 379, 382, 383, 431.
Litolff, H., his cheap music, 453.
Liturgical dramas, 17.
Lobgesang of Mendelssohn, 353, 357.
Lobkowitz, Prince, 173, 292.

INDEX. 473

Locatelli, P. (1693—1764), 106.
Lock, Matthew (1628[?]—1677), 180, 181.
Loder, E. J. (1813—1865), 441.
Lodoiska, opera by Cherubini, 306.
Lohengrin, opera by Wagner, 345, 383, 385.
Lord, for Thy tender mercies' sake, anthem by R. Farrant, 82.
Loreley, finale to, by Mendelssohn, 357.
Lorenzo de Medici, 60.
Lortzing, G. A. (1803—1852), 340.
Lotario, opera by Handel, 217.
Lotti, Antonio (1667[?]—1740), 101, 219.
Louis XI. of France, 59.
—— XII. of France, 60.
—— XIII. of France, 114.
—— XIV., his musical acquirements, 122.
Louis Ferdinand, Prince of Prussia, 368.
Love in her eyes, air in Handel's *Acis and Galatea*, 210.
Lowe, Edmund (1610[?]—1682), 181, 186.
Lucia di Lammermoor, opera by Donizetti, 315.
Lucrezia Borgia, opera by Donizetti, 315.
Ludwig II., King of Bavaria, 385.
Lully, Jean Baptiste (1633—1687), 121; protected by Louis XIV., 122;. composes ballets, *ib.*; obtains Perrin's privilege for performing opera, 124; his career as a writer of opera, 125; his death, 127; his Church music, 128, 182; 202, 241, 249.
—— Jean Louis de, 130.
—— Louis, 130.
Lurline, opera by W. V. Wallace, 441.
Luscinius (Nachtigall), Ottomar (1487—   ), 75.
Lustigen, Weiber von Windsor, Die, opera of O. Nicolai, 341.
Lute, the, 47.
Luther, Martin, his love for music, 73.

Lvoff, Alexis (1799—1870), 402.
Lyre, the, 23, 38.

Macbeth, music to, 181, 190.
Maccabees, opera by Rubinstein, 400.
Mace, Thomas (1613—1709), his *Musick's Monument*, 199.
Macfarren, Sir G. A. (1813—1887), 441.
Mackenzie, Sir A. C., 449.
Maçon, Le, opera by Auber, 411.
Madden, Sir F., on manuscript of *Sumer is icumen in*, 79.
Madrigalian Era in England, 82, 246; in Netherlands, 61.
Madrigals, rareness of complete printed sets of, 61, 86.
Magnum Opus Musicum of Orlando di Lassus, 65.
Maid of Artois, The, opera by Balfe, 439.
Mainwaring, Rev. John, his translation of Mattheson's *Life of Handel*, 164.
Malek-Adhel, opera by Costa, 443.
Malibran, Madame (1808—1836), 433.
Manfred, incidental music to, by Schumann, 365.
Manon, opera by Massenet, 429.
Manon Lescaut, opera by Auber, 411.
—— opera by Puccini, 323.
Maometto secondo, opera by Rossini, 310, 312.
Marais, Martin (1656—1728), 130.
Marcello, Benedetto (1686—1739), 101.
March from Handel's *Rinaldo*, 206.
Marchand, Louis (1669—1732), 142.
Marenzio, Luca (1550[?]—1599), 70.
Mariages Samnites, Les, opera by Grétry, 264.
Maritana, opera by W. V. Wallace, 440.
Marmontel, J. F. (1723—1799), 259, 260, 264.
Marot, Clément (1495—1544), his translation of the Psalms, 112.
Marot, Clément, Lettre de (satire on Lully), 128.

INDEX.

Marpurg, F. W. (1718—1795), his critical and theoretical writings, 168.
Marschner, H. (1795—1861), 338.
Martha, opera by Flotow, 341.
Martini, G. B., Padre (1706—1784), 177, 239, 278, 303, 329.
Martyr of Antioch, The, oratorio by Sullivan, 449.
Masaniello, opera by Auber, 411.
Mascagni, Pietro, 323.
Mass in D, Beethoven's, 293.
—— by Rossini, 314.
Massenet, Jules, 429.
Ma Tante Aurore, opera by Boieldieu, 408.
Matrimonio Segreto, Il, opera by Cimarosa, 305.
Mattei, S. (1750—1825), 303, 309.
Mattheson, Johann (1681—1764), 157; his opera *Cleopatra*, 158; his critical and theoretical writings, 163, 172.
Mauduit, Jacques (1557—1627), 116.
Maximilian I., Emperor, 60, 73.
—— II., Emperor, ennobles Orlando di Lassus, 63.
May Queen, cantata by Sir W. S. Bennett, 445.
Mayr, Simone (1763—1845), 308.
Mayseder, Josef (1789—1863), 301.
Mazarin, Cardinal, introduces Italian opera into France, 116; enormous sums spent on it by him, 117.
Médecin malgré lui, Le, opera by Gounod, 425.
Méhul, E. N. (1763—1817), 405.
Mefistofele, opera by Boito, 322.
Meistersinger, Die, opera by Wagner, 385.
Meistersingers, The, 15; their election, 16.
Melothesia, Lock's, 182.
Melusina, overture by Mendelssohn, 357.
Mendelssohn Bartholdy, Fanny (Madame Hensel) (1805—1847), 349, 356.
—— Bartholdy, Felix (1809—1847), his birth and education, 347; early compositions, 348; C minor symphony, *ib.*; visits Paris, 349; *Camacho's Wedding*, *ib.*; his overtures, 350, 359; visits England, 350; settles in Düsseldorf, 352; conducts Gewandhaus Concerts, *ib.*; his marriage, 353; *St. Paul*, *ib.*; his organ-playing, *ib.*; the Academy of Arts in Berlin, 354; his psalms, 355; foundation of the Leipzig Conservatorium, 355; *Elijah*, *ib.*; his illness and death, 356; —— 362.
Merbecke, John (1512[?]—1585), 80.
Mercadante, S. (1795—1870), 315.
Mersenne, Marin (1588—1648), 134.
Messiah, The, Handel's oratorio, 152, 224, 226, 236.
Metastasio, 170, 270.
Meyerbeer, G.(1791[1794[?]]—1864), 330, 339, 349; his Italian style, *ib.*; his French operas, 413; *Robert le Diable*, *ib.*; *Les Huguenots*, *ib.*; *Le Prophète*, *ib.*; *Dinorah*, 415; *L'Africaine*, *ib.*
Midsummer Night's Dream, overture by Mendelssohn, 350; incidental music by do., 355.
Mignon, opera by Amb. Thomas, 423.
Military trumpet, 36.
Milton, John, father of the poet (c. 1576—1647), 90.
——, John, the poet, 179.
Minnesingers, the, 15.
Minstrels, 15. See also "Menestriers."
Mirelle, opera by Gounod, 426.
Missa Papæ Marcelli, by Palestrina, 68, 94.
Mitridate, opera by Mozart, 166.
Mizler, Lorenz (1711—1778), his *Neueröffnete Musikalische Bibliothek*, 168, 172.
"*Modern Church Musick, Preaccused*," etc., by Matthew Lock, 182.
Moïse, opera by Rossini, 312.
Molière, his intimacy with Lully, 122.
Molinara, La, opera by Paisiello, 304.

INDEX. 475

Monday Popular Concerts, 453.
Monochord, 55.
M. de Porceaugnac, incidental music to, by Lully, 122.
Monsigny, P. A. (1729—1817), 256.
Montano et Stephanie, opera of Berton, 407.
Monte, Philippe de (1521—1603), 61.
Montéclair, M. P. de (1666—1737), 134, 246.
Monteverde, Claudio (1568—1643 [?1651]), 94; his instrumentation, 96, 118.
Morales, Cristoforo (16th century), 70.
Morlacchi, F. (1784—1841), 335.
Morley, Thomas (1563—1604), his madrigals, ballets, and canzonets, 84; his *Plaine and Easie Introduction to Practicall Musicke*, 85.
Mornington, Lord (1735—1781), 239.
Mors et Vita, oratorio by Gounod, 426.
Mort d'Adam, La, opera by Lesueur, 407.
Moscheles, Ignaz (1794—1870), 337, 348, 357, 438; his description of Mendelssohn when a boy, 349.
Moscow, great bell of, 26.
Mosé, opera by Rossini, 310, 312.
Moses, opera by Rubinstein, 400.
Motets, collection of, by O. di Lassus, 65.
Motteville, Madame de, her opinion of the Italian opera, 117.
Mount of Olives, oratorio by Beethoven, 291.
Mountain Sylph, opera by J. Barnett, 441.
Mouton, Jean (16th century), 61.
Mozart, J. C. W. A. (1756—1791), his childhood, 276; visits Vienna, Paris, and London, 277; *La Finta Semplice*, 278; his visit to Italy, *ib.*; Allegri's *Miserere, ib.*; *Mitridate, ib.*; friction with Archbishop of Salzburg, *ib.*; second visit to Paris, 279; Aloysia Weber, *ib.*; *Idomeneo, ib.*; *Entführung aus dem Serail*, 280; his marriage, 281; *Der Schauspiel Director*,

ib.; *Le Nozze de Figaro, ib.*; its reception at Prague, *ib.*; *Don Giovanni*, 282; his symphonies in E flat, G minor, and C, 283; *Cosi fan tutte, ib.*; *Zauberflöte, ib.*; Requiem, *ib.*; *La Clemenza di Tito*, 284; his death, *ib.*; Von Köchel's Catalogue, *ib.*; his *Ave Verum*, 286; ——, 70, 166, 233, 266, 437, 445.
Mozart, J. G. Leopold (1719—1787), 276, 278, 280.
—— Maria Ann (1751—1829), 276.
Muette de Portici, opera by Auber, 411.
Mulliner, Thomas (15th century), 80.
Muses Galantes, Les, opera by J. J. Rousseau, 253.
Musette, 30, 134.
Music, early treatises on, 72; in England, 79; widespread knowledge of, during the 16th and 17th centuries, 85.
Musica Antiqua, J. Stafford Smith's, 239.
Musica Getutscht, by S. Virdung, 75.
Musica Transalpina, published by N. Yonge, 83.
Musical Antiquarian Society, 86.
Musical Century, Henry Carey's, 230.
Musicalische Patriot, Der, by Mattheson, 163.
Musick's Monument, Mace's, 198.
Musikalische Bibliothek of Mizler, 168.
Muzio Scevola, opera by Ariosti, G. B. Buononcini, and Handel, 212.
My heart is inditing, coronation anthem by Handel, 215.
Mynheer van Dunck, glee by Bishop, 438.
My Pretty Jane, song by Bishop, 438.

Naaman, oratorio by Costa, 443.
Nablum, 39.
Nacaire, 23.

Nachtigall. See " Luscinius."
Nadeshda, opera by A. Goring Thomas, 447.
Naiades, overture by Bennett, 444.
Nanini, Bernardino (1545[?]—1620[?]), 70.
—— Giovanni, Maria (1530[?]—1607), 70.
Napoleon, the Emperor, 290, 304, 307.
Narciso, opera by D. Scarlatti, 211.
Nardini, P. (1722—1793), 107.
Nares, Dr. James (1715—1783), 195.
Nel cor più, air by Paisiello, Beethoven's variations on, 304.
Ne plus ultra, sonata by Woelfl, 369.
Neri, St. Philip, his intimacy with Palestrina, 69; founds order of Oratorians, 98.
Nero, opera by Handel, 159, 162.
——, opera by Rubinstein, 400.
Netherlands, musical influence of, 56.
Neue Zeitschrift für Musik (founded by Schumann), 361, 364, 382, 390.
Neukomm, Sigismund (1778—1858), 300.
Neums, invention of, attributed to St. Gregory, 4; suggested origin of, 6; nomenclature of, 7; used for both sacred and secular music, 8.
Nicolai, Otto (1810—1849), 340.
Nicolo. See " Isouard, N."
Niedermeyer, L. (1802—1861), 417.
Night Dancers, The, opera by E. J. Loder, 441.
Nina, opera by Paisiello, 304.
Noces de Thétis et de Pélée, opera by Colasse, 130, 140.
Nonne sanglante La, opera by Gounod, 425.
Norma, opera by Bellini, 315.
Nourmahal, opera by Spontini, 316.
Nouveau Système de Musique Théorique, by Rameau, 294.
Novello and Co., their introduction of cheap music, 453.
Nozze de Figaro, opera by Mozart, 281.

Numitor, opera by Giovanni Porta, 211.
Nun danket alle Gott, the chorale, 73.

Oberon, opera by Weber, 336, 338.
Oberto, opera by Verdi, 319.
Occasional Oratorio, Handel's, 227.
Ode for St. Cecilia's Day, Handel's, 223.
—— by Parry, 450.
O du mein holder Abend-Stern, air from *Tannhäuser*, 381.
Odysseus, cantata by Max Bruch, 395.
Œdipe in Colone, opera of Sacchini, 304.
Œdipus Coloneus of Mendelssohn, 355.
Oesterlein, his *Wagner Katalog*, 389.
Offenbach, Jacques (1819—1880), 416.
Oft on a plat, air from Handel's *L'Allegro*, 223.
Okenheim or Okeghem (1415[?]—1513[?]), 57, 59, 60, 111.
Oliphant, 34.
Olympie, opera by Spontini, 316.
Onslow, George (1784—1853), 349, 421.
Opera, origin of the, 92; first theatre for, in Venice, 97; foundation of, in France, 118; in Germany, 154; in England, 191, 202; in Italy, 303; in France, 405.
" Opera of the Nobility," 220.
Oper und Drama, by Wagner, 382.
Oratorio, origin of the, 98; Handel's oratorios, 223.
Orfeo performed in Paris in 1647-8, 116.
—— opera by Gluck, 174, 259.
Organ, 22, 30; hydraulic, 22, 31; in Italy, 107; in Germany, 152; in England, 195.
—— concertos, Handel's, 231.
Organistrum, 52.
" Organizing" taught by the Roman singers to the French, 12.

INDEX.   477

Organum, or diaphony, 13.
Oriana, Triumphs of, 85.
O Richard! ô mon roi! air in Grétry's *Richard Cœur de Lion*, 264.
Orlando, opera by Handel, 217, 218.
O'Rourke. See "Rooke."
Orphée aux Enfers, opera bouffe by Offenbach, 417.
O ruddier than the cherry, air in Handel's *Acis and Galatea*, 210.
Osborne, G. A. (1806—1893), 431.
Otello, opera by Rossini, 310 ; opera by Verdi, 321.
O the pleasures of the plains, chorus in Handel's *Acis and Galatea*, 210.
Ottone, opera by Handel, 212.
Oury, Madame (1806—1881), 301.
Overtures of Mendelssohn, 351, 357.
O where shall wisdom be found! anthem by Dr. Boyce, 195.

PACHELBEL, Johann (1653—1706), 137, 140.
Pacini, G. (1796—1867), 315.
Paer, Ferdinand (1771[1774?]—1839), 308.
Pagan influence on early Christian music, 2.
Paganini, N. (1782[1784?]—1840), 325.
Pagliacci, I, opera by Leoncavallo, 323.
Paisiello, G. (1741—1815), 304.
Palestrina, Giovanni Pierluigi da (1524[?]—1594), 68, 70, 94 ; summary of his works, 69.
Pammelia, by T. Ravenscroft, 88.
Pan's pipes or syrinx, 27.
Paolucci, Padre G. (1727—1777), 303.
Paradise and the Peri, overture by W. Sterndale Bennett, 445.
—— cantata by Schumann, 365.
Paradise Lost, opera by Rubinstein, 400.
Parallèle des Italiens et des Français, Raguenet's, 251.

Pardon de Ploermel, Le (*Dinorah*), opera by Meyerbeer, 415.
Paride ed Elena, opera by Gluck, 176.
Parry, C. Hubert H., 449.
Parsifal, opera by Wagner, 387.
Part du Diable, La, opera by Auber, 411.
Partenope, opera by Handel, 217.
Parthenia, 86.
Pasdeloup, J. E. (1819—1887), 430.
Pastorale, La, opera by Cambert, 119.
Pastor Fido, opera by Handel, 207.
Paton, Miss, 337.
Patrocinium Musices of Adam Berg, 65.
Paul IV., Pope, deprives Palestrina of his post in the Sistine Chapel, 69.
Pauline, opera by Cowen, 451.
Paul's, St., Cathedral, Smith's organ in, 197.
Paxton, Stephen (1735—1787), 239.
—— William (—1781), 239.
Pêcheurs, Les, opera by Gossec, 256.
Peer Gynt, incidental music and suite by Grieg, 402.
Pellegrin, Abbé (1661—1745), 246.
Pépin receives an organ from Constantine Copronymus, 32.
Pepusch, Dr. (1667—1752), 203, 209, 216.
Pepys, Samuel, extracts from his diary, 183, 184, 196.
Percussion, instruments of, 23.
Pergolesi, G. B. (1710—1737), 100, 255, 262.
Peri, Jacopo (16th century, living 1610), 94, 99.
Perle du Brésil, La, opera by Félicien David, 422.
Perrin, Abbé (—1676), 127 ; joins Cambert in founding the first opera-house in Paris, 118 ; quarrels with his partners, 121 ; sells his patent to Lully, 124.
Peter's, St., at Rome, organs in, 107.

Peters and Co., their cheap music, 453.
Petit Chaperon rouge, Le, opera by Boieldieu, 409.
"Petits violons du Roi," 122.
Petrucci, Ottaviano dei (1466—1524), music-printer, 59, 62.
Phaeton, poème symphonique by Saint-Saëns, 427.
Phalèse, Pierre (1510[?]—), music-printer, 62.
Philémon et Baucis, opera by Gounod, 426.
Philharmonic Society, 293, 294, 452.
Philidor (Danican), the family of the, 264.
Philosophes and the opera, 248.
Pianoforte concerto in G minor, by Mendelssohn, 352.
—— invention of, 46.
—— works of Schumann, 367.
Pianto d'Armonia, cantata by Rossini, 309.
Piccinni, Nicolo (1728—1800), 259, 261.
Pierson, H. Hugo (1815—1873), 446.
Pilgrim of Love, The, song by Bishop, 438.
Pills to purge Melancholy, D'Urfey's, 200.
Pimmalione, opera by Cherubini, 307.
Pius IV., Pope, 68.
Pixis, J. P. (1788—1875), 370.
Plain-chant or plain-song, 4 ; treatises on, 72.
Playford, John (1623—1693), 187, 197, 237.
Pleyel, Ignaz J. (1757—1831), 300.
Plus ultra, sonata by Dussek, 369.
Poèmes symphoniques of Saint-Saëns, 427.
Poisson, Père, translates Descartes' *Compendium Musicæ* into French, 134.
Polly Peachum in the *Beggars' Opera,* 216.
Polyeucte, opera by Gounod, 426.
Pompadour, Madame de, 251.
Pontifical Chapel, the, 57, 60.

Popelinière, Leriche de la, 245, 253, 256.
Poro, opera by Handel, 217.
Porpora, N. A. (1686—1767), 104, 165, 219, 220, 270.
Porta, Costanzo (1520[?]—1601), 61, 72.
—— Giovanni (1690[?]—1740), his opera *Numitor,* 211.
"Portative" (small organ), 33.
"Positive" (small organ), 33.
Postillon de Longjumeau, Le, opera by Ad. Adam, 416.
Pougin, Arthur, 436.
Power of Sound, symphony of Spohr, 344.
Prætorius, Michael (Schultz) (1571—1621), his *Syntagma Musicum,* 75, 137.
Pré aux Clercs, Le, opera by Hérold, 412.
Preciosa, incidental music to, by Weber, 335.
Préludes de l'Harmonie Universelle, by Mersenne, 135.
Premier Jour de Bonheur, Le, opera by Auber, 411.
Près, Josquin de. See "Josquin de Près."
Printers, early music, 62.
Prodigal Son, The, oratorio by Sullivan, 449.
Projet concernant de Nouveaux Signes pour la Musique, by J. J. Rousseau, 253.
Prophète, Le, opera by Meyerbeer, 413.
Proserpine, opera by Saint-Saëns, 428.
Protestantism, influence of, in France, 112.
Prussia, Prince Louis Ferdinand of, 368.
Prynne's *Histrio-Mastix,* 115.
Psalmody, metrical, in the English Church, 89 ; the "old" version, *ib.* ; the "new" version, 90.
Psalms, Marcello's, 102 ; Mendelssohn's, 355, 357.
Psalms, Sonets, and Songs of Sadnes and Pietie, by W. Byrd, 82.

INDEX. 479

Psalms, Songs, and Sonnets, by Byrd, 82.
Psalterium, 22, 38.
Psaltery or dulcimer, 51.
Psyche, Matthew Lock's, 182.
Puccini, Giacomo, 323.
Puits d'Amour, Le, opera by Balfe, 439.
Purcell, Henry (1658—1695), 188; his youth and education, 189; his early works, 190; his *Dido and Æneas*, 191; *Te Deum* and *Jubilate, ib.* 193; *The Tempest, Dioclesian,* and *King Arthur,* 192; *Indian Queen, ib.*; his death, 194; his *Orpheus Britannicus, ib.*; —— 208.
—— Thomas (—1682), 190.
Pur dicesti, song by Lotti, 101.
Puritani, I, opera by Bellini, 315.

Quæstiones Celeberrimæ in Genesim, by Mersenne, 135.
Quantz, Johann Joachim (1697—1773), 144.
Quatre Fils d'Aymon, Les, opera by Balfe, 439.
Quinault (1635—1688) writes most of the books of Lully's operas, 125, 259.
Quinto Fabio, opera by Cherubini, 306.

RACINE, his *Iphigénie en Aulide* arranged as an opera and set to music by Gluck, 176; his *Hippolyte et Aricie* (Phèdre), by Rameau, 246; music to *Athalie* by Mendelssohn, 355.
Radamisto, opera by Handel, 211.
Raff, Joachim (1822—1882), 373.
Raguenet, Abbé (1660[?]—1772[?]), 250.
Rameau, Jean Philippe (1683—1764), 174, 176, 241; his theoretical publications, 243; his career as a composer, 245; opinion of Italian music, 252.
Randegger, Alberto, 444.

Rappresentazione di Anima e di Corpo, oratorio by E. del Cavaliere, 99.
Ravenscroft, Thomas (1582[?]—1635), 88; his *Psalms*, 90.
Reber, H. (1807—1880), 417.
Recitative, accompanied, invented by Carissimi, 100.
Recorder, 37.
Redford, John (16th century), 81.
Reed, the, 35.
Redemption, The, oratorio by Gounod, 426.
Reform in Church music effected by Palestrina, 68.
Reformation, effect of the, on music, 73; in England, 89.
"Regal" (small organ), 33.
Reine de Chypre, La, opera by Halévy, 416.
Reine de Saba, La, opera by Gounod, 426, 427.
Reinecke, Karl, 396.
Reissiger, C. G. (1798—1859), 371.
Requiem of Mozart, 283, 284; of Verdi, 321.
Restoration, music in England at the, 179.
Resurrezione, oratorio by Handel, 160.
Return, blest days, glee by J. Stafford Smith, 239.
Return, O God of Hosts, air in Handel's *Samson*, 226.
Reuchlin, Johann (1455—1522), his *Scenica Progymnasmata*, 154.
Revenge, The, Choral Ballad, by Stanford, 450.
Reyer, Ernest, 430.
Rheims, House of Musicians at, 23, 31.
Rheinberger, Josef, 396.
Rheingold, Das, opera of Wagner, 383.
Rhenish, symphony by Schumann, 366.
Ricciardo Primo, opera by Handel, 215.
Richard Cœur de Lion, opera by Grétry, 264.
Rienzi, opera by Wagner, 377, 380.

Ries, Ferdinand (1784—1838), 300.
Rietz, Julius (1812—1877), 365.
Rigoletto, opera by Verdi, 319.
Rimsky-Korzakow, 401.
Rinaldo, opera by Handel, 159, 205; Rossi's excuse for the libretto, *ib.*; —— 208, 209, 215.
Rinck, J. C. H. (1770—1846), 372.
Ring der Nibelungen, Der, series of operas by Wagner, 383, 385, 386.
Rinuccini, Ottavio, poet, 94 : his *Dafne* set to music by H. Schütz, 154.
Robert le Diable, opera by Meyerbeer, 413.
Rode, Pierre (1774—1830), 433.
Rodelinda, opera by Handel, 213.
Rodrigo, opera by Handel, 160.
Roeckel, August (1814—1876), 382.
Roi de Lahore, Le, opera by Massenet, 429.
Roi d'Ys, Le, opera by Lalo, 430.
Roland, opera by Piccinni, 259, 260.
Rollet, Bailli du, his relations with Gluck, 176, 258, 261.
Romans, music among the, 1 ; musical instruments of the, 22.
Romberg, Andreas (1767—1821), 371.
—— Bernard (1767—1841), 371.
Romeo et Juliet, opera by Steibelt, 369.
—— Symphony by Berlioz, 420.
—— opera by Gounod, 426.
Rooke, W. M. (O'Rourke) (1794—1847), 439.
Rore, Cipriano di (1516—1565), 61, 72.
Rosamund, Addison's, set by Clayton and subsequently by Arne, 204.
Rose of Castile, The, opera by Balfe, 439.
Rose of Sharon, The, oratorio by Mackenzie, 449.
Rose Pilgerfahrt, Der, cantata by Schumann, 366.
Rossini, Gioacchino (1792—1868), his early years, 308 ; first successes, 309 ; visits Paris and London, 312 ; *Guillaume Tell, ib.*; his *Stabat Mater*, 313 ; Mass, 314 ; —— 349, 413.
Rota, or hurdy-gurdy, 49.
Rotta, or crwth, 48.
Rouet d'Omphale, Le, poème symphonique by Saint-Saëns, 427.
Roulstan and Ludmila, opera by Glinka, 399.
Rousseau, J. J. (1712—1778), 252, 253.
Rowbotham, Mr. J. F., his classification of instruments, 22.
" Royal Academy of Music " (opera), foundation of, 211.
Royal Academy of Music, 453.
—— College of Music, 453.
—— Society of Musicians, 235.
Rübezahl, opera by Weber, 333.
Rubinstein, Anton (1830—1895), 400.
Rudolph, Archduke, pupil of Beethoven, 289, 292.
Rule Britannia, air by Dr. Arne, 230.
Ruler of the Spirits, overture by Weber, 333.
Russian bells, 26.
Russian Church Music, 397.
Ruth, oratorio by César Franck, 429.
Ruy Blas, overture by Mendelssohn, 357.

SABATINI, Padre L. A. (1739—1809), 303.
Sacchini, A. M. G. (1734—1786), 262, 304.
Sachs, Hans (1486—1567), 16.
Sackbut, 37.
Sacrati, Francesco Paolo (—1650), 98.
Sacred Harmonic Society, 235, 353, 356, 452 ; its library, 89.
—— music, corruptions of, 68.
St. *Cecilia*, oratorio by Benedict, 442.
St. Gall, its M.S. of Gregory's *Antiphonarium*, 3 ; facsimile of a portion of, 5.

INDEX. 481

Saint-Huberty, Madame (1756—1812), singer, 267.
St. John the Baptist, oratorio by Macfarren, 441.
St. Ludmilla, oratorio by Dvořák, 394.
St. Paul, oratorio by Mendelssohn, 353, 357.
St. Peter, oratorio by Benedict, 442.
Saint-Saëns, Camille, 427.
Salaries of singers in time of Handel, 214.
Salieri, Antonio (1750—1825), 261, 280, 301, 305.
Sally in our alley, song by Henry Carey, 230.
Salmon, Jacques (living 1582), 114.
Salomon, J. P. (1745—1815), 286.
Sambuca, 22.
Sammartini, G. B. (about 1700[?]—living in 1770), 173, 177.
Samson, Handel's oratorio, 226.
—— opera by Rameau, 246.
Samson et Delila, opera by Saint-Saëns, 427.
Sapho, opera by Gounod, 425.
Sarti, G. (1729—1802), 304, 305.
Satanella, opera by Balfe, 439.
Saul, oratorio by Handel, 223.
Scarlatti, Alessandro (1659—1725), 99, 165.
—— Domenico (1683—1757), 108, 161, 211.
Scenica Progymnasmata of Reuchlin, 154.
Schauspiel Director, Der, opera by Mozart, 281.
Scheibe, J. A. (1708—1776), his *Kritischer Musicus*, 168.
Schickaneder, E. J. (1751—1812), 283, 284, 291.
Schicksalslied, by Brahms, 392.
Schmidt, Bernard ("Father Smith") (1630[?]—1709), 196.
Schmoll Peter, opera by Weber, 332.
Schneider, J. G. (1789—1864), 372.
Schools, choir-, established by St. Gregory, 4.
Schröder-Devrient, Madame (1804—1860), 291, 377, 380, 381.

Schubert, Franz (1797—1828), his early years, 295; Mass in F, 296; the *Erlkönig* and *Wanderer, ib.*; lives in Court Esterhazy's family, 298; publication of his first songs, *ib.*; his productiveness, 299; the Symphony in C and other instrumental works, 300;—362.
Schütz, Heinrich (Sagittarius) (1585—1672), 154.
Schumann, Clara, 367.
—— Robert (1810—1856), his youth, 358; studies law at Leipzig, *ib.*; acquaintance with Wieck, *ib.*; injury to his hand, 360; founds the *Neue Zeitschrift für Musik*, 361; Florestan and Eusebius, *ib.*; the Davidsbündler, *ib.*; Clara Wieck, 362; his marriage, 363; his songs, *ib.*; symphonies, *ib.*; chamber music, *ib.*; illness, 364; *Genoveva* and *Manfred*, 365; Düsseldorf, 365; insanity and death, 366; his chamber music and songs, 367; —— 299, 355, 444.
Schuppanzigh quartet, 288.
Schunke, Ludwig (1810—1834), 361.
Scipio, opera by Handel, 213, 217.
Scotch Symphony of Mendelssohn, 351, 352, 357.
Scotto, Girolamo (—1573), music-printer, 62.
Seasons The, oratorio by Haydn, 273.
Semiramide, opera by Rossini, 310, 311.
Senesino (Francesco Bernardi)(1680—1750), singer, 211, 212, 214, 217, 218.
Senfl, Ludwig (1490[?]—1555), 73.
Serva Padrona La, opera by Pergolesi, 101, 251, 255, 256, 262.
Sesostrate, opera by Hasse, 166.
Seven Last Words, by Haydn, 274.
Sgambati, Giovanni, 326.
Shamus O'Brien, opera by Stanford, 450.
Shawm, 37.
Shepherds' trumpets, 35.

31

Sheppard, John (16th century), 80.
Sheridan, R. B., 233.
Shield, William (1748—1829), 233.
Shophar, 34.
Should he upbraid, song by Bishop, 438.
Siège de Corinth, opera by Rossini, 312.
Siege of Belgrade, opera by Storace, 233.
Siege of Rochelle, opera by Balfe, 439.
Siegfried, opera by Wagner, 383.
Siena, ancient bell at, 24.
Silas, E. 444.
Silver Swan, madrigal by Orlando Gibbons, 84.
Simone Boccanegra, opera by Verdi, 320.
Simpson, Christopher (1640[?]—), *Chelys; or, The Division Violist*, 199; *Compendium of Practical Musick*, 198.
Singers, Italian, 316.
Siroe, opera by Handel, 215.
Sistine Chapel, performance of the *Missa Papæ Marcelli* in, 69; Palestrina appointed composer to, *ib.*; unaccompanied vocal music in, 70; music in Holy Week, *ib.*
Sistrum, the, 22, 24.
Sixtus IV., Pope, 60.
Sleep, gentle Lady, glee by Bishop, 438.
Slide-trumpet, 37.
Smith, J. Stafford (1746[?]—1836), 239.
Smithson, Miss, wife of Berlioz, 418.
Soissons, Count of, 14.
Solomon, Handel's oratorio, 227.
Son and Stranger, opera by Mendelssohn, 351.
"Sonata," the word first used by G. Gabrieli, 107.
Sonatas, Purcell's, 192.
Songe d'une Nuit d'Eté, opera by Amb. Thomas, 423.
Songs of Sundrie Natures, some of Gravitie and others of Myrth, by W. Byrd, 82.

Songs without Words, by Mendelssohn, 358.
Sonnambula, La, opera by Bellini, 315.
Sonnleithner, L. von (1797—1873), 298.
Sontag, Henrietta, (1806—1854), 416.
Sourdéac, Marquis de, joins Perrin, Cambert, and Champeron in founding the French Opera, 120.
South Kensington Museum, C. Engel's catalogue of musical instruments at, 21.
Spectre's Bride, cantata by Dvořák, 394.
Spinet, 45.
Spofforth, Reginald (1768—1827), 239.
Spohr, Louis (1784—1859), 333, 341; his early years, *ib.*; *Faust*, 343; *Zemire and Azor, ib.*; moves to Dresden, *ib.*; settles in Cassel, *ib.*; *Jessonda*, 344; *Last Judgment, ib.*; *Violin School, ib.*; symphony, *Der Weihe der Töne, ib.*; *Calvary* and *Fall of Babylon, ib.*; his death and characteristics, 345.
Spontini, G. L. P. (1774—1851), 312, 316, 334, 335, 349, 412.
Stabat Mater, by Astorga, 234; by Dvořák, 394; by Pergolesi, 100; by Rossini, 313.
Stadt-pfeiffer, or town musicians in Germany, 137.
Staff, musical, development, of, 9.
Stainer, Sir John, 451.
Standard Bearer, song by Lindpainter, 339.
Stanford, Dr. C. V., 450.
Steffani, Abbate (1655—1730), 162.
Steibelt, Daniel (1755[1764?]—1823), 369.
Stephens, Miss (Countess of Essex), 337.
Sternhold and Hopkins' *Psalms*, 90.
Stevens, R. J. S. (1753—1837), 88, 239.

INDEX. 483

Storace, Anna S., singer (1765[?]—1817), 233.
—— Stephen (1763—1796), 233.
Storm Rondo, by Steibelt, 370.
Strada, Anna, singer, 217, 219, 222.
Straduarius, Antonius, 55.
Stratonice, opera by Méhul, 406.
Stringed instruments, 38.
Suard, J. B. A. (1734—1817), 260.
Suite de Pièces pour le Clavecin, by Handel, 210.
Sullivan, Sir Arthur, 447.
Sumer is icumen in, round, 79.
Supplément au Roman Comique of Jean Monnet, 250.
Susanna, Handel's oratorio, 227.
Süssmayer, F. X. (1766—1803), 284.
Sweelinck, J. P. (1540[?]—1621), 152.
Sweet bird, air from Handel's *L'Allegro*, 223.
Swieten, Baron von, 288.
Sylvana, opera by Weber, 333, 334. See also *Waldmädchen, Das*.
Symphonic Poems, by Liszt, 374.
Symphonie espagnole, by Lalo, 429.
Symphonie fantastique, by Berlioz, 418.
Syntagma Musicum, of Michael Prætorius, 75.
Syrinx or Pan's pipes, 27.

Tableau Parlant, Le, opera by Grétry, 264.
Tabour and pipe, 23.
Tallis, Thomas (1520—1585), 81, 82; his forty-part canon, 81; his Evening Hymn, *ib.*; his patent for music-printing with Byrd, 82.
Tambourin, 23.
Tambourine, 23.
Tamerlano, opera by Handel, 213.
Taming of the Shrew, opera by Goetz, 396.
Tancredi, opera by Rossini, 309, 311, 339.
Tannhäuser, opera by Wagner, 345, 381, 383, 384.

Tappert, his Wagner Lexicon, 389.
Tarare, opera by Salieri, 301, 305.
Tartini, Giuseppe (1692—1770), 106.
Tate, Nahum, his *Dido and Æneas* set by Purcell, 191.
Taverner, John (first half 16th century), 80.
Taylor, Edward (1784—1863), 344.
Teatro alla moda, Marcello's, 103.
Te Deum, by Dvořák, 394; by Graun, 168; by W. Jackson of Exeter, 195; by Handel, 208, 209, 226; by Purcell, 191, 193.
Telemann, G. P. (1681—1767), 142, 152.
Tempest, The, music to, by Purcell, 192; proposed opera by Mendelssohn, 352.
Tempesta, La, opera by Halévy, 416.
Temple Church organ, 197.
Temple Musick, Rev. A. Bedford's 200.
Templer, Der, und die Jüdin, opera by Marschner, 338.
Teseo, opera by Handel, 207.
Thalberg, Sigismund (1812—1871) 301, 372.
The dead shall live, chorus from Handel's *Ode for St. Cecilia's Day*, 223.
The Glories of our Blood and State, ode by Parry, 450.
The king shall rejoice, coronation anthem by Handel, 215.
The mighty conqueror, glee by S. Webbe, 238.
The soldier tired, air by Dr. Arne, 230.
The trumpet's loud clangour, chorus from Handel's *Ode for St. Cecilia's Day*, 223.
The ways of Zion do mourn, anthem by M. Wise, 182; anthem by Handel, 222.
Theater of Musick, Playford's, 198.
Theile, Johann (1646—1724), 154.
Then round about the starry throne, chorus in Handel's *Samson*, 226.
Theodora, oratorio by Handel, 227.
Theorbo, 48.

Thésée, opera by Lully, 128.
They that go down to the sea in ships, anthem by Purcell, 191.
Thibaut, King of Navarre (1201—1254), 14.
—— A. F. J. (1772—1840), his *Purity of Musical Art*, 360.
"Third sound" of Tartini, 107.
Thirty Years' War, its effect on music in Germany, 137.
This Magic-wove Scarf, trio in Barnett's *Mountain Sylph*, 441.
Thoinan, Ernest (A. E. Roquet), 59, 253.
Thomas, A. Goring (1851—1892), 447.
Thomas, Ambroise (1811—1896), 423.
Thomyris, Queen of Scythia, opera, 203.
Thun, Countess, 270, 288, 293.
Tibia or flute, 27.
Tieffenbrücker. See "Duiffoprugcar."
Tinctoris, J. (1434[?]—1511), 57, 59.
Tod Jesu, Der, oratorio by Graun, 168.
Tofts, Mrs. (17th century), singer, 203.
Tolomeo, opera by Handel, 215.
Tom Bowling, song by Dibdin, 234.
Tonic Sol-Fa, 453.
Torvaldo, opera by Rossini, 310.
Tosi, P. F. (1680[?]—1762[?]), 170.
Total eclipse, air from Handel's *Samson*, 226, 228.
Tower of Babel, The, opera by Rubinstein, 400.
Town-musicians, or *Stadtpfeiffer*, in Germany, 137.
Traité de l'Harmonie reduite à ses Principes Naturels, by Rameau, 243.
Travenol, Louis (1698[?]—1783), 252.
Travers, John (1706—1758), 195.
Traviata, La, opera by Verdi, 320.
Treasury of Musick, Playford's, 198.
Treatises on music, ancient, all in Greek language, 1.

Tremolo invited by Monteverde, 97.
Trent, Council of, 68.
Triangle, 24.
Tribut de Zamora, Le, opera by Gounod, 426.
Trionfo del Tempo, cantata by Handel, 161.
Tristan, opera by Wagner, 383, 385.
Triumph of Time and Truth, cantata by Handel, 161.
Triumphs of Oriana, 85.
Troubadour, The, opera by Mackenzie, 449.
Troubadours, their origin and constitution, 14.
Trovatore, Il, opera by Verdi, 319.
Troyens, Les, opera by Berlioz, 418.
Trumpet, 22, 34.
Trumpet-marine, 55.
Tschaikowsky, P. (1840—1893), 400.
Tschudi maker of harpsichords, 46.
Tuba, St. Jerome's description of, 22.
Tye, Dr. Christopher (1508[?]—1570[?]), 81.
Tympanum, 22.

Under the greenwood tree, air by Dr. Arne, 230.
Une fièvre brûlante, air in Grétry's *Richard Cœur de Lion*, 264.
Unterbrochene Opferfest, Das, opera by Winter, 330.
Utrecht *Te Deum* and *Jubilate*, Handel's, 208.

Val d' Andorre, Le, opera by Halévy, 416.
Vallotti, F. A. (1697—1780), 329.
Vampyr, Der, opera by Marschner, 338.
Vecchi, Orazio (1530[?]—1605), 72.
Veiled Prophet of Khorassin, opera by Stanford, 450.
Venice, early school of music at, 61, 71.
Vêpres Siciliennes Les, opera by Verdi, 320.

INDEX. 485

Veracini, F. M. (1685[?]—1750), 106.
Verdelot, Philippe (1490—1567), 61.
Verdi, Giuseppe, birth and education, 317; early operas, 319; *Ernani*, *Rigoletto*, *Il Trovatore*, etc., *ib.*; *La Traviata*, *Les Vêpres Siciliennes*, etc., 320; *Aïda*, *ib.*; *Requiem*, *ib.*; *Othello*, 321; *Falstaff*, *ib.*
Verse anthem, introduction of, 186.
Vestale, La, opera by, Spontini, 316.
Vie pour le Czar, La, opera by Glinka, 399.
Vielle (small hurdy-gurdy), 52.
Vienna, music in, 269.
Vieuxtemps, H. (1820—1881), 433.
Vincenti, music-printer, 62.
Viol, 52.
"Viola da Gamba," 53.
Violin School, Spohr's, 344.
Viols, Mace's advice on their preservation, 199; abandoned in favour of violins in France, 266.
Virdung, Sebastian (16th century), his *Musica Getutscht*, 75.
Virginal, 44.
Vita Caduca, La, madrigal by A. Lotti, 101, 219.
Vittoria, T. L. (1540[?]—1608), 70.
Vivaldi, A. (1685—1743), 106.
Vive Henri IV., the air, 116.
Vogler, J. C. (1698—1765), 151.
—— Abbé G. J. (1749—1814), 328; his pupils, 330.
Vollkommene Kapellmeister, Der, Mattheson's, 163.
Voltaire, 245, 248, 263.

WAELRENT, Hubert (1517—1595), 61.
Waft her, angels, song from Handel's *Jephtha*, 227.
Wagner, Richard (1813—1883), birth and education, 375; early operas, 376; engagements at Magdeburg, Königsberg, and Riga, 377; visits Paris, *ib.*; *Rienzi* produced at Dresden, 380; flies from Dresden, 382; friendship with Liszt, 383; *Tannhäuser* and *Lohengrin* produced at Weimar, *ib.*; visits London, 384; his letters, *ib.*; *Tannhäuser* in Paris, *ib.*; Ludwig II. of Bavaria, 385; the Bayreuth Theatre, 386; *Der Ring der Nibelungen*, *ib.*; concerts in London, *ib.*; *Parsifal*, 387; his death, *ib.*; his musical principles, *ib.*; the "Leit-motif," 96, 388.
Wagner, literature, 389.
Waldmädchen, Das, opera by Weber, 332, 333. See also *Sylvana*.
Waldstein, Count, 287, 290.
Walküre, Die, opera by Wagner, 383.
Wallace, W. Vincent (1814—1865), 440.
Walpurgis Nacht, Die, by Mendelssohn, 352.
Walsh, John, music-publisher (— 1736), 206.
Wanderer, Der, song by Schubert, 296, 299.
Ward, John (1580[?]—), 84.
Warren-Horne, E. T. (1730—1794), secretary of the Catch Club, 239; his MS. collection of glees, etc., *ib.*; his published collection, *ib.*
"Water Music," Handel's, 208.
Water parted from the sea, air from Arne's *Artaxerxes*, 230.
Watson, Thomas (1557[?]—1592), his *Italian Madrigalls Englished*, 84.
Webbe, Samuel (1740—1816), 237, 238.
Weber, Aloysia (Madame Lange) (1750—1839), 330.
—— Bernhard Anselm (1766 — 1821), 330.
—— Carl Maria von (1786—1826), early years, 330; operas *Das Waldmädchen*, *Peter Schmoll*, 332; *Rübezahl*, 333; *Sylvana*, *ib.*; *Abu Hassan*, 334; marriage, 335; Patriotic songs, *ib.*; settles in Dresden, *ib.*; *Preciosa* and *Der Freyschütz*, *ib.*; *Euryanthe*, 336; visit to England and death, 336;

remains removed to Dresden, 337; ——330, 358.
Weber, Gottfried (1779—1839), 330.
Weelkes, Thomas (1578—1640[?]), 84.
Weihe der Töne, Die, symphony by Spohr, 344.
Weldon, John (1676[?]—1736), 195.
Wesley, Samuel (1766—1837), 445.
—— Samuel Sebastian (1810—1876), 446.
Westminster Abbey, Smith's organ in, 196; St. Margaret's, Smith's do. at, *ib.*
We will rejoice, anthem by Dr. Croft, 188.
When winds breathe soft, glee by S. Webbe, 238.
Where the bee sucks, air by Dr. Arne, 230.
While fools their time, glee by J. Stafford Smith, 239.
Whitehall Chapel, organ in, 196.
Widor, C. M., 430.
Widow of Nain, The, oratorio by Lindpaintner, 339.
Wieck, Clara (Madame Schumann) (—1896), 362, 363, 367.
—— Friedrich (1785—1872), 358, 360, 361, 363.
Wilbye, John (1564[?]—1612[?]), 84.
Wilderness, The, anthem by S. S. Wesley, 446.
Willaert, Adrian (1480[?]—1562), 61, 72.
Winchester, early organ in cathedral, 33.
Wind instruments, 26.
Winter, Peter von (1755—1825), 330.
Wise, Michael (1638—1687), 181, 183.

Wise and Foolish Virgins, liturgical drama of the, 18.
Wit and Mirth; or, Pills to purge Melancholy, D'Urfey's, 200.
Woelfl, Josef (1772—1812), 369.
Wohltemperirte Clavier, of J. S. Bach, 148.
Wolstan, description of organ in Winchester Cathedral, 33.
Woman of Samaria, The, oratorio by W. Sterndale Bennett, 445.
Wood Nymphs, The, overture by W. Sterndale Bennett, 445.
Wretched lovers, chorus from Handel's *Acis and Galatea*, 210.

Ye Mariners of England, part song by Pierson, 487.
Ye twice ten hundred deities, from Purcell's *Indian Queen*, 192.
Yonge, N. (1550[?]—), 83.

Zadok the Priest, coronation anthem by Handel, 215.
Zampa, opera by Hérold, 412.
Zampogna, or Calabrian bagpipes, 30.
Zarlino, Gioseffo (1519—1590), 61, 72, 152.
Zauberflöte, Der, opera by Mozart, 283, 284.
Zelter, C. F. (1758—1832), 348, 350.
Zemire and Azor, opera by Spohr, 343.
Zémire et Azor, opera by Grétry, 264.
Zéphyre et Flore, opera by Louis and Jean Louis de Lully, 130.
Zingarelli, N. A. (1752—1837), 315, 442.

www.ingramcontent.com/pod-product-compliance
Lightning Source LLC
Chambersburg PA
CBHW021414300426
44114CB00010B/492